ALASTAIR
SPECIAL PLACES

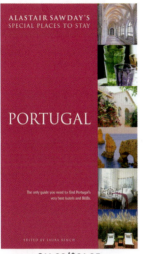

£11.99/$21.95

£14.99/$23.95

£11.99/$21.95

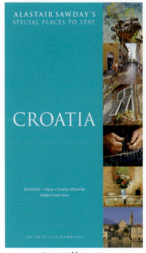

£11.99/$21.95

Credit card orders (free p&p for UK orders) **01275 395431**
www.specialplacestostay.com

In US: credit card orders (800) 243-0495, 9am–5pm EST,
24-hour fax (800) 820-2329 www.globepequot.com

Seventh edition
Copyright © 2007
Alastair Sawday Publishing Co. Ltd

Published in 2007
Alastair Sawday Publishing,
The Old Farmyard,
Yanley Lane, Long Ashton
Bristol BS41 9LR
Tel: +44 (0)1275 395430
Fax: +44 (0)1275 393388
Email: info@specialplacestostay.com
Web: www.specialplacestostay.com

A catalogue record for this book is
available from the British Library.

Design:
Caroline King

Paper and Printing: We have sought the lowest
possible ecological 'footprint' from the production
of this book, using super-efficient machinery,
vegetable inks and high environmental standards.
Our printer is ISO 14001-registered.

Maps & Mapping:
Maidenhead Cartographic Services Ltd

Printing:
Butler & Tanner, Frome, UK

UK Distribution:
Penguin UK, 80 Strand, London

ISBN-13: 978-1-901970-82-1

ALASTAIR SAWDAY'S
SPECIAL PLACES TO STAY

SPAIN

Contents

Alastair Sawday Publishing

Our main aim is to publish beautiful guidebooks but, for us, the question of who we are is also important. For who we are shapes the books, the books shape your holidays, and thus are shaped the lives of people who own these 'special places'. So we are trying to be a little more than 'just a publishing company'.

New eco offices

In January 2006 we moved into our new eco offices. With super-insulation, underfloor heating, a wood-pellet boiler, solar panels and a rainwater tank, we have a working environment benign to ourselves and to the environment. Lighting is low-energy, dark corners are lit by sun-pipes and one building is of green oak. Carpet tiles are from Herdwick sheep in the Lake District.

Environmental & ethical policies

We make many other gestures: company cars run on gas or recycled cooking oil; kitchen waste is composted and other waste recycled; cycling and car-sharing are encouraged; the company only buys organic or local food; we don't accept web links with companies we consider unethical; we bank with the ethical Triodos Bank.

We have used recycled paper for some books but have settled on selecting paper and printing for their low energy use. Our printer is British and ISO14001-certified and together we will work to reduce our environmental impact.

In 2005 we won a Business Commitment to the Environment Award and in April 2006 we won a Queen's Award for Enterprise in the Sustainable Development category. All this has boosted our resolve to promote our green policies. Our flagship gesture, however, is carbon offsetting; we calculate our carbon emissions and plant trees to compensate and support projects overseas that plant trees or reduce carbon use.

Carbon offset

SCAD in South India, supports the poorest of the poor. The money we send to offset our carbon emissions will be used to encourage village tree planting and, eventurally, low-carbon technologies. Why India? Because the money goes a long way and admin costs are very low. www.salt-of-the-earth.org.uk

Ethics

But why, you may ask, take these things so seriously? You are just a little publishing company, for heaven's sake! Well, is there any good argument for not taking them seriously? The world, by the admission of the vast majority of scientists, is in trouble. If we do not change our ways urgently we will

Who are we?

doom the planet and all its creatures – whether innocent or not – to a variety of possible catastrophes. To maintain the status quo is unacceptable. Business does much of the damage and should undo it, and provide new models.

Pressure on companies to produce Corporate Social Responsibility policies is mounting. We are trying to keep ahead of it all, yet still to be as informal and human as possible – the antithesis of 'corporate'.

The books – and a dilemma
So, we have created fine books that do good work. They promote authenticity, individuality and good local and organic food – a far cry from corporate culture. Rural economies, pubs, small farms, villages and hamlets all benefit. However, people use fossil fuel to get there. Should we aim to get our readers to offset their own carbon emissions, and the B&B and hotel owners too?

We are gradually introducing green ideas into the books: the Fine Breakfast scheme that highlights British and Irish B&B owners who use local and organic food; celebrating those who make an extra environmental effort; gently encouraging the use of public transport, cycling and walking. Last year we published *Green Places to*

Stay focusing on responsible travel and eco-properties around the globe.

Our Fragile Earth series
The 'hard' side of our environmental publishing is the Fragile Earth series: *The Little Earth Book*, *The Little Food Book* and *The Little Money Book*. They consist of bite-sized essays, polemical, hard-hitting and well researched. They are a 'must have' for anyone who seeks clarity about some of the key issues of our time. Last year we have also published *One Planet Living*.

Lastly – what is special?
The notion of 'special' is at the heart of what we do, and highly subjective. We discuss this in the introduction. We take huge pleasure from finding people and places that do their own thing – brilliantly; places that are unusual and follow no trends; places of peace and beauty; people who are kind and interesting – and genuine.

We seem to have touched a nerve with thousands of readers; they obviously want to stay in special places rather than the dull corporate monstrosities that have disfigured so many of our cities and towns. Life is too short to be wasted in the wrong places. A night in a special place can be a transforming experience.

Alastair Sawday

Acknowledgements

Jose Navarro is passionate about traditional customs and their survival. So he took a few weeks off the vast labour of assembling this edition to follow and photograph what may have been one of the last 'transhumantes', the shepherded migration of thousands of sheep, on foot, across a great swathe of Northern Spain. I admire such devotion and deep interest, and this book reflects it. For Jose has brought dedication and integrity to the compilation of this guide. He knows and loves his Spain.

So if you enjoy these special places, then thank Jose – and all those upon whose shoulders he stands, especially Guy Hunter-Watts who started us off in Spain.

Thanks go too to the guide's other inspectors and writers, to Maria Serrano for her administrative support, to Jo Boissevain for her always thorough copy editing, to Jackie King for her calm management, Russell Wilkinson for his masterly web skills, Julia Richardson and her production team for such a handsome work, and to Bridget Bishop's industrious accounts team.

Alastair Sawday

Series Editor Alastair Sawday

Editor Jose Navarro

Editorial Director Annie Shillito

Writing Jose Navarro, Jo Boissevain, Jon Clarke, Matthew Hilton-Dennis, Gail McKenzie, Kate Shepherd, Rebecca Stevens

Inspections Jose Navarro, Jon Clarke, Guy Hunter-Watts, Billy Kite, Rob Paterson, Maria Serrano

Accounts **Bridget Bishop,** Jessica Britton, Christine Buxton, Sandra Hasell, Sally Ranahan

Editorial **Jackie King,** Jo Boissevain, Florence Oldfield, Maria Serrano, Rebecca Stevens, Danielle Williams

Production **Julia Richardson,** Rachel Coe, Tom Germain, Rebecca Thomas

Sales & Marketing & PR Andreea Petre Goncalves, Sarah Bolton

Web & IT **Russell Wilkinson,** Chris Banks, Isabelle Deakin, Joe Green, Brian Kimberling

Previous Editor Guy Hunter-Watts

And many thanks to those people who did the odd inspection or write-up.

A word from Alastair Sawday

As I write, in January 2007, I have just returned from a fortnight in Spain, neatly avoiding the grey of England's New Year. Dancing before my eyes are memories of long and beautiful views, of the Grazalema National Park, of the hills and forest of cork oaks beyond Aracena, of countryside stretching as far as the eye can see. I can smell the 'jabugo' ham made from acorn-fed pigs, the 'fino' that glistens gold in the glass, and the thyme plucked from the hillside. I can hear the gravelly cacophony of men pontificating below the hanging hams in the bars, the genial chatter of women bent on nothing in particular. Spain is a sensual place, and the trick when travelling is to stay with the people who can get you under its skin.

Yet all is not entirely well in southern Spain. The drought is a real worry, less urgent in winter, of course, but lurking nonetheless. Economic growth is frantic, and, as elsewhere, is crushing some of the character and countryside that we love. We English have much to answer for, invading the coast in our hordes, speculating obsessively in property and driving demand for golf courses in places that cannot support them. Yet there may be redemption. This week, developers are taking to court in Ronda a trio of noble expatriates who have criticised their plans for a golf course, 800 houses and three hotels on the edge of the national park. They are suing for £14 million of investment lost because of the criticism. It sounds mad, but it is true. If the developers lose, then perhaps golf courses all over Spain will tremble. If they win, then pity the believers in democratic resistance.

If this book does anything, it opens the eyes of the traveller to the real Spain. You cannot but learn to sympathise with those three expats. You cannot stay in Special Places without seeing the best of 'old Spain' – and wanting to protect it. At the same time, of course, as having a terrific time.

Alastair Sawday

Introduction

FROM THE GRAND AND THE GRACIOUS TO THE SMALL AND THE INTIMATE

Our Spanish guide to Special Places to Stay, launched in 1992, is one of our most popular titles. And not just with readers but with owners, whose feedback is overwhelmingly positive (they love our readers!).

As for the Spanish accommodation scene, interesting things have happened in recent years. Small hotelier associations are springing up to encourage good taste and good practice, while the more established groups, such as Rusticae and Pacos Galicias, are going from strength to strength. At present they are targeting the home market, but it's only a matter of time before they will be promoting these properties beyond Spain.

There is fierce competition: new *casas rurales* (country houses) and *hoteles con encanto* (charming hotels) open every week. We have included 90 new places in this edition, many of which provide not only extraordinary value for money, but also a very special experience. Spanish standards of accommodation are on the rise; places that seemed acceptable five years ago may be less so now. Increasingly, guests expect beds to be king-size and bathrooms en suite. This is not to say that a Special Place has to promise all that, plus lifts and porters, room service and stars. On the contrary, the star system uses criteria very different from ours, and is incapable of accounting for the very things we rate most highly: character, style and warmth of welcome.

In short, we do not offer an 'exclusive product', but an 'inclusive' one, and our choices are subjective, almost entirely so. Special places range from the grand and the gracious to the small and the intimate, and we happily include some of the new wave of boutique hotels so keenly promoted by the travel press. If such places are run with genuine warmth, we are delighted to invite them.

Photo left Ca'n Reus, entry 349
Photo right Caserío del Mirador, entry 185

Introduction

More and more Spaniards speak English; they want to communicate, and they love their Sawday's guests. At the same time, there is an increasing pride in Spanish history and heritage. The result is a burgeoning species of upmarket B&B. Some have been started by retired couples tired of the rat race and seeking purer, quieter waters, others by Spanish – sometimes non-Spanish – families who have left the worlds of media or finance. All have led interesting lives, enjoy meeting new people and are passionate about their adopted corner of Spain. They often work hard to become part of their communities, and enjoy sharing their regional secrets.

There is also a growing awareness of environmental issues. Positive environmental thinking is catching on, and many of our non-Spanish owners – Dutch, Germans, British – are leading the way.

How we choose our Special Places

We select the places that, first and foremost, we like; and that means choosing our inspectors – our 'eyes and ears' – with care. We like places that buzz with humanity and individuality, where the smiles spring from a genuine interest in people and where the fabric of the building reflects a real feel for place. We look, too, for a sense of fun.

Expect this book to lead you to places that are original, individual and welcoming. We hope it will bring you closer to the Spain that we love, a country whose people are convivial and spontaneous, impossibly chatty and, at times, beautifully mannered.

What to expect

You cannot judge Spain by your own cultural yardsticks. So, in hotels, bars and restaurants, be quick to pardon what might at first seem brash or abrupt. The Spanish language can be as rich and convoluted as it is economical, almost austere. And don't be surprised or put off by how rarely the words 'please' and 'thank you' are used in daily conversations. No rudeness is meant. Politeness is implied.

Relax

We all know that the Spanish conception of time can be fairly loose. Spaniards firmly believe they determine the course of time and not the other way round. You will have to take this on board and relax about time when in Spain. Enjoy all those little things that can make life so enjoyable, with which the Spaniards regularly indulge themselves. The 'sobremesa', the ubiquitous chat over coffee after lunch; a siesta to cope with the rigours of the hot summers; or 'el paseo', the stroll down the main avenue at dusk with no specific purpose in mind.

Standards of living

Spain is not the cheap place to travel that it used to be. If standards are going up, so too are prices. While some things, such as petrol and transport, are cheaper than in the UK, others – including accommodation – have become more expensive. Cheap 'menús del día' (set menus) are becoming harder to find. A full trolley at the local supermarket will not be any cheaper than in the UK – apart from the wine and the olive oil, perhaps. Books are definitely more expensive than in the UK. Tickets for the theatre and exhibitions are much more expensive.

Noise

One of the first things you will certainly notice is the Spaniards' built-in tolerance to noise – from riotous 2-stroke mopeds whooshing up and down late at night to charming, albeit annoying, pre-dawn church bells, from distant barking dogs to vociferous bar conversations. The best attitude towards this issue is to consider it one of the country's idiosyncrasies and part of your travel experience. Or bring ear plugs.

Finding the right place for you

We have sought out beautiful homes and hotels throughout Spain. But we have also chosen some good places where the charm factor may, at first glance, be low. But choose your hotel on looks alone and you will miss out on some remarkable places to stay. Don't be too put off by, say, a vast and noisy restaurant – the food may be tremendous. Likewise, be prepared to tolerate a sugary taste in decoration. The rooms will be comfortable and come with a reasonable price tag. We want to get you to places that you will like and aim to write honest descriptions. Hotels, like people, are never perfect, so read the descriptions carefully!

Special green entries

For the first time we have chosen, subjectively, places that are making a particular effort to be eco-friendly. The entry numbers are 34, 36, 101, 260 and 285.

Photo The Hoopoe Yurt Hotel, entry 260

Introduction

This does not mean there are no other places in the guide taking green initiatives – there are many – but we have selected just a few examples.

Maps

Plan your trip by starting with the maps at the front of the book; pages and entry numbers correspond. Many roads, including new dual carriageways, do not appear on the maps. Bear in mind that our maps are for guidance and not for detailed route planning; for this you need a proper road map. In Spain you have the toll motorways, and the 'autovias', or dual carriageways. For example, between Zaragoza and Huesca there is an 'autovia' which, to all intents and purposes, acts as a motorway, except it's free.

Road nomenclatures

A = motorways (usually with a toll)
E = new European nomenclature for motorways or free dual carriageways
N = national roads (equivalent of British A roads), some of which have been converted into dual carriageways.

For minor roads, each region has its own number system, the letter(s) usually standing for the particular region eg. CV = Communidad Valenciana; A = Aragón.

Characteristic of most roads in Spain are the km markers – invaluable in the more remote areas.

Photo Posada La Preda, entry 55

Rooms

We tell you the range of accommodation in single, double, twin, family rooms and suites; in self-catering entries, we mention the number of people who can sleep comfortably (eg. 2-3) in the apartment, cottage or house. Suites may mean rooms big enough to contain a sitting area, or even with an extra room; we do not distinguish between suites and junior suites. Extra beds can often be added for children. Check when booking.

Bathrooms

Do not assume bath and shower rooms are en suite. If it is important to you that they are, ask when booking. In some of the simpler places, a bathroom may be shared.

It seems that Spaniards prefer an invigorating and refreshing shower to a long soak in a foaming bath. Hence the plug may be missing from your bathroom. Just in case, pack one of those handy universal bath plugs you can buy.

Children

The majority of Spanish hotels and B&Bs love having families to stay. However, a percentage of our Special Places do not welcome children of all ages: perhaps the hotel is a peaceful couples' retreat, or the grounds contain an unfenced pond. Check important details before booking.

Introduction

Weddings, conferences and courses

We try to say when a place is a popular wedding or conference place; in any event, it is best to ask if a large party is likely to be present when you book. The same goes for courses. More places are encouraging relaxation or painting breaks (for example) but you may find your peaceful haven does not turn out to be quite as peaceful as you'd expected. Again, pick up the phone and check.

Prices

The prices that we quote for rooms are exclusive of VAT at 7%. When VAT is included we say so. Note that prices are per room not per person, and assume breakfast is included; if it's not, we give the price.

Meal prices are per person. Half-board prices may be quoted per room or per person; if in any doubt, check.

The prices we quote were applicable at the time that this book went to press. We publish every two years so expect prices to be higher if you are using this book towards the end of 2007 or in 2008.

A word about the Balearic & the Canary islands

Expect to pay about 50% more here than in the rest of Spain. We promise that we haven't sought out expensive places – that's just the way it is.

Symbols

There is an explanation of our symbols on the last page of the book. Use these as a guide, not as a statement of fact.

Opening hours

As a general rule:
• Shops open 9am-1.30pm, 4.30/5pm-8/8.30pm Monday-Friday; 9am-1.30pm on Saturdays.
• Banks are usually open 8am-3pm, Monday-Friday.
• Post Offices generally open at 8.30am and close at 2.30pm, Monday-Friday.

Many restaurants still traditionally close on Mondays; which can be frustrating if the place you are staying at does not offer meals – plan ahead or contact your host.

Phones and phone codes

Emergency number 112, wherever you are in Spain.

From Spain to another country: dial 00 then the country code and then the area code without the first 0. eg. ASP in England, from Spain: Tel: 01275 395430 becomes 00 44 1275 395430.

Within Spain: all nine digits are needed whether intra or inter-provincial.

Calling Spain from another country:
• From the USA: 011 34 then the

nine-digit number
• From the UK: 00 34 then the nine-digit number.

Most mobile numbers begin with 6. This is the best clue as to when you're dialling an (expensive) mobile number.

Buy telephone cards from tobacconists or post offices (coin-operated boxes are few and far between). The cheapest card starts at about €10.

Abbreviations

Co – camino = pathway or track (camí in Catalán language)
c/ – calle = street (carrer in Catalán; rua in Galician)
Ctra – carretera = road
s/n – sin número = un-numbered
Avda. – avenida = avenue
Pza. – plaza = square
Apdo – apartado (de correos) = post office box no. eg. Apdo. 34 = PO Box 34

Types of properties

Can A farmhouse in Cataluña or the Balearic Islands, often isolated.
Casita Cottage or small house.
Casona A grand house in Asturias or Cantabria; many were built by returning emigrants
Cortijo A free-standing farmhouse, generally in the south
Finca A farm; many of those in this book are on working farms

Photo Casa Blas, entry 77

Fonda A simple inn which may or may nor serve food.
Hacienda A large estate; originally a South American term
Hostal Another type of simple inn where food may or may not be served
Hostería A simple inn which often serves food
Hostelería An inn which may or may not serve food
Mas or *masía* A farmhouse in the north-east of Spain.
Posada Originally a coaching inn, with beds and food available
Palacio A grand mansion
Palacete A slightly less grand version of the above
Pazo A grand country or village manor in Galicia
Venta A simple restaurant, usually in the countryside; some have rooms

Introduction

Regional spelling of place names

Where there are two languages (as in Galicia, the Basque Country, the Balearic Islands, Valencia and Cataluña) place names will often have two spellings. Orense will be Ourense in Galicia. Lerida will be spelt Lleida on road signs in Cataluña – Catalunya in Catalán language. In the Basque Country, regional spellings usually accompany the Spanish one eg. Vitoria will be signposted Vitoria-Gasteiz. We try to use the ones that you are most likely to see: this may mean one version in the address, another in the directions on how to get there. We have no political agenda!

Meals

The Spanish eat much later than we do: breakfast often doesn't get going until 9am, lunch is generally eaten from 2pm and dinner rarely served before 8.30pm.

Breakfast

The 'continental' in larger hotels tends to be uninspired: coffee, toast (perhaps cakes), butter and jam. Marmalade is a rare sight and freshly squeezed juice the exception. Fortunately, wholesome breakfasts with homemade jams, cheese, eggs and cold meats are very often served in rural areas. Your hotelier may assume that you prefer a blander, more northern-European offering. Tea tends not to be widely available,

and the tea you are offered may have been on the shelves for years; take your favourite brew with you and ask for hot water! Ask for it 'con leche' if you like it with milk or 'con limón' for a slice of lemon. Bars nearly always serve camomile tea ('manzanilla') – it can be a useful evening drink because the coffee is very strong. If you want a hot chocolate then ask for a 'Cola-Cao'; you'll be served hot milk and a sachet with drinking chocolate. Traditional Spanish chocolate is considerably thicker than its British counterpart; it's served with delicious deep-fried pastry sticks called 'churros' to dip in ('chocolate con churros').

Lunch and dinner

The daily set meal – 'el menú del día' – is normally available at lunch time and occasionally at dinner, when waiters may present you simply with the à la carte menu. But do ask for it; it tends to be great value and will often have fresher ingredients. Many restaurants serve only à la carte at weekends.

Tapas and raciones

A tapa is a small plate of hot or cold food served with an aperitif before lunch or dinner: it remains an essential part of eating out in Spain. It could be a plate of olives, anchovies, cheese, spicy chorizo, fried fish... portions vary as does the

Introduction

choice. It is a delicious way to try out local specialities and don't worry if your Spanish is poor – tapas are often laid out along the bar for you to see. If you would like a plateful of any particular tapa then ask for 'una ración de queso' (cheese), for example. Many bars will also serve you a half portion – 'una media ración'.

Some historians attribute the Spanish love of meat to the rationing that followed the Spanish Civil War. The truth is that meat is a ubiquitous element in the Spanish diet. Outside main towns it might be difficult to arrange for vegetarian meals; salads may be the only vegetarian alternative on offer.

Tipping

Leaving a tip is not unusual, but do not feel obliged, particularly when you've just had a few tapas and a couple of drinks in a busy bar. If you are given your change on a small saucer, you could leave a couple of small coins. For lunch or dinner leave 5%-10%. You would rarely be made to feel embarrassed if you don't tip. Taxi drivers don't expect a tip, but welcome the gesture of leaving the change with them.

Seasons

Prices given range from low to high season. In most of Spain, high season includes Easter, Christmas, public holidays and the summer. Some hotels, especially city hotels, classify weekends as high and weekdays as low.

Public Holidays

Apart from the public holidays nationwide, there is an array of local festivities in the honour of one saint or another in every town and village in Spain. You may find this frustrating – shops and restaurants might be shut – or you may enjoy joining the locals in the celebration. Either way, it may be difficult for you to find out the relevant dates beforehand. As a rule, August tends to be filled with local festivities. National holidays are 1 January, 6 January (the Epiphany), Good Friday, 1 May, Corpus Christi (usually early June), 24 June, 25 July, 12 October, 1 November, 6 December, 8 December, 25 December. In some parts of Spain, 15 August and Easter Monday are also holidays. Be aware of the very Spanish phenomenon known as 'puentes' (bridges). When a

Photo La Casa Vieja, entry 191

bank holiday falls on Thursday or Tuesday it's not unusual for businesses and shops to take the Friday or Monday off. 'Puentes' trigger mass escapes of town dwellers to nearby countryside areas, worth knowing if you plan to stay near a large town during one.

Booking

Try to book well ahead if you plan to be in Spain during any of these holidays. August is best avoided unless you are heading somewhere remote. Certain regions are particularly busy at specific times of the year: the Jerte valley in Extremadura will be fully booked during the spring cherry blossom; Valencia won't have a single room to spare during the exciting Fallas fiestas in mid-March. Many hotels will ask you for a credit card number when you book. And remember to let smaller hotels and B&Bs know if you want dinner. There's a bilingual booking form at the back of the book. Hotels may send back a signed or stamped copy as confirmation. Do not assume that you will get a speedy reply, not even by email.

Arrival & registration

Many city hotels will only hold a reservation until the early evening, even though you might have booked months in advance. Ring ahead if you are planning to arrive late.

It remains law that you should register on arrival. Hotels sometimes insist on holding on to identity cards or passports, but they have no right to keep your passport, however much they insist.

Payment

The most commonly accepted credit cards are Visa, MasterCard and Eurocard. We found that American Express is rarely accepted in the properties we list. Many smaller places don't take plastic because of high bank charges. But there is nearly always a cash dispenser (ATM) close at hand; again, Visa and MasterCard are the most useful.

Plugs

Virtually all sockets now have 220/240 AC voltage (two-pin). Pack an adaptor if you travel with electrical appliances. Note that telephone plugs are also different from the ones in the UK; you will also need an adaptor if you intend to bring your laptop.

Driving

Foreign number plates attract attention so never leave your car with valuables inside. Use a public car park; they are cheap and safe. It is compulsory to have in the car: a spare set of bulbs, a car jack, a spare/emergency wheel, two warning triangles, a visibility jacket – which you must carry at the front, not in

Introduction

the boot – and a basic first aid kit. It is also compulsory to carry on you your UK driving license and the car documents, whether you have a rental car or your own. Impromptu road checkpoints are a not unusual occurrence. These are usually carried out by the Guardia Civil – in green fatigues – who, however intimidating (and armed) they may look, are courteous and extremely helpful should you have an emergency.

Public transport

Trains, buses and taxis are cheap in Spain. You meet people, can start a good conversation, and get much more of a feel for the country by travelling this way. Spain has a high-speed rail link (known as AVE) between Lleida and Madrid, via Zaragoza. In Madrid it splits and one branch goes to Malaga, while the other one goes to Seville. From Zaragoza there is also a service to Huesca. Some regional lines would bring a tear to a rail buff's eye, such as the one between Ronda and Algeciras.

In the north the FEVE company runs several narrow-gauge trains, which usually travel through extraordinary landscapes and have retained the magic and the romance of old railway journeys. You can travel by FEVE trains from Bilbao all the way to El Ferrol, in Galicia, or to Léon. Visit www.feve.es for more info.

Look out for the national coach company if you want to travel by public transport. ENATCAR (Empresa Nacional de Transportes por Carretera) underwent a massive restructuring some years ago and established concessions in every major town. As a result of this it has some of the most comfortable coaches you will find in Europe. And they are relatively cheap. The rarity of roundabouts in the road network and the existence of motorway tolls – which deter drivers from using the faster roads – mean that coach journeys tend to be swift, too.

Subscriptions

Owners pay to appear in this guide. Their fee goes towards the high costs of inspecting and producing an all-colour book and maintaining a sophisticated web site. We only include places that we like and find special for one reason or another. It is not possible for anyone to buy their way onto these pages.

Internet

www.specialplacestostay.com has online pages for all the special places featured here and from all our other books – around 5,000 in total. There's a searchable database, a taster of the write-ups and colour photos.

And look out for our dedicated web site on self-catering in England,

Scotland and Wales,
www.special-escapes.co.uk.
For more details, see the back of
the book.

Disclaimer

We make no claims to pure
objectivity in choosing our Special
Places. They are here because we like
them. Our opinions and tastes are
ours alone and this book is a
statement of them; we hope that
you will share them. We have done
our utmost to get our facts right and
we apologise unreservedly for any
errors that may have crept in.

We do not check such things as fire
alarms, swimming pool security or
any other regulation with which
owners of properties receiving
paying guests should comply. This is
the responsibility of the owners.

Feedback

Feedback from you is invaluable and
we always act upon comments,
which may be sent by letter or email
to info@sawdays.co.uk. Or you can
visit our web site and write to us
from there. With your help and our
own inspections we can maintain
our reputation for dependability –
and do be patient with us at busy
times; it's sometimes difficult to
respond immediately.

Poor reports are followed up with
the owners in question: we need to
hear both sides of the story. Really
worrying reports lead to incognito
visits, after which we may exclude
a place. As a general rule, do
mention any problems that arise to
the relevant people during your
stay; they are the only ones who
can do anything about such things
and may be able to resolve them on
the spot.

Owners are informed when we
receive substantially positive reports
about them and recommendations
are followed up with inspection
visits where appropriate. If your
recommendation leads us to include
a place, you receive a free copy of
the edition in which it first appears.

So tell us if your stay has been
a joy or not, if the atmosphere
was great or stuffy, whether the
owners or staff were cheery or
bored. We aim to celebrate human
kindness, fine architecture, real
food, history and landscape, and
hope that these books may be a
passport to memorable experiences.

And finally

Thank you to all those who have
taken the time to share your
opinions with us. You have helped
make this edition of the book even
better than the last!

Jose Navarro

©Maidenhead Cartographic, 2007

Please remember: our maps are designed to be used as a guide, not as road maps for navigation.

On the following map pages:
self-catering properties are marked in blue   **30**

catered properties are marked in red   **12**

properties with a mixture are marked with both   **79**

Photo Jose Navarro

Map 1

Catered properties
Self-catering properties
Mix of catered/self-catering
Special green entry

0   10   20   30 kilometres
0   10   20 miles

Map 2

27

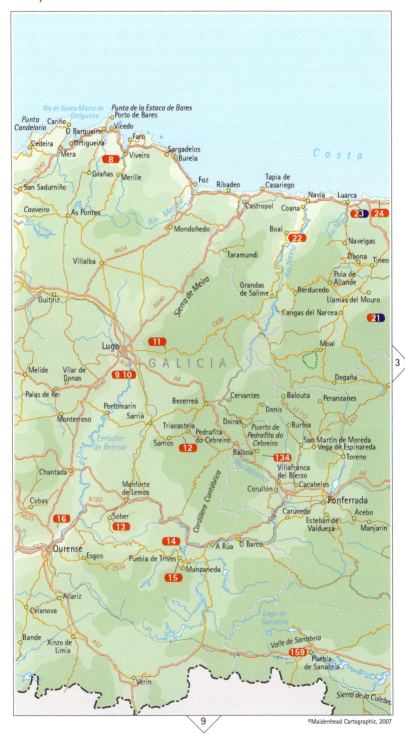

Río de Santa Marta de Ortigueira
Punta de la Estaca de Bares
Porto de Bares
Punta Candelaria
Cariño
O Barqueiro
Vicedo
Cedeira
Ortigueira
Faro
Mera
Viveiro
Sargadelos
Burela
8
Grañas
Merille
San Sadurniño
Foz
Ribadeo
Tapia de Casariego
Navia
Luarca
Costa
Caaveiro
As Pontes
Castropol
Coana
23
24
Río Eume
Mondoñedo
Boal
22
Navelgas
Villalba
Taramundi
Óbona
Tineo
Guitiriz
Sierra de Meira
Grandas de Salime
Berducedo
Pola de Allande
Llamas del Mouro
C630
Cangas del Narcea
Lugo
11
Moal
21
GALICIA
3
Melide
Vilar de Donas
9 10
Degaña
Palas de Rei
Becerreá
Cervantes
Balouta
Peranzanes
Portomarín
Sarriá
Donis
Burbia
Monterroso
Triacastela
Doiras
Puerto de Pedrafita do Cebreiro
San Martín de Moreda
Embalse de Belesar
Samos
Pedrafita do Cebreiro
Balboa
134
Vega de Espinareda
Toreno
12
Villafranca del Bierzo
Chantada
Cacabelos
A6
Monforte de Lemos
Corullón
Cobas
N120
Ponferrada
16
Sober
13
Carucedo
Esteban de Valdueza
Acebo
Manjarín
14
A Rúa
O Barco
Ourense
Esgos
Puebla de Trives
Manzaneda
15
Allariz
Celanova
Bande
Xinzo de Limia
Lago de Sanabria
Vérin
Valle de Sanabria
159
Puebla de Sanabria
Sierra de la Culebra

Map 3

Map 4

29

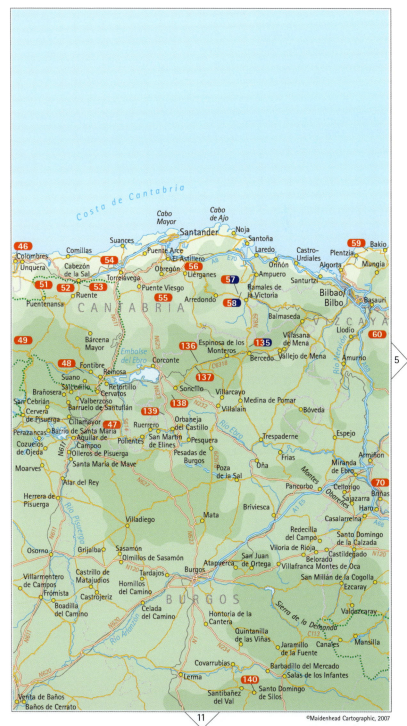

Bay of Biscay

Costa Vasca

Bermio 64 63
Lekeitio
Gernika 65 Ondarroa Getaria
VIZCAYA Deba
Markina Orio 66 Oiartzun
62
San Sebastián
Donostia
Fuenterrabia
Irún
Bera Zugarramurdi
Urdazubi
Lesaka
Etxalar
Azpeitia
Eibar
Durango Elorrio Bergara Régil
Ituren
Arizkun
Elizondo
EUSKADI 61 Tolosa
GUIPÚZCOA
Arrasate
Oñati Beasain
Zubieta
Leitza 67
Valcarlos
Otxandio Betelu
Segura Azpirotz
Lekunberri
Burguete Roncesvalles
Auritzberri Orbaitzeta
Altsasu 68
Uharte Arakil
Ochagavía
Argómaniz Eguilaz
Gaceo Salvatierra
Pamplona/
Iruñea
Vitoria/ Alaiza
Gasteiz
Treviño
COUNTY OF Zudaire
TREVIÑO Baquedano
Urroz Agoitz
Noam Artaiz
Navascues
Antoñana
Puente la Reina
Estella Obanos
Ciraqui Lumbier Sierra de Leyre
Yesa
NAVARRA Javier
Sorlada Artajona
Abalos Sangüesa
San Vicente de la Sonsierra Los Arcos
Biasteri Tafalla Ujué
Sos del Rey Católico
Villabuena Torres
Elciego del Río Olite
Cenicero Viana
Lodosa
Navarrete Logroño
Tricio
Sorzano 69 Calahorra 81
Viguera Clavijo Uncastillo
LA RIOJA Sádaba
Arnedillo Arnedo
Muñilla Alfaro Ejea de los
Préjano Caballeros
Enciso Corella
Cornago Cintruénigo
Fitero Tudela
Cervera del Cascante
Río Alhama
Inestrillas
Vinuesa Aguilar del Tarazona Tauste
Río Alhama

4

Map 6

31

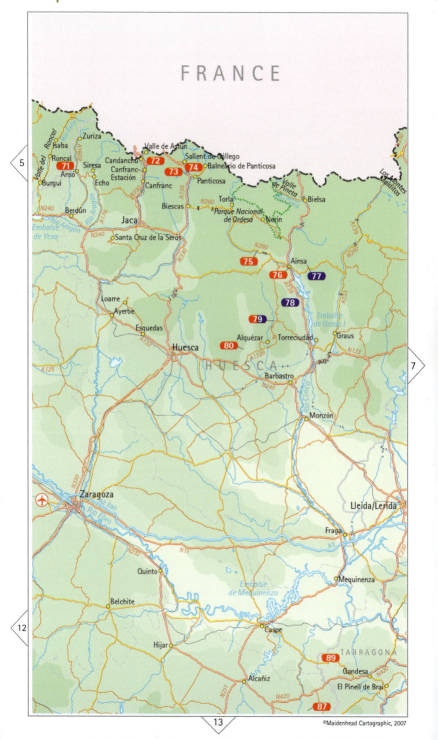

Map 7

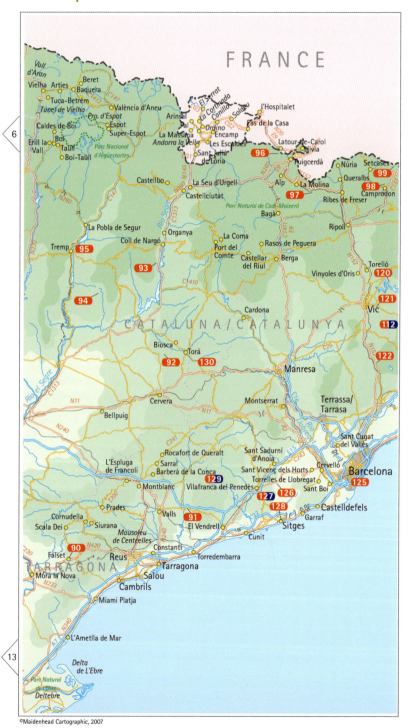

FRANCE

Vall d'Aran

Vielha Arties Beret
Baquera
Tuca-Betrèm
Túnel de Vielha València d'Aneu
Pro. d'Espot Arinsal
Caldes de Boí Espot Pal
Boí Super-Espot Ordino
Erill la Taüll La Massana Encamp
Vall Boí-Taüll Andorra la Vella Les Escaldes
Parc Nacional Sant Julià 96
d'Aigüestortes de Lòria

El Serrat
La Cortinada Conillo
Soldeu l'Hospitalet
Pas de la Casa

Latour-de-Carol
Nívia
Puigcerdà Núria Setcases
Castellbo La Seu d'Urgell Alp 99
Castellciutat La Molina Queralbs
97 98
Parc Natural de Cadi-Moixeró Camprodon
Ribes de Freser
La Pobla de Segur Bagà
Organya Ripoll
La Coma
Tremp Coll de Nargó Port del Rasos de Peguera
95 Comte Berga Torelló
93 Castellar 120
del Riu Vinyoles d'Oris
94 Vic 121

Cardona 112

CATALUÑA / CATALUNYA
Biosca 122
92 Torá
130 Manresa
Cervera Terrassa/
Bellpuig Montserrat Tarrasa
Sant Cugat
del Vallès
Rocafort de Queralt Sant Sadurní
L'Espluga Sarral d'Anoia
de Francolí Barberà de la Conca Sant Vicenç dels Horts Cervelló
129 Torrelles de Llobregat Barcelona
Montblanc Vilafranca del Penedès Sant Boi 125
Prades Valls 127 126
128
El Vendrell Garraf Castelldefels
90 91 Sitges
Cornudella Siurana Mausoleu Cunit
Scala Dei de Centcelles Constantí
Falset Reus Torredembarra
TARRAGONA
Mora la Nova Salou Tarragona
Cambrils
Miami Platja

L'Ametlla de Mar

Delta
de L'Ebre
Deltebre

Map 8

33

MEDITERRANEAN SEA

Map 9

Alcañices

Fermoselle

Embalse de Almendra

Saucelle

P O R T U G A L

Ciudád Rodrigo

Casares de las Hurdes

202 Fragosa

Caminomorisco
Pinofranqueado

CS76

EX004

EX205

EX370

203

Rio Verte

Coria

Rio Alagón

Torrejoncillo

N630

EX372

EX109

Cañaveral

Embalse
de Alcántara

Alcántara

Rio Tajo

EX207

Garrovillas

208

207

C A C E R E S

Map 10

35

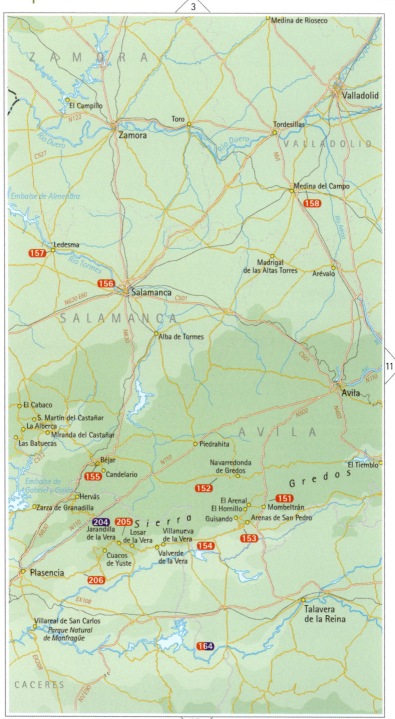

©Maidenhead Cartographic, 2007

Map 11

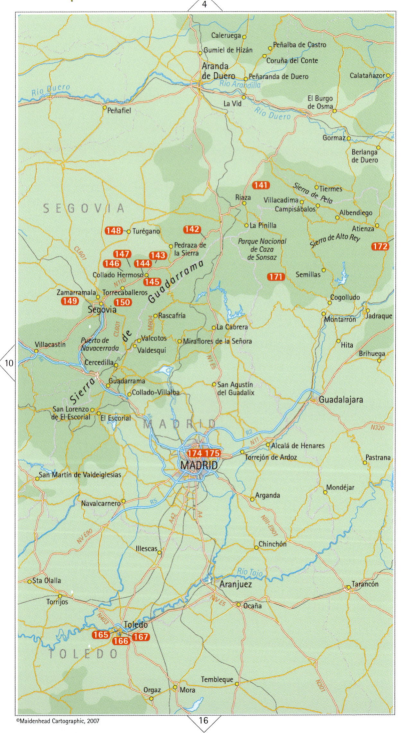

Map 12

37

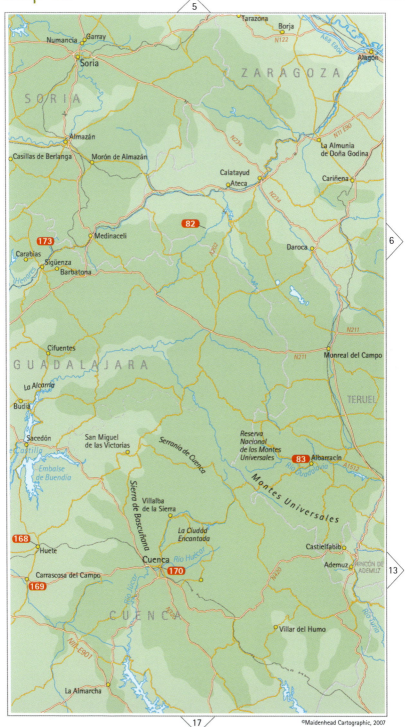

Map 13

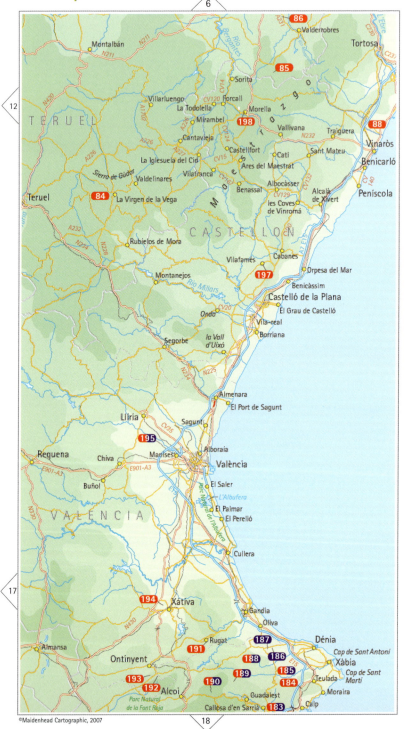

©Maidenhead Cartographic, 2007

Map 14

Map 15

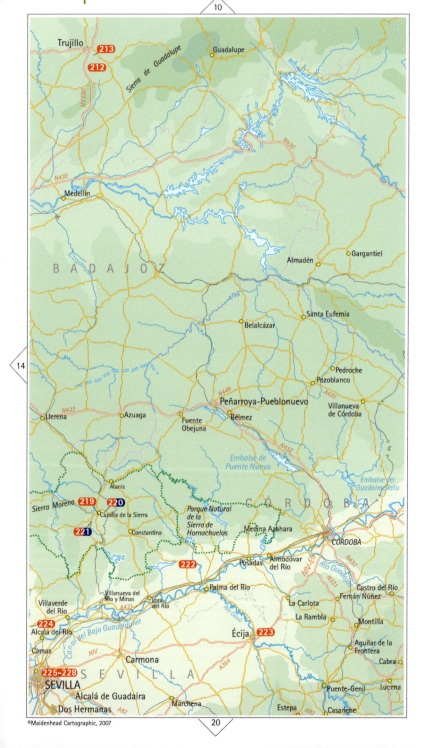

Map 16

41

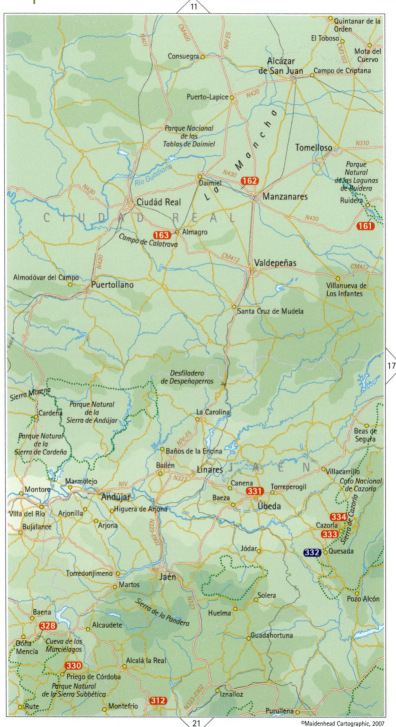

Map 17

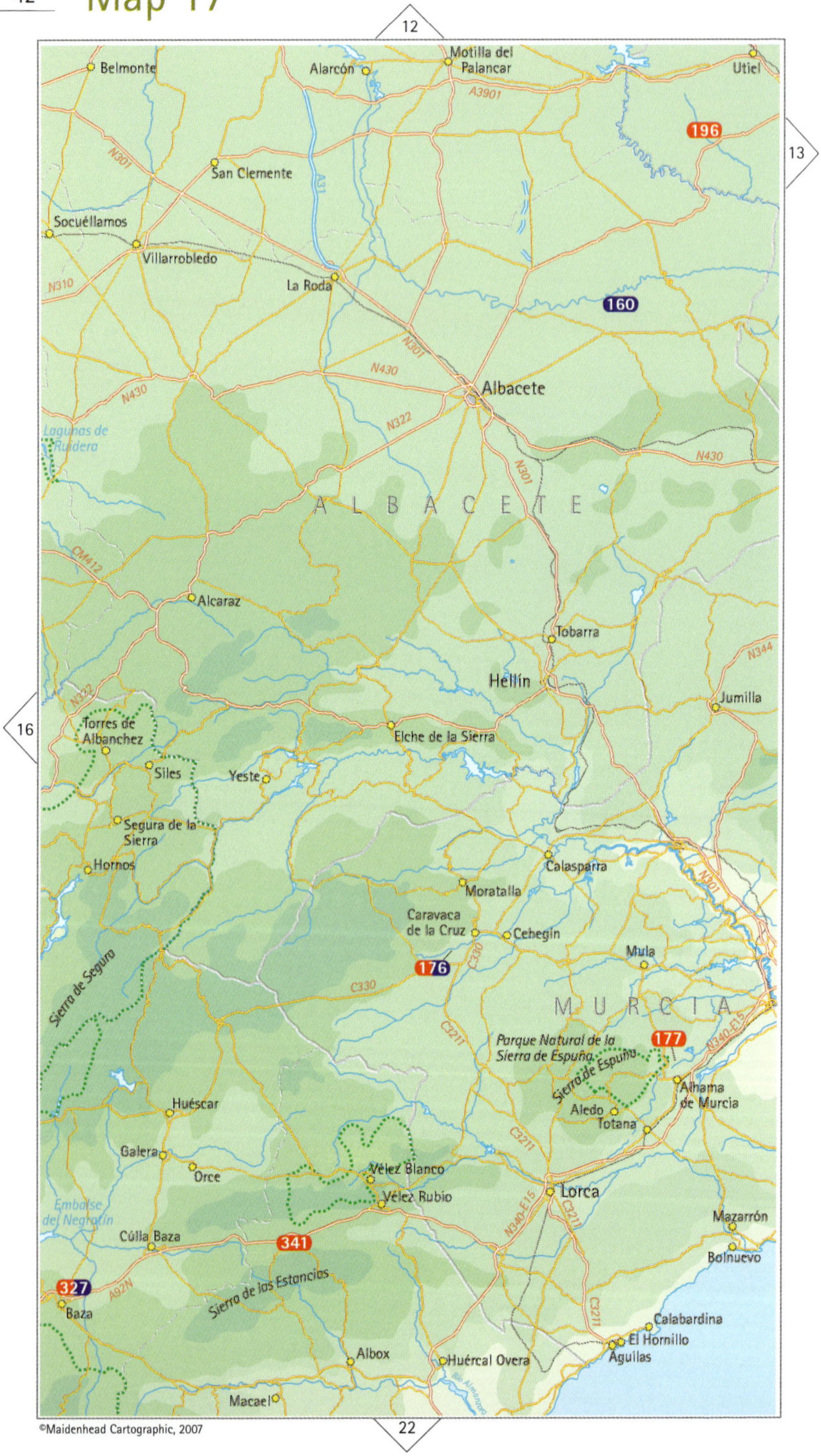

Belmonte
Alarcón
Motilla del Palancar
Utiel

A3901

196

San Clemente

N301

13

Socuéllamos

N310

Villarrobledo

La Roda

160

N430

N430

Albacete

N301

N430

N322

Lagunas de Ruidera

N430

A L B A C E T E

CM412

Alcaraz

Tobarra

N344

N322

Hellín

Jumilla

16

Torres de Albanchez

Elche de la Sierra

Siles

Yeste

Segura de la Sierra

Hornos

Calasparra

Moratalla

Caravaca de la Cruz

Cehegín

Mula

Sierra de Segura

176

C330

M U R C I A

C3211

N340-E15

Parque Natural de la Sierra de Espuña

177

Huéscar

Sierra de Espuña

Aledo

Totana

Alhama de Murcia

Galera

Orce

Vélez Blanco

Vélez Rubio

Lorca

C3211

Mazarrón

Embalse del Negratín

Cúlla Baza

341

N340-E15

Bolnuevo

327

A92N

Baza

Sierra de los Estancios

Calabardina

El Hornillo

Águilas

Albox

Huércal Overa

C3211

Macael

Map 18

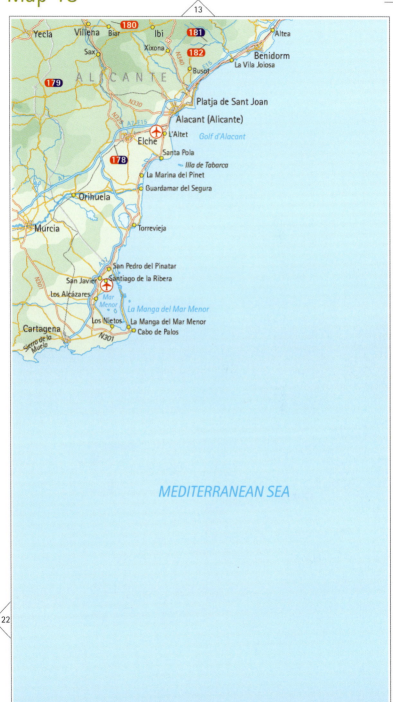

Yecla Villena Biar **180** Ibi **181** Altea

Sax Xixona **182** Benidorm

La Vila Joiosa

179 A L I C A N T E Busot

N330

N340 A7 E15 Platja de Sant Joan

Alacant (Alicante)

Elche L'Altet *Golf d'Alacant*

178 Santa Pola

~ *Illa de Tabarca*

La Marina del Pinet

Orihuela Guardamar del Segura

Murcia Torrevieja

A7 San Pedro del Pinatar

San Javier Santiago de la Ribera

Los Alcázares *Mar Menor*

N301 *La Manga del Mar Menor*

Los Nietos La Manga del Mar Menor

Cartagena Cabo de Palos

Sierra de la Muela

22

MEDITERRANEAN SEA

14

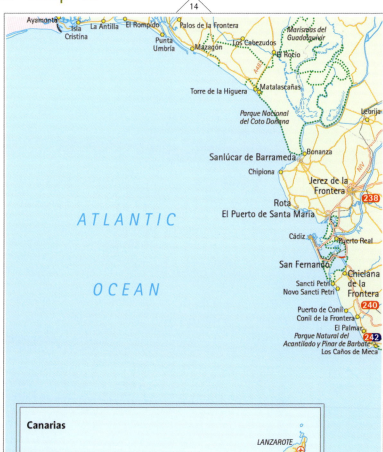

Ayamonte
Isla Cristina
La Antilla
El Rompido
Palos de la Frontera
Punta Umbría
Mazagón
Los Cabezudos
El Rocío
Marismas del Guadalquivir
Torre de la Higuera
Matalascañas
Parque Nacional del Coto Doñana
Lebrija
Sanlúcar de Barrameda
Bonanza
Chipiona
Jerez de la Frontera
238
Rota
El Puerto de Santa María
Cádiz
Puerto Real
San Fernando
Chiclana de la Frontera
Sancti Petri
Novo Sancti Petri
240
Puerto de Conil
Conil de la Frontera
El Palmar
242
Parque Natural del Acantilado y Pinar de Barbate
Los Caños de Meca

ATLANTIC

OCEAN

Canarias

LA PALMA
Santa Cruz de de la Palma
362-364
Santa Cruz de Tenerife
361
Las Palmas de Gran Canaria
HIERRO
GOMERA
TENERIFE
GRAN CANARIA
LANZAROTE
Arrecife
FUERTEVENTURA
Puerto del Rosario

Map 20

45

Map 21

Map 22

47

Sierra de los Filabres

A L M E R I A

Palomares

340 Garrucha

Gérgal

Sorbas

Turre

Mojácar

339

A370

Tabernas

Mini Hollywood

Sierra Alhamilla

Níjar

Carboneras

338

A344

ALMERIA

336

335

337

Aguadulce

Retamar

Parque
Natural
de Cabo
de Gata-
Níjar

Costa de Almería

Cabo de Gata

Roquetas de Mar

Almerimar

Cabo de Gata

MEDITERRANEAN SEA

ALGERIA

MOROCCO

Map 23

MEDITERRANEAN SEA

Cap de Formentor

344 Port de Pollença
Pollença **343**
Alcúdia
C710 **345** Port d'Alcúdia
Sa Calobra
350 **349** **347**
Port de Sóller **348** **346**
Deià *C713*
Sóller Arta **355** Cala Ratjada
351 Inca *C712*
Valldemossa Binissalem **353**
Esporles **352** Sineu Petra *C715*
354
Palma de Mallorca Manacor
Porto Cristo
C715 Porreres **356**
Felanitx
Magaluf Llucmajor **357** Porto Colom
359 **358**
MALLORCA Porto Petra
Colònia de Sant Jordi Santanyí

Cabrera

EIVISSA

San Antonio **342**

MENORCA

Sant Francesc

Mahón
360 San Luis

FORMENTERA

photo right Jose Navarro

Galicia

Pazo de Sedor

Castañeda, 15819 Arzua, La Coruña

One of a number of grand Galician *pazos* open to guests, and a delectable place to stay if you're on the road to Santiago. It is an imposing, 18th-century country house in a fairly remote position, surrounded by wooded hillsides and fields of maize and cattle. Inside you get a proper sense of its aristocratic past: great big rooms and a beautiful wide stone staircase between the two floors. Equally memorable is the open fireplace that spans an entire wall of the dining room, with bread ovens at each side; an airier second dining room has been created in an outbuilding with sweeping views. The bedrooms are a treat; high-ceilinged and parquet-floored, they have family antiques (some Art Deco, some older) and embroidered bedcovers. Some come with a balcony; all have space for an extra bed. Meals are as authentic as the house, and promise the flavours of Galicia – most of the vegetables are home-grown and the meats free range. Your hosts are charming, and fill the house with garden flowers. Superb value. *A Pazos de Galicia hotel.*

rooms	7 twins/doubles. Extra beds.
price	€56–€70. Singles €43–€53.
meals	Breakfast €5. Dinner €13.
closed	February.
directions	From Lugo N-540, then N-547 for Santiago. 400m past km57 marker, right to Pazo.

	Joaquín Saavedra
tel/fax	+34 981 501600
mobile	+34 675 080818
email	info@pazodesedor.com
web	www.pazodesedor.com

Hotel

Map 1 Entry 1

Casa Hotel As Artes

Travesia de Dos Puertas 2, 15707 Santiago de Compostela, La Coruña

Where would you want to stay when visiting Santiago? As close as possible to the cathedral, of course. Look no further than this delightful small hotel, in the quietest area of a busy city (the bars round the cathedral close at 10pm). It is the creation of two friendly and energetic Galicians, entirely inspired by Carlos's six-month stay in an intimate Parisian hotel. Guest bedrooms look to music and the arts for their leitmotif: choose between Rodin, Dante, Vivaldi, Gaudí, Picasso, Duncan and Chaplin. All are stylishly furnished with new wrought-iron bedsteads on polished parquet, fashionable fabrics, paintings and prints on exposed stone walls; beds have embroidered sheets, bathrooms sport dressing gowns and thick towels. There's a little sauna, too, and physiotherapy on request. It's fantastic value, and what makes it even better is the professionalism of your hosts. Breakfast – fresh orange juice, fruit salad, charcuterie, cakes, several breads – is served at pretty red-clothed tables. The setting is unbeatable: the cathedral two steps away, restaurants outside the door. *Parking is at some distance.*

rooms	7 twins/doubles.
price	€52–€98.
meals	Breakfast €8.
closed	Rarely.
directions	In Santiago head for Praza do Obradoiro; Rua de San Francisco to left of cathedral. Hotel 50m past cathedral on right. Detailed directions on web site.

	Esther Mateos & Carlos Elizechea
tel	+34 981 572590
mobile	+34 657 813713
fax	+34 981 577823
email	recepcion@asartes.com
web	www.asartes.com

Hotel

Map 1 Entry 2

Casa Grande de Cornide

Teo, 15886 Santiago de Compostela, La Coruña

This very special B&B 15 minutes from Santiago centre is surrounded by Galician green. Casa Grande may be likened to a good claret: refined, select, worth paying a bit more for. Owner José Ramón wrote *The Way to Compostela*) and a love of culture is evident throughout his home, today run by Javier Goyanes. It houses a large collection of modern Galician paintings, hundreds of ceramic pots, a huge library and decoration that is a spicy cocktail of old and new: exposed granite, designer lamps, wooden ceilings, and, everywhere, art. A place to come to read, to paint in the beautiful mature garden full of ancient trees – and a surprising number of palms for so far north – and to cycle: bikes are provided free for guests. The studied décor of the lounges and library is mirrored in the bedrooms and suites, some of which are in a separate building. They have all mod cons and the same mix of modern and old; there are books, ornaments, paintings and exquisite little details such as handmade tiles in the bathrooms to create a special feel. "A glorious place," enthused one reader. *A Pazos de Galicia hotel.*

rooms	8: 6 twins/doubles, 2 singles.
price	€50–€100. Singles €40–€68.
meals	Breakfast €7. Lunch & dinner €15.
closed	January-March.
directions	From Santiago, N-550 for Pontevedra. Follow sign for hotel; at roundabout, turn left.

	Javier Goyanes
tel	+34 981 805599
fax	+34 981 805751
email	cornide@casasgrandesdegalicia.com
web	www.casasgrandesdegalicia.com

Guest house

Map 1 Entry 3

Casa Grande do Bachao

Monte Bachao s/n, Sta. Cristina de Fecha, 15898 Santiago de Compostela, La Coruña

In a recently widened clearing in the forest… not a gingerbread cottage nor the home of Red Riding Hood's grandmother, but a solid, four-square house. Much of the wood has been cleared but you'll still need to like eucalyptus trees to stay here… stands of them, many recently cropped, surround Bachao on all sides. Inside, the house has been soberly furnished without eclipsing the original bones of the place. Bedrooms are uncluttered and distinct. The dining room is huge and light, with a high raftered ceiling, slab-stone floor and the odd sculpture dotted about; as if to emphasise the importance of food, there's a vast stone feeding trough next door. If you like splendid isolation you'll love it here – and you can actually walk to Santiago de Compostela (it's 35 kilometres). There are sauna, gym, a library stacked with books on flora and fauna, and bikes to borrow. A spot of trout fishing can also be arranged. On wet days families will appreciate the games and TV room; on fine ones, the swimming pool. And the freedom to explore. Good value. *A Pazos de Galicia hotel.*

rooms	12: 9 twins/doubles, 2 singles, 1 suite.
price	€50-€85. Singles €40-€68. Suite €65-€100.
meals	Breakfast €7. Lunch & dinner €15.
closed	24/25 December.
directions	From Santiago, CP-0701, Santa Comba road. Pazo signed on right at 11km marker before village. Follow road for 5km; signed.

	Javier Goyanes
tel	+34 981 194118
fax	+34 981 192028
email	bachao@pazosdegalicia.com

Hotel

Map 1 Entry 4

Hotel Rústico Santa Eulalia

Santa Baia s/n, 15256 Chacín-Mazaricos, La Coruña

If you're sporty and you don't demand luxury, this modest hotel between Santiago and the Atlantic could be for you. The young owners are keen to promote 'adventure tourism' on their patch so you can fish for trout, hike, mountain-bike or ride the St James's Way, sail or, perhaps most tempting of all, swim in the Atlantic off the lovely sands at Carnota. Bedrooms are in the original stone farmhouse and are surprisingly smart considering the price, the best with their own covered galleries. All are cheerfully decorated with attractive wooden furniture and floors, and central heating in bedrooms and bathrooms, a comfort when the days turn chilly. The restaurant is just across the way, new and strictly functional, its culinary philosophy to keep things "simple and local". Try the local specialities stuffed peppers and *empanada*, the Galician equivalent of Cornish pasty. The wine list is surprisingly good. Although this is a no-frills hotel, the young owners' kindness and hospitality has convinced us that Santa Eulalia deserves a place in this guide.

rooms	10 twins/doubles.
price	€45-€55. Singles €33-€45.
meals	Breakfast €5. Lunch €10. Dinner €12.
closed	Rarely.
directions	From A-9 exit Santiagojor/Noia. Signs for Noia, then right to Serra de Outes. Here, road towards Mazaricos. Hotel on right after 8km.

John Pritchard & María Angeles Cuadrós

tel	+34 981 877262
mobile	+34 647 694848
fax	+34 981 852062
email	reservas@andanzasrural.com
web	www.hotelsantaeulalia.com

Hotel

Map 1 Entry 5

Pazo de Souto

Lugar de la Torre 1, 15106 Sisamo-Carballo, La Coruña

The fine old manor, lost among fields of maize and wooded glades, was built by a member of the Inquisition in 1672; the inquisitor's safe still lurks in one wall. Later it became the school that José attended as a boy. Now he and young Carlos have one of the best small hotels in this little-known corner of Galicia. The house is dark and labyrinthine; the vast sitting room has a *lareira* (inglenook), old-fashioned fauteuils and chunky beams, the dining room is lovely, with a gallery; lighting is subtle and the bar is deliciously cosy. Some bedrooms are on the ground floor; a granite staircase leads to more above. Those on the first floor have classic Spanish beds and a certain decadent flair, while the smallest and plainest are in the attic. A few rooms have waterbeds; bathroom suites are new. Dinners are better than breakfasts and locals come for the fresh fish from Malpica – a good sign. Carlos is eager to please and has impeccable English; it would be hard to find more charming hosts. Fine views from the palm-treed garden – and all the rugged beauty of the north coast. *A Pazos de Galicia hotel.*

rooms	11 twins/doubles.
price	€50-€83. Singles €36-€66.
meals	Lunch & dinner €15. À la carte from €22.
closed	Rarely.
directions	From Santiago C-545 for Santa Comba & Carballo; after 27km, through Carballo for Malpica; left 100m after BP petrol station, for Sisamo. Pazo 2.5km beyond, on right after church.

	Carlos Taibo Pombo
tel	+34 981 756065
fax	+34 981 756191
email	reservas@pazodosouto.com
web	www.pazodosouto.com

Hotel

Map 1 Entry 6

Casa Entremuros

Cances Grandes 77, 15107 Carballo, La Coruña

Here are long stretches of fine, sandy beaches, hidden coves and a number of old fishing villages where the seafood is among the best in Spain. Rest awhile at Santiago and Rosa's solid old granite house and B&B, and let them unlock the secrets of this wonderfully unspoilt region. You approach through the pretty stable yard, with an annexe to one side, lawns, flowers and a fold-away swimming pool in one corner. There are six bedrooms, not huge but handsome; expect shining parquet-clad floors, fitted wardrobes, white bedspreads and matching rag rugs, carefully restored antique beds, a modern upholstered chair or two, and good (though somewhat small) bathrooms. There is a large, light-filled lounge with a dresser and a wood-burner in the huge stone *lareira*. Rosa makes fresh fruit juices and gives you local cheeses and honey and cake. No meals apart from breakfast but the popular Casa Elias is only two miles away — you can have a great meal there at any time of year. A quiet, unassuming and good value place to stay on the wild, indented coastline of the Rías Altas, little known beyond Galicia.

rooms	6 twins/doubles.
price	€42-€53. Singles €36-€45. VAT included.
meals	Breakfast €4. VAT included. Restaurants nearby.
closed	15 December-15 January.
directions	From Santiago de Compostela, by Alameda, road for 'Hospital General'. On to Carballo, then towards Malpica to Cances; house signed by petrol station.

	Santiago Luaces de La-Herrán & Rosa Alvarez
tel/fax	+34 981 757099
mobile	+34 678 605443
email	entremuros@finisterrae.com
web	www.casaentremuros.com

B&B

Map 1 Entry 7

Pazo da Trave

Galdo, 27850 Viveiro, Lugo

Plants scramble over old stone, the garden laps up to the house, vines hang heavy under the trellis, big trees give shade. The lovely gardens, where sculptures – discreetly for sale – are dotted amonst the greenery, is an integral part of this place. There is also an old *hórreo* outside – a wooden storage area where food was traditionally stored – and a chapel exhibiting more art. Food, too, is taken seriously at Pazo da Trave and dinners are a delight, served by kind and attentive staff in a sympathetically lit dining area, accompanied by an excellent selection of wines. Beautiful bedrooms have big oak beds, beamed ceilings and more art; children are thoughtfully taken care of, with small beds and cots. There is a lovely whitewashed beamy sitting room with an open fire – perfect for cosy winter nights – and a gallery on the first floor with a chaise-longue and armchairs so you can gaze over the gardens or dip into a book (there's quite a collection). A sauna, gym and billiard room are further reasons to stay in this friendly, artistic and unstuffy hotel. *A Pazos de Galicia hotel.*

rooms	20: 17 twins/doubles, 1 single, 2 suites.
price	€66-€105. Single €45-€60. Suite €115-€145.
meals	Breakfast €8. Lunch & dinner €22. Restaurant closed 1-15 November.
closed	Rarely.
directions	From N-642 to Viveiro, C-640, Lugo road. After 2km, Galdo signed right. Pazo on right after village.

	Alfonso Otero Regal
tel	+34 982 598163
fax	+34 982 598040
email	traveregal@interbook.net
web	www.oteroregal.com

Hotel

Map 2 Entry 8

Casa Grande de Camposo
Lugar de Camposo 7, 27364 O Corgo, Lugo

Inside and out – a rare, intriguing place. A high stone wall encloses the four-square farmhouse and its grounds, fortifying Casa Grande against the outside world. The stables have been turned into a quirky covered patio – usable in even the wettest Galician weather – and the unfussy garden is a brilliant place for children. The house itself, built in the 1740s by a wealthy farmer, is a fascinating labyrinth of passages, landings and rooms. María Luisa – whose father inherited the place – presides, priding herself on the family atmosphere and the traditional cooking. You'll be welcomed into a softly lit, stone-floored hall, with oak and chestnut beams and a massive traditional open fireplace. Big, airy bedrooms have pretty rugs on shining wooden or terracotta floors, solid original furniture and bright immaculate bathrooms. The village is tiny – 14 inhabitants – and grew up around the house. The area is not yet on the tourist trail and there's plenty to explore: you're within easy reach of the Sierra de los Aucares and the river Miño has monasteries and churches dotted all along its banks.

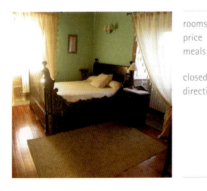

rooms	8 twins/doubles.
price	€57–€78. Singles €42–€52.
meals	Breakfast €4. Lunch & dinner €18.
closed	15 January–15 February.
directions	Lugo-Salida A-6, exit 479 onto DP-1611 for Puebla de San Julián. After 10km, signed on right.

	María Luisa Sánchez
tel	+34 982 543800
mobile	+34 696 641230
fax	+34 982 543937
email	camposo@terra.es
web	www.casagrandecamposo.agatur.es

Guest house

Map 2 Entry 9

A Fervenza

Ctra. Lugo-Páramo km11, 27163 O Corgo, Lugo

The river Miño laps at the walls of this house and ancient, working mill. Girdled by 18 hectares of magnificent ancient woodland, it's precious enough to have been declared a UNESCO Biosphere Reserve. The Casa, named after the amazing rocky waterfall outside, is both hotel *and* museum, and the foundry, in perfect working order, is fascinating; they'll happily give you a guided tour. The restaurant with glorious open fireplace is in the oldest part and dates from the 17th century, and the menus are based on the sort of food that was around when the building was built… such as beef and wild boar stew with chestnuts in winter. Wines are outstanding, the region's best. After a day on the river (with canoe or traditional *batuxo*) return to quiet, simple, stylish bedrooms in this house where the miller once lived. Restoration has been meticulous in its respect for local tradition and lore, yet there's no stinting on creature comforts. Antiques have been beautifully restored, rugs woven on their looms, there are linen curtains, chestnut beams and floors and hand-painted sinks. A gem. *A Rusticae hotel.*

rooms	9: 8 doubles, 1 suite.
price	€56–€70. Singles €39–€49. Suite €80–€100. VAT included.
meals	Breakfast €5. Lunch & dinner €15. A la carte €15–€30. VAT included.
closed	Rarely.
directions	From Madrid, N-VI for Lugo. 2km to Conturiz & left at Hotel Torre de Núñez for Páramo; 11km; right at A Fervenza sign; 1km.

Germán Pérez Mourenza

tel/fax	+34 982 150610
email	info@fervenza.com
web	www.fervenza.com

Hotel

Map 2 Entry 10

Pazo de Vilabade

Villabade, 27122 Castroverde, Lugo

In a delectably quiet corner of Galicia, on one of the old routes to Santiago, the deeply rural Pazo de Vilabade is worth at least two nights. Behind the sober façade and fine granite entrance of the manor house by the church waits a charming family home. And heirlooms at every turn. In the corridors: statues, a chaise-longue and family portraits above the grandest of stairwells; in the big, airy bedrooms, named after beloved family members, stacks more lovely pieces: old brass or walnut beds (beware old sizes too), dark wardrobes, huge mirrors. Most seductive of all: the lofty breakfast room with its enormous *lareira* (inglenook) and two tables at which you will be served cheeses, homemade cakes and jams and delicious coffee. The heart and soul of it all is Doña Teresa Arana, an entertaining and sprightly lady, so determined to get it right that she studied rural tourism in France before opening her historic house. Meet her – just a few words of English but her French is very good – and share a wonderful home and gardens. "Totally special, a fascinating place," wrote a reader.

rooms	6: 5 twins/doubles, 1 single.
price	€89. Single €75.
meals	Breakfast €5.25.
	Restaurants in Castroverde.
closed	November–May.
directions	From Madrid for La Coruña on A6. Exit onto C-630 for Castroverde. At exit of town, left signed 'Pazo de Villabade'. House 2km, by prominent church.

	Teresa Arana
tel/fax	+34 982 312063
mobile	+34 637 776737
web	www.elpazo.com
email	pazovilabade@telefonica.net

B&B

Map 2 Entry 11

Casa de Labranza Arza

Reigosa-San Cristobo do Real, 27633 Samos, Lugo

Glorious views, a farmhouse-family welcome, the smell of newly baked bread... this place is special. The views really *are* something, the 6,000-foot-high peaks strung together like a dowager's diamonds; in the foreground is a rural patchwork of green fields and hedgerows. On a clear day you can see as far as Portugal. Casa Arza is on the slopes of Monte Oribio and is a working dairy farm – hence the delicious butter and soft cheeses served at breakfast. Rosy-cheeked Ramona, who seems to belong to another age, makes jams, butter, bread, cooks meat in a wood-fired oven and vegetables straight from the farm. (The bread is kneaded in an old bread chest and baked daily in a 1700s stone oven.) This is back to basics in the best possible sense, and the warmth of the hospitality is the cherry on the cake. The slate walls and roof of the Casa are typical of the area; spotless bedrooms have rafters and exposed stone walls and beds are wooden and antique, widened to take modern mattresses. Be sure to visit the Monasterio de Samos nearby – it's the biggest monastic cloister in Spain. Stunning value.

rooms	9 twins/doubles.
price	€35. Singles €28. VAT included.
meals	Breakfast €4. Dinner with wine, €11.
closed	Rarely.
directions	From Lugo, N-VI for Ponferrada; C-546 to Sarria-Monforte. Left at Sarria on LU-633 to Samos. Through San Cristobo; signed to right at end of village; 4km uphill on left, on entering Reigosa.

	Cristina Arza Río
tel	+34 982 216027
fax	+34 982 187036
email	arza@mundo-r.com

Guest house

Map 2 Entry 12

Casa Grande de Rosende
Rosende, 27466 Sober, Lugo

This monument to medieval life is full of fascination – from its suits of armour to its vast stone-walled rooms. The tower dates from 1511, the rest is noble 18th century, and several of the bedrooms are stupendously raftered, with furnishings to match. The charming personalities of Pauloba, Manuel and son Alesandro, who has recently studied tourism, add to fun of being here – and Manuel's knowledge of history is a delight. His grandmother left this, the long-standing family home, to become a celebrated pastry chef of the Ritz in Madrid; she returned to share her knowledge with the locals, and now the area is renowned for its pastries and cakes! (Pauloba's fresh almond pudding is worth a detour alone.) Guests are also invited to sample *aguardiente*, a homemade digestif, before dinner, in a sitting room magnificent with neo-classical paintings and a piano crowded with family photos. You are in the heart of the Ribeira Sacra, one of the most beautiful corners of Galicia; from here you can visit any number of bodegas. A great treat. *A Pazos de Galicia hotel.*

rooms	13: 12 twins/doubles, 1 suite.
price	€65. Suite €84.
meals	Breakfast €5.50. Lunch €19. Dinner €16.
closed	15 December–15 January.
directions	From Orense, N-120 for Monforte. At km530, exit for Canaval. Right at 1st T-junc., following signs for house. Casa Grande 3km down road.

	Manuel Vieítez
tel	+34 982 460627
fax	+34 982 455104
email	rosende@infonegocio.com
web	www.casagrandederosende.com

Hotel

Map 2 Entry 13

Pazo Paradela

Carretera Barrio km2, 32780 Puebla de Trives, Orense

An utterly bucolic retreat: a 17th-century manor house with views to the Galician hills. Your host: delightful Manuel, who speaks superb English. He grew up in the States, dreamed of returning to his native soil, and ended up restoring the imposing old granite house, close to sleepy Trives, that his father bought years before. Manuel's natural generosity is reflected in the renovation; "be proud of your work," is his philosophy. Bedrooms and bathrooms have been treated to the simple best: chestnut floors and furniture, Portuguese marble, antique mirrors, rustic stone walls. There's central heating for winter, air conditioning for summer, views are long and green and the peace supreme. The treats continue at table: in the vast granite-hearthed dining room you get homemade honey and jams for breakfast and, for dinner, the best of Galician country cooking: perhaps roast leg of lamb from the wood-fired oven and vegetables straight from the kitchen garden. And the ultimate in hospitality: a *queimada* shared with your hosts, the local hot brandied brew that keeps evil spirits at bay.

rooms	8: 7 twins/doubles, 1 suite.
price	€60. Singles €45. Suite €70. VAT included.
meals	Breakfast €8. Dinner with wine, €22. VAT included.
closed	22 December–2 January.
directions	From León, N-VI to Ponferrada; N-120 into A Rua Petin; C-636 to Trives. Through centre of town, cross bridge, 1st right; follow signs.

	Manuel Rodríguez Rodríguez
tel/fax	+34 988 330714
mobile	+34 679 429873
email	1pa712e1@infonegocio.com

Hotel

Map 2 Entry 14

Casa Grande de Trives

c/Marqués de Trives 17, 32780 Pobra de Trives, Orense

This noble village house with its own chapel (mass held every Wednesday) was one of the first to be restored with government help and open to guests; like good claret it has got better and better. Rooms are filled with antique pieces, many exquisitely upholstered or carved, and a very fine restored piano, rained on for years in this once-derelict house – a present from Elizabeth II of Spain. Bedrooms in a separate wing are a quiet delight, big with polished floors and (in some cases) French windows to the gardens. And the garden is huge, straight out of a fairytale, full of shady hidden corners and heaven for kids. There's a lovely sitting room where you can have a quiet drink, and an unforgettable dining room where breakfast is served. Here the richness of the furnishings, the cut flowers and the classical music vie with the homemade cakes, fresh fruits, big pots of coffee and croissants that make their way up from the kitchen via a dumb waiter. Fine bone china adds to the elegance of the meal. A marvellous place and a most gracious and charming welcome from mother and son.

rooms	9 twins/doubles.
price	€51–€72. Singles €41–€60.
meals	Breakfast €5.60.
	Dinner €18, on request.
closed	Rarely.
directions	Madrid A-6 for La Coruña. Exit 400 for N-120 Monforte de Lemos. At km468, branch off for Pobra de Trives, signed Terra de Trives; right at lights onto C-536 Trives. On left in village.

	Alfredo Araujo & Adelaida Alvarez
tel/fax	+34 988 332066
email	info@casagrandetrives.com
web	www.casagrandetrives.com

Guest house

Map 2 Entry 15

Casa Grande de Soutullo

Soutullo de Abaixo, 32152 Coles, Orense

Come for charming owners and stylish country living. This was Benito's great-grandfather's house, a pile of stones in 1973; then Gill and Benito nurtured it back to life. From the breezy and beautiful internal courtyard – with unusual stone settee – radiate a series of elegantly raftered galleries and rooms decorated with Gill's paintings and many wonderful antiques. The breakfast room is inviting, its several tables set with white china. Wooden-floored bedrooms are equally good, enhanced with period pieces and lively colours; no need for air conditioning: they are naturally cool. Bathrooms have hand-painted washbasins: the attention to detail is a delight. Outside, vast grounds through which a 100-year-old tortoise roams, a sun loggia, a serene pool and a tennis court. Hard to tear yourself away… but make time for Orense with its seven-arched bridge, one of the finest in Spain, and its amazing Bishop's Baths. Its three outdoor pools, Japanese stove garden and treatments galore are your passport to heaven, modestly priced. *A Pazos de Galicia hotel.*

rooms	8 twins/doubles.
price	€69–€79. Singles €55–€61.
meals	Breakfast €6.50.
	Restaurants nearby.
closed	Rarely.
directions	From Orense, N-525 for Santiago to Gustei; CP-6 to A Peroxa; 1st turning on right to Soutullo de Abaixo.

	Benito Vázquez
tel	+34 988 205611
mobile	+34 669 826223
fax	+34 988 205694
email	pazosoutullo@yahoo.com

Hotel

Map 2 Entry 16

Hostal Restaurante Asensio

Rua do Tollo 2, 36750 Goian, Pontevedra

At first glance you may wonder how this unassuming restaurant with rooms earns its place in the pages of this guide. But there are two excellent reasons for coming here: delightful Dolores ('Loli') and her husband Fernando, who lived for many years in the UK and who love receiving English-speaking guests – and the food. Fernando's claim that he can satisfy even the most demanding of palates is no idle boast. With the river Miño a hop away and the sea not much further the menu naturally gravitates towards fish, but there's tasty duck à l'orange too, and sirloin of pork with blue cheese. To match it all is a small and judiciously chosen list of wines (and the wine from the village is superb). Pink and white tables are crisply laid in the small, pine-clad dining room; the bar area next door is where you breakfast. Bedrooms could be just an afterthought but they're as spruce as can be, not hugely memorable but comfortable and clean; chose between the newest ones grafted onto the original building, and the coolest in the old part. All have fans. It's cheerful, friendly and the value is superb.

rooms	6 twins/doubles.
price	€42. Singles €36.
meals	Breakfast €2. Lunch €9. Dinner from €30 à la carte.
closed	16 September-16 October.
directions	E-1 Vigo to Tuy; exit at km172 onto N-550 La Guardia & A Guarda. On for 15km. Hostal on left on passing through Goian.

	Fernando Asensio
tel/fax	+34 986 620152
mobile	+34 686 962884
email	asensio1988@msn.com
web	www.restauranteasensio.com

Guest house

Map 1 Entry 17

Finca Río Miño

Carril 6, Las Eiras, 36760 O Rosal, Pontevedra

It's like being on holiday in two countries at the same time. Portuguese Vila Nova de Cerveira (worth a visit for its Saturday market alone) is ten minutes by car; on this side of the water, one of the most lushest areas of Spain. And what a position, up on the bank of the Miño with views to the Alto Minho on a clear day. Robin fell in love with Galicia many years ago, returned with Deborah on their 25th wedding anniversary and booked into Finca Río Miño; now they own the whole lovely place. This 'hidden finca', as locals know it, includes two simple, comfortable pine-clad lodges in a large, verdant garden and a small cottage attached to the 350-year-old farmhouse. Plus... a breakfast room, a bar, a pool with a view and an unforgettable terrace with a rambling passion fruit to give shade. One of the big attractions here is the proximity of river and sea, so anyone interested in fishing, kayaking, surfing or white water rafting will be in clover. Hiking, riding and biking too can be arranged – and pets Dylan and Kat are very much part of the family. Such peace.

rooms	1 + 3: 1 twin. 2 lodges for 4; 1 cottage for 2-4.
price	€60. Lodges €80-€99. Cottage €75-€99. VAT included.
meals	Breakfast €8. Restaurants within walking distance.
closed	Lodges December & January.
directions	Vigo E1/A-3 to Tui; La Guardia/O Rosal exit onto CS50/POSS2; bypass Goian; left at Eiras sign just past Adegas Tollodouro; thro' forest to T-junc; right; Finca 100m on left.

	Robin & Deborah Winterhalder
tel	+34 986 621107
mobile	+34 660 930 313
fax	+34 986 621035
email	info@fincariomino.com
web	www.fincariomino.com

B&B & Self-catering

Map 1 Entry 18

Os Bravos I

Estas, 36730 Tomiño, Pontevedra

Pluck fresh kiwi, peaches and nectarines for breakfast. Stroll around your walled garden – yes, you will feel proprietorial – before breakfasting on your bedroom balcony with its views to Portugal. Slipped into this unspoilt pocket of Spain, this is a genuine hideaway. Several notches above the average self-catering villa, the sprawling, five-bedroom, colonial-style house combines modernity with Galician charm. Locally-made chestnut furniture, sloping ceilings and splashes of chintz give a hint of 'country' while the modern sofas and owner's bold paintings add panache. The kitchen is so well-equipped you'll want to take it home. Judith (English and the artist) and Karl (half-Galician) are warm, engaging, fun and know all the best beaches, walks and romantic ruins. But often it's just too tempting to do anything but drift around the garden and pool, or perhaps sketch or paint (studio and materials available for budding artists). At night, you'll be hard pushed to hear anything more than the soft plop of an over-ripe peach.

rooms	5 + 1: 3 twins, 2 family. 1 villa for up to 12.
price	€70. Villa £900–£1,500 (sterling) per week. VAT included.
meals	Restaurants nearby. Maid service optional, £200 (sterling) per week.
closed	Rarely.
directions	From Vigo N-550 for Tui. Pass yellow bar, El Paso; next right for Estas; through village for 2km.

Judith Mary Goater & Karl Abreu

tel	+34 986 623337
mobile	+34 667 497914
fax	+34 986 623338
email	osbravos@telefonica.net

B&B & Self-catering

Map 1 Entry 19

Rectoral de Cobres 1729

San Adrian de Cobres, 36142 Vilaboa, Pontevedra

Mussel platforms, fishing boats and the majestic sweep of the Ría de Vigo – a special site for a special place. The house was built for a priest in 1729 and has been beautifully renovated by vivacious Randi, a Norwegian architect, and her husband, the equally hospitable Juan Carlos. Relax in the long living room divided by an old stone arch and graced with a delicate Persian carpet and red sofas; dip into a tome from the library (3,000 books and almost as many maps), take a drink to the terrace with the estuary views. Bedrooms are sensitively designed and reveal a designer's love of clean lines and uncluttered spaces. One lovely double has a sweep of polished parquet, French windows to a balcony (more views) and an entire wall of ancient stone. Gravitate to the bar, where strong Galician beer is served; Juan Carlos may pick up the guitar or the Gallic pipes and serenade you. The stunning outdoor *hórreo* (granary) has been converted into a further sitting area: a magical place to watch the sun go down. And there are some wonderful fish restaurants close by. *A Pazos de Galicia hotel.*

rooms	8 twins/doubles.
price	€80-€150.
meals	Breakfast €8. Restaurants 500m.
closed	Rarely.
directions	From Pontevedra, A-9 for Vigo; exit 146 Cangas. After toll, left following signs for Vilaboa & Cobres. 2km from junction, at km8 marker, take track on left; 100m from road.

	Juan Carlos Madriñán & Randi Hanssen
tel	+34 986 673810
mobile	+34 607 210209
fax	+34 986 673803
email	info@rectoral.com
web	www.rectoral.com

Hotel

Map 1 Entry 20

Asturias & Cantabria

La Corte

33843 Villar de Vildas, Asturias

Here you are *cerca del cielo* – close to heaven. Up the scenic road to a delightful working village deep in the Somiedo Natural Park. The inn is a 19th-century wood and stone farmhouse, converted by its charismatic owner into a small restaurant with rooms. You enter via a small courtyard, then up old stone steps to a wooden-floored sitting room. Here are books and photographs (some of your host as a young boy), a brass-studded chess of drawers, old crockery, a handsome hearth and a gallery with amazing mountain views. A metal spiral staircase leads to the bedrooms, some big, some small. All have good bathrooms, new pine furniture and comfy beds; two have dormer windows so you can study the stars from your bed. The self-catering studio in the 150-year-old granary has a Heidi feel, the apartment comes with an open-plan living room. Locals pop in for a drink or a fine meaty meal in the restaurant – cosy, low-ceilinged, beamed and with basket lamps. No simpler or sweeter place from which to go walking in the Pigüeña Valley, where some of Europe's last bears roam free.

rooms	5 + 2: 5 doubles. Studio for 2. Apartment for 4.
price	€60. Studio €65. Apartment €100. VAT included.
meals	Breakfast €4. Lunch & dinner €15.
closed	Rarely.
directions	From Oviedo N-634 west. Just before Cornellana, left on AS-15 to Puente de San Martín. Here, AS-227 south to Aguasmestas. Here, right to Pigüeña; up via Cores; 11km to Villar.

	Adriano Berdasco Fernández
tel	+34 985 763131
mobile	+34 696 605400
fax	+34 985 763117
email	lacorte_somiedorural@hotmail.com
web	www.somiedorural.com/lacorte

B&B & Self-catering

Map 2 Entry 21

Palacio de Prelo

33728 Prelo-Boal, Asturias

Rediscover the meaning of silence. It is broken only by the echo of footsteps on ancient floors. Alicia will guide you through reading rooms and vaulted doors to your room, relating on the way the story of the professor of economics who has so beautifully restored this 16th-century palace to its former glory. Your room will be large, plush and outrageously comfortable. Noble old wardrobes and delicately embroidered bedspreads reflect the owner's delight in fine antiques and rich fabrics, but our favourite room is the one in the tower, its contemporary furnishings enhanced by a feast of ancient rafters. Or choose a room at the front of the house, for pastoral views and the sound of cowbells. If you are in the tower bedroom, no excuse not to write that novel: the mezzanine gallery has writing desks strategically positioned in front of tiny windows. In-palace entertainment includes an atmospheric billiard room and a home cinema with a fine selection of classic and foreign films. You may be a 30-minute drive from fine Asturian beaches but this feels a million miles away.

rooms	5: 3 twins/doubles, 2 suites.
price	€126-€140. Suites €160-€200.
meals	Dinner €24. Lunch on request only.
closed	10 January-10 February.
directions	From Navia on AS-12 through Boal to San Luis. Here, follow signs to Villalón/Castrillón. After 1.4km, Palacio on hillside on left.

	Alicia Alvarez
tel	+34 985 620718
fax	+34 985 620038
email	info@palaciodeprelo.com
web	www.palaciodeprelo.com

Hotel

Map 2 Entry 22

Hotel Villa La Argentina

Parque de la Barrera, Villar de Luarca 33700, Luarca, Asturias

This aristocratic villa was constructed in 1899 by an emigrant who'd made his fortune in South America – hence the name. It was later abandoned, then rediscovered by the González Fernández family who saw in the crumbling stucco a brighter future. Once again it breathes an air of light-hearted elegance and optimism. The breakfast room is parquet-floored and high-ceilinged, with beautiful stained-glass windows; gilt-framed oil paintings, candelabras and tall mirrors add to the lofty feel. The best bedrooms are in harmony with the house and have glorious garden views; most are large with stuccoed and corniced ceilings and king-sized beds. Good mattresses and hydromassage tubs add to the feel-good factor, bathrooms are quirky and Antonio and his staff are delightful. After a light tapas lunch in the coffee bar, slip off for a swim or a game of billiards, then wander the Villa's overgrown gardens with their 100-year-old sequoias brought all the way from America. There's also a faded and charming little chapel.

rooms	12 + 4: 9 twins/doubles, 3 suites. 4 apartments for 4.
price	€69-€95. Suites €81-€102. Apartments €150.
meals	Breakfast €5.50-€9.50. Tapas available. Restaurant 100m.
closed	7 Jan-end Feb; open 14 Feb.
directions	From Oviedo & Gijón on A-8/N-632 for Avilés. Exit onto N-634 for Luarca. At AGIP petrol station just before Luarca, right on LU-1; yellow signs to hotel.

	Antonio González
tel	+34 985 640102
fax	+34 985 640973
email	villalaargentina@villalaargentina.com
web	www.villalaargentina.com

Hotel & Self-catering

Map 2 Entry 23

La Torre de Villademoros

Villademoros s/n (Cadavedo), 33788 Valdés, Asturias

In meadowland high above the coast stands this elegant retreat – hike down to undiscovered shingle beaches. Young, welcoming Manolo designed La Torre with his brother, and the 18th-century Asturian exterior, with a medieval tower to one side, gives little hint of the delights within. It is intimate, cosy and hugely appealing. Old granite walls, chunky rafters and gleaming wooden or slate floors are the background to sleek sofas and sculpted lighting, while warm colours, modern paintings and an open hearth add depth. Serene bedrooms and private sitting rooms are finished with polished chestnut and pine; bathrooms are rustic-contemporary. Views are grand – over the sea or the lush eucalyptus forests. Dinner is an inexpensive and convivial affair with traditional dishes (stuffed tuna a seasonal delicacy), good wines and delicious desserts. Breakfasts are equally scrumptious – pastries, cakes, crêpes, homemade jams, a cooked breakfast on request – and will set you up for the superb coastal path to Cudillero (return by train). Not easy to find, but well worth the effort. *A Rusticae hotel.*

rooms	10 twins/doubles.
price	€74-€105. Singles €56-€81.
meals	Breakfast €7. Dinner €16.
closed	7 January-2 March
directions	From Oviedo, N-632/E-70 for La Coruña; exit for Cadavedo. Through village & into Villademoros. 30m after Villademoros road sign, right; signed.

	Manolo Santullano Méndez
tel	+34 985 645264
fax	+34 985 645265
email	correo@torrevillademoros.com
web	www.torrevillademoros.com

Hotel

Map 2 Entry 24

La Casona de Pío

c/Riofrío 3, 33150 Cudillero, Asturias

Hard to believe Pío ever had a fish-salting factory here, in this elegant little hotel one street back from the main square. Cudillero is one of the prettiest fishing villages of the Asturian coast, a huddle of houses around a sheltered cove where you can still watch the catch being landed first thing. La Casona de Pío is one of the area's best fish restaurants and is hard to fault — beautifully presented tables and food, an extraordinarily crafted wooden ceiling, and a chef who knows his stuff. We were ushered through to the kitchen to see all kinds of good things on the go in boiling pots and sizzling pans. Steep steps climb from the street to the reception hall, where out of season Pío's charming owners will give you a choice of rooms. We might choose no. 104 for its private terrace, or a top-floor room for its light. All the rooms are compact but smart, with chestnut furniture, matching bedcovers and drapes, rugs on gleaming tiled floors and swish bathrooms with hydromassage baths. Picnics can be prepared for walks and other sorties. Excellent value, lovely people.

rooms	11: 10 doubles, 1 suite.
price	€50–€78. Singles €39–€62. Suite €75–€94.
meals	Breakfast €6. Lunch & dinner €20–€30.
closed	7 January–7 February.
directions	From Oviedo, N-634 for La Coruña; on for Luarca. Turn right off road for Cudillero. Hotel in town centre, just off main square. Park in front of bollards to unload. Car park 250m, by harbour.

	Rosario Fernández Martínez
tel	+34 985 591512
fax	+34 985 591519
email	casonadepio@arrakis.es
web	www.arrakis.es/~casonadepio/

Hotel

Map 3 Entry 25

Casona de la Paca

El Pito, 33150 Cudillero, Asturias

Worth coming here for the breakfasts alone… Asturian cheeses, smoked meats, *torrijas*, *maranuelas*, *frixuelos*, doughnuts and crêpes – all superb. The Casona's strawberry-coloured façade and exotic gardens packed with New World species grab the attention on arrival – as was intended. This is one of Asturias's many flamboyant edifices built by emigrants who made their fortune in the Americas, then returned home. Revived from ruin only 15 years ago, the house contains an elegant mix of classic and colonial styles in sympathy with the spirit of the place. There's mahogany and teak in abundance, contemporary fabrics and handmade, Deco-style floor tiles. The conservatory is exquisite, the well-upholstered lounge is a lovely place to read and there are plenty of books in the library. Bedrooms are divided between the main house and the annexe; it's worth paying more for the Tower Suite with its wraparound terrace. There are also ten immaculate self-catering studios. Casona de la Paca runs on well-oiled wheels, and the fishing town of Cudillero lies delightfully nearby. *A Rusticae hotel.*

rooms	19 + 10: 16 twins/doubles, 1 single, 2 suites. 10 studios for 2-4.
price	€66-€105. Singles €54-€76. Suites €95-€117. Studios for 2, €60-€82; for 4, €82-€105.
meals	Breakfast €6.90. Restaurants 600m.
closed	11 December-end January.
directions	From Oviedo/Gijón on A-8/N-632 for La Coruña. After Soto de Barco, right at signs for Cudillero. House on right after 1km.

Montserrat Abad

tel	+34 985 591303
mobile	+34 671 607670
fax	+34 985 591316
email	hotel@casonadelapaca.com
web	www.casonadelapaca.com

Hotel & Self-catering

Map 3 Entry 26

La Quintana de la Ería

La Eria, 33449 Luanco, Asturias

Members for years of the guest-exchange organisation SERVAS, good-natured Clara and Guti make delightful hosts. Be prepared for a traditional welcome: a glass of local cider poured from an impossible height! Their Asturian farmhouse is surrounded by dairy farms and big skies, while cool sea breezes help build up appetites for hearty breakfasts of fried eggs, chorizo and… cider. All this is cheerfully served on old wooden tables in a cosy sitting room with roughly plastered mauve and terracotta walls, robust beams and a roaring stove. Simple but spacious bedrooms are colour coordinated and named after herbs found in Clara's garden; we like the Rosemary Room best, with its own balcony. A rustic and earthy feel runs throughout, complemented by delicate embroidered covers and old wrought-iron bedsteads; all around you are views of rolling hills to the serrated skyline of the Picos de Europa. Plan trips to fishing villages or to the awesome Cabo de Peñas, as you rest awhile under the courtyard's weeping willow, your sole companions a clutch of contented free-ranging hens.

rooms	4 twins/doubles.
price	€40–€60.
meals	Breakfast €4.
	Dinner €11, on request. VAT included.
closed	Rarely.
directions	A-8/E-70 from Gijon; exit 404 for Luanco onto AS-238/AS-239a. At km7.5, right to La Ería, opposite Bar Peláez. Follow track for 400m; house has tarmac driveway.

Clara Sierra & Guti Lagares

tel/fax	+34 985 882023
mobile	+34 600 526570
email	clara@quintanadelaeria.com
web	www.quintanadelaeria.com

B&B

Map 3 Entry 27

Hotel Quinta Duro

Camino de las Quintas 384, 33394 Cabueñes-Gijón, Asturias

The family estate is a haven of greenery and mature trees, girdled by a high
stone wall. It and its stately house lie just to the east of Gijón and you overlook
the city; though 800m from the main road, you hear nothing but birds. Carlos,
a delightfully warm presence, has redecorated house and large veranda and the
result is stylish yet homely. Panelled walls and period Portuguese and English
furniture show the family's love of quality and detail, and bedrooms are
distinguished, one with its own terrace. The bronze statue in the lovely gardens
is of Carlos's grandfather who casts a wistful eye on all those who visit – he
would surely approve of his grandson giving the house this new lease of life.
Breakfasts are excellent and there are two restaurants close by – or head for
the lively resort. The beach gets busy, but on the harbour front you'll find two
Asturian specialities in abundance: fish and cider. The former comes in varieties
distinct to the Cantabrian sea, the latter poured from a bottle held above the
waiter's head into a glass held at knee height – huge fun. *Pottery courses available.*

rooms	11 twins/doubles.
price	€88–€140. VAT included.
meals	Restaurants 400m.
closed	Rarely.
directions	A-8 exit 385 Gijón, then to Jardín Botánico at 1st & 2nd r'bouts. At r'bout by Jardín Botánico 1st right for Santurio y Cefontes; after 200m left for Santurio; 200m, right for Deva; 350m on right.

	Carlos Velázquez-Duro
tel/fax	+34 985 335815
email	info@hotelquintaduro.com
web	www.hotelquintaduro.com

Hotel

Map 3 Entry 28

La Quintana de la Foncalada

Argüero, 33314 Villaviciosa, Asturias

Severino greets you with unaffected simplicity at this honeysuckle-clad farmhouse in the flat, coastal *mariña* area of Asturias. The shady, breezy front garden is a delight, while the inside of the house is light, bright and simple. Bedrooms have basic furniture and artistic splashes of colour, bathrooms are small; the stable apartment with open fire is the most atmospheric. Make yourself a hot drink in the big, rustic kitchen whenever you like; enjoy the games room – popular with families; find out about the area and its traditions in the guest lounge filled with leaflets and books. Your hosts encourage adults and children to try potting in their workshop: every plate, lamp and tile in the house is homemade. You may also help with the Asturian ponies and the organic veg patch. Much is home-produced: honey, cheese, juices, cider, jam. Make the most of the delectable beaches nearby, the good eateries and the excursions from La Quintana by bike or pony. Equinophiles should know that Severino has created a museum dedicated to the Asturian pony, the *asturcón*; he also breeds them.

rooms	5 + 1: 5 twins/doubles. 1 apartment.
price	€45-€55. Singles €40. Apartment €90-€120. VAT included.
meals	Breakfast €5. Lunch & dinner €17. VAT included.
closed	Rarely.
directions	A-8 Santander-Oviedo, at exit to Villaviciosa AS-256 for Gijón. Arguero 8km further; follow signs.

Severino García & Daniela Schmid

tel	+34 985 999001
mobile	+34 655 697956
fax	+34 985 876365
email	foncalada@asturcon-museo.com
web	www.asturcon-museo.com

B&B & Self-catering

Map 3 Entry 29

El Correntiu

c/Sardalla 42, 33560 Ribadesella, Asturias

It must be the swishest grain silo in Spain. Set in nine acres, it stands to one side of the Asturian farmhouse – a stunning renovation. It is stylishly simple: a crisp use of wood, ochre tones to impart warmth, discreet lighting to give character, lots of space. There are two apartments here, each with a circular bedroom upstairs and its own kitchen garden – pick to your heart's content. There is also an abundance of kiwi, avocado and citrus trees: in this micro-climate everything thrives. Inside, a feast for the eye – chunky rafters, chestnut floors, country furniture, bright cushions – and all you need: books, games, linen, towels. If you're a traditionalist you may prefer the little cottage, just as beautifully equipped. A stream babbles by: *escorentía* means 'place that collects rain water'. It's a long, steep walk down to the lovely fishing village of Ribadesella at the mouth of the Sella, and the beaches are magnificent. Your hosts couldn't be nicer and keep rare Xalda sheep. María Luisa, who speaks very good English, can supply you with fresh eggs every morning. An irresistible place.

rooms	2 apartments for 2, 1 cottage for 4.
price	Apts €55-€70. Cottage €85-€110. VAT included.
meals	Self-catering.
closed	Rarely.
directions	From Santander A-8/N-632. At Ribadesella N-632 for Gijón. Immediately after bridge, left for Cuevas & Sardalla. From here, 2km to El Correntiu.

	María Luisa Bravo & Jose Luis Valdés
tel	+34 985 861436
mobile	+34 651 582440
email	elcorrentiu@fade.es
web	www.correntiu.com

Self-catering

Map 3 Entry 30

La Corte de Lugás
c/Lugás s/n, 33311 Villaviciosa, Asturias

The road ends at Lugás! Secluded it is, remote even, surrounded by eucalyptus and walnut forests, off the lushly beaten track. The young owners used to own a soft furnishings business, and their new venture is a showcase for their decorative talent. Bedrooms, named after the kings of Asturias, are divided between the 17th-century house (including attic) and the former bakery (where spaces are loftier). They vary in size and theme and there's a stylish rusticity at play: some rooms feel darkly medieval, others bohemian, one has a seaside air; all are bold, eye-catching, simple and luxurious. Some of the wrought-iron furniture was commissioned by local artists, a few beds are country antiques; fabrics are subtle and of fine quality, the attention to detail is superb, and real art adds an original touch. Note that windows tend to be small. Outside, huge lawns and wide-ranging field and forest views. Venture forth to discover the estuary town of Villaviciosa, famous for its migratory birds; return to suave leather armchairs before a fire, and dinner worth waiting for.

rooms	10: 7 twins/doubles, 3 suites.
price	€100-€130. Singles €70-€90. Suites €130-€160.
meals	Lunch & dinner €30.
closed	7 January-7 February.
directions	From Villaviciosa towards Infiesto; at km3 marker, left for Lugás. Hotel 2km.

	Daniel González Alvarez
tel/fax	+34 985 890203
email	info@lacortedelugas.com
web	www.lacortedelugas.com

Hotel

Map 3 Entry 31

Casona de Bustiello

Ctra. Infiesto - Villaviciosa s/n, 33535 Infiesto, Asturias

Cave paintings and monasteries, beaches and mountains, towns and tranquillity. All are within easy reach of this fine *casona* built by a returned emigré from Mexico. The original opulence has scarcely faded in 150 years. The grand, balustraded entrance patio is fringed by mature cherry trees – and you're welcome to pick the cherries! Rooms are painted in warm colours and furnished with confidence and restraint, never losing their cosy, rural feel. The shallow roof is dominated by a large, dormer window; in the attic is a particularly delightful room with rosy walls, sloping ceilings and a mass of beams. From the sitting room, furnished with big sofas and impressive bookcases, a door leads to a long windowed gallery – a peaceful from which to sit and contemplate the views that stretch over the orchards all the way to the Sierra de Ques. Excellent stress-busting treatments are on the menu here, and horse riding for beginners. Head south for the magnificent wilds of the Picos de Europa, or north for Villaviciosa Estuary Natural Reserve, an ornithologist's delight. *A Rusticae hotel.*

rooms	10: 9 twins/doubles, 1 suite.
price	€76–€97. Suite €95–€126.
meals	Breakfast €7.50. Dinner €18.
closed	January/February.
directions	From Oviedo, N-634 for Santander. 2km before Infiesto, left on AS-255 for Villaviciosa. On right after 4km.

	José Luís Sánchez
tel	+34 985 710445
mobile	+34 677 414957
fax	+34 985 710760
email	info.hcb@hotelcasonadebustiello.com
web	www.hotelcasonadebustiello.com

Hotel

Map 3 Entry 32

El Babú

Carrales s/n, 33343 Caravia, Asturias

Light and landscape flood into this refreshingly contemporary hotel. Glass walls in the living room pull in extraordinary views of the El Suave range, while a telescope allows you to explore the mountain tops – from the comfort of a smart leather sofa. Rugged terrain contrasts with smooth steel and concrete lines. Books on art and photography are seductively served for you to browse. Corridors carry interesting works of art: a framed collection of bright T-shirts, an installation of reject road signs. Beautiful modern furniture and gleaming old wood combine to create serene bedrooms in which to unwind. If art feeds your soul, then adventurous cuisine feeds the rest. Exquisite dishes and exclusive wines are served in the terrace restaurant, where boundaries between indoor and out blur: Josef Koudelka's dramatic black and white photographs to one side, the soaring peaks to the other. Walk off your indulgence in the hills, or take a comfy perch in the home cinema. It's all so strikingly different you'll long to return.

rooms	7: 5 twins/doubles, 1 family, 1 suite.
price	€67–€85. Family €110–€129. Suite €88–€110. Half-board extra €28 p.p.
meals	Breakfast €8. Dinner €23.
closed	17 January–15 March.
directions	Oviedo/Gijón on A-8, exit 337 for Caravia; onto N-632. Thro' Caravia Alta to Caravia Baja; 2.6km from m'way exit is Carrales; near stilt granaries & green building, hotel has flags outside.

	Pilar Arroyo
tel	+34 985 853272
email	elbabu@elbabu.com
web	www.elbabu.com

Hotel Posada del Valle
Collia, 33549 Arriondas, Asturias

After two years spent searching the hills and valleys of Asturias, Nigel and Joann Burch found the home of their dreams — a century-old farmhouse just inland from the rugged north coast, with sensational views to mountain, hill and meadow. Find a seat in the green hillside garden and gaze! Now they are nurturing new life from the soil — theirs is a fully registered organic farm — while running this small and beguiling hotel. The apple orchard has matured, the sheep munch the hillside, the menu celebrates the best of things local, and guests delight in this sensitive conversion. Bedrooms are seductive affairs with shutters and old beams, polished wooden floors, exposed stone, colourful modern fabrics and washed walls to match. There's a stylishly uncluttered living room with an open brick fire, and a dining room with glorious views. You are close to the soaring Picos, the little-known sandy beaches of the Cantabrian coast and some of the most exceptional wildlife in Europe. Your hosts have compiled well-researched notes on self-guided walks. Great food, great people, great value.

rooms	12: 10 twins/doubles, 2 family.
price	€58–€80. Singles €46–€56.
meals	Breakfast €7.50. Dinner €20.50.
closed	Mid-November to end March.
directions	N-634 Arriondas; AS-260 for Mirador del Fito. After 1km, right for Collia. Through village (don't turn to Ribadesella). Hotel 300m on left after village.

SPECIAL
GREEN ENTRY
see page 13

Hotel

		Nigel & Joann Burch
tel	+34 985 841157
fax	+34 985 841559
email	hotel@posadadelvalle.com
web	www.posadadelvalle.com

Map 3 Entry 34

  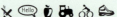

Palacio de Cutre

33583 Villamayor, Asturias

Javier worked for one of Spain's big hotel chains but is now a firm convert to the 'small is beautiful' school. He and his wife Alejandra have lavished energy and care on this intimate, luxurious, 16th-century hotel. Part of the spirit is captured by the hotel's own literature, fancifully written as if all were overseen by the ancient oak that towers over the lovely gardens. In the beautifully decorated bedrooms are flounced and beribboned curtains, lavish cushions, Tiffany-style lamps, antique bedsteads and plush fabrics. The toile de Jouy suite sits under white-painted rafters, the bathrooms are fittingly fabulous. But we give Alejandra herself the final word: she insists that what makes Cutre so special is the cuisine, an innovative mix of traditional Asturian dishes and more elaborate fare, such as duck breast with red peppers. Enjoy breakfast in elegance on rush-seated chairs in a dining room with astonishing views; there'll be ham and eggs, tortilla, many different jams. And the lovely old town of Villamayor-Infiesto is just down the road.

rooms	17: 11 twins/doubles, 4 family, 2 suites.
price	€99-€144. Family €110-€177. Suites €185-€199.
meals	Breakfast €9.50. Lunch & dinner €35-€45.
closed	24/25 December.
directions	A-8 exit 326 for Ribadesella; N-634 dir. Arriondas. Just before Villamayor, right onto AS-259, Bolines/Colunga. After 500m, right; signs to hotel for 2.5km.

	Javier Alvarez Garzo
tel	+34 985 708072
fax	+34 985 708019
email	hotel@palaciodecutre.com
web	www.palaciodecutre.com

Hotel

Map 3 Entry 35

L'Ayalga Posada Ecológica
La Pandiella s/n, 33537 Piloña (Infiesto), Asturias

Abandon the car and take a train on the narrow-gauge railway to Infiesto. Or come by bus. Either way, if you let them know beforehand, Luis or Concepción will be there to meet you. They are a friendly, caring couple who've taken infinite pains in restoring their farmhouse and use only healthy, non-contaminating materials. Sand is used as sound insulation between floorboards and ceiling and the cleaning products are homemade from borax and essential oils. Herbs scent the garden, a pair of Asturcon ponies graze quietly and green slopes lead the eye inexorably to dramatic mountain profiles. The rooms are attractive and unadorned, with simple white walls, plain wood and warm-coloured fabrics. Thanks to solar panels, the showers have constant hot water and the wooden beds, treated with natural oils, are fairly comfortable. Your hosts, who manage without staff, give 1% of their income from guests to charity. If you crave a massage in peace, your children will be looked after – you may even find them harvesting watermelons for lunch...

rooms	5 twins/doubles.
price	€47. Singles €41.
meals	Vegetarian dinner €11.
closed	21 December-8 January.
directions	From Santander/Bilbao on A-8; exit 326 for Ribadesella/Arriondas. At r'bout, exit N-634 for Arriondas. At km361, turn towards Infiesto; then AS-254 for Campo de Caso. After 3km, left for La Pandiella; FEVE railway to Infiesto for pick-up.

Luis A. Díaz & Conchi de la Iglesia

mobile	+34 616 897638
email	layalga@terrae.net
web	www.terrae.net/layalga

SPECIAL GREEN ENTRY
see page 13

B&B

Map 3 Entry 36

Los Cuetos

Santianes s/n, 33537 Infiesto, Asturias

The 16th-century farmhouse has a commanding position and uninterrupted views – best appreciated from its covered gallery. All is warm and friendly inside and blends serenely with the majestic setting. Furnishings are smartly stylish with well-matched fabrics, rugs on tiled floors, pictures, plants – plastic and real – and porcelain figurines. Seila, a 'hands on' hostess, is happy in the kitchen cooking breakfast, or creating one of her special fish dishes for dinner. The sweeping curved staircase takes you up to the first floor where that great galleried window lets the light in; there's a sizeable sitting room and five regal guest rooms. Each one is themed, well-lit and furnished with good-looking repro furniture and rugs. Central heating and air conditioning add to the comfort; Les Mimoses with its sparkling jacuzzi occupies an entire wing. In the gardens, a lazy swing and a pool-with-a-view, tennis, racquets and a marquee with a great round table that spins. The old *hórreo* (a granary on stilts) is listed and striking. And the glorious Parque Natural de Redes is no distance at all.

rooms	5 twins/doubles.
price	€55–€90. VAT included.
meals	Breakfast €5. Dinner €15. VAT included.
closed	Rarely.
directions	From Santander A-8 junc. 326; N-634 for Arriondas. There, on towards Infiesto. Enter village & left for Lozana on PI–III. Los Cuetos on right after 1.5km; large black entrance gate.

	Seila Sánchez Barro
tel	+34 985 710656
fax	+34 985 710874
email	loscuetos@loscuetos.com
web	www.loscuetos.com

B&B

Map 3 Entry 37

La Reserva Lodge
33996 Bezanes, Asturias

The village where you left your car and jumped into the hotel's 4x4 lies far below. Be glad you're no longer driving! And close your eyes if the precipice proves too much to bear; this is the closest you come to flying. Deep in the Redes Natural Park, an official biosphere reserve, is this hunters' lodge. At 1,200m, its position is extraordinary. Shepherds' huts dot the landscape, horses graze. It is special in all seasons, from sweet spring to snowbound winter. As for the lodge, its arty, quirky, colourful décor has much charm. A roaring woodburner boosts centrally heated cast-iron radiators; sisal-carpeted rooms have fine patterned fabrics and panelled walls; eclectic artwork – paintings and sculptures – lines corridors and stairs. A free daily 4x4 shuttle service connects the lodge with the village of Bezanes, and Veneros and its wood carving museum are a short drive. But you'd be just as happy staying put; all your meals can be eaten here, and there's the Park to discover. Circular walks start from the door. *Minimum stay two nights.*

rooms	10: 8 doubles, 2 suites.
price	Half-board €190. Suites €240.
meals	Half-board only. Lunch & dinner €30. Packed lunch €18.
closed	January-March. Call to check.
directions	Madrid A6 to Benavente; A66 for León & Oviedo to Mieres; take AS-1, exit at sign to Langreo, AS-17 to Bezanes. Call hotel in advance for pick-up.

	Javier Alvarez Garzo
mobile	+34 680 608332
email	hotel@lareservalodge.com
web	www.lareservalodge.com

Hotel Aultre Naray

Peruyes, 33547 Cangas de Onis, Asturias

You'll be captivated by the views. The green-sloped, grey-peaked Cuera mountains have the quality of a life-size pop-up book: every tree, every rock, every gully appears with such clarity that you feel you could reach out and touch them. This grand *casona* dates from the time when 19th-century Spanish emigrants invested the gains of their adventures overseas in deliberately ostentatious houses. The transition from grand home to fine hotel has been a seamless one here. Vintage flags greet you on arrival, and an exquisite chestnut staircase leads from reception to cosy, comfortable rooms upstairs. The name comes from a medieval motto meaning, 'I'll have no other' and the hotel flourishes under new ownership, the mood remaining warm and relaxed. Designer prints, fabric and furniture marry well with the core elements of beams and stone walls. And it is a treat to breakfast on the terrace in the English-style garden faced with a choice of crêpes, homemade cakes – and eggs and bacon! – to accompany those out-of-this-world views. *A Rusticae hotel.*

rooms	10: 9 twins/doubles, 1 family.	
price	€70–€115. Singles €60–€85. Family €113–€163.	
meals	Breakfast €4.50–€9. Lunch & dinner €20–€25 à la carte.	
closed	Rarely.	
directions	From Oviedo for Santander on m'way, then N-634. After passing Arriondas at km335 marker, right for Peruyes. Climb for 1km to village; hotel on left after 150m.	

	Iñaki Sabando & Susana Marcos
tel	+34 985 840808
mobile	+34 629 732192
fax	+34 985 840848
email	aultre@aultrenaray.com
web	www.aultrenaray.com

Hotel

Map 3 Entry 39

Bajo los Tilos

Santianes del Agua 6, 33569 Ribadesella, Asturias

The hamlet materialises, as if by magic, out of nowhere. As do steep green mountainsides and lush chestnut forests; a wild and wonderful eco-system thrives outside Elena and Juan Luis's front door. These two ex-bankers left Madrid mayhem for memories of childhood summers spent here. Now, bold colour schemes enliven interior spaces; uncluttered bedrooms with sweeping wooden floors reveal deep hues and dazzling white crochet covers. Indian and south-east Asian pieces of furniture add intriguing ethnic touches; paintings and canvasses by Juan Luis's brother strike a bold note. You are only two miles from the nearest FEVE train station, so drop the car and take a trip into the mountains or along the coast. Elena can also tell you about walks in search of hidden springs. Return to a pretty, shady garden and woodpeckers at work; get out the binoculars and spot a few deer. Come evening, there's a huge selection of DVDs, including many classics, to choose from. Charming hosts are the cherry on this very special cake.

rooms	6 twins/doubles.
price	€55–€70.
meals	Breakfast €5. Dinner €16.50.
closed	Rarely.
directions	From Santander/Oviedo on E-70; exit fpr Ribadesella/Picos de Europa onto N-634. At r'about, signs for Arriondas. After 1km, Santianes del Agua; left into village opposite church. Bear left; 300m to hotel.

	Elena de Haro & Juan Luis Toribio
tel	+34 985 857527
mobile	+34 669 460544
email	info@bajolostilos.com
web	www.bajolostilos.com

B&B

Map 3 Entry 40

La Montaña Mágica

El Allende, 33508 Llanes, Asturias

Wedged between beaches and the mighty Picos mountains, the hill-perched farmstead has a privileged position and the approach is sensational. Ecologically-minded Carlos, who has his own tree-planting programme, has sensitively restored the old ruins, and the finish is rustic and cheerful. Warm colours and robust furniture in walnut and oak mingle beautifully with stonework and rafters. The reception leads to a log-fired sitting room and library, and a map room for walkers – just what you need in trekking country. The riding too is superb. There are six lovely suites in this part of the house, some split-level with huge woodburning stoves, all with a modern alpine feel. Words cannot do justice to some of the views… ask for a room facing south. A second large building has good, well-insulated, pine-finished rooms with big bathrooms – clean, practical, bright. The dining room stands on its own beside the old *horreo* (granary), now converted into a children's playroom. Lunches and dinners are great value, there's a small bar where you can enjoy a digestif, and Carlos and his staff are wonderful.

rooms	16: 10 twins/doubles, 6 suites.
price	€50–€85. Suites €70–€105.
meals	Breakfast €4.80. Lunch & dinner €12.80.
closed	Rarely.
directions	From Santander W on E-70/N-634. Past Llanes; at km307 right for Celorio; AS-263 to Posada. Here left on AS-115 for Cabrales to La Herreria. At Allende right over bridge; right, following signs; 3km.

	Carlos Bueno & Pilar Pando
tel	+34 985 925176
fax	+34 985 925780
email	magica@llanes.as
web	www.lamontanamagica.com

Guest house

Map 3 Entry 41

La Posada de Babel
La Pereda s/n, 33509 Llanes, Asturias

Demure, quaint, unobtrusive it is not. But what a sensation for the eye. The cool lines, bold colours and extravagant glass of the three buildings that dot these lawns are a modernist's dream. Designed with an architect's attention to detail, it has views from within as exciting as those from without: floor to ceiling windows look onto undulating lawns and meadows while the foothills of the Cuera rise behind. White walls, bursts of cobalt blue, polished tiles, understated furnishings, sleek lighting. (Lucas and Blanca are from Madrid, and it shows.) The open-plan design of the dining and drawing rooms is languorous, large and washed with the light; shade your eyes and you might wonder if you're inside or out. Bountiful breakfasts include homemade breads, pastries, local fruits and cheeses; in the evening, the dining room takes on a cool elegance. Blanca and Lucas are inventive cooks, giving modern twists to the local Asturian cuisine. Gentle and knowledgeable, they will also point you to the best local walking, riding or fishing. Or you might prefer simply to unwind in these uniquely beautiful spaces.

rooms	12: 10 twins/doubles, 2 suites.
price	€78-€100. Suite €120-€138.
meals	Breakfast €8.50. Dinner €27.
closed	November-February.
directions	A-8 m'way exit for Llanes; right for La Pereda. Over railway tracks & left at village. Posada 300m down road, signed.

Lucas Cajiao & Blanca Fernández

tel	+34 985 402525
mobile	+34 606 808374
fax	+34 985 402622
email	laposadadebabel@retemail.es
web	www.laposadadebabel.com

Hotel

Map 3 Entry 42

Hotel El Habana

La Pereda s/n, 33509 Llanes, Asturias

Lush meadows, grazing cows, dry-stone walls – such is the rural beauty of Asturia, where gently rolling farmland gives way to the foothills of the Cuera Mountains. The hotel is a contemporary version of the traditional Asturian house, and is charming within. Plants, rugs on warm terracotta floors, modern art, subtle lighting. Much of the furniture comes from Mariá Eugenia's home in New Delhi and an air of colonial elegance – touched with modern Deco – prevails. The friendly atmosphere goes up a notch in the dining room, the elegant hub of the hotel. Here, regulars and visitors congregate to sample excellent Asturian dishes, served from 9pm. Bedrooms are big and light, the two with patios leading to the garden (Sirio's creation, with 300 species of trees, shrubs, ferns and stunning pergola) being our favourites. Spin off on one of the bikes, take a put on the golf course by the sea, set out on a coastal pony trek, dip into the pool. Your multi-lingual hosts will advise – and if sporting pursuits do not appeal, head for nearby Llanes with its handsome galleried buildings. *A Rusticae hotel.*

rooms	12: 9 twins/doubles, 3 suites.
price	€81–€116. Suite €123–€145.
meals	Breakfast €6.50.
	Dinner from €24 à la carte.
closed	November–mid-March.
directions	Santander-Oviedo on N-634; at km301 marker, Llanes exit, do a U-turn & cross over N-634 for La Pereda, following signs on right for Prau Riu Hotel. 1.5km; signed.

	María Eugenia Caumel & Sirio Sáinz
tel	+34 985 402526
fax	+34 985 402075
email	hotel@elhabana.net
web	www.elhabana.net

Hotel

Map 3 Entry 43

Casa de Aldea La Valleja

Rieña, 33576 Ruenes, Asturias

If you fancy turning your hand to preserve-making or mountain honey-gathering, then head for La Valleja. Tending the livestock and pottering in the garden are also a must: Paula is passionate about rural tourism and loves guests to muck in. The house was built in 1927 and the original materials – bricks, tiles, stones and chestnut beams – maintain the rustic charm. Each bedroom, gaily coloured, has been named after wild berries; if yours feels sombre, throw open the shutters and drink in the views – sensational. La Valleja is a working homestead where they produce organic cider but there's comfort too; all is spotless yet not over-polished, there are orthopaedic mattresses, good heating and scrumptious food. After a rugged walk in the Peñamellera Alta – don't miss the spectacular Cares gorge – you'll be well fortified: meals are hearty and the food organic and lovingly prepared. So whether you want to sit and enjoy the views, join in the chestnut harvest or birdwatch with binoculars, this is the place. Be sure to buy some of the jams and preserves to take home.

rooms	5 twins/doubles.
price	€49.
meals	Packed lunch €7. Dinner €12.
closed	ChrisTmas & January.
directions	N-634; at Unquera, left for Panes. Here, right onto AS-114 for Cangas de Onís. 10km beyond, at Niserias, right to Ruenes. Through Alles; 800m after Pastorias, right up a steep track to Rieña. Park at top.

	Paula Valero Sáez
tel/fax	+34 985 415895
email	valleycas@yahoo.es

B&B

Map 3 Entry 44

Casona D'Alevia

LG. Alevia s/n, 33579 Peñamellera Baja, Asturias

An improbable setting for a village: a pocket of greenery, an old church and a cluster of lovely old buildings — until this year, at the end of a recently widened vertiginous mountain road! The eagle-eye views are breathtaking. Step into the 15th-century farmhouse and you step back in time; the house could be a museum of ethnography. If you ask, softly-spoken Gregorio will tell you all about his family, who have been basket-makers for generations. The hall is decorated with tools that belonged to his father-in-law, the bedrooms sport damask-covered tables and kilims on chestnut boards, and in the sitting room are fascinating curios and an old piano. Such rustic interiors are timeless and enchanting and the homely feel is epitomised by displays of family items on each landing, including some of Gregorio's daughter's beautiful, symbolic sculptures. New mattresses on old wrought-iron beds guarantee a good night's sleep, and you wake to a breakfast as good as any in Spain. It is a privilege to stay in such a place.

rooms	9: 6 twins/doubles, 3 suites.
price	€70-€85. €85-€100.
meals	Breakfast €7.
	Restaurants in Panes, 3km.
closed	7 January-7 February.
directions	N-634 to Oviedo-Santander; exit for Unquera onto N-621. At Panes, right to Cabrales on the AS-114, right again at sign to Alevia; follow new road for 3km to Alevía. House on left of main square.

Gregorio Sánchez Benito

tel	+34 985 414176
mobile	+34 616 159837
email	alevia@casonadalevia.com
web	www.casonadalevia.com

Hotel

Map 3 Entry 45

Casona de Villanueva

Apdo. de Correos 30, 33590 Villanueva de Colombres, Asturias

In the east of Asturias, a charming place from which to discover romanesque churches and sleepy fishing villages, walk the rocky coastline or go horse riding in the Picos de Europa. Thanks to careful restoration and imaginative decoration of the Villanueva – the oldest house in the village – this is an exceptional place to stay. Bedrooms, not grand, vary in size and have smallish bathrooms – but what a sense of history! Ancient walls and floors are scattered with rugs and cushions from Morocco, paintings and rare etchings, unusual colours and heaps of antiques. Then there are the details: the homemade preserves and flowers at breakfast, the classical music at mealtimes, and the wi-fi in every room. Food is good – Argentinian beef and lamb, fish fresh from the slate, cream and fudge pudding, exotic fruits, good wines. More joy outside, in the organic walled garden full of tropical plants, fruit trees, roses and scented climbers; retreat here with a book. Villanueva's new owner, an Argentinian, is more than happy to help you plan your forays.

rooms	8: 6 twins/doubles, 2 suites.
price	€85–€100. Singles €75–€85. Suites €100–€130. Extra bed €30.
meals	Breakfast €7. Dinner €30.
closed	27 December–31 January.
directions	From Santander N-634/E-70 for Oviedo. 3km after Unquera, at km283 marker, left for Colombres. Through village; 2km to Villanueva. At T-junc. hotel opp. on left.

	Ariel Rios Gloviar
tel	+34 985 412590
mobile	+34 600 099568
fax	+34 985 412514
email	info@lacasonadevillanueva.com
web	www.lacasonadevillanueva.com

Hotel

Map 4 Entry 46

Posada Casa Centenera

Barrio Monasterio 23, 39419 Valdeprado del Río, Cantabria

Spaniards say clergymen always chose the best land – and the best site for their houses. Here is a fine example. Posada Casa Centenera has a beautifully elevated position opposite the church, in a forgotten corner of Cantabria. You negociate dual carriageways and pass factories to get here, but please persevere – it is worth it! Javier and Angela are lovely hosts: she a former stewardess, naturally caring, he a music teacher, cultivated and charming, and they have restored their 19th-century house with loving attention to detail. Oak window frames and shutters, sliding doors, hand-painted tiles, dressers brimming with crockery – all have had new life breathed into them. Delightfully rustic bedrooms are enlivened with warm dashes of colour, thick duvets top comfortable beds. Top-floor rooms have stunning high roof structures, their old timbers occasionally wailing in wild weather. Let the region unravel its secrets slowly: the waymarked walks that follow abandoned villages, the rock churches, the anthropomorphic graves, the Romanesque chapels.

rooms	4 twins/doubles.
price	€58–€66. VAT included.
meals	Restaurants in Fombellida, 8km.
closed	Rarely.
directions	From Reinosa on A-67; exit 122 onto CA-272 direction Polientes. After 8km, right for Mataporquera & Valdeprado.

	Angeles Calero & Javier Centenera
tel	+34 942 745694
mobile	+34 620 254456
email	reservas@casacentenera.com
web	www.casacentenera.com

B&B

Map 4 Entry 47

Casona de Naveda

Plaza del Medio Lugar 37, Hermandad de Campóo de Suso, 39211 Naveda, Cantabria

Step out of the front door and follow the river to the village – or skip through pastures of cows and wild flowers. The *casona* was built 300 years ago by one of those enterprising indianos who returned from Cuba to build a dwelling grand enough to announce his newfound riches. Floors, ceilings and fire surrounds of rich walnut and oak have the soft patina that only centuries of polishing can achieve. Ancient stone pillars in the sitting room would not look out of place in one of Cantabria's churches. An Edwardian fireplace from a Scottish castle and Austrian panelled chairs add to the distinguised feel. Rooms 6 and 7, with their wooden galleried sitting areas, have a *Romeo and Juliet* charm, but every room is distinctive in its own way. The menu is a celebration of simple food beautifully cooked, accompanied by some of Spain's treat wines. The area is studded with romanesque churches, nearby Reisona, with its galleried houses and fine central square, is quite a find, and you are only a short drive from the ski terrain of Alto Campóo. *A Rusticae hotel.*

rooms	9: 2 twins/doubles, 1 single, 6 suites.
price	€78–€86. Single €63–€69. Suite €85–€105.
meals	Breakfast €8. Dinner €21.
closed	2 weeks in November.
directions	From Santander on A-67; exit 136 onto CA-183 for Alto Campóo. Drive through Nestanes, Salcos & Fontibre. In Náveda, hotel on village square.

Paloma López Sarasa

tel	+34 942 779515
fax	+34 942 779681
email	info@casonadenaveda.com
web	www.casonadenaveda.com

Hotel

Map 4 Entry 48

Posada La Trébede

Perrozo, 39573 Cabezón de Liebana, Cantabria

The smell of wood smoke seduces you even before your eyes adjust to the light. Gnarled old beams still stand strong, eagle-eye views take in distant mountains. La Trébede gives you this – and more. It's a child-friendly house that tucks itself into the steep hillsides of the Liebana Valley, a rich forested landscape of cork, chestnut and oak with a thriving eco-system. Hens, dogs and children roam freely on the quaint cobalt and stone patio and even the dogs have personalities here (John Wayne with bow legs, Fermín who looks like a muppet). The solid old house, named after the hearth above which the very young and the very old would sleep when winters were winters, is as authentic as can be. Comfortable rooms have a homely, rustic feel, good fabrics, woollen blankets and crisp white sheets guarantee deep sleep, bathrooms sparkle, stone and terracotta brickwork on the walls is a treat for the eye, and attic rooms have sloping roofs and dormer windows – mind your head! The Liébana Monastery, a major pilgrimage site, is nearby, as are the Picos de Europa; Manuel was a National Park ranger so you are in excellent hands.

rooms	6 twins/doubles.
price	€45–€58.
meals	Breakfast €4. Dinner €12.
closed	Rarely.
directions	From Santander E-70 to Oviedo, then N-630 Unquera to Potes. Continue for Cervera/Pto. de Piedrasluengas. 1km after Puente Asni, left for Perroza. Signed.

	Manuel Bahillo & María Eugenia Herrero
tel/fax	+34 942 735085
mobile	+34 608 025202
email	manelbahillo@hotmail.com
web	www.perrozo.com

B&B

Map 4 Entry 49

Casa Gustavo Guesthouse

Cillorigo de Liébana, 39584 Aliezo, Cantabria

In the beautiful Liébana valley lies the hamlet of Aliezo and this very old farmhouse. Lisa, Mike and their children have taken on their adopted land, have learned its language, know its history and its footpaths. Within the thick stone walls of their house are low beams, steps up, sidewards and down, and good smells wafting out from the kitchen. For home it is: don't expect hotelly trimmings. Rather, the house is organic and shambolic; some rooms are small, some large, some have balconies. But walkers will be more than happy with the country cooking, hot showers and decent beds. Redstarts nest beneath the eaves, there are dogs and cats, a cosy lounge with woodburner, balcony, toys and books, and a shaded patio with awesome views; the main protagonist is Nature and her Picos mountains. Mike and Lisa offer free transport to the beginning of walks, will advise according to what the weather is doing and should be able to provide you with the best maps of the area. Great for ornithology and botany buffs – ski-mountaineering courses in winter – and spot on for families.

rooms	7: 5 twins/doubles; 1 single, 1 family sharing bathroom.
price	€44–€68. Singles €22–€44. VAT included.
meals	Packed lunch €5. Dinner €15.
closed	Rarely.
directions	From Santander A-67/N-634 for Oviedo. Left at Unquera onto N-621 for Potes. Shortly before Potes, through Tama; after 200m, left to Aliezo. Follow bend to top of village; 2nd house.

	Lisa & Michael Stuart
tel	+34 942 732010
fax	+44 (0)1629 813346
email	stuartsinpicos@terra.es
web	www.picos-accommodation.co.uk

Guest house

Map 3 Entry 50

Fuente de las Anjanas

Canal de los Bueyes s/n, Val de San Vicente, 39549 Estrada, Cantabria

It's hard to miss: a medieval tower stands by the road 50 metres from this *casa de colonos*. Inside, charming, caring Nieves has put together modern country furniture with sumptuous fabrics to dramatic effect. The first impression is that of a hunter's lodge: roaring fire, checked armchairs, mounted wild boar's head. Animated dinners take place around a large wooden table. On the stairs is a bizarre collection of masks from West Africa and Venice, agricultural yokes, and photos of Nieves in regional dress. Comfortable, cool bedrooms are eye-catching, with their dark wooden beams, pristine bed linen and vibrant walls; bedsteads from Seville and embroidered fabrics coexist with rather more twee furnishings. Choose a colour to match your mood, or a Cantabrian fairy after which each room is named; Nieves will tell you – in Spanish – about their quirks and qualities. Most rooms overlook rolling meadows and indigenous forest; we like best those with balconies over the young front garden. Charming San Vicente de la Barquera is nearby, and the famous Camino de Santiago slips just by the house.

rooms	12 twins/doubles.
price	€55–€90.
meals	Breakfast €6. Dinner €18.
closed	7-31 January.
directions	From Santander on E-70; exit 264 for San Vicente de la Barquera. At 2nd r'about, CA-843 for Abanillos. After 4.5km, right at tower. House 100m beyond.

	Miguel & Nieves Cuevas-Villar
tel	+34 942 718539
email	fdelasanjanas@hotmail.com
web	www.fuentedelasanjanas.com

Guest house

Map 4 Entry 51

El Jardín de Carrejo

Carrejo, 39500 Cabezón de la Sal, Cantabria

Swings and sequoias in the grounds, the odd swaying palm and weeping willow, vast lawns and ancient trees. Everyone loves this small hotel, with its clean lines and modern design. The huge 1901 stable and hayloft have been stylishly re-crafted into a comfortable haven between the Cabuérniga Valley and the golden beaches of Comillas. Expect a cool symphony of creams, taupes and warm hues, stone floors and polished parquet. Over 100 photographs by contemporary Spanish photographers enliven the interor spaces; there is masses of light, not a curlicue in sight, and suave leather sofas and chestnut and walnut pieces represent the best of modern design. Bedrooms, two with balconies, all with garden views, are serene. Bathrooms are chic and lack nothing. The new garden suites are the swishest of all: high ceilings, black slate and an open-plan layouts with sliding doors to private gardens. Hire a tandem from the hotel, practice your golf in the grounds, head off for a Parque Natural (there are two nearby), laze under a posh parasol. And the staff are great. *A Rusticae hotel.*

rooms	12: 8 twins/doubles, 4 suites.
price	€78-€112. Singles €70-€90. Suites €120-€210.
meals	Breakfast €9. Dinner €25.
closed	3 January-3 February.
directions	A-8 exit 249 for Cabezón de la Sal; right at entrance of town following signs for Reinosa. Drive through town & into Carrejo. Pass narrow section & traffic lights, turn immediately left. Hotel signed.

	Isabel Alvarez García
tel	+34 942 701516
fax	+34 942 701871
email	info@eljardindecarrejo.com
web	www.eljardindecarrejo.com

Hotel

Map 4 Entry 52

Posada La Casona de Cos

Pueblo de Cos 87, 39509 Mazcuerras, Cantabria

In a quiet village of Cantabria, just a short drive from Santillana, is a great place
to stay on the way to the ferry. The Posada is small, friendly, unpretentious and
Spanish to the core. In the village, locals far outnumber visitors still. Bright-eyed,
ever-smiling Natalia and daughter Sebita have built up the reputation of this little
hotel over the past 30-odd years. And what is so refreshing is not just Natalia's
pride in her 400-year-old home but the relish with which she greets her guests.
The dining room is the hub of the place; low, beamy, with marble-topped tables
and a fire in the hearth, there's something about it that tells you that you will eat
well. As indeed you do; the kitchen promises good, old-fashioned and slow-paced
cooking. Natalia's *cocido montañés*, a traditional meat-rich stew (made with
vegetables from their own plot) is renowned, and the chocolate and orange tart is
irresistible. Upstairs are simple, spotless bedrooms, and a quiet guest sitting room
along the corridor. Great hosts, great value for money.

rooms	11 twins/doubles.
price	€60. Singles €35.
meals	Breakfast €4. Lunch & dinner €30. Restaurant closed in August.
closed	Rarely.
directions	Santander A-67 to Torrelavega; A-8 exit 249 Cabezón de la Sal; N-634, then CA-180 for Reinosa. Past Carrejo; over bridge just past Parque Santa Lucía; left on CA-812 to Cos. Casona on right, 100m before church.

Sebita Puente

tel	+34 942 701550
mobile	+34 618 577320
fax	+34 942 702434
email	lacasonadecos@mixmail.com
web	www.lacasonadecos.com

Guest house

Map 4 Entry 53

Casona Torre de Quijas

Barrio Vinueva 76, 39590 Quijas de Reocín, Cantabria

This is a grand yet intimate little hotel within striking distance of Santander and minutes from the beach. Pilar and her husband bought it as a family home, then transformed it into a delightful hotel. Fresh fruit and dried flowers set the welcoming mood. A log fire and deep, comfortable chairs upholstered in white cotton make for an attractive sitting room, while polished chestnut floors run throughout. Bedrooms, mostly pale with a fresh cotton theme, are elegantly furnished with towering Art Deco wardrobes and embroidered linen, reflecting your hosts' taste and flair. Our favourite is the Lemon Room, big, light and airy, with French windows to a balcony renovated in such a way that the original arches still stand. The cosiest bedrooms are in the upper part of the house where ceilings are beamed. Inviting, too, is the small bar, with its cane furniture and lace-covered lamps. Outside is a peaceful and covered patio aglow with potted plants and shrubs. No dinner, but there is a smart restaurant over the road. Perfect for a first or last night in Spain.

rooms	19 twins/doubles.
price	€48-€115.
meals	Breakfast €6. Restaurants in village.
closed	15 December-15 January.
directions	From Santander/Bilbao on A-8; exit 238 for Quijas. Hotel on left, next to medieval tower.

Pilar García Lozano

tel	+34 942 820645
fax	+34 942 838255
email	informacion@casonatorredequijas.com
web	www.casonatorredequijas.com

Hotel

Map 4 Entry 54

Posada La Preda

Barrio Acereda 9, 39698 Santiurde de Toranzo, Cantabria

Undiscovered Spain. This is the Toranzo valley, carved by the river Pas, from which the local word for farmer – *pasiego* – derives. It is also the home of those delicious, soft, buttery cakes, *sobaos pasiegos*. Pleasant meadows surround La Preda, perfect for cows; if you have children, join Ramón on his milking round. He and Emi, doctor and nurse, have found a charming outlet here for their natural inclination to care for guests. The breakfast room has a homely feel, with an Irish ceramic sink and a wood-burning stove, and the rustic mood is accentuated by attractive copper pans, old coffee grinders, and a glass-topped table filled with dried leaves and fruit. Arab brickwork lining the stairs guides you to your room, though two are downstairs and open to the breakfast room. The rooms are simple and delightful, some with lofty ceilings; ancient woodwork contrasts with exposed stone walls, and there are pretty finishes, such as Emi's hand-painted leaves on basins. Simple, wholesome breakfasts, hens' eggs to collect and videos for children make this a wonderful stopover for families.

rooms	4: 2 twins/doubles, 2 triples.
price	€50–€70.
meals	Restaurant 5-minute drive.
closed	Rarely.
directions	From Santander on A-67 to Torrelavega. Follow signs for Bilbao; exit onto N-623 for Burgos. At Borleña, left for Santiurde de Toranzo. Over bridge; at crossroads, signs for 1.7km to Posada.

	Emilia Morate & Ramón Centenera
tel	+34 942 597702
mobile	+34 605 678905
email	posada@lapreda.com
web	www.lapreda.com

B&B

Map 4 Entry 55

La Casona de Hermosa

Barrio Palacio 142, 39724 Hermosa (Solares), Cantabria

Hermosa means 'beautiful' and this peaceful hillside enclave of sober houses, crowing cockerels and smoke-wafting chimneys is aptly named. In the grand casona, delighfuly eccentric Begoña has created her own interior, a sophisticated and elegant environment with artistic surprises. Sculptures dot the garden; local artwork decorates the walls; ethnic objets are shown off on polished floors. A glass cabinet on the landing displays silverware and metalwork by a prominent Cantabrian artist, another one a collection of old coins. Drinking chocolate soirées are held in the relaxing sitting room where window shutters, wooden lintels, tartan armchairs and an old-fashioned globe set the scene… Albinoni's *Adagio* is playing in the background. Spacious and refreshingly bold bedrooms ooze charm and comfort: lace bedcovers, rocking chairs, rose-patterned walls; in some are balconies, in others, a feast of beams above your pillow. All this and hostess Begoña, former director of the local tourist office: make the most of her in-depth knowledge.

rooms	9 twins/doubles.
price	€80-€125.
meals	Supper on request.
closed	15-30 November; 6-31 January.
directions	From Santander A-8; exit 13A for Solares (from Bilbao A-8 exit 197). Drive into town & follow signs for Pueblo de Hermosa & Casona.

	Begoña Gabiola
tel	+34 942 522322
mobile	+34 670 738820
fax	+34 942 521168
email	info@casonadehermosa.com
web	www.casonadehermosa.com

Hotel

Map 4 Entry 56

La Torre de Ruesga

La Barcena s/n, 39810 Valle de Ruesga, Cantabria

On the lush banks of the Asón, the 1610 stronghold matches elegance with sobriety, and is surrounded by pretty gardens. Through a glazed arch you enter the stone-finished hall with a charming bar to your right. The grander rooms have been embellished with frescos by the Catalan painter, Leon Criach, the finest in the pink-washed banqueting hall on the first floor. On either side are special rooms for videos, games or quiet reads – a nice touch – and there's a piano to play. The bedrooms in the palacio itself have a delightfully rustic feel, with their terracotta floors, chunky rafters and antique beds. In the ornate restaurant dinner is an accomplished mix of Cantabrian and international, accompanied by fine wines from the well-stocked bodega. Take tea on the terrace or lounge on the lawns; the views of Torre de Ruesga are stunning. There's also a large outdoor pool with a gym and sauna, and five new 'corporate' garden suites with hydromassage baths. Every possible need has been anticipated, from babysitting to room service, and vivacious, charming Carmen is the star of the show. *A Rusticae hotel.*

rooms	10 + 5: 6 twin/doubles, 4 suites. 5 apartments.	
price	€90-€115. Singles €60-€80. Suite €108-€130. Apartment €125-€145.	
meals	Lunch & dinner €21. A la carte €35-€40.	
closed	Last 3 weeks in January.	
directions	From Santander, S-10 for Bilbao. Exit 173 for Colindres; N-629 for Burgos to Ramales de V. Right on C-261 to Arredondo & Valle; right at sign. On right just over bridge.	

	Carmen Caprile & Giorgio García de Leaniz
tel	+34 942 641060
mobile	+34 639 614241
fax	+34 942 641172
email	reservas@t-ruesga.com
web	www.t-ruesga.com

Hotel

Map 4 Entry 57

Hotel Posada Aire de Ruesga
Mentera, 39813 Valle de Ruesga, Cantabria

Amazing to think you are 20 minutes from some of the best beaches in Spain.
Up here, in glorious 180-degree mountain scenery, is Josu's casona, a beautifully
restored 17th-century country-house hotel that beats with a modern heart. On
a clear day you can distinctly see five layers of mountain ridges; in autumn, four
shades of brown on the highest slopes. It is a place that encourages meditation, and
the San Esteban hermitage opposite shows that you are not the first one to feel the
magic. Big, comfortable, contemporary bedrooms are loosely themed: 'Arab' has
mint walls and Moroccan furniture, 'Colonial' a Balinese four-poster and wardrobe.
Eight bungalows are due to be finished soon, constructed with families in mind.
Josu's sister, a professional chef, buys fish and seafood from Laredo's market, her
special menus and the *menú del día* – superb value – served in an elegant restaurant
with Añil-blue walls and nicely dressed tables. Enjoy a wild mushroom and prawn
pie in full view of the mountains: all-glass walls pull in the Collados del Asón
Natural Park. The sunsets are to die for and the staff are wonderful.

rooms	18: 10 twins/doubles, 8 bungalows for 4.
price	€68-€120. Bungalows €90-€140. VAT included.
meals	Dinner €12-€30.
closed	6-31 January.
directions	From Santander/Bilbao on A-8; exit 173 Colindres/Burgos onto N-629. At Ramales, right for Valle/Arreonda. After 5km, just before Valle, right for Mentera. Hotel at entrance of village, on left.

Josu Madariaga Páez

tel	+34 942 641000
mobile	+34 618 641035
email	airederuesga@telefonica.net
web	www.airederuesga.com

Hotel

Map 4 Entry 58

Basque Country, Navarra – La Rioja

Hotel Arresi

c/Portugane 7, 48620 Armintza, Vizcaya

Driving off the ferry into a foreign land as night falls, fractious children in tow, can be a stressful start to a holiday. So, whether you're arriving at Bilbao or Santander, this hotel is a godsend: close at hand and friendly. From the outside, it may not look that special. Step in and you feel as though you have entered the home of a gracious friend. The approach is informal; the interior is anything but. An imposing staircase leads to an equally impressive landing and on to the bedrooms: all smart, roomy and comfortable, with excellent bathrooms. In the morning, a fine panorama – taking in the hotel's beautiful gardens and vineyard (try their wine!), the cliffs and the hills, Armintza harbour and the sea. The children will by now have found the big Wendy house in the lush garden and the swimming pool (safely fenced off). You'll head for the shaded pergola by day, the cosy reading room by night. There's no restaurant as such, but they may well rustle up a meal for you if you ask in advance. An excellent little stopover.
A Rusticae hotel.

rooms	10: 9 twins/doubles, 1 suite.
price	€105-€127. Singles €85-€102. Suite €163. VAT included.
meals	Restaurants 300m.
closed	24 December-8 January.
directions	From Bilbao for Mungia on N-631. At Mungia exit for Plentzia (BI-2120). On to Andraka on BI-3153. Here, right to Armintza. At entrance of town, hotel signed on left; at end of 200m uphill.

Arantza Aranbarri Uresandi

tel	+34 946 879208
mobile	+34 605 711428
fax	+34 946 879310
email	hotelarresi@hotelarresi.com
web	www.hotelarresi.com

Hotel

Map 4 Entry 59

Ametzola

Barrio Ametzola 1, 48499 Zeberio, Vizcaya

This fine Basque farmhouse has risen like a phoenix after destruction by fire three centuries ago – the result of a family feud. Mikel, your unfailingly affable host, has undertaken a laborious and sympathic restoration. And the serenity of the setting is extraordinary; watch the early mists lift from the valley below and an idyllic pastoral scene unfolds. The ancient wooden structure of the house is revealed in beams, walls and ceilings; look closely at the wafer brickwork and you'll see evidence of a time when tools were simple but ingenuity compensated. Bedrooms here are rustic affairs but with plenty of comfort, thanks to plump duvets and hydromassage showers, while shelved, curtained alcoves make simple storage space. After one of several circular walks starting from the door, how comforting to return to Mikel's hearty dishes, accompanied by robust wines. Savour his port-flavoured chicken and raisins, or his quails' legs in chocolate sauce; you'll be glad this former economist swapped his spreadsheets for an apron. Friendly, authentic, charming and special.

rooms	6 twins/doubles.
price	€60-€75.
meals	Breakfast €6. Dinner €18.
closed	Rarely.
directions	AP-68 Burgos-Logroño, exit 1 for Arrigorriaga onto A-625. Cont. dir. Laudio-Llodio on BI-625. After 3km, right for Ugas/Miraballes onto BI-3524. At Ermitabarri, sharp left by church for Ametzola; 1km; left again on very steep road to house.

	Mikel Azaola
tel	+34 944 046076
mobile	+34 629 429870
email	house@ametzola.net
web	www.ametzola.net

B&B

Map 4 Entry 60

Mendi Goikoa

Barrio San Juan 33, 48291 Axpe-Atxondo, Vizcaya

Donde el silencio se oye: a place of silence. Peaceful it is, and beautiful. The hotel is made up of two handsome 19th-century farm buildings surrounded by meadow, with mountain views from almost every room: extraordinary. The main restaurant, once the old barn, is vast and high-ceilinged and packed with fine country antiques; the emphasis is on traditional Basque cooking with a few of the chef's own creations, and recent reports tell us the food is good. There is a smaller breakfast room and a gem of a restaurant/bar in the stables, rustic with open-stone walls and rafters. The bedrooms on the hayloft floor, not huge, are equally good-looking: original rafters and small windows, exposed stones, some lovely old pieces of furniture, carpeting and seductive views. Shower rooms are functional. There are great walks up to (or towards!) the surrounding peaks, so make sure you work up an appetite for dinner. Do book – it's a popular place – but note, this is a wedding-feast venue and can get lively at weekends.

rooms	11 twins/doubles.
price	€90. Singles €60.
meals	Lunch & dinner €23.50. A la carte from €50. Restaurant closed Sun evening & all Monday.
closed	November–March.
directions	From A-8, exit 17 for Durango. N-636 for Elorrio. In Atxondo, right to Axpe. After 1km, right following signs; through village. House above village, at foot of mountain.

Agurtzane Telleria; Iñaki & Jose Luís Ibarra

tel	+34 946 820833
fax	+34 946 821136
email	reservas@mendigoikoa.com
web	www.mendigoikoa.com

Hotel

Map 5 Entry 61

Ziortxa-Beitia

Goiherria 13, 48279 Bolibar, Vizcaya

Our inspector arrived with a bag of pears and green peppers and asked the owner
– known as 'Paco' to all and sundry – whether they could be incorporated into his
evening meal. Without batting an eyelid, Paco whisked the ingredients off to the
kitchen. The peppers later appeared with some freshly cooked pork and the pears
poached in wine. This is not so much an example of Basque hospitality, rather
an illustration of your gentle host's no-fuss-no-frills attitude. His old farmhouse
sits in remote countryside below a Cistercian monastery on the famous pilgrim
route to Santiago de Compostela; the drive here is stunning. Bedrooms are basic
modern but comfortable and squeaky clean – fine for pilgrims and walkers –
and there's a laundry on the top floor. Food is of the home-cooked variety and
although the bar can get quite lively in the evenings, the nights are blissfully quiet
– just the hoot of the owl to lull you to sleep. Nearby Bolibar is the birthplace
of Simon Bolivar, the liberator of South America, and the museum is well worth
a visit – as is a stroll round the grounds of the monastery.

rooms	12: 6 twins/doubles, 6 dormitories for 6.
price	€48–€53. Singles €39–€43. Bunkbed €15 p.p.
meals	Breakfast €5.50. Lunch & dinner €25.
closed	Christmas.
directions	Directions on booking. Not easy to find.

	Francisco Rios Urbaneja
tel	+34 946 165259

Urresti

Barrio Zendokiz 12, 48314 Gautegiz de Arteaga, Vizcaya

A dream come true for Urresti's two friendly young owners – they have transformed the ruins of the farmhouse they found in green Vizcaya. From the outside it looks 17th century; inside is more contemporary in feel. Breakfast is excellent value, served in the large sitting/dining room: local cheeses, homemade jam, fruits from the farm, plenty of coffee. For other meals guests share an open-plan, fully-equipped kitchen/living area. Smart, impeccably clean little bedrooms have laminate floors and new, country-style furniture; the one under the eaves (hot in summer!) has a balcony; another is big enough for an extra sofabed. En suite bath and shower rooms are excellent. Outside: a small organic plot – you can buy the vegetables. The house stands in beautiful rolling countryside with stunning beaches not far away – bring buckets and spades. Gernika, too, is close. A brilliant place for families, with emus, sheep, goats, horses and hens to fuss over, and ancient forests of oak and chestnut to explore (borrow the bikes). The whole area is a Parque Natural and many come just for the birdlife.

rooms	6 + 2: 6 twins/doubles. 2 apartments: 1 for 2, 1 for 4.
price	€47–€55. Apartments €71–€77.
meals	Breakfast €6.50.
closed	Rarely.
directions	From Gernika for Lekeitio. At fork, lower road for Lekeitio. After 6km, left for Elanchobe. On right, below road level, after 1.2km at sign 'Nekazal Turismoa Agroturismo'.

	María Goitia & Jose María Ríos
tel/fax	+34 946 251843
email	urresti@wanadoo.es
web	www.toprural.com/urresti

Guest house

Map 5 Entry 63

Atalaya Hotel

Itxaropen Kalea 1, 48360 Mundaka, Vizcaya

Fernando, Jesús and Alaín go out of their way to make your stay a happy one, here in one of the most 'family' of Vizcaya's small hotels. You couldn't better the position, either, right by the fish market and a step from the beach of a deep inlet carved by the Cantabrian sea. The house was built in 1911 and is listed. An open galleried frontage lets in the ever-changing light, encouraging contemplation of sand, sea and the church tower of Santa María. The owners and staff are kind, straightforward people who proudly maintain their small hotel, and cheerfully help you plan your visits. The best rooms have sea views but they're all worth a night: quiet, clean and comfortable with new oak furniture, king-size beds and every gadget in the book. A smart little bar serves sandwiches and snacks. This would be the perfect place to spend a last night before the ferry ride home, and car and belongings should be safe in the car park. It's a great base from which to explore the Urdaibai Biosphere Reserve, while the stunning Guggenheim Museum is just over an hour by train — and the station is five minutes away.

rooms	12: 10 twins/doubles. 2 family.
price	€88-€97. Singles €70-€77.
meals	Breakfast €8.30.
	Bar meal around €25.
closed	Rarely.
directions	From Bilbao, A-8/E-70 exit 18 onto N-634. BI-635 via Gernika to Mundaka; left to village centre. Hotel near Santa María church; one way system, narrow roads. Park at free hotel car park.

Fernando Rodriguez & Jesús Alkorta

tel	+34 946 177000
fax	+34 946 876899
email	hotelatalaya@hotel-atalaya-mundaka.com
web	www.hotel-atalaya-mundaka.com

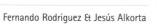

Hotel

Map 5 Entry 64

Hotel Zubieta

c/Portal de Atea s/n, 48280 Lekeitio, Vizcaya

The inauspicious surroundings are misleading; through the arch, up the drive to the former stables, and you arrive at somewhere special. The hotel, enfolded by forests of eucalyptus, is a temple to stylish rusticity. Smart sofas, old teracotta brick floors, carved wooden columns, a small library: the atmosphere is that of an old inn touched with a contemporary elegance, a place where you would happily settle in for the day. Bedrooms match crisp patterned fabrics with some fine pieces of old family furniture – wrought-iron bedsteads, armoires, delicate four-posters – while subdued lighting adds to the immaculate but warm feel. After a deep sleep, start the day with homemade pastries on a large terrace that overlooks the family's 18th-century manor house. Venture further and you enter Lekeitio, a town where, according to owners Mikel and Zenaida, "tourism is only accidental." It's an authentic Basque fishing town with a startling energy; fishermen pull in the catch daily, women mend nets by the sea. Local 'fiestas' have special ethnographic interest and local Basque tapas – 'pintxos' – are particularly good.

rooms	24: 22 twins/doubles, 2 family.
price	€74-€102. Family €96-€120.
meals	Breakfast €9.50.
closed	November-early February.
directions	In Lekeitio, right at main x-roads for Ondarroa. After 500m, at the end of tree-lined avenue, on left.

	Zenaida & Mikel Solano
tel	+34 946 843030
fax	+34 946 841099
email	hotelzubieta@hotelzubieta.com
web	www.hotelzubieta.com

Hotel

Map 5 Entry 65

Villa Soro

Avda. de Ategorrieta 61, 20013 San Sebastián, Guipúzcoa

Classy, different and in San Sebastián. Built in 1898 for a prominent Basque family, the conversion from house to hotel was completed in 2003. Only three of the original 20 chimneys remain – but this is a small price to pay for an exquisite transformation. The carpeted and carved oak staircase sets the tone of elegance and grace; drawings by the contemporary artist Orteiza adorn the walls; the radiators are not merely radiators, but beautiful examples of what can be done with cast iron… Parquet floors gleam, chandeliers glisten, staff glide. Retreat with tea or cocktail to one of two sitting rooms, light-filled in summer, fire-lit in winter. Big, serene bedrooms – some in the main house, others in the carriage house, equally good – have pure-wool carpets, classic furniture and exemplary beds. Marble bathrooms come with fine toiletries (for sale) and dressing gowns, while double glazing ensures peace from the nearby motorway to France. Michelin stars are a ride away, but don't motor in when the parking is tricky: spin off on one of the hotel's city-shoppers instead. *A Rusticae hotel.*

rooms	25: 23 twins/doubles, 2 singles.
price	€142–€230. Singles €125–€160.
meals	Breakfast €13. Room service available.
closed	Rarely.
directions	A-8 exit Donostia/Ondarreta. At Ondarreta up c/San Martín; over bridge & drive up c/Miracruz, which becomes Avda. de Ategorrieta. Hotel on left; on to next r'bout & turn around; very busy road.

	Pablo Carrington & Jaione Gastañares
tel	+34 943 297970
fax	+34 943 297971
email	info@villasoro.com
web	www.villasoro.com

Hotel

Map 5 Entry 66

Donamariako Benta

Barrio Ventas 4, 31750 Donamaría, Navarra

A mouthwatering address! Donamaría is hidden away off to one side of a pass through the mountains between France and Spain, within striking distance of Pamplona; it was a farmers' rest until this family arrived. They are sophisticated and delightful people, proud of their guest house and restaurant – and rightly so. These two old village houses (guest rooms in one, restaurant in the other) are packed full of old furniture, vintage toys, dried flowers and a few surprises to boot; the atmosphere is intimate, genuine, laid-back. This is a place to linger long over lunch or dinner; connoisseurs rave about the traditional Navarra cooking with a modern French touch. Menus change according to season; mushroom salad with foie gras is a speciality, all of it is memorable. Bedrooms are basic, clean and well looked after, bathrooms are pristine but small; one room has a superb little terrace overlooking the river. Mother, father and daughters welcome you most graciously into their home, set among old oak forests to make the heart soar. *Wine-tasting courses available; also salmon fishing.*

rooms	5 twins/doubles.
price	€60.
meals	Breakfast €5. Lunch & dinner €12. A la carte €25–€30. No meals Sunday evenings or Mondays.
closed	Rarely.
directions	From San Sebastián, N-121-A for Pamplona. Right into Santesteban (Doneztebe); here, just before bridge, left for Saldías. On for 2km to junc. with Donamaría road; hotel opp. junc. on right hand side.

	Elixabet Badiola & Imanol Luzuriaga
tel/fax	+34 948 450708
email	info@donamariako.com
web	www.donamariako.com

Guest house

Map 5 Entry 67

Etxatoa

31879 Oderitz, Navarra

The stunning forests are an open invitation to walkers, the old railway track is a gift for cyclists (horses, wheelchairs and pushchairs too), and the road up to the Santuario de San Miguel caves is spectacular. The house is a listed 17th-century building with a coat of arms and a three-sided roof; its plain stone exterior, awaiting renovation, conceals the charms of this young guest house. Inside, as much has been recycled as possible – the washstand made of reclaimed oak is charming – and a fine restoration job has been done on the antique pieces so carefully collected. The large, frill-free living/dining/kitchen area has both comfort and style, and the simple double rooms, with their chunky rafters, open-stone walls, new wrought-iron beds and country antiques, have a fresh, rustic appeal. Note that the suite, impeccably restored and with a small bathroom, has a private terrace under the plum trees. The new owner promises breakfasts as delightful as all the rest, and there are restaurants aplenty in Pamplona (a 20-minute drive) where Basque, Spanish and French cuisines meet.

rooms	6: 4 twins/doubles, 2 suites.
price	€64–€75. Suites €96–€192.
meals	Breakfast €9.10.
closed	Rarely.
directions	From S. Sebastián A-15 for Pamplona; exit 127. Through Lekunberri; at exit of town NA-7510 for Baraibar; 500m, left at junc. for Madotz on NA-7500; 6.5km to Oderitz. House opp. as you drive into village.

	Iñaki Etxebarria
tel	+34 948 504449
mobile	+34 669 886558
email	info@etxatoa.com
web	www.etxatoa.com

B&B

Map 5 Entry 68

La Casa del Cofrade

Ctra. Nalda km 9, 26120 Albelda de Iregua, La Rioja

You could drive past this and not take a second look. But this roadside hotel, opened in 2004 on the outskirts of a small Riojan town, has its fair share of surprises. Yes, you have a good bed for the night, in a stylish room that is double glazed, air conditioned, internet-wired and vastly comfortable. What makes La Casa del Cofrade special is what lies below: a warren of vaulted galleries containing the hotel's own bodega. They produce their own highly regarded Riojan wines here, of which '200 Monges' ('200 Monks') is the star. One hundred thousand bottles are arranged in eye-catching rows in the underground alcoves. A tour is a must; you'll see the process from start to finish, from burgundy fruits to nectar maturing in 900 wooden barrels. Leticia, the sparky young director, will tell you all. She can also book you on the Vinobus, a bodega-themed tour that leaves from Logroño daily – a fantastic idea. Back above, bedrooms sport bold stripes and gleaming parquet, our favourite being La Tentación (Temptation). Groups of 12 may book the old wine cellar for meals.

rooms	18: 17 twins/doubles, 1 single.
price	€72-€97.
meals	Restaurant 10-minute walk.
closed	24 December-1 January.
directions	From Bilbao on AP-68; exit 12 for Logroño. Continue on N-111 for Soria. After 7km, left to Albelda de Iregua; through here, following signs for Nalda/Soria. Hotel at exit of town, on left. Hotel car park 100m, on left.

	Leticia Villegas
tel	+34 941 444426
fax	+34 941 444427
email	reservas@lacasadelcofrade.com
web	www.lacasadelcofrade.com

Hotel

Map 5 Entry 69

Hospedería Señorío de Briñas

Travesía de la Calle Real 3, 26290 Briñas, La Rioja

Briñas is one of the prettiest villages of La Rioja. Its stately houses and ornate churches pay witness to its golden age, the 16th century, when the region reached its economic zenith and noble families set up house. The stern façade of this *casona* gives no hint of the character and classiness that lie within. Charming, gregarious Angela is a designer who embarked on this project when the building was little more than a ruin; impossible to believe now! A rustic elegance prevails – chunky terracotta floors, antique chairs, embroidered linen, chandeliers. Most intriguing of all are the trompe l'oeil frescos, the surreal creations of a Polish artist that will have you gazing out of an imaginary window or pulling back a lavish drape… Treasures and treats galore: a vast, individually decorated, blissfully quiet bedroom with an old and creaky pine floor, a mezzanine suite perfect for families, good breakfasts with freshly squeezed juices, and a cosy bar where you can get to grips with Rioja's most famous export, its oaky red wine. *A Rusticae hotel.*

rooms	14: 11 twins/doubles, 3 suites.
price	€117. Singles €89. Suite €137-€170.
meals	Evening snacks available. Restaurants in Haro.
closed	Rarely.
directions	From A-68, exit 8 for Zambrana; N-124 for Logroño. Through tunnel, up hill; after 8km, left for Briñas. After 300m right; 50m down dead-end road. Park in front, or in car park.

	Angela Gómez
tel	+34 941 304224
fax	+34 941 304345
email	info@hotelesconencantodelarioja.com
web	www.hotelesconencantodelarioja.com

Hotel

Map 4 Entry 70

Aragón
Cataluña

Posada Magoría

c/Milagro 32, 22728 Ansó, Huesca

This 1920s family home has a genuine mood and has been caringly restored by the much-travelled Enrique. It's a warm and well-insulated house, where ancient radiators belt out the heat, louvred shutters let in the light, the pale interior is finely furnished, and the traditional bedrooms are uncluttered and soberly attired. Good quality mattresses lie on 1920s beds and bathrooms have glass-brick walls to let the daylight in. But the heart of the place is the communal dining area where a huge rock juts into the room beside the long table and the full-length wall tapestry lends the space weight. Here you are served the most delicious, organic, vegetarian food – salads, soups, cheeses, homemade bread and lashings of cider. Breakfast is a purifying selection of muesli, cereals and mountain honey. Enrique, a pioneer of eco-tourism and a perfect host, has an intimate knowledge of the region and will deepen your understanding of this undiscovered peak; it is a joy to listen to him. Walking, mushroom-picking, yoga… make a trip to this wonderfully remote place. The village, too, is special. *Vegetarian food only.*

rooms	6 twins/doubles.
price	€48–€53. VAT included.
meals	Breakfast €6. Dinner €12. VAT included.
closed	Rarely.
directions	Pamplona-Jaca N-240. Left at Berdun on HU-202 to Ansó. Here, 2nd left into village past mill; left along narrow street to church; last house on right. Steep walk from car park: unload at house first.

Enrique Ipas & Teresa Garayoa

tel	+34 974 370049
fax	+34 974 370003
email	posadamagoria@gmail.com

B&B

Map 6 Entry 71

Hotel Santa Cristina

Ctra. Astún-Candanchú km.669, 22880 Canfranc-Estación, Huesca

The Pyrenees tower majestically before you, and from this idyllic valley you can walk straight into France. In a former headquarters of the 19th-century *carabineros* (whose joyful role it was to seize smugglers) is this stunning hotel. Friendly and attentive staff have replaced the armed police, stylish rooms have supplanted spartan soldiers' quarters and the former canteen is a celebrated restaurant. Roomy, relaxing bedrooms reveal clean lines, earthy hues and a warm minimalism. Stunning views of the Aragón Valley flood the spa (sauna, gym and heated pool – no charge for residents.) The pilgrim's way to Santiago meanders beside the hotel and if you're fit, you could walk the 20 kilometres to Jaca, a town with an active cultural agenda and a romanesque cathedral. Return on the scenic train, to a charming welcome and a delightful dinner: red-shrimp and monkfish carpaccio perhaps, or slow-roasted lamb shoulder with thyme. This would make a superb winter sporting base: you're a snow-ball's throw from two of the best ski resorts in the Pyrenees – Candanchú and Astún.

rooms	56: 54 twins/doubles, 2 singles. Extra beds available.
price	€95–€172.50. Singles €71–€86. Half-board option available.
meals	Lunch & dinner €19.
closed	14 October–November.
directions	From Zaragoza A-23 to Nueno; m'way becomes N-330. Continue on N-330 to Canfranc Estación; follow direction Francia/Astún/Candanchú. Hotel signed after 2km.

Conchita Murrieta
tel +34 974 373300
fax +34 974 373310
email hotel@santacristina.es
web www.santacristina.es

Hotel

Map 6 Entry 72

El Privilegio de Tena

Plaza Mayor, 22663 Tramacastilla de Tena, Huesca

The name of this gorgeous place echoes the privileges granted long ago by the Kingdom of Aragón. Because of the valley's isolation, it suffered terrible hardship in the long winter months; there's still a remoteness and silence but you'll find the privations hard to credit now. Big, beautiful bedrooms and quirky, designer bathrooms have a generous, stylish comfort, but the history of the place is still apparent in the ancient detail, rough golden stone and huge great beams. Juan inherited the two buildings – one a 15th-century abbey, the other a hotel – from his family; until ten years ago they were used to shelter cows... If you really want to push the boat out, book the Suite Privilegio – it's quite something. There's even a brass telescope so you can make the most of the stunning views (the breathtakingly sheer rockface of Peña Telera down in the valley is an iconic landmark). Juan and his wife are thoroughly nice people – she's from Zaragoza and used to teach Italian – and very proud of their collaboration with top Spanish chef Martín Berasategui. *Reserve parking at time of booking.*

rooms	26: 19 twins/doubles, 7 suites.
price	€114–€154. Singles €77–€100. Suite €140–€600. VAT included.
meals	Lunch & dinner €25. A la carte from €30.
closed	Rarely.
directions	From Huesca N-136 for Jaca. Follow road round to Biescas. 12km on, at junc. for Biescas, on towards France. 10km after junc. left; 1.5km to Tramacastilla. Through village; hotel behind 'Ayunatmiento'.

	Anabel Costas & Juan Ignacio Pérez
tel	+34 974 487206
fax	+34 974 487270
email	info@elprivilegio.com
web	www.elprivilegio.com

Hotel

Map 6 Entry 73

La Casueña

c/El Troniecho 11, 22640 Lanuza, Huesca

A story of fate and survival. Some 30 years ago the inhabitants of Lanuza were evicted: the reservoir, they were told, would swallow their houses. But a design fault in the dam – it leaks – confounded these prophets of doom. Now seven of the families are back and the old stone houses returned to their owners. This is one of them. Flanked by the towering Foratata mountain, near ski resorts and mountain spas, the hamlet's lakeside position is exceptional. And Marián's family have sympatheticaly restored their house adding an unusual literary twist: each room is named after a Spanish-speaking writer – Lorca, Márquez, Isabel Allende, Pallaruelo. A biography of each writer awaits you in your dramatically contemporary bedroom, while book excerpts are engraved on glass in stylish shower rooms. Fine reproductions of medival paintings and abstract/geometric frescos enwrap walls, ceilings and even doors; bold colours and striking graphics catch the eye at every turn. Furniture is custom-made by Aragonese craftsmen, and the restaurant is as unique as all the rest. Fun in all seasons.

rooms	10 twins/doubles.
price	€110–€136. VAT included.
meals	Lunch & dinner €20.
closed	3 weeks in November.
directions	From Zaragoza/Huesca E-7/N-330 to Sabiñánigo. Here, N-260 and A-136 for Biescas/Portalet/France. Through tunnel outside Escarrilla; right over dam to Lanuza. Hotel next to church.

Marián Pérez

tel	+34 972 146367
fax	+34 972 146169
email	info@lacasuena.com
web	www.lacasuena.com

Hotel

Map 6 Entry 74

Casa de San Martín

22372 San Martín de la Solana, Huesca

A retreat that manages to be chic and rustic. Once you've left the main road, prepare to stay in second gear for a tortuous three-mile track: the hotel rests on a little green knoll surrounded by the foothills of the Pyrenees. A dwelling is said to have stood here since 1200 but the tall, stone, galleried front is 500 years older. Pass the Spanish water dogs sunning themselves on the patio and enter the hall, where pride of place is given to a real Goya on the wall: it's the portrait of a one clergyman owner who gave the artist shelter during the War of Independence. In the chunky beamed sitting room – once a chapel – are voguishly clad tartan sofas and country chairs, exposed stones, soft lighting, a big fire – a rustic contemporary décor. Bedrooms, too, are decorated in glowing good taste. The scent of lavender lingers in the lawned gardens where cool breezes caress the trees, and food is a mix of regional Spanish and Brazilian, with some produce straight from the garden; it couldn't be fresher. The Somontano wines are delicious, too, and Mario is a gracious and welcoming host. A gem. *A Rusticae hotel.*

rooms	9 twins/doubles.
price	€120–€180. Singles €90.
meals	Breakfast €10. Dinner €30.
closed	Rarely.
directions	Barcelona A-2/E-90 for Lleida; N-240 for Huesca. Before Barbastro, right on N-123, then A-138 Aínsa. Left for Boltaña onto N-260; 10km after Boltaña, right for San Martín. Rough track 4km; right onto tarmac; for 1km to hotel.

	Mario Reis & David Robinson
tel	+34 974 503105
mobile	+34 902 010560
fax	+34 974 341456
email	info@casadesanmartin.com
web	www.casadesanmartin.com

Hotel

Map 6 Entry 75

Hotel Los Arcos

Plaza Mayor 23, 22330 Aínsa, Huesca

At the heart of the enchanting village of Aínsa is a cobbled square overlooked by a fine church tower. Tucked away down its medieval alleys, many tempting restaurants and cafés – no wonder Aínsa is so popular. On one side of the square is a delightful terrace of old houses, built of warm stone, with shuttered windows and tiny iron balconies. Oscar, an engineer born in Aragón who decided to return to his roots, has turned one of these tall, slender houses into a charming little hotel. He is gentle and eager to ensure that his guests are comfortable. The communal areas are of necessity small, but the spaces have been cleverly used and on the walls are paintings by a Barcelona artist. Exposed stone, reclaimed beams and quarry tiles coexist with ultra modern steel and glass; soft, tawny colours and fabrics contrast with dazzling white linens. The bedrooms are generous and pleasing, some facing the square, others the Peña Montañesa. The 'special' room has a splendid four-poster. Ordesa National Park is close by: go there for great walking and, perhaps, a glimpse of wild boar, vultures and deer.

rooms	7 twins/doubles.
price	€70–€150.
meals	Restaurants in village.
closed	Rarely.
directions	From Barcelona to Lleida (Lérida) on A-2; exit 458 onto N-123 for Huesca. Before Barbastro right for Aínsa. Left at main x-roads in Aínsa. After 250m, right at sign 'casco historico'; 500m to car park; 5-min walk to hotel.

Oscar Fantova & Carlota Dorado

tel	+34 974 500016
mobile	+34 696 590852
fax	+34 974 500136
email	info@hotellosarcosainsa.com
web	www.hotellosarcosainsa.com

Hotel

Map 6 Entry 76

Casa Blas

c/Sta Agueda 9, 22330, Banastón-Usana, Huesca

The scent of bodega envelops you as you walk through the vaulted stone archway that leads to Casa Blas, a 17th-century farmhouse in an elevated village with sweeping mountain views. Your front door, inscribed with an engraving of St Jacques pilgrims' shell, opens into a labyrinthine interior with a marked ethnographical feel. Step through the hall – a rustic extravaganza of old farming implements and original stone vats – and up a solid stone staircase with a wrought-iron banister to simple, authentic spaces with plain but good furniture. This is perfect for large families or group of friends. An evocative scent pervades the well-equipped Aragonese kitchen, speaking of a gentle attention to food down the ages. Next door is an open fireplace guarded by benches on each side – nice to imagine a roaring fire on a crisp blue-sky winter day. Our favourite rooms are the bedrooms on the top floor, with their white walls, decorative floor tiles and terrace with superb views. Medieval Ainsa is an hour's walk along a waymarked path, and the mighty Pyrenees are a day trip away. *Minimum stay three nights.*

rooms	House for 2-10 (6 doubles).
price	€960-€1,200 p.w. VAT included.
meals	Self-catering.
closed	Rarely.
directions	From Barbastro on A-138 to Aínsa; in Ainsa, right at main crossroads onto A-260. Village signed after 2km; park in village & walk 80m to house (no car access).

	Jayne Calvert
mobile	+34 690 039999
email	info@populationsix.com
web	www.populationsix.com

Self-catering

Map 6 Entry 77

La Antigua Abadía

Plaza Mayor, 22330 Coscojuela de Sobrarbe, Huesca

Barely 20 souls live in this sleepy, charming village in the Sobrarbe. To the north, the rugged contours of Monte Perdido can be seen; to the south, the waters of the Mediano reservoir glitter in the sun. This former abbot's manse, seamlessly integrated into the church – climb the church for spectacular views – has become a home of character. A rustic, low-vaulted living area – the former stable and bodega – welcomes you in, its kitchen with a large Aragonese table. Squishy floral sofas sit alongside older, more attractive pieces. More rusticity in the bedrooms: simple, spotless, awash with light, they have comfortable beds, fat white duvets and a tranquil feel in keeping with the setting. Off one of the bedrooms is a free-standing bath – gaze on the Pyrenees as you soak! But the quirkiest spot in the house is the original kitchen upstairs, complete with its flagstone basin for washing clothes. Antique cooking and farming implements and Moroccan touches create a cosy atmosphere throughout; families would like it here. A great escape – and medieval Ainsa is a short drive. *Minimum three nights.*

rooms	House for 9 (4 doubles, extra single bed).
price	€1,120-€1,400 per week. VAT included.
meals	Self-catering.
closed	Rarely.
directions	A-138 from Barbastro to Ainsa. At km38 marker, right for Coscojuela. Right again after 1km into village. Park opposite church in main square. Abadía next to church.

	Jayne Calvert
mobile	+34 690 039999
email	info@populationsix.com
web	www.populationsix.com

La Choca

Plaza Mayor 1, 22148 Lecina, Huesca

It is a vertiginous arrival – but worth it. In a privileged positon on the village square, in a tiny (yet easily accessible) hamlet in a wild part of Huesca, Miguel and Ana restored this centuries-old fortified farmhouse for themselves... but La Choca cried out to be shared so they opened to all. Fall asleep to the hooting of the owl, wake to the sound of the church bells: the peace is intoxicating. Inside, stone walls, ancient timbers, stone stairs and an attractive rusticity. The bedrooms are simple: without air conditioning (it gets hot in summer) but with captivating views... The lightest are the twins at the front, three are big enough for a family, and the top one has its own terrace. You'll eat well (perhaps to background classical music): homemade jams at breakfast, regional dishes with a French twist at main meals, and Ana's own recipes. There's a garden flanked by the church, and an ancient green oak for shade. Cave paintings nearby, bikes in the hamlet, walks from the door, and exceptionally kind hosts. The delightful self-catering apartments were added three years ago.

rooms	9 + 2: 9 twins/doubles. 2 apartments for 4.
price	Half-board €80. Singles €50. Apartment €40–€54 (min. 2 nights, self-catering only).
meals	Half-board only. Lunch (weekends only) €25–€30 à la carte. Picnic lunch on request.
closed	November to Christmas.
directions	Directions on booking.

	Ana Zamora & Miguel Angel Blasco
tel	+34 974 343070
mobile	+34 659 633636
fax	+34 974 343304
email	chocala@wanadoo.es
web	www.lachoca.com

Guest house

Map 6 Entry 79

Hostería de Guara

c/Oriente 2, 22144 Bierge, Huesca

There's inn-keeping in the family: this well-established roadside hosteria was started by Ana and Eva's parents. A spectacular drive on narrow scenic roads brings you to the unassuming village of Bierge; the Guara Natural Park, criss-crossed with canyons of emerald waters, is a short drive away. The front garden, packed with thyme, rosemary, lavender and roses, provides an explosion of Mediterranean colour against the perennial blue sky. Hotel-smart bedrooms have polished tiles, beds have white metal bedheads and flowing muslin drapes, and perhaps an armchair or two. Take a sundowner to the terrace for views of the hilltop church, floodlit at night. In the restaurant some dishes are cooked over an open fire; and don't miss the 'olive oil menu' – they produce their own. At the back is an almond orchard, a cloud of white and pink in February when the blossom begins. Delightful Eva can arrange guided tours of the many bodegas of the Somontano region, and then there's rafting, riding, climbing and ravine-spotting. Or book onto a birdwatching tour and see eagles and vultures feeding. *A Rusticae hotel.*

rooms	14 twins/doubles.
price	€70–€120. Singles €58. Half-board €100–€160 for 2.
meals	Lunch & dinner €25.
closed	January.
directions	From Huesca, N-240 for Lleida. 5km after Angües, left to Abiego, then left to Bierge. Hostería on left, at entrance to village.

	Ana & Eva Viñuales Ferrando
tel/fax	+34 974 318107
email	info@hosteriadeguara.com
web	www.hosteriadeguara.com

Hotel

Map 6 Entry 80

Posada La Pastora

c/Roncesvalles 1, 50678 Uncastillo, Zaragoza

Uncastillo, as the name implies, is an attractive castle-topped town – all too often passed by – in the Sierra de Santo Domingo. Just behind the beautiful, romanesque Iglésia Santa María is this grand, 18th-century house: the nicest place to stay in town. The traditional elements of old flagstones, wrought-iron grilles, terracotta tiles and wooden beams have been preserved and restored. Massively thick outer walls mean that even at the height of the Spanish summer it remains cool inside; in winter, a woodburner keeps the little lounge as warm as toast. Inma and Miguel are as charming and unassuming as the guest house they have created. Guest rooms have no delusions of grandeur but, with those heavy stone walls, checked bedspreads and antique washbasins they feel wonderfully snug. Another medieval town to visit is Sos del Rey Católico; its claim to fame is that the local-boy-made-good was Fernando II, whose marriage to Isabela would so radically change the course of Spanish history. *A Rusticae hotel.*

rooms	10 twins/doubles.
price	€66-€105. Singles €48.
meals	Breakfast €5.50.
closed	Rarely.
directions	From Pamplona N-121 south, then N-240 Huesca; NA-127 to Sangüesa. There, A-127 to Uncastillo. Here, round church of S. María; park in small cobbled square. 20m to house.

	Inma Navarro Labat & Miguel Pemán
tel/fax	+34 976 679499
email	lapastora@lapastora.net
web	www.lapastora.net

Guest house

Map 5 Entry 81

Hotel Monasterio de Piedra

Afueras s/n, 50210 Nuévalos, Zaragoza

This 800-year-old monastery up in the hills is one of those gems of Spanish culture that ravish the senses and make exploring Iberia a joy. Impressive corridors still invite contemplation but there's not a horsehair mattress in sight: uncluttered bedrooms, each converted from a quartet of monks' cells, are smart with antiques and cool in scorching summer. Best of all, they overlook a monastic garden. Vaulted sitting areas echo; food is mouthwatering; ancient cream stone walls and alabaster windows soothe the soul. Unwind, and take a guided tour of the cloisters, altars and tombs – and the first European kitchen where chocolate was made. (There's an exhibition attached.) In one of the former cellars, the Wine Museum gives another glimpse of life in days gone by, and there's the Life of the River Centre with its 3D audio-visual presentation of the life cycle of the trout. But the dense natural ecosystem of the park is the jewel in this particular Aragonese crown. A 174-foot waterfall, a mirror lake, a sunken grotto... go and lose yourself in the gardens and walkways. *Regular bird of prey demonstrations.*

rooms	61 twins/doubles.
price	€126. Singles €67–€94.
meals	Breakfast €9. Lunch & dinner €24.
closed	Rarely.
directions	From Barcelona & Zaragoza exit 231 for Monasterio de P. In Nuévalos, signs for Monasterio de P. Hotel 2.5km outside village in monastery grounds.

	Antonio Carmona Fernández
tel	+34 902 196052
fax	+34 976 849054
email	hotel@monasteriopiedra.com
web	www.monasteriopiedra.com

Hotel

Map 12 Entry 82

Hostal Los Palacios

c/Palacios 21, 44100 Albarracín, Teruel

Albarracín is one of Teruel's most amazing walled towns, its medieval streets tumbling down the hillside to a beautiful square and blue-domed cathedral. Los Palacios is a tall, balconied building just outside the city walls whose earthy colours appear to fix it to the hillside on which it stands. The 50-year-old building was not long ago thoroughly revived and thus was born this small *hostal*. Bedrooms are furnished with workaday wooden furniture, floors are decked in modern tiles and the fabrics are a shade satiny, but forgive this little lapse – these are authentically Spanish rooms, impeccably clean and, from their small balconies, have views that are second to none. More breathtaking views from the breakfast room/bar. An unpretentious little place, amazingly cheap, and wholeheartedly recommended if you are happy in simple surroundings. Make time for the new animal farm nearby, Masía Monteagudo, with its horse riding and restaurant. *Meals available July/August, Easter & bank holidays only.*

rooms	16: 15 twins/doubles, 1 single.
price	€36–€40. Singles €23–€25. VAT inc.
meals	Breakfast €3. Lunch & dinner €10. VAT included.
closed	Rarely.
directions	From Teruel N-234 north for Zaragoza. After 8km, left on TE-901 to Albarracín. Here, through tunnel, right after 150m. Hostal 2nd house on right.

	Valeriano Saez & Maite Argente
tel	+34 978 700327
fax	+34 978 700358
email	hostallospalacios@montepalacios.com
web	www.montepalacios.com

Guest house

Map 12 Entry 83

Hotel Esther

44431 Virgen de la Vega, Teruel

The high mountains and villages of the Maestrazgo are beginning to awaken the curiosity of those in search of new pastures to walk and ski. At its heart: the little Esther inn. Though the family may not always be present this is a family affair, run by father, mother and son, and the focus is on the restaurant. Expect a good meal in a modern but semi-rustic room, whose sloping timbered ceiling lends an intimate feel. Specialities are dishes from Aragón: roast lamb, pork and kid, stewed broad beans with chorizo, junket with honey for dessert – wholesome home cooking. There is a decent choice of wines and you can trust Miguel's recommendations. Decoration is the same upstairs and down – tiled floors, light pine; bedrooms have small bathrooms and printed drapes. The settlement of Virgen de la Vega is nothing to write home about, virtually deserted out of season, but there are some pretty villages nearby – head for Mora de Rubielos. Skiing is at Valdelinares, five miles away. Honest prices, and you may well be the only foreigner staying here.

rooms	22: 15 twins/doubles, 3 singles, 2 family, 2 suites.
price	€66-€112. Singles €46. Suites €132.
meals	Breakfast €6. Lunch & dinner €18. A la carte from €30.
closed	8-25 September.
directions	From Valencia for Barcelona; at Sagunto, left on N-234 for Teruel. A-232 to Alcalá de la Selva. V de la Vega 2km before Alcalá. 200m before church, on right.

	Miguel Andrés Rajadel García
tel	+34 978 801040
fax	+34 978 808030
email	hotelesther@sierradegudar.com
web	www.sierradegudar.com

Hotel

Map 13 Entry 84

Masía del Aragonés

44586 Peñarroya de Tastavins, Teruel

Its 16th-century tower rising majestically above open pastures, at the end of a long, long track, is this lovingly restored farm. It was once a weekend retreat for wealthy Aragonese; today it is more simply furnished. Its airy, sitting/dining room has stone walls hung with old farm implements, contemporary tiles, pine furniture and a fine wood-burning stove. This is where you enjoy Pilar's cooking with nearly all ingredients home-grown or reared: wholesome soups and stews, simple puddings and pastries accompanied by her liquers and home-brewed wine (and she doesn't mind a bit if you bring your own!). Bedrooms, some basic, are a good size and have iron bedsteads, homespun curtains, spotless bathrooms, exposed stone walls. With arched windows and an open layout (sharing an open bit of wall), we liked those on the top floor best, in spite of the steep stairs. The scenery is epic, the mountains home to ibex and eagles, there are crystalline rock pools above Beceite, and Valderrobres is worth a visit. The Andreu family go out of their way to make sure your stay is memorable.

rooms	6 twins/doubles.
price	€33–€45. VAT included.
meals	Lunch & dinner €12–€16, on request. VAT included.
closed	Rarely.
directions	Barcelona A-7, exit 38 for L'Hospitalet de L'Infant. On to Valderrobres. There, left to Fuentespalda, on for Monroyo, left for Peñarroya de T. After 500m, right to Herbes; signs to Masía. After 2km, right for 3km track.

	Pilar Andreu & Manuel Lombarte
tel	+34 978 769048
mobile	+34 637 115814
web	www.masaragones.com

B&B

Map 13 Entry 85

Hotel El Convent

c/Convento 1, 44596 La Fresneda, Teruel

Its massive front door is set in a creamy stone archway, flanked by a pair of cypresses; one quarter of the door swings open to admit you. The site was acquired around 1900 by a forebear of today's owners; with the land came the ruins of a church built in 1613. By the time the said forebear arrived on the scene, little more remained than the church's outer walls – the shell for an elegant new dwelling. Now it's a delightful hotel run by a smiling family. Spaces are lofty and unexpected, and there's an arresting mix of ancient and modern: beamed, vaulted ceilings and glass walls, exposed stone and contemporary fittings, conventual austerity and secular comfort. The bedrooms have huge period appeal and old frescos; those on the top floor are more contemporary and have terrific views. Particularly striking are the central patio and restaurant in the old choir and nave, the former side chapels providing intimate dining areas. The food is Mediterranean with an elegant, contemporary slant. Gardens are vast, sunny and tranquil, watery sounds abound and there's a modest pool.

rooms	13: 11 twins/doubles, 2 suites.
price	€90–€110. Suites €125–€150. VAT included.
meals	Lunch €40–€60. Dinner €40–€50.
closed	10-27 December.
directions	5km before Valderrobres, right to La Fresneda. There, left fork to square; park. Hotel 50m below square on right, at bottom of dead-end alley; staff will show you how to get to hotel car park.

	Ana & Diana Romeo Villoro
tel	+34 978 854850
mobile	+34 679 671472
fax	+34 978 854851
email	hotel@hotelelconvent.com
web	www.hotelelconvent.com

Hotel

Map 13 Entry 86

La Parada del Compte

Finca la Antigua Estación, 44597 Torre del Compte, Teruel

The 1940s railway station in the forested valley has been given a new lease of life. At the end of the road cutting down from the village a surprising, original and luxurious hotel awaits. Public spaces are large, cool and airy, colourful not cosy: high rafters, sweeping glass and metal, designer sofas and chairs. In contrast, bedrooms and bathrooms are intimate and enticing – among the best in this book. Each room is inspired by a different place – 'themed', but in the chic-est way. Istanbul has sloping rafters and a bright red wall; New York is purple and metropolitan; Seville is a symphony of rose, citrus and white; Valencia has sliding doors to the garden. It's hard to choose a favourite but we would go for França because it gets the sun first thing. Bathrooms are state of the art, lights sparkle, cushions tumble; this is Spanish contemporary design at its best. Head off along the old railway track, on foot or by bike, to discover the wilderness and wonders of this part of Spain; return to Mediterranean food so good looking you hesitate to consume it. Amazing. *A Rusticae hotel.*

rooms	11: 6 twins/doubles, 5 suites.
price	€100-€125. Suites €160-€200.
meals	Breakfast €12. Lunch & dinner €30. On request.
closed	10-31 January.
directions	Zaragoza-Alcañiz N-232. A-231 for Valderrobres. Turn left into Torre del Compte. Exit village & follow road to left. Signed.

	José María Naranjo & Pilar Vilés
tel	+34 978 769072
mobile	+34 689 786788
fax	+34 978 769074
email	hotel@hotelparadadelcompte.com
web	www.hotelparadadelcompte.com

Hotel

Map 6 Entry 87

Tancat de Codorníu

Ctra. 340 km1059, 43530 Les Cases d'Alcanar, Tarragona

Families will love this young, laid-back, fuss-free hotel, with its pretty rural backdrop and its proximity to the Delta d'Ebra — full of bird life, paddy fields and wide, empty, sandy beaches. At the end of an impressive palm-lined driveway, past a hidden crazy-golf course, you arrive at the vast, lovely, 150-year-old castle-style house — fantastically revamped by a Barcelona architect. Run by María, the hotel feels fresh, quirky and fun. There is a huge swimming pool, and another for children, and the garden backs on to working farmland — source of organic fruit and vegetables for the restaurant. If you step out to dine you'll find seafood restaurants nearby, serving fish straight from the Delta. The hotel's bedrooms announce the best of new, from walk-in hydromassage showers with wooden decking to designer products and robes, striking contemporary art and metal-wired spotlights illuminating walls. Some bedrooms have private saunas, jacuzzis and terraces with views over the sea. There's also a comfortably rustic living room, and a big summer house for celebrations. *A Rusticae hotel.*

rooms	11: 7 twins/doubles, 4 suites.
price	€120-€200. Suites €200-€300.
meals	Breakfast €9-€12. Lunch & dinner €28.
closed	Rarely.
directions	A-7 exit 41 towards Les Cases d'Alcanar. Right at port; hotel signed.

	María Ramos
tel	+34 977 737194
mobile	+34 696 544801
fax	+34 977 737231
email	info@tancatdecodorniu.com
web	www.tancatdecodorniu.com

Hotel

Map 13 Entry 88

Venta de San Juan

Ctra. P-723 Batea-Nonaspe km 7.3, 43786 Batea, Tarragona

Wonderful, the sort of place that some of us dream of finding in this apparently empty – and vast – Spanish countryside. If you begin your search for the *venta* in Batea you will be in benign mood, for it is a beautiful little town. There is a long drive up to the solid old house, deserted-looking among the fields and woods. Jorge and Clotilde are filling it with life, having inherited it from a grandfather who made his fortune in Cuba but decided to cut his losses and return after Independence... if you love faded old houses you'll love it here. The entrance is full of country clutter, flagstone-floored with doors leading into ancient rooms still dressed in flock wallpaper and exactly as they were when first sparked into life. Some might focus on the (minor) inconveniences; others will appreciate the sheer authenticity and thank us for bringing them here. The food alone makes the trip worthwhile and much of what you eat will have been grown on the farm. Jorge and Clotilde are young, modern, Catalan and charming – addicted to this chaotic old house. *Minimum stay two nights. Payment by cash only (no cheques).*

rooms	4 + 1: 3 twins/doubles sharing bath. 1 apartment for 4.
price	€44. Singles €22. VAT included.
meals	Breakfast €4. Dinner €12. VAT incl.
closed	December-Easter.
directions	Barcelona A-7 Valencia. Exit 38 L'Hospitalet de L'Infant y Móra & Gandesa. There to Alcañiz, right to Batea; P-723 for Nonaspe. At km7.3 before boundary sign for Zaragoza, left on dirt track. At each fork bear left; house 2km.

	Clotilde de Pascual
mobile	+34 649 644724
fax	+34 934 143854
web	www.ventadesanjuan.com

B&B & Self-catering

Map 6 Entry 89

Cal Mateu

c/Mayor 27, 43372 La Bisbal de Falset, Tarragona

To stay at Cal Mateu is rather like rediscovering a lost relative; guests have been known to shed a tear when they take their leave. Carmen has created a warm and comfortable home in the little medieval town of La Bisbal – known for its olive oil and its mansion houses. Cal Mateu is of more recent construction but has the spirit of an older building. Its sitting room, dining room and kitchen are low-beamed and connected by stone arches; two more sitting rooms on the upper floors have splendid views of the Montsant, a region known for its canyons and dry-stone terraces. The six little bedrooms take their decorative cue from the rest of the house, with their rough plaster walls, simple iron or wooden beds and red or mint-checked fabrics. Basic bathrooms have showers or sit-up-and-beg baths. The whole house breathes an air of unaffected charm, while meals are tasty and wholesome. The sleepy village produces prize-winning olive oil – pop into the Agrituebda and take some home. Extraordinarily good value, a peaceful setting, and the most *simpática* of hostesses. *Self-catering option for large group.*

rooms	6: 4 twins/doubles, 2 family, all sharing bathrooms.
price	€35. Singles €21. VAT included.
meals	Breakfast €6. Lunch & dinner €15. VAT included.
closed	Rarely.
directions	From Reus N-420 to Falset; there, right on T-710 to Gratallops then La Vilella Baixa. On via Cabassers (Cabacès) to La Bisbal de Falset. House on right at dead end of main street, past church.

	Carmen Perelló Masip
tel	+34 977 819185
mobile	+34 637 922435
fax	+34 977 819370
email	casapagesmateu@terra.es

B&B

Map 7 Entry 90

Hotel Rural Les Vinyes

c/Vilardida 13, 43812 Vilardida-Montferri, Tarragona

Josep and Manja's backgrounds in property and interior design have transformed
a former hostel for mill workers into a hotel of imagination and personality.
A quirky candelabra key-holder is the first of many surprises, and each themed
bedroom and suite is individual, colourwashed walls inspired by the name: reds
and greens for La Vinya, warm yellows for El Sol, soft blues and whites for El
Cielo… Manja has added handmade soft furnishings and lampshades, prettily
painted antique furniture and many more touches, making each room special.
Bathrooms are brilliant with marble basins and powerful showers; the high
standards carry through to the elegantly comfortable dining and sitting rooms.
You're in the heart of a small wine-making community and vineyards surround
you. Make the most of Manja's Spanish and Dutch dishes – organic vegetables
come fresh from the garden – and the local wines: such tiny vintages that each
bottle is numbered. If you want to explore, borrow bikes – nothing is too much
trouble for these enthusiastic and friendly hosts.

rooms	8: 4 twins/doubles, 4 suites.
price	€110–€150. VAT included.
meals	Dinner €20–€30 à la carte.
closed	Rarely.
directions	AP-2, exit 11 onto C-51 to Vendrell. After 2km, in hamlet on left.

	Josep Ruiz Camps & Manja Jonker
tel/fax	+34 977 639193
email	info@lesvinyes.com
web	www.lesvinyes.com

Hotel

Map 7 Entry 91

Can Cuadros

c/Major 3, 25211 Palouet-Massoteres, Lérida

Arriving in the dreamy silence of siesta time, you'd never imagine the hamlet of Palouet could contain such a place as Can Cuadros. The labyrinthine, 900-year-old castle is more museum than hotel, each room a step back in time. New young owners Roger and Isabel are seeking to relive the traditions of this corner of Cataluña. Not even the shower rooms escape the hand of history – each has beams and antique fittings – while bedrooms, darkish yet appealing, mercifully cool in summer, have fine old beds, good mattresses and many fascinating curios and drawings. Ancient stone walls and floors, no air con, no TV; the comforts are spartan but the place is steeped in character. There's a living room full of antique armchairs, books and some fascinating CDs (flamenco, old blues, ragtime) and, in the old cellar (once a prison!) a dining room with a wine press for a fireplace, beautifully illuminated at night. For summer suppers there's a patio, and the food is a big draw: peach jams at breakfast, delicious game in winter, local organic wines. A unique place.

rooms	7: 6 twins/doubles, 1 family, with separate or shared shower rooms.
price	€70. Singles €45. Family €75.
meals	Breakfast €5. Lunch & dinner €22.
closed	Rarely.
directions	From Barcelona N-II to Cervera. Here, right to Guissona; right to Massoteres; follow signs to Palouet.

	Roger Puiggròs & Isabel Navascués
tel	+34 973 294106
mobile	+34 654 239884
email	info@cancuadros.com
web	www.cancuadros.com

Hotel

Map 7 Entry 92

Can Boix de Peramola

Can Boix s/n, 25790 Peramola, Lérida

Ten generations of the Pallarés family have lived and worked at Can Boix; three of them have turned this seductively sited hotel into something of an institution. It is well-loved and well-run, with a real buzz. The restaurant is busy, fun and popular with Spanish families, and the menus are a celebration of what is locally grown or raised. The presentation is superb, the wine list long and the accompanying views are as satisfying as the food. Bedrooms are big, immaculate and awash with modern comforts: air conditioning, DVDs, snowy towels and jacuzzis. Those in the main building have a small balcony or terrace, those in the annexe a larger terrace overlooking gardens or stunning valley, along with direct access to the sauna and solarium. There's a new ornamental garden by the large pool, and the pool has 'wow' views; the ridge towering above the hotel is a reminder of the sublime scenery of the Pyrenees. The hotel's décor may not be the most original but this is an immensely friendly place which confidently caters for business people, outdoorsy people *and* families. *A Rusticae hotel.*

rooms	41 twins/doubles.
price	€93-€129. Singles €75-€103. Half-board €75-€131 p.p.
meals	Breakfast €9. Lunch & dinner €19. A la carte €39-€49.
closed	2 weeks November; 4 weeks January/February.
directions	Barcelona-Lleida (Lérida) on A-2. Exit Cervera & on through Cervera to Ponts; there, right on C-14 to Oliana. 3km after bridge, left to Peramola. 4km to hotel.

	Carles Muñoz
tel	+34 973 470266
fax	+34 973 470281
email	hotel@canboix.cat
web	www.canboix.cat

Hotel

Map 7 Entry 93

Casa Pete y Lou

Toló, San Salvador de Toló, 25638 Tremp, Lérida

Crystal clear air, heady views, snug farmhouse — Pete and Lou serve up an intoxicating mix at their traditional Catalan home perched high in the foothills of the Pyrenees. Every day a tough decision: trekking, rock climbing, whitewater rafting, hang-gliding, horse riding, swimming in cascade ponds... Pete will help you, with maps and routes, transport and his own good company. But there's nothing to stop you staying put here, gazing from the terrace on the alpine flowers, perhaps spotting a griffon vulture or short-toed eagle. The stone-built farmhouse, surrounded by colourful gardens, is warmly rustic inside. The three bedrooms have beamed ceilings, rugs on wooden floors and colourful wall-hangings, and you share a bathroom and sitting room. In the brightly cluttered kitchen it's all too easy to linger over one of Lou's suppers; dine in several nights a week on home-grown organic fruit and veg (and homemade bread and preserves breakfast). The site may be remote, but there are other eateries to discover. Warm, friendly, laid-back, the mood is one of 'mi casa, tu casa'.

rooms	3: 2 doubles, 1 twin.
price	€46.
meals	Dinner €12. Packed lunch available.
closed	December-February.
directions	A-2 Barcelona-Lérida, to Tárrega; C-14 to Agramunt; on to Artesa de Segre; L-512 for Tremp; at Col de Comiols, left for San Salvador; after 6km, past bridge over river, left track for 1km. Signed Tolo, then hotel.

	Peter Dale & Lou Beaumont
tel/fax	+34 973 252309
email	lou@casapeteylou.com
web	www.casapeteylou.com

B&B

Map 7 Entry 94

Casa Guilla

Santa Engracia, Apartado 83, 25620 Tremp, Lérida

A matchless position, a magical place. As you soar higher and higher to the hamlet perched on a rocky crag you can only wonder at the tenacity of Santa Engracia's earliest inhabitants. Richard and Sandra Loder, who have a head for heights, restored the old buildings that make up Casa Guilla two decades ago. A fortified Catalan farmhouse, parts of which go back 1,000 years, the labyrinthine dwelling twists and turns on multi levels… all is deliciously organic. There's a large sitting room with an open hearth, a library on the mezzanine floor and bedrooms that are plainly but comfortably furnished: terracotta tiles, heavy old beams, low ceilings, en suite showers. In the dining room or on the terrace, tuck into big breakfasts with home-baked bread and five-course dinners with lots of game — accompanied by that incomparable view. Geologists, lepidopterists, ornithologists and botanists will be in their element, but anyone seeking seclusion in a fascinating part of Cataluña will adore it here. Richard and Sandra are caring and informative hosts, and suppers at the big table are feasts.

rooms	4: 2 twins/doubles, 2 family.
price	Half-board €118. Singles €59. VAT included.
meals	Half-board only. Packed lunch €6.
closed	1 November-29 February.
directions	C-13 Tremp to Pobla de Segur; 1.5km, left at sign 'Santa Engracia 10km'. House next to church, reached via own road. Parking.

	Richard & Sandra Loder
tel	+34 973 252080
mobile	+34 620 911935
email	info@casaguilla.com
web	www.casaguilla.com

B&B

Map 7 Entry 95

Can Borrell

c/Retorn 3, 17539 Meranges, Gerona

Can Borrell was once the shelter of mountain shepherds who brought their flocks up to the high slopes of La Cerdanya for the rich summer grazing. This rambling old Pyrenean farmhouse of granite and slate is in the tiniest of villages, with meadows to the front (so children can roam) and conifer-clad mountains behind. Wood is all about in beam, shutter and chair, while slate floors mirror the building's exterior. Its conversion from home to hotel has been sensitively accomplished; it is not over-prettified but has a delightful intimacy. And there are board games for families and paintings on the walls. Bedrooms are inviting with polished floors, fabulous views and excellent beds. They vary in size, following the idiosyncrasies of an old house, and are simple and characterful. Expect something special at your well-dressed table in the popular restaurant: the mouthwatering cooking is "Catalan with a special touch". Uniformed waiting staff add a surprising note for such an off-the-beaten-track place. There are waymarked walks to neighbouring hamlets and cycle trails aplenty.

rooms	9: 7 twins/doubles, 2 family.
price	€73–€145. Singles €61–€67.
meals	Lunch & dinner €24. A la carte from €33.
closed	November: Wed; December–April: Mon–Thurs. Open daily summer & Easter.
directions	From Barcelona, A-18; C-1411 to Berga. Through Tunel del Cadí, then dir. Andorra. After 5km, right for Puigcerdá on N-260; left at Ger to Meranges. Signed in village.

Laura Forn Solé

tel	+34 972 880033
mobile	+34 629 794758
fax	+34 972 880144
email	info@canborrell.com
web	www.canborrell.com

Hotel

Map 7 Entry 96

Cal Pastor

c/Palos 1, 17536 Fornells de la Muntanya-Toses, Gerona

Ramón and Josefina are gentle folk whose families have farmed this valley for generations. Two rooms next to their house were originally opened to guests; now four new guest rooms have been added. They are simple, not cosy but spotless, with tiled floors, modest Spanish fabrics and comfortable beds. Those in the attic have a warmer feel and bigger windows. The dining room is slightly soulless but don't be put off: there's eggs and bacon at breakfast – just ask – and Josefina's dinners are hearty and delicious; don't miss her *croquetas*. She's happy to cook vegetarian dinners, too, and there's a little restaurant you could also visit next door. The trans-Pyrenean, Mediterranean-to-Atlantic footpath runs right by the house and you may feel inspired to do part of it – or go trout fishing in the hills. This is a good place to come back to – unpretentious, authentic, peaceful – and the hamlet is delightful and friendly. Be sure to visit the Museo del Pastor – a testimony to the work of four generations of Ramón's farming family.

rooms	6: 3 twins/doubles, 3 triples.
price	€48-€60.
meals	Breakfast €8. Dinner €14.
closed	Rarely.
directions	From Barcelona, N-152 for Puigcerdà via Vic & Ripoll. Just past Ribes de Freser, left at km133.5 marker; 2km to village. House by restaurant.

	Josefina Soy Sala
tel	+34 972 736163
fax	+34 972 736008
email	apartrural@hotmail.com

B&B

Map 7 Entry 97

Hotel Grèvol SPA

Ctra. Camprodón-Setcases s/n, Vall de Camprodón, 17869 Llanars, Gerona

Close to ski slopes, mountain trails and a swag of romanesque churches. Carved pine balconies and exposed stone – it's the Alps without the cuckoo clocks and the perfect backdrop for après-ski. The high-raftered sitting and dining rooms have the best of modern: central hearths and big windows to pull in the light. Pine-panelled, carpeted bedrooms, each named after an alpine flower, are four-star swish; those on the first floor open onto the balcony that wraps itself around the building; attic rooms have little ones you can stand up on. *Grèvol* means 'holly' in Catalan (a protected species here) and the décor uses the leaf for its leitmotif. The hotel has a warm, enveloping feel and the food is really special: a mix of regional, international and 'haute'. "It tastes good and looks good," says Antonio. There is also a vast choice of wines: a rare treat in this quiet corner of the Catalan Pyrenees. The hotel, bustling in season with skiers heading for the slopes in Vallter, has an indoor pool and bowling alley, and, new this year, a spa: a serious pull for skiers and walkers.

rooms	36: 28 twins/doubles, 2 family, 6 suites.
price	€134–€182. Family €163–€257. Suites €188–€277.
meals	Lunch & dinner €32.
closed	2 weeks in May; 2 weeks in November. Phone for dates.
directions	From Barcelona A-7 for France; C-17 (former N-152) via Vic to Ripoll. There, C-151 to Camprodón. Hotel 1.5km from Camprodón, on Setcases road.

	Antonio Solé Fajula
tel	+34 972 741013
fax	+34 972 741087
email	info@hotelgrevol.com
web	www.hotelgrevol.com

Hotel

Map 7 Entry 98

Hotel Calitxó

Passatge el Serrat 1, 17868 Molló, Gerona

Molló is a pretty mountain village, 3,000 feet up in the Pyrenees, on the edge of the French border. Hotel Calitxó has more than a hint of the Tyrolean chalet; strange to say, this building was once was a warehouse for the potatoes for which the village is famous. It's well set back from the road with a balconied façade brightened by summer geraniums. You enter through the bustling, barn-like restaurant, where the food, which is, in the main, hearty traditional Spanish, is ferried by cheery staff. The living room is less enticing, but has a wood-burning stove for winter. Bedrooms, named after trees, are a good size, and comfortable. You get new pine, matching floral curtains and bedcovers, and views – green in summer, white in winter. We prefer the suites: in smart mountain lodge style, they have space, terraces and views. Breathe in the mountain breezes as you listen to the cowbells. There's no garden to play in (just a plastic slide for tots) but there is free entry to the municipal pool next door. Orchid-strewn fields in spring, skiing in winter, romanesque churches all year round.

rooms	26: 14 twins/doubles, 12 suites.
price	€78–€96. Singles €40–€79. Suites €100–€138. VAT incuded.
meals	Breakfast €9. Lunch €15–€20. Dinner €25–€30.
closed	Rarely.
directions	From Ripoll C-151 to Camprodón, then C-38 to Molló. In village on left.

	Josep Solé Fajula
tel	+34 972 740386
mobile	+34 690 691423
fax	+34 972 740746
email	info@hotelcalitxo.com
web	www.hotelcalitxo.com

Hotel

Map 7 Entry 99

Mas el Guitart

Santa Margarida de Bianya, 17813 La Vall de Bianya, Gerona

Toni and Lali are young, friendly hosts; he left television and she design to launch themselves into the restoration of this old dairy farm. Thanks to their hard work and unpretentious good taste they have succeeded in creating one of Cataluña's very best *casas rurales*. We loved the rooms, each decorated in a different colour with Lali's stencilled beds to match; there are wooden floors and old rafters, window shutters and washstands, little rugs, decent bathrooms and good views. The two sitting rooms are decorated in a similar vein. Although no breakfast or meals are available, there are two fully-equipped kitchens as well as a washing machine at your disposal: this would be a great choice for a longer stay. Gaze on the gorgeous green pastures from the hammock, drift off by the safely fenced pool, explore the surrounding mountains. Delightful Toni knows everything: restaurants, walks, history, reflexology – why not book in for a massage? Swings, slides and a mini football pitch in the garden, cows and cow bells, kittens, ducks and hens – it's heaven for families. *Minimum stay two nights.*

rooms	4 + 2: 4 twins/doubles. Kitchens & extra beds available. 2 apartments for 4.
price	€50. Apt €100. VAT included.
meals	Self-catering. Restaurant 2km.
closed	Rarely.
directions	From Gerona, C-66 to Besalú. On to Castellfollit de la Roca. Here, signs for Camprodón on C-26. House signed in La Vall de Bianya.

	Lali Nogareda Burch & Antoni Herrero Perez
tel	+34 972 292140
email	guitart@guitartrural.com
web	www.guitartrural.com

Self-catering

Map 8 Entry 100

Mas Colom

17857 Sant Joan les Fonts, Gerona

Stay here and your conscience will be squeaky-clean. Soap is hand-made, food organic and furniture recycled. Pilar and Jodi, an enthusiastic and friendly young couple, care about the environment yet are never preachy. And their 14th-century mas, perched on the forested hills outside St Juan les Fonts, has an easy mood: a cat curled up in the sun, Greenpeace magazines scattered around, help-yourself biscuits and teas. Rooms are earth-coloured with exposed stonework, tiled floors and chunky furniture. The sitting room has an open wood fire, comfy sofas and hand-sewn cushions; the dining room, in the former stable, colourful shutters and fabulous food at one big table. Paintings and sculptures by an artist friend add character. The bedrooms are similarly bright and rustic with appealing touches, perhaps a polished antique bedhead or rush-seated chair. Bathrooms are small but well-designed. Walk, cycle, hunt for medicinal mushrooms, visit the botanical gardens of Olot, ask Pilar to point you towards secret rock pools for swimming. Return to peace, views and a wholesome tranquillity.

rooms	7: 3 twins/doubles, 4 family (2 sharing bathroom).
price	Half-board €48 p.p. VAT included.
meals	Half-board only.
closed	Rarely.
directions	A-7 exit 6 for Gerona Nord-Olot. N-260 & GI-522 to St Joan les F. Through village; right for 'Residencia Torreblanca'; there, left. On for 500m; sign for Mas Colom on left. Follow road for 300m; on left.

Pilar Quintana Laduz

tel	+34 972 290802
mobile	+34 627 419679
email	mascolom@telefonica.net
web	www.mascolom.com

SPECIAL GREEN ENTRY
see page 13

Guest house

Map 8 Entry 101

Rectoría de la Miana

17854 Sant Jaume de Llierca, Gerona

Not for those looking for luxury – but poets, romantics and history buffs will love it. In the middle of a vast stand of beech and oak, at the end of three miles of rough, winding track, a former rectory in a fabulous setting. History is ever present: in the eighth century there was a fortified manor; in the 1200s a monastery was built, complete with escape tunnel and chapel. It took courage and vision for Frans to embark on the restoration – and from the ruins has emerged an unusual and simple hostelry. Flagged floors and undressed walls have been left intact; old sepia photographs are touching in their directness (a group of locals marvelling at the first radio to arrive at La Miana). Spartan bedrooms, some with bunk beds, vary in shape and size; all have high ceilings, stone walls and floors, and one, a terrace with views. Shower rooms are tiny. The food is regional/international and innovative, served in a vaulted dining room with century-old pews. Watch the sunset from the sitting room terrace, drink in the history and the peace. Best visited in summer – unless you are decidedly hearty!

rooms	9: 6 twins/doubles, 3 family rooms, most sharing showers.
price	Half-board €82. VAT included.
meals	Half-board only. Picnic-style lunch €10.
closed	Rarely.
directions	Figueres N-260 to Besalú & Sant Jaume de Llierca. Left into village, 2nd left into c/Industria. 6km track to house following signs. Just past Can Jou farmhouse.

	Frans Engelhard & Janine Westerlaken
tel	+34 972 190190
email	rectoriadelamiana@yahoo.com

Hotel

Map 8 Entry 102

Can Jou

La Miana, 17854 Sant Jaume de Llierca, Gerona

You won't forget your arrival at Can Jou: as you drive up the three-mile track you feel you are leaving the world behind. Round the final bend you catch sight of the farm, high on a hill, overlooking miles of forest of oak and beech – superb. No wonder Mick and Rosa were inspired to revive this old place in search of the good life: by working the land, by giving the house a family (they have four children), and by restoring the once-derelict barn. Bedrooms are basic with a mix of old and new and lively colour schemes; six come with balconies. It's a good place for a family holiday: a farm to explore, horses to ride (ideal for beginners, and with marked forest bridleways) and, close by, a beautiful spring-filled rock pool. Rosa does shiatsu and aromatherapy; Antonio has taken over the cooking reins and offers an inventive take on Catalan cuisine. Dinners are friendly affairs around one vast table. Riders and hikers, families and those looking for nature without luxury would enjoy a stay here.

rooms	15 twins/doubles.
price	€88. Half-board €59 p.p. Full-board €72 p.p. Half-price for under-8s. VAT included.
meals	Lunch & dinner available.
closed	Rarely.
directions	From Figueres, N-260 to Besalú & Sant Jaume de Llierca. Left into village; 2nd left into c/Industria. 6km track to house; signed.

Rosa Linares & Mick Peters

tel	+34 972 190263
fax	+34 972 190110
email	canjou@turismerural.net
web	www.canjou.com

Guest house

Map 8 Entry 103

Mas Salvanera

17850 Beuda, Gerona

In a blissfully quiet corner of the wooded Pyrenean foothills this solid, semi-fortified farmhouse has been transformed into a small luxury hotel. Your hosts still glow with enthusiasm for the project that changed their lives. The guest bedrooms, in an olive mill next to the main house, are named after signs of the zodiac and are large and elegant. Beneath old, darkening beams are colourful fabrics and antiques, many of which Ramón has restored himself, while Rocío's decorative flair is on show throughout. Bathrooms are generous and lovely. The main building has a pretty old well, vaulted ceilings, open hearths, exposed stone, an authentic country feel; the dining room is up one level, its centrepiece a fine 18-place dining table. Everyone eats together (though no meals in summer) and many of Rocío's recipes are Basque. Paella and rabbit are specialities, rioja is the wine of choice. Breakfasts are big and buffet, taken whenever you like. Outside, a peaceful walled garden and a big sculpted pool beneath the olive trees, great for families.

rooms	9 twins/doubles.
price	€125. Half-board €175.
meals	Dinner €25. No meals July–Sept. Restaurant in Beuda, 1.5km.
closed	1–10 January; 1–10 July; 11–19 September.
directions	Barcelona A-7 Gerona. Exit 6 Gerona Norte; C-150 to Banyoles & Besalú. Right on N-260 Figueres; left for Maià de Montcal. Follow signs to Beuda; 1.6km to hotel.

	Ramón Ruscadella & Ana Degollada
tel	+34 972 590975
mobile	+34 606 326398
fax	+34 972 590863
email	salvanera@salvanera.com
web	www.salvanera.com

Hotel

Map 8 Entry 104

Mas Falgarona

17742 Avinyonet de Puigventós, Gerona

This easy, engaging couple spent years searching for Mas Falgarona and what a find it is; built from golden stone, the 11th-century farm is said to be the oldest in the region. The restoration is a deft blend of ancient and modern: light, modern colours lift the spirits as does their passion for old things. If the interior is a minimalist's dream, then cypresses, olives and palms, an aquamarine pool and stunning views over the Pla d'Estany are the gilding on the lily. Dominated by beautiful arched ceilings, lounge and dining room have cool, neutral tones; good, plain fabrics blend with old flagstones and terracotta tiles. Bedrooms and bathrooms are exquisite, their walls dotted with photographs taken by an artist son. A small, chic and cosy room has been set aside for aperitifs; in summer you eat under the stars. Cooking, based on aromatic herbs and olive oil, is inventive and Mediterranean, and vegetarians are well looked after. Wines are local and delicious. After more than 30 years in the business Severino has achieved his dream, summarised by a favourite quote: "One eye sees, the other feels".

rooms	11: 5 twins/doubles, 6 suites.
price	€168–€195. Suites €240–€315. VAT included.
meals	Dinner €29–€58. Restaurant closed Monday & Tuesday.
closed	January.
directions	From Figueres N-260 for Besalú & Olot. After 5km, right to Avinyonet; follow signs to Mas Falgarona.

	Severino Jallas & Brigitta Schmidt
tel	+34 972 546628
fax	+34 972 547071
email	email@masfalgarona.com
web	www.masfalgarona.com

Hotel

Map 8 Entry 105

Can Xiquet

Afores s/n, 17708 Cantallops, Gerona

Stylish modernity on ancient foundations. And the views are among the finest in this book. This whole region is steeped in the art of the early 20th century; Matisse and the Fauves spent time up the coast at Collioure, Dali loved Cadaques, and works by local artists hang here – the tradition lives on. This immaculately reconstructed farmhouse takes full advantage of its lofty site, its huge windows keeping the sea and the hills permanently in view. In the entrance hall: gleaming tiles, chunky rafters, contemporary wicker. The living area has gorgeous sofas, teak tables, a lovely old stairwell, logs for winter. Bedrooms are awash with natural light and neutral colours; some open onto private terraces, all are slickly yet rustically furnished, most have a sun terrace. If you like space, splash out on a suite. Dine under the cork oaks by candlelight, laze by the pool on a perfect lounger, dream in the sculpted garden, make the most of the gleaming new gym. Young and energetic staff add to the fun – a chic, comfortable, unassuming country retreat. *A Rusticae hotel.*

rooms	17: 14 twins/doubles, 3 suites.
price	€140–€210. Suites €250–€270. Half-board €42 p.p. extra.
meals	Breakfast €12. Lunch & dinner €35.
closed	Rarely.
directions	From Figueres, N-II for La Jonquera. Before La Jonquera, right to Cantallops. Hotel signed on left after 5km. Follow track.

	Josep Font
tel	+34 972 554455
fax	+34 972 554585
email	info@canxiquet.com
web	www.canxiquet.com

Hotel

Map 8 Entry 106

El Molí

Mas Molí, 17469 Siurana d'Empordà, Gerona

Here is an inviting new farmhouse set among fields of barley and wheat, modelled on the traditional Gerona *mas*. Big bedrooms have rustically tiled floors, wafer-bricked and ochre-washed walls, floaty curtains, king-size beds, super showers and views across the garden to the fields and woods beyond. And there's a beautifully furnished terrace. Young María and Josep's welcome is warm, and their food exceptionally good value. Vegetables, chicken and beef come straight from the farm – pigs grunt, hens potter – accompanied by a good local red wine and a *hierbas* infusion to finish. For breakfast there are delicious breads, organic eggs, salamis, tomatoes, watermelon and homemade jams. This would be a great place in which to break the journey travelling north or south, and smiling young María, who speaks excellent English, will help you plan your trips. Choose between the Roman ruins at Empuries, the pretty fishing village of Cadaqués, the Dalí Museum at Figueres or the beach at San Pere Pescador, a ten-minute drive.

rooms	6: 4 twins/doubles, 2 suites. Extra beds available.
price	€70–€85. Suites €70–€85. VAT included.
meals	Dinner €15. VAT included.
closed	1 week in January.
directions	AP-7 exit 4 for Figueres on N-II. After 3km, right on C-31 Vilamalla; there, signs for Siurana & then for hotel.

	Maria Sanchís Pages
tel/fax	+34 972 525139
mobile	+34 661 237613
email	casaelmoli@teleline.es
web	www.elmolidesiurana.com

Guest house

Map 8 Entry 107

Can Navata

Baseia 2, 17469 Siurana d'Empordà, Gerona

Amparo has lived among this small farming community all her life, and has named her 19th-century farmhouse after her father's native village. Enter through a shady porch a warren of living areas, darkish but cool, arched and decorated in colourful regional style. Bedrooms are furnished with family heirlooms and kitschy touches, four with a seasonal theme; the 'summer' room is light and airy with an antique embroidered sheet for a curtain, a warm red and yellow colour scheme and French windows that open to the upstairs terrace. Bathrooms are functional. Winter suppers are served at a long table in the vaulted basement, and dishes are hearty. Families can truly unwind: there's a playroom on the ground floor, swings and boules in the garden, and farm animals to meet. Amparo has also provided those in need of peace, a quiet refuge with a room full of books. Ever obliging, she will send you details of places to visit, make bookings and prepare cycling and walking routes. Can Navata and its delightful owner are as Catalan as it's possible to be – full of *amistat* (Catalan for friendship).

rooms	6 twins/doubles.
price	€60-€70. Half-board €90. VAT included.
meals	Dinner €13. VAT included.
closed	Rarely.
directions	From Figueres N-II, then GI-31 (C-252) for L'Escala. After 4km, right for Siurana. On left as you enter Baseia.

	Amparo Pagés
tel	+34 972 525174
mobile	+34 605 619580
fax	+34 972 525756
email	turisme@cannavata.com
web	www.cannavata.com

B&B

Map 8 Entry 108

San Bartomeo de Torres

17833 Fontcorberta, Gerona

It's easy to settle into a lush Catalunyan foothill of the Pyrenees, easier still in a 13th-century Benedictine priory. Views of La Garrotxa's volcanic hills are best considered from the courtyard or during a patio breakfast by the peaceful pool. The original fortified *masia* was bequeathed to Guillem de Torres in 1212 after a successful bash in the Holy Land, where one of the spoils was a thorn plucked from Christ's coronet. Steve tells how he covets it for his party trick, but it's Bea who puts on the real show with her sleight of interior design, creating an open-plan marvel of kitchen and living space. Whether you B&B or self-cater, you will be delighted by sculptures, couches, rugs, Steve's photography on the walls, a snooker table... all warmly framed between terracotta and wooden beams. Each mezzanine bedroom has its distinguishing features: an African statue here, an Indian wardrobe there, pewter lamps, a stone bath, graceful mosquito nets, and hand-made blankets in the fun-loving children's room. The hardest thing to do is hand back the keys. *Minimum stay three nights. Chef available.*

rooms	House for 12. B&B (1 double, 1 twin) available September–May.
price	Email for self-catering rates. B&B €110. VAT included.
meals	Self-catering. Restaurant 15-minute drive.
closed	Rarely.
directions	Directions on booking.

	Bea & Steve Garforth
tel	+34 972 576264
mobile	+34 616 394095
email	info@sanbartomeo.com
web	www.sanbartomeo.com

B&B & Self-catering

Map 8 Entry 109

Hostal Empuries

Platja Portitxol s/n, Apartado Correos 174, 17130 L'Escala, Gerona

You couldn't be closer to the beach. A hundred years ago, this was a snack bar; then a vast Roman necropolis was discovered in L'Escala. Archaeologists flocked and rooms were added to accommodate them. Later, in the 40s and 60s, the place acquired the reputation of a love nest, and its decline began. No longer! Since Cinta and Guillermo stepped in four years ago, its fortunes have been transformed. Today Hostal Empuries is a fascinating beachside hotel with a shabby-chic style all of its own. Don't be disappointed by the approach; once you're on that terrace overlooking the sands, the view is unforgettable. The atmosphere is friendly, relaxed and charmingly assured; the walls are pale and the décor subtle, with dashing floor tiles and comfortable sofas and chairs dressed in linen. There's a woodburning stove in the big sitting room, an enticing reading room and a dining terrace overlooking the beach. Cinta and Guillermo, their two young children and their delightful staff make you feel at home. The food is local, unpretentious and extremely good

rooms	38: 27 twins/doubles, 10 family, 1 suite.
price	€90-€140. Singles €70-€100. Suite €100-€150. Half-board extra €26 p.p.
meals	Breakfast €10. Lunch & dinner €26 a la carte.
closed	Rarely.
directions	From Barcelona on A-7; exit 5 for L'Escala. At L'Escala follow signs for Ruinas de Empuries. Hostal on right on beach; car park.

	Cinta Fernández Camps
tel	+34 972 770207
fax	+34 972 982936
email	info@hostalempuries.com
web	www.hostalempuries.com

Guest house

Map 8 Entry 110

Can Massa

c/Vell s/n, 17120 La Pera, Gerona

This old peasant farmhouse is not swanky but charming. Outside are plants, urns and an old cart, a nod to 50 years ago when Josep's father worked the land. The sound of youngsters is never far off here; the warmth of strong family ties permeates this ramshackle place. The family have recently moved out of the main building to free up two more bedrooms for guests; unobtrusive hosts, they are extremely helpful and kind – walking books, maps, bikes, table tennis, toys: yours to share. Bedrooms are traditional, comfortable, unexceptional and well-priced. 'Chestnut' is the parents' old bedroom and just as it was; 'Blue' has a large terrace with views; 'Green' sports a fine antique bed and a mezzanine for two singles. Bathrooms are simple and small. After a day's walking in the green countryside, return to an *aperitivo* on the covered terrace – or to a winter sofa, log fire and dominoes. The medieval village of Pubol is a marked walk away – famous for Dali's Castillo Gala and gardens. We love the simplicity of this place. *Minimum stay two nights weekends, one week peak season.*

rooms	6: 3 twins/doubles, 1 triple, 2 quadruples.
price	€45–€65. Triple €55–€65. Quadruple €65–€85.
meals	Breakfast €5.
closed	Rarely.
directions	A-7 exit Gerona Nord; signs for Pálamos. At km15 marker, right to La Pera; house signed just past phone box.

Josep Massa Roura

tel/fax	+34 972 488326
email	canmassa@canmassa.com
web	www.canmassa.com

B&B

Map 8 Entry 111

Casa Rural Magnolia Blanca

Avda. Marcos Redondo 5, 17406 Viladraú, Gerona

For active families, this is perfect. Table tennis, games and a gorgeous pool here, and the National Park of Montseny beyond, with its great rivers and sweeping forests of pine. The elegant house was built in 1934, a cool retreat for wealthy Catalans. A stone arch and a wooden gate open to three outdoor levels rampant with magnolias, roses and vines, stone statues, hammocks and secret ponds – lovely, peaceful, charming. Inside are large African paintings and bright Mediterranean colours; Helena and her family promise a happy, bright and welcoming home. Guests have a charming, high-ceilinged sitting room, its windows roundly arched, its furniture comfortably minimalist, all natural fabrics and big pale sofas. The kitchen is rustic, tasteful and self-contained; the dining room has one long table. Bedrooms are less spacious but equally polished, up in the loft with a simple, chalet-like feel. Bathrooms have large sinks and antique oval mirrors. If you're doing B&B, you'll be treated to homemade cakes and local *embutidos* at breakfast. But this is special all round.

rooms	5 twins/doubles (2 sharing bathroom). Whole house available to rent.
price	€75–€85. Singles €65–€75.
meals	Self-catering option. Restaurants in main square.
closed	2 weeks in February; 2 weeks in March.
directions	From Girona on C-25; exit 202 on GI-543 to Viladraú. In town follow signs to hotel.

	Elena Cardenal & Luis Salinas
tel	+34 938 849495
mobile	+34 630 750603
email	info@magnoliablanca.com
web	www.magnoliablanca.com

Self-catering & B&B

Map 7 Entry 112

Mas Salvi

c/Carmany s/n, 17256 Pals, Gerona

You may opt for privacy and peacefulness in the new annexe, where contemporary, light-filled suites have private terraces onto the gardens, or stay in one of the truly spacious rooms in the main house, soaking up the history and the grandeur. Whatever you choose, you will have a cossetting stay. The hotel is a beautifully restored 17th-century manor house, in verdant grounds overlooked by acres of Mediterranean forest. The food is the finest (wild hare, catch of the day, hazelnut soufflé), the bedrooms ooze comfort, the public spaces have three bars – one of which has a vaulted ceiling and a vast window looking onto those gardens – and the staff are attentive and friendly. You are within easy reach of forests, coves, medieval villages, even the Pyrenees, while active types have cycling, trekking and golf. Return to a game of tennis on the hotel's courts, or a swim in one of two pools. And there's a jacuzzi, a sauna, and many beauty and alternative therapies to choose from. *Minimum stay two nights at weekends.*

rooms	22: 6 suites. Annexe: 16 suites.
price	€198–€353.
meals	Lunch & dinner €35–€65.
closed	January–mid-February.
directions	AP-2 from Barcelona; exit 6 for Palamós onto C-66; 7.5km after La Bisbal, left onto GI-652 for Pals. Drive into town; hotel signed half way up main street.

	Javier Josa
tel	+34 972 636478
fax	+34 972 637312
email	info@massalvi.com
web	www.massalvi.com

Hotel

Map 8 Entry 113

Hotel Restaurant Aiguaclara
St Miguel 2, 17255 Begur, Gerona

Back from a shoreline once awash with pirates lies a treasure. Down a chic, cobbled street, behind a time-worn façade, waits a civilised hotel. The moment your weary feet hit the cool old Catalan floor tiles, you begin to wind down. Keeping faith with the past, there's an old fireplace and many original features – a reflection of the sympathetic nature of the owners. Local coves lend their names to ample bedrooms, and from Aiguaclara's grand old terrace of urns, you peer down to the village and up to the crumbling castle. The setting is beautiful. Up a floor, elegant double doors lead you through to another fine bedroom. Bathrooms are in simple retro style, not massive but charming, and there's WiFi throughout. You can almost smell the sea from here, and from nearby villages comes today's tantalising catch – given a modern twist and served up deliciously in the colonial restaurant, or under a 100-year-old cherry tree on the walled patio. After dinner, allow yourself a little nightcap from the honesty bar, sink into a deep leather sofa and let the classical music wash over you.

rooms	10: 8 twins/doubles, 2 suites.
price	€95–€145. Suites €120–€170. VAT included.
meals	Tasting menu €39.
closed	Rarely.
directions	A-7 Barcelona-Girona; exit 6 Bisbal/Palafrugell. Begur signed before reaching Palafrugell. Hotel can be seen from the square by the church.

	Clara Dato & Joan Lluis
mobile	+34 619 253692/609 118087
fax	+34 972 623286
email	aiguaclara@aiguaclara.com
web	www.aiguaclara.com

Hotel

Map 8 Entry 114

Hotel Aigua Blava

Platja de Fornells, 17255 Begur, Gerona

It's something of an institution in Cataluña, this large hotel – but, thanks to exceptional management and clever design, manages to feel as intimate and as welcoming as the best B&B. The bedrooms are individually decorated and ranged on several terraced wings that look out across gardens to a delicious hidden cove; so rugged a coastline would be hard to spoil. Run by the same family for four generations, nourished by the same chef, tended by the same gardener for 40 years, the hotel has a long history of personal attention. Señor Gispert genuinely cares for – and remembers – each one of his guests. Breathe in deeply the sweet pinewoods, bask beside the pool, tuck into lobster straight from the cove; views from the immaculately dressed tables sail across the sparkling waters. So many places to relax: the pub-like bar, the comfortable lobby, the trellised terrace, the parasoled garden, the beach bar just below. The village is one of the prettiest on the Costa Brava, and you are close to the medieval towns of Pals and Palafrugell. Spain at its best – light-years from Benidorm.

rooms	85 + 10: 77 twins/doubles, 5 singles, 3 suites. 10 apartments for 2-6.
price	€133-€214. Singles €99-€130. Suites €174-€269. Apts €176-€340. VAT included.
meals	Breakfast €14.50. Lunch & dinner €37.50. VAT included.
closed	November-February.
directions	From Gerona C-255 to Palafrugell. From here, GE-650 to Begur. Signed on entry to village.

	Josep María de Vehí Falgás
tel	+34 972 624562
fax	+34 972 622112
email	hotelaiguablava@aiguablava.com
web	www.aiguablava.com

Hotel & Self-catering

Map 8 Entry 115

Hostal Sa Rascassa
Cala d'Aiguafreda 3, 17255 Begur, Gerona

Pungent pine on the nose and glimpses of rocky shores send you spiralling down to a cove. What immediately strikes you as a really old establishment was in fact built in 1916 by an eccentric millionaire. Forget the unpacking, make a beeline for that special little table and chairs on a pine-needled carpet and gaze out to sea. Scuba divers are in paradise, as are walkers following the spectacular Costa Brava coastline. So unfold the maps on offer and let Oscar 'walk' you through them with his boundless enthusiasm. At the end of the day, it's an easy path up to comfy, attractive and immaculate bedrooms with russet or sea-blue walls and creamy white armchairs. The whole feel of this sophisticated little hotel will win you over, and if you're lucky, the prickly local rock fish, *rascassa*, will make an appearance at dinner (for special celebrations it takes over the menu!). The food is the best of Catalan: rock mussels, sardines, salads of roasted peppers. As light fades, easy music wafts through the bar and beyond; 'chilled' is the word – until the flamenco hits the terrace on a sultry summer night.

rooms	5 twins/doubles.
price	€69-€96.
meals	Lunch & dinner €25-€30.
closed	November-February.
directions	From Begur 3km to Aiguafreda. Straight on at first crossroads towards Aiguafreda & Las Terrasses. Parking 800m ahead & hotel beyond.

	Oscar Górriz Bonhora
tel	+34 972 622845
mobile	+34 619 921088
email	info@hostalsarascassa.com
web	www.hostalsarascassa.com

Hotel

Map 8 Entry 116

Hotel Sant Roc

Plaça Atlàntic 2, 17210 Calella de Palafrugell, Gerona

The Costa Brava remains a stunning stretch of coastline and this quiet little hotel could restore your faith in seaside holidays in Spain. It's a family affair – not only family-run but a place where guests are treated like old friends. Many return. The setting is marvellous: a perch at the edge of a cliff, surrounded by pine, olive and cypress, the sea ever present. Its colours change with every hour, and from the dining room and large canopied terrace are delightful views across the bay: bobbing boats, hillsides and and the village beyond. The best rooms have seaward terraces but we like them all, so light and pretty with their hand-painted headboards and watercolours painted by an artist friend. Bathrooms are new. With Franco-Catalan owners you can expect something special from the kitchen; fish is a speciality and the fairly-priced wines are good. A path from the hotel winds down to the beach and there are longer walks around the bay. Young Bertrand and Teresa are humorous and charming, even in high season: their generosity permeates this exceptional, family-friendly hotel.

rooms	47: 44 doubles, 3 suites.
price	Half-board €140–€260.
	Suites €250–€320.
meals	Breakfast €11.80.
	Lunch & dinner €24–€35.
closed	End November–mid-March.
directions	From Barcelona A-7 north to exit 6 (Girona Norte); signs for La Bisbal via Palamos, then on to Palafrugell; then Calella. Hotel signed.

	Teresa Boix & Bertrand Hallé
tel	+34 972 614250
fax	+34 972 614068
email	info@santroc.com
web	www.santroc.com

Hotel

Map 8 Entry 117

Xalet La Coromina

Ctra. de Vic 6, 17406 Viladraú, Gerona

Viladraú is an aristocratic, elegant little town close to the stunning Montseny
Natural Park – known for the best drinking water in Spain! Woodlands
are grandiose, water flows and falls, rare plants flourish, and the climate is
delightfully cool in summer. This building dates from the 1900s when wealthy
Catalans started to build summer retreats away from Barcelona; the building
has kept its elegant exterior. Inside is unexpectedly formal. Turn-of-the-century
furnishings are sober, the immaculately tiled and sofa'd sitting room has its
original fireplace (lit in winter) and bedrooms combine paintings of pastoral
scenes with a smart Seventies' décor. Bathrooms are white, with good showers.
The rooms vary in size but we would choose the suite, for its terrace. New
owners Salvador and his wife Belen are full of enthusiasm for their new venture.
He is an experienced chef and there are Michelin standards to live up to, so you
may expect the best. Outside are gentle gardens and a pretty hexagonal, stone-
riveted pool. *A Rusticae hotel.*

rooms	8: 7 twins/doubles, 1 suite.
price	€98–€105. Singles €80–€90. Suite €150–€170.
meals	Breakfast €10. Lunch €20. Dinner €25–€35.
closed	Rarely.
directions	From Girona C-25. Exit km202, then GI-543 to Viladraú. In village towards Vic: hotel on right after 50m. From Barcelona on AP-7, then C-17; exit to Seud/Viladrau.

Salvador Casaseca Almaraz

tel	+34 938 849264
mobile	+34 686 452849
fax	+34 538 848160
email	xaletcoromina@xaletcoromina.com
web	www.xaletcoromina.com

Hotel

Map 8 Entry 118

Mas Vilarmau

Ctra. de Sant Marçal s/n, 17406, Viladraú, Gerona

Delightfully idiosyncratic. That just about sums up Pep and Pilar's approach
to interior design. In just two years, they've added verve and fun to a secluded
12th-to-18th-century farmhouse that was already crammed with character. Each
bedroom has a theme: *mimbré* means 'rushes' so, if this is your room, you'll find
a rush canopy over the bed, a wicker-framed mirror and chair, a bouquet of
rushes in the bathroom… you get the idea. The beds may be blissful but comfort
and cosiness spread right through this house; on each floor is a sitting area with
old wooden beams and planked floors, stone walls and an open fire. "Park your
car and forget it for your whole stay", says Pep. Take his advice. You're on the
edge of the mountainous Montseny Natural Park, a rambler's paradise and yours
to discover – if you can drag yourself away from your hammock in the garden.
Or the swimming pool, the chickens and the ducks, the game of ping-pong, the
fresh seasonal dishes… or that great bottle of red that Pep has just brought up
from the cellar. *Two nights minimum at weekends. Near Gerona Airport.*

rooms	8 twins/doubles.
price	Half-board €60 p.p. Full-board €75 p.p. VAT included.
meals	Half- or full-board only.
closed	Never.
directions	From Barcelona on C-17; exit for Seva. Through Viladraú; right for Campins. Hotel signed after 1km; follow lane for 2km to hotel.

	Pep Bochaca & Pilar Masmuntal
mobile	+34 659 446613
email	info@masvilarmau.com
web	www.masvilarmau.com

Guest house

Map 8 Entry 119

El Jufré

08511, Tavertet-Osona, Barcelona

The hilltop villages of this part of Cataluña rival those of Provence. And the drive up to Tavertet, past craggy limestone outcrops and stands of forest, is an adventure in itself. El Jufré is perched over a craggy ledge and the views are superb: look out over the plain below and be captivated. Wonderful to stay with Josep and sweet Lourdes and their two children in this very old house; rebuilt in the 1600s, some parts date back as far as 1100, and Lourde's family have been in residence for over 800 years! Bedrooms are simple and attractive, marrying together ancient beams and exposed stones with new beds, baths and lighting. We liked best the big room with the iron bedstead and the mountain-drop view. Linger later on the terrace over an aperitif, distant cowbells signalling the end of the day. The food is another reason to come: good, simple dishes make full use of their own organic beef, pork and vegetables. At breakfast there's milk from the cows. El Jufré is for lovers of high places and tranquillity (full-time residents in the village number 40), and walkers will be in heaven.

rooms	8 twins/doubles.
price	Half-board €90-€95. VAT included.
meals	Half-board only.
closed	22 December-7 January; 1-15 September.
directions	From Vic C-153 for Olot & Roda de Ter to L'Esquirol & Santa María Corco. Here, right to Tavertet. House on left as enter village.

Josep Roquer & Lourdes Rovira

tel/fax +34 938 565167

Guest house

Map 7 Entry 120

Hotel Torre Martí

c/Ramón Llull 11, 08504 Sant Julia de Vilatorta, Barcelona

Wow! This boutique hotel, opened last year by father Pere and son Roger, is, quite simply, stunning. You may think you'd pulled up to a Tuscan villa – the solidity and the squareness, the porticoed first floor, the rich red exterior. Enter a world of more reds – and ochres, pistachios and Moroccan blues. A classy, chic backdrop for flamboyant furnishings: gilt mirrors, twinkly chandeliers, Asian and modern art (including Pere originals), old theatre seats for dining on, a barber's chair on the landing – it's eclectic in the nicest possible way. Be soothed by soft classical music and incense as you float down for dinner; Pere's sublime cooking lures locals, ever a good sign. (Breakfasts, too, are delectable.) Big windows allow views onto the terrace and lawn with its fountained pond. Bedrooms, some in the main house, some with balconies, the rest in the old guards' house next door, are surprising, original and come with sparkling bathrooms. And there's more: the vivid blue library with its traditional leather chairs, the open fires, the magnificent grounds, the warm and charming staff... *A Rusticae hotel.*

rooms	8: 6 twins/doubles, 1 single, 1 suite.
price	€120-€150. Singles €95-€120. Suite €235.
meals	Lunch & dinner €35.
closed	Rarely.
directions	From N-II exit for Cervera on C-25. After Vic, signs to Sant Julia de V. From Barcelona on C-17 towards Vic, follow signs to Sant Julia de V.

	Roger Morral Palacín
tel	+34 938 888372
mobile	+34 666 762317
fax	+34 93 8888374
email	hoteltorremarti@yahoo.es
web	www.hoteltorremarti.com

Hotel

Map 7 Entry 121

Masía El Folló

Ctra. C-17 km36, 08593 Tagamanent, Barcelona

So unexpected, this mountain-top farmstead one hour from Barcelona. A Catalan *casa pairal* (father's house), it has been masterfully restored by Merce and Jaume. Rustic bedrooms have huge charm, their rough stone or pine-clad walls invigorated by bold colours and a fruit and flower motif throughout. Hues range from the vibrant red of the 'Strawberry' room to the gentler tones of 'Mallow'. Lighting is subdued and complements the beamed ceilings, the muslin curtains, the natural fabrics, and there are flip-down bunkbeds for kids. Two bathrooms, one with astonishing views, have amazing antique tubs and oodles of towels. Outside, chickens, horses, ducks, dogs… reminders of a rural past are never far away. One of the dining rooms, dominated by a long table, is in the old stable. There's a feeling of abundance and well-being, and Mercè is proud of her robust, organic cooking – the number one interest here. Don't miss out on the amazing breads – granary, onion, courgette, rye – or the goat's cheese with quince jelly. Board games, TV, an open fire; it's equally cosy in winter. *Cookery school attached.*

rooms	8 twins/doubles, 2 sharing bathroom.
price	€70–€85. Singles €60. Half-board €70 p.p. Full-board €85 p.p.
meals	Breakfast €10. Restaurant closed Sun evening & all Monday.
closed	Rarely.
directions	From north A-7 for Barcelona, exit 14; C-17 for Vic. At km36 (opp. petrol station) right, then over r'bout. Follow signs for 2km to El Folló.

	Merce Brunés & Jaume Villanueva
tel/fax	+34 938 429116
web	www.elfollo.com

Guest house

Map 7 Entry 122

Hotel Masferrer

08474 Gualba, Barcelona

It takes boldness and sensitivity to turn a grand Catalan *masía* into a young contemporary hotel without losing its charm. Montserrat and her husband spent two years restoring Masferrer, in the little town of Gualba on the edge of the Parque Natural, and have achieved a beguilingly simple blend of ancient and modern. Rustic oak beams and exposed stones have been invigorated with earthy and pastel coloured walls and designer lighting. Elegant antiques mix with modern sofas. Bedrooms are pared down but not chilly: a cream rug on polished tiles, muslin curtains at a stone window. Bathrooms are a stunning mixture of designer-sleek and rough-cast. Choose the split-level suite for huge windows onto a private terrace. The dining room is breezily elegant with white linen and simple vases of flowers. Montserrat has gained a reputation for her *cocina de temporada*, using produce from the garden whenever possible. In several acres of woodland and garden – with a pool – it's hard to believe the coast is 15 minutes away and Barcelona half an hour. Peace without the isolation. *A Rusticae hotel.*

rooms	11: 9 twins/doubles, 2 suites.
price	€120. Singles €100. Suites €145–€170.
meals	Breakfast €12. Lunch & dinner €25.
closed	Rarely.
directions	From Barcelona AP-7 to Gerona; exit 11 onto C-35 to Hostalric; left at r'bout to Gualba. Hotel siged on right, after 200m.

	Montserrat Guinovart
tel	+34 938 487705
mobile	+34 630 921213
fax	+34 938 487084
email	hm@hotelmasferrer.com
web	www.hotelmasferrer.com

Hotel

Map 8 Entry 123

Can Rosich

Camí de la Riera, 08398 Santa Susanna, Barcelona

Handy for Barcelona, close to the beach, yet deep in 20 hectares of bucolic loveliness. This *masía* is two centuries old but has been virtually rebuilt. Tiled bedrooms, named after the birds and animals of the region, are a good size and large enough to take a third bed. Beds are antiques, mattresses are new, and you'll find a be-ribboned, neatly-ironed bundle of towels on your duvet – a typical touch from a gracious hostess. To one side of the large hallway is the rustic, white-walled dining room, its tables decked in bright checks; there's a new second room for groups and an enchanting dining area outside. Cooking is wholesome, delicious and superb value. Among Montserrat's specialities are rabbit, pork from the farm and *asado de payés*, a thick stew with three different meats, plums and pine nuts (order this one in advance!). Breakfast, too, is delicious: cheese and charcuterie, fruits, fresh juice. You are a five-minute drive to the station and trains that get you to Barcelona in an hour. Mateo and Montserrat are the loveliest hosts; it's no surprise this is a favourite with our readers.

rooms	6 twins/doubles.
price	€50–€55.
meals	Breakfast €7. Dinner with wine, €15.
closed	2 weeks in October/November.
directions	From AP-7, exit 9 Maçanet; N-II for Barcelona to Santa Susanna; here, right at 1st r'bout for 'nucleo urbano'; signs for 2km to Can Rosich.

	Montserrat Boter Fors
tel/fax	+34 937 678473
email	canrosich@canrosich.com
web	www.canrosich.com

Hotel

Map 8 Entry 124

Hotel Duquesa de Cardona
Paseo de Colón 12, 08002 Barcelona

Where would you choose to stay in Barcelona? Near Las Ramblas, by the atmospheric marina? The Duquesa de Cardona has a near-perfect site – vibrant until the small hours! – and a sophistication to match that of the city. You can safely expect the best of everything here: service, comfort, food, and a high-ceilinged, columned and vaulted restaurant that is quite something. This imposing 19th-century building, in palm-lined Paseo de Colón in the city's famous gothic quarter, was once home to nobles and kings. The aristocratic mood is reflected in original chequered marble floors and stone arches and carvings, while elegant bedrooms, some small, some large, come in contemporary chocolates and taupes with carpeted floors and high ceilings... ask for a harbourside view. Bathrooms are stunning. After a day exploring one of the world's best-loved cities, return to a sleek teak table on the top terrace, sip a cocktail beneath a vast parasol, take a dip in the splash pool and watch the sun going down. The way to get here may not be the easiest; everything else is close to perfection.

rooms	44: 35 twins/doubles, 9 suites.
price	€140-€345.
meals	Lunch & dinner €30.
closed	Rarely.
directions	From airport, C-32 dir. Barcelona; exit 'Ronda Litoral' onto B-10; exit 21 'Ciutat Vella direction Paseo Colón/Puerto'. Hotel opp. marina, with parking. See map on hotel web site.

	Daniel Carretero
tel	+34 93 2689090
fax	+34 93 2682931
email	info@hduquesadecardona.com
web	www.hduquesadecardona.com

Hotel

Map 7 Entry 125

Cal Mestre

c/Torre Romana 2-4, 08793 Les Gunyoles d'Avinyonet, Barcelona

Breakfast overlooking the rugged outline of Mount Montserrat, then toss up whether to spend the day on the beaches or lapping up Barcelona's riches: this very old village house is within easy reach of both. Marian and Martin (multi-lingual Dutch) lovingly restored the house, smoothly blending old with new to create sleek, understatedly stylish rooms. Polished wooden floors, timber beams and exposed stonework mix with oversize lampshades, abstract art and elegant bedcovers. Modern, clean-lined furniture stands next to handsome originals, perhaps a grandfather clock or an old school desk. Choose Penedès for its free-standing bath or Horse Stable for its shuttered doors to the village street – perfect for walkers with dogs. Spend the day exploring Roman Tarragona, hiking in Garraf Nature Park or wine-tasting in the Penedès vineyards. Or relax with a book from Marian and Martin's library in the terraced gardens around the house, Spanish guitar music drifting from inside. Suppers are served around the communal dining table, and your hosts are gentle, friendly and immensely helpful.

rooms	5 twins/doubles.
price	€90–€120. VAT included.
meals	Lunch & dinner €14–€20.
closed	Winter months.
directions	From Barcelona N-340 to Vilafranca. At Avinyonet, signs to Olessa-Gavà-Begues. After 100m, right, signed Los Gunyoles. Hotel 1km: yellow house near church.

	Marian & Martin Badoux
tel	+34 938 970761
mobile	+34 660 455843
email	info@cal-mestre.com
web	www.cal-mestre.com

B&B

Map 7 Entry 126

Hotel Masía Sumidors

Ctra. de Vilafranca km2.4, 08810 Sant Pere de Ribes-Sitges, Barcelona

The crumbling, 400-year old *venta*, perched quietly on its own upon a hill, surrounded by pine trees and vineyards, oozes charm. New English owners have introduced a bohemian yet classical style, laced with African and oriental undertones. Scattered around are interesting objets d'art – Japanese umbrellas, a saxophone, a clarinet, and paintings old and new on low, thick walls. Bedrooms are atmospheric, showers are simple and the suite has a rustic four-poster. For self-caterers, the bungalow is bright and cool. Outside on the upper terrace, a Bedouin tent hung with lamps protects intimate clusters of wrought-iron tables and chairs; sit out by the blue crescent-shaped bar for sunset drinks before a candlelit dinner. There is also a barbecue, which is often used. On the lower terrace, the figure-of-eight pool is fabulous and the views awesome. Explore the surrounding countryside on foot or by mountain bike. For day trips there's classy Sitges and the medieval towns of Olivella or Montserrat, while Tarragona and Barcelona are a short drive. A simple but special place – relax and revive.

rooms	8 +1: 7 twins/doubles, 1 suite. 1 bungalow for 4-5.
price	€95-€115. Suite €130. Bungalow €200.
meals	Dinner €25.
closed	Rarely.
directions	Barcelona C-32 to Sitges; exit 28 onto C-15B dir. Sant Pere de Ribes/Vilafranca. 2km past turning to Sant Pere de Ribes, immed. after Restaurant Carnivor, right onto 1km track; hotel signed on apex of bend.

	Neil Stock & Iain Murray
tel	34 938 962061
email	info@sumidors.com
web	www.sumidors.com

Hotel & Self-catering

Map 7 Entry 127

Hotel Santa María

Passeig de la Ribera 52, 08870 Sitges, Barcelona

Sitges has been fashionable among wealthier Catalans for years. The crowd is international now, but the place has kept its intimate feel and life still centres on the promenade and beach. At the heart of it all: the Santa María. It is a pretty building, its white façade enhanced by apricot awnings, the largest one spanning the entire front terrace. There's a glistening array of fresh seafood from the modern open kitchen – and it's truly child-friendly. The sea almost laps to the table and everything ticks over beautifully – thanks to the indefatigable Señora Ute, who manages to switch between half a dozen languages at any given time. Some bedrooms have beautiful shuttered balconies and a view across the palm trees to the bay; all are light and well furnished, some with modern furniture, others with floor tiles and traditional pieces. There are prints on the walls and vases of fresh flowers. For Sitges it's well priced – but you must book ahead in season; if there's no room here, there may be space in the sister hotel, La Niña.

rooms	57: 51 twins/doubles, 6 family rooms.
price	€80–€120. Singles €68–€91. Family rooms €115–€140.
meals	Lunch & dinner €12. A la carte from €25.
closed	20 December–1 February.
directions	From Barcelona, A-16 through Tuneles de Garaf. 2nd exit for Sitges centre, follow signs to Hotel Calipolis. On sea front; car park.

Antonio Arcas Sánchez

tel	+34 938 940999
fax	+34 938 947871
email	info@lasantamaria.com
web	www.lasantamaria.com

Hotel

Map 7 Entry 128

Arianella de Can Coral

Avenida Can Coral s/n, Alt Penedés, 08737 Torelles de Foix, Barcelona

Sample a slice of Catalan life with Ariane and Rayner who count local winemakers and members of Vilafranca's Castellet team – human-tower racers – among their friends. The sun ripens olives and almonds and this particular 19th-century farmhouse a crisp burnt-yellow. Great stone floors in the living room surround a huge sandstone pillar that glows in firelight during winter. Outside, the mulberry trees grow, now plucked to make a delicious sweet sauce for ice cream. Fruity by name, charming by nature, rooms like 'Melecton' have slanted ceilings that shelter sweet wrought-iron four-poster beds and little sinks in the corner. Swimming pool, mountains and vines fill the view before it plunges toward Vall de Penedés. The self-catering apartment is a smart modern renovation with a fabulous terrace overlooking vineyards. Catalan specialities like *fideua* and *butifarra* are enjoyed outside under the tree by candlelight. On one night of the year, all 150 flowers of the cactus that climbs the wall suddenly burst into bloom; come morning, they're gone. Stay another night.

rooms	6 + 1: 5 twins/doubles, 1 family suite. 1 apartment for 4.
price	€69. Apartment €118–€134 (€610–€840 per week).
meals	Breakfast €5.50. Dinner €15–€20, on request.
closed	2 weeks in January/February.
directions	A-7 Barcelona-Tarragona; exit Vilafranca del Penedés & follow signs & Sant Martí BP-2121. On to Torrelles de Foix; right 50m after church; hotel 1.5km, signed.

	Ariane Paasch
tel/fax	+34 93 8971579
mobile	+34 670 068395
email	arianella@cancoral.com
web	www.arianella.com

B&B & Self-catering

Map 7 Entry 129

Cal Ros

Apartat de Correus 45, 08281 Calonge de Segarra, Barcelona

Meandering through Cava country, you finally stumble upon this far-flung working farm. Wagging dogs escort you past terraces of cereals, almonds and, most lately, chickpeas, to the door of a perfect rural retreat. Mercé's family have cared for the land for decades, and their imposing farmhouse exudes comfort and warmth. Anyone would love it here. It's a solid home, spotless and spacious, with all-round endless views. For a 'room with a view' pick any one: La Font is all linen and light, with beams, L'Era is country-classy, with two singles in the alcove, ideal for families. All ooze charm and their shuttered windows pull in the views. Bathrooms are hugely stylish, with hydro-showers or baths. Suitably refreshed and relaxed, admire Mercé's impressive *huerto* (vegetable garden) and wander at will. As the day cools, take a pew by the big fireplace and relax to an impromptu piano recital. Or drift off to one of the upstairs terraces. Here is a slice of real Catalan life, where you share home-grown food with delightful people, and feel you've been part of the family forever. Terrific value.

rooms	5: 2 twins/doubles, 3 family.
price	€56–€76. Family €72–€120. Half-board extra €46–€59 p.p. VAT included.
meals	Breakfast €7.80. Lunch €19. Dinner €16. VAT included.
closed	Rarely.
directions	From Barcelona on A-2; exit 545 for Pons-Andorra on C-1412. After 25km, right for Calonge de Segarra. At end of tarmac drive, guest house signed.

	Mercè Centellas Junyent
tel	+34 93 8699241
mobile	+34 617 426091
email	calros@bsab.com
web	www.calros.info

B&B

Map 7 Entry 130

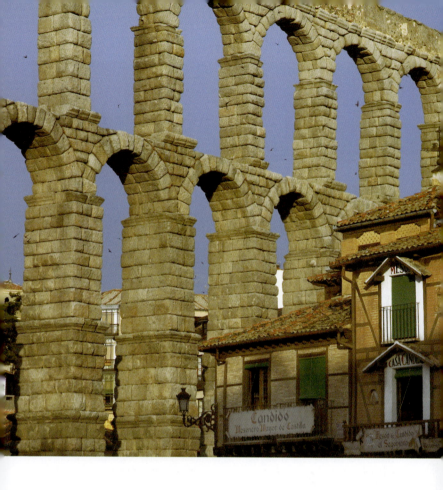

Castilla-León
Castilla – La Mancha
Madrid

Posada del Marqués

Plaza Mayor 4, 24270 Carrizo de la Ribera, León

Never mind the ordinariness of the town, there are few places to stay in Spain as special as this historic pilgrim's hospital. Pass through the fine portal to a pebbled cloister and beautiful, mature gardens with a gurgling brook, a big old yew and walnut trees: with its high walls and rambling roses it may remind you of an English rectory garden. Sombre but charming bedrooms are set around a gallery on the first floor and are filled with family heirlooms: Portuguese canopied beds, oil paintings, old lamps and dressers. One has a terrace over the cloisters for summer, there are big old radiators to tackle the winter months, and spotless marble bathrooms. The sitting and games rooms downstairs are similarly furnished – antique Castillian doors, carved chests, tapestries, comfy armchairs and an English sofa in front of the hearth. For summer dinners there's regional food from a short menu (roast leg of pork, trout with red peppers) washed down with robust wines. Afterwards, a post-prandial game of snooker. Kind and erudite hosts in the most peaceful, beguiling of hotels. *Balloon flights available.*

rooms	11 twins/doubles.
price	€76-€102. VAT included.
meals	Dinner €16. VAT included. Book ahead.
closed	2 January-end March.
directions	AP-71 (León-Astorga) exit 23 to Hospital de Orbigo; cross old N-120 for La Madalena on LE-420; Carrizo de la Ribera on km16. In Carrizo, follow wall around monastery; left into Plaza Mayor; through archway.

Carlos Velázquez-Duro

tel	+34 987 357171
mobile	+34 606 831337
fax	+34 987 358101
email	info@posadadelmarques.com
web	www.posadadelmarques.com

Hotel

Map 3 Entry 131

Camarga

c/La Ermita s/n, 24732 Santiago Millas, León

Your chance to discover this unjustily overlooked corner of Spain, where once the enigmatic Maragatos thrived. Over a century ago they developed an idiosyncratic culture of Christian rites with a pagan twist. Marga, your bilingual host, restored this 1890 house following the Maragato architectural style: dry stone walls, terracotta brickwork, traditional colours of mustard yellow, burnt sienna and cobalt blue 'añil'. Walk through the vaulted wooden doors into the cool, birdsung courtyard, where wicker furniture invites you to rest after a day of discovery in Castilla. Rooms, overlooking the courtyard, have refined touches: embroidered bedspreads, English linen, lace curtains made by Marga's mother. Impressive rusticity survives in the living areas – impossibly large flagstones and old dignified beams. The 24ft-high restaurant still has its bread oven; robust chains support its structure from the ceiling. You'll relish Marga's innovative cooking, which blends local meats with seafood from Galicia. If you have a sweet tooth, don't miss Astorga's chocolate museum and the many sweet shops in town.

rooms	9 twins/doubles.
price	€65. Singles €55.
meals	Breakfast €3-€7.20.
	Lunch & dinner €17.50.
closed	8-31 January.
directions	Madrid A-6 for Coruña; exit 326 signed Morales de Arcediano. Past Morales; at km9 marker you arrive in Santiago Millas. House on right.

	Margarita Quintana Boza
mobile	+34 656 395158
email	info@camarga.es
web	www.camarga.es

Hotel

Map 3 Entry 132

Guts Muths

c/Matanza s/n, Barrio de Abajo, 24732 Santiago Millas, León

This and other villages in the area drew their wealth from the transport of merchandise by horse and cart throughout Spain. The coming of the railways put an end to all that, but what remains are some grand old village houses of which Guts Muths is a fine example. Enter through the imposing arch to find yourself in a large gravelled courtyard, dotted with shrubs and a couple of palms. The interior is bohemian and bold, cosy and warm; these effusive hosts have created an easy feel. Expect exposed stone and heavy beams, dried and fresh flowers, potted plants and pictures, sofas round a rustic, well-used hearth. The dining room comes with a stocked bodega and an old bread oven – a proper backdrop for Mari Paz's delicious cooking and homemade liqueurs. Bedrooms could be better soundproofed, but new pine beds are comfortable and murals and modern art add an individual touch. Sjoerd is great fun, and interested in local history and folklore. He may even be persuaded to take you out to explore the gorges on foot or bike… or attached to the end of a rope. *A Rusticae hotel.*

rooms	8 twins/doubles.
price	€67.
meals	Breakfast €8. Dinner €17.
closed	Rarely.
directions	From Astorga, LE-133 for Destriana. 1km before S. Millas, left at sign Barrio de Abajo. Into village past playground; signed on left past triangle in centre; 1st left; 2nd house, 2nd on left.

| | Sjoerd Hers & Mari Paz Martínez |
| tel/fax | +34 987 691123 |

El Tiempo Recobrado

Avda. de Villanueva 33, 24550 Villamartín de la Abadía, León

What used to be two modest workers' houses is now an attractive and astonishingly good-value place to stay. The hotel, a gentle mix of rough stone, apricot plaster and gleaming slate roofs, is proving a draw, as is its restaurant. What a delight! The food is superb, from the starter of leeks with Cantabrian anchovies to the delectable homemade puddings. The wine list, too, is worth going out of your way for: this region is famous for its fine Bierzo wines. The buildings have been well and stylishly renovated, the big, airy bedrooms are simple and natural – exposed stone, polished wooden floors, chestnut beams, wrought-iron bedheads – and everything is of the highest quality. It's quiet, too, the only sound that of the river pulsing past. This is a relatively unknown part of Spain yet there is so much to see and do. The village is full of interesting and ancient houses, and a good road network gives easy access to a whole host of places, including the Médulas, the church at Peñalba de Santiago and the thatched houses of Campo de Agua.

rooms	9: 5 twins/doubles, 4 suites.
price	€65. Suites €80.
meals	Lunch & dinner €15.
closed	7-31 January.
directions	From León A-6 for Coruña. After Ponferrada exit at km399 for Villamartín. Hotel signed at village entrance.

	Juan Jóse Alonso
tel/fax	+34 987 562422
mobile	+34 630 284081
email	eltiempo@eltiemporecobrado.com
web	www.eltiemporecobrado.com

Hotel

Map 2 Entry 134

Casa Zalama

c/La Fuente s/n, 09569, San Pelayo de Montija, Burgos

In a farming village in a little known area of northern Spain, the wonderful Casa Zalama is a place in which to linger. María, originally from the Basque country, and her partner Graeme, uprooted from Brighton in search of a guest house, and found this. Maria's attractive furnishings in the carefully converted house are matched by Graeme's green fingers, and the landscaped garden is dotted with Graeme's wood sculptures. Beamed bedrooms have comfortable beds and lovely earthy colours; those with balconies have stunning views of the hills. Dinners, served in the chunky-raftered dining room (once the stables) are country Spanish and delicious: local sausage, home-grown veg, pear tart. Opposite the house there is a cosy and colourful self-catering cottage, perfect for couples or a small family. Your hosts are hugely helpful about where to go and what to do, and set you up with wholesome and hearty breakfasts. The views are bucolic, the birdwatching is brilliant, and the Ojo Guareña Nature Park is nearby. Wonderful value, just an hour from Bilbao and Santander.

rooms	6 + 1: 5 twins/doubles, 1 suite. 1 house for 4.
price	€50. Suite €70. House €80 (€500 per week).
meals	Breakfast €5. Dinner €15.
closed	2 weeks in January/February.
directions	From E-70 for Bilbao, exit km173 for Colindres. N-629 up over Alto de los Tornos. At Aguera, left for San Pelayo. Past church, on left.

	Maria Cruz Totorika & Graeme Hobbs
tel	+34 947 565961
mobile	+34 653 714336
email	info@casazalama.com
web	www.casazalama.com

B&B & Self-catering

Map 4 Entry 135

El Prado Mayor

Quintanilla del Rebollar 53, 09568, Merindad de Sotoscueva, Burgos

The impressive façade of the 16th-century Prado Mayor is concealed behind a solid arched gateway. Via a small garden with a columned terrace – perfect for summer breakfasts – you enter a warm home. The cream-coloured stone gives the house a sheltered and peaceful air and the stylish, understated décor is in perfect harmony with the architecture. Wooden-floored bedrooms are rustic and inviting: expect period antiques, rocking chairs, colourful blankets, dried flowers, pretty country cabinets under basins, ornate framed mirrors. All have their own shower rooms. Breakfast is a must: your gentle host, who lives on the upper floor, serves homemade cakes, biscuits, fruits, local bread baked in a wood oven. Lunch and dinner are superb affairs with organic home-grown vegetables and good local meats; the rabbit is excellent. The lush landscape is one of Spain's best-kept secrets, breathing culture and history – and the Ojo Guareña cave system, from where you can trace humanity's religious expression from Paleolithic times, is one of the biggest in the world. Great value.

rooms	8: 6 twins/doubles, 2 suites.
price	€50–€56. Singles €36–€42. Suite €70–€75.
meals	Breakfast €5. Dinner €18. Packed lunches available.
closed	Rarely.
directions	Burgos N-623 Santander. At Cilleruelo de Bezana, C-6318 Bilbao. Village 7km before Espinosa de los Monteros. Left at entrance of village; on for 500m to fountain. 50m to hotel, right at no. 52.

	Olga Fernández
tel/fax	+34 947 138689
mobile	+34 627 364378
email	info@pradomayor.com
web	www.pradomayor.com

Hotel

Map 4 Entry 136

Casa La Engaña

Ctra. de la Estación 5, 09574 Pedrosa de Valdeporres, Burgos

Duncan and Mila – experienced trekkers, enthusiastic hosts – spent two years restoring their handsome 20th-century manor, keeping the character and adding comforts galore. Oak beams and pillars, exposed stones, old floorboards, flagstones and polished terracotta work their magic to create a warm, relaxing and sophisticated place to stay. On the ground floor: a massive open-plan living area with sofas and wood-burner, piano, flute, trumpet, Spanish guitar, French horn! On the first floor, a library (100 books in English alone). Most alluring of all is the glass-and-wood gallery that spans several floors. Read in the sun, watch birds of prey coming in to land; 112 species nest within a bike's ride of here. Bedrooms could not be simpler – pale-washed walls, period beds, a bentwood chair, an antique wardrobe, perhaps a colourful bedspread or abstract print to add a homely touch. Bathrooms are classic, white, sparkling. Your lovely hosts, who specialize in English immersion courses for the Spanish, will tell you all about the area over delicious dinner, and much of their produce is organic.

rooms	6 twins/doubles.
price	€50–€60. Singles €40–€46.
meals	Breakfast €5. Dinner €15.
closed	January/February.
directions	From Santander N-623; N-232; BU-526 to Santelices. After 400m left to Casa La Engaña; over level crossing 300m & follow road round for 50m; on left. From Bilbao by road or scenic FEVE railway to Pedrosa; station 300m from house.

	Duncan Holt & Milagros García
tel	+34 947 138073
email	turismo@laengana.com
web	www.laengana.com

B&B

Map 4 Entry 137

Posada Molino del Canto

Molino del Canto s/n, Barrio La Cuesta, 09146 Valle de Zamanzas, Burgos

This jewel of a place is remote and heavenly in an Eden-like valley, lapped by the river Ebro. It is a 13th-century millworkers' home, restored by the young owner Javier, and the simplicity of the façade is reflected inside — authentic and exquisite. Through the dim little entrance hall — cool for summer, warm for winter — to a chunkily beamed, stone-walled sitting room scattered with country furniture, kilim, sofa and good log fire. Then to bedrooms upstairs, a splendid surprise: a cosy, delightful sitting room down, a sofabed for children, and sleeping quarters up (hot in summer). There are generous beds, large classic wardrobes, stylish white-and-terracotta bathrooms, big sky windows to gaze at the stars... drift off to the sound of the river. Breakfast is a great start to the day and the regional cooking is good. Javier will happily advise on birdwatching routes — and will show you how the watermill works. On a promontory down by the river it's a thousand years old and still contains the old flint wheels that spin into action when the sluice gate is opened. You'll fall in love with this place.

rooms	6: 3 twins, 3 doubles.
price	€84. Singles €70. VAT included.
meals	Tapas-style lunch €20. Dinner €23. VAT included.
closed	Rarely.
directions	From Burgos N-623 for Santander. North of Quintanilla de Escalada, at km66, exit for Gallejones. On for Villanueva Rampally. There left for Arreba. Posada signed to right after 2.6km.

	Javier Morala
tel	+34 947 571368
mobile	+34 689 891749
fax	+34 947 571176
email	info@molinodelcanto.com
web	www.molinodelcanto.com

B&B

Map 4 Entry 138

La Gándara

c/La Paloma s/n, 09572 Crespos, Burgos

The biggest noise around here is cicada hum and birdsong. The road stops at the village; remote, rustic, relaxed. The old farmhouse reflects this simplicity but there is a generous degree of comfort. Floors are oak, stairs creaky, windows shuttered, and walls are a pleasing mix of stone and plaster. The low-beamed bedrooms are furnished in elegant cottage style – brass or carved bedheads, embroidered covers, muslin curtains, perhaps a china basin or pine wash stand – even an old-fashioned typewriter. Bathrooms are elegant with their buttercup or sage walls. The top-floor suite is heaven: spot deer from the windows or gaze at the stars from the your tub. This is a place of simple pleasures – canoeing on the river, forest walking, exploring romanesque churches or visiting the spectacular gorge at Palancas. In the early evening, drink in hand, spot vultures from the balcony that overlooks the house's inner courtyard. Owners Javier and Isabel serve delicious meals with vegetables from their organic garden, and join their guests for supper. With no television, conversation lingers well into the night.

rooms	6: 5 twins/doubles, 1 suite.
price	€54-€58. Suite €75-€80.
meals	Breakfast €5. Dinner €18.
closed	6-31 January.
directions	From Santander N-623; left at km70 for Arreba & Manzanedo; on for 4km. Left; 1km to Crespos. House 1st on right.

	Javier Moyano & Isabel Villullas
tel	+34 947 573184
mobile	+34 689 034671
email	lagandara@teleline.es
web	www.lagandara.com

B&B

Map 4 Entry 139

Hotel Santo Domingo de Silos II
c/Santo Domingo de Silos 14, 09610 Santo Domingo de Silos, Burgos

Catch vespers at 7am: the highlight of a stay is the Gregorian chant in the monastery chapel. For this reason alone it's worth stopping off at Santo Domingo on the journey north or south; the stunning church with its magnificent bells is one of the finest in Spain. Consider staying a night at this simple family hotel, recently doubled in size thanks to its extension. Its real raison d'être is its restaurant: delicious meats roasted by Eleuterio in a wood-fired oven pull in a family crowd at weekends. On weekdays you might feel a touch lonely in this vast space, but you can always ask for dinner to be served in a second, smaller dining area, or in the cosy bar next door. The cuts of lamb, kid and suckling pig are worthy of a medieval banquet, and the prices astonishingly low. The bedrooms in the new extension are the best: lavish and a good size, spotlessly clean and with hydromassage showers or tubs. This is a good, down-to-earth place to stay: hearty food, great value for money – and exquisite Gregorian chant.

rooms	50 twins/doubles.
price	€50-€60. Singles €38-€45.
meals	Breakfast €3. Lunch & dinner from €10.
closed	Rarely.
directions	From Burgos, A-1 for Madrid; N-234 for Soria. Right in Hacinas on BU-903 to Santo Domingo. Hotel on right on passing through village.

Eleuterio del Álamo Castillo

tel	+34 947 390053
fax	+34 947 390052
email	reservas@hotelsantodomingodesilos.com
web	www.hotelsantodomingodesilos.com

Hotel

Map 4 Entry 140

Molino de la Ferrería
Camino del Molino s/n, 40512 Villacorta, Segovia

In a clearing in a wood, a delicious weekend bolthole for Madrileños: a river setting for summer, a ski resort (La Pinilla) for winter. Just outside the village of Villacorta, this smartly renovated flour mill, active until the 1970s, has become a stylish small hotel. Naturally the river flows right by, and the great old grinding stones are still at the heart of the place, perfectly preserved. Be welcomed by this charming young couple who lived and worked in Madrid before they swapped city buzz for a place in the country. The restaurant is a delight, with its chunky stone walls, circular white-clothed tables and friendly country furniture. A treat to dine in, it's packed at weekends and Mónica does most of the cooking. Peaceful bedrooms, some in the old mill, others on the ground floor of the new (but traditional) wing, all pristine and with every mod con, manage to be rustic and cosy. Be charmed by old bedsteads, new mattresses, chic lampshades on energy-saving bulbs (it's an eco-friendly place) and aromatic touches in super bathrooms.

rooms	12 twins/doubles.
price	€95-€110.
meals	Dinner €16.
closed	Rarely.
directions	From Madrid N-I for Burgos. At km103 marker follow signs for Soria-Riaza. At Riaza take lane on right between church & main square; this links with SG-V-1111. Continue to Villacorta; follow main road; right after village; hotel signed.

	Mónica Otero & Alejandro Mujica
tel	+34 921 125572
mobile	+34 639 216757
email	info1@molinodelaferreria.com
web	www.molinodelaferreria.es

Hotel

Map 11 Entry 141

Posada del Acebo

c/Rafael Matesanz 7, 40165 Prádena, Segovia

Prádena sits snug in the lee of the Sierra de Guadarrama, the high chain of mountains just north of Madrid. Its older houses are surprisingly grand, built in an age when villagers were granted royal privileges for the quality of their sheeps' wool. You enter through the small dining/sitting room, with its rustic bench seating, scents of seasoned timber, small open fire and family photographs of semi-nomadic shepherds. Ramón will usher you up the fine old banistered staircase to your rooms, passing a charming collection of working antique clocks on the way. Vintage washstands, wrought-iron bedsteads and old lamps fill the rooms – named after places special to the family – while central heating and double-glazing keep the fearsome winters of the Meseta at bay. There are mountains outside the door, the mighty Duratón river gorges to explore on foot or by canoe, and romanesque churches and the medieval town of Sepúlveda to visit. Then back to dinner in that cosy dining room. Rooms and food are excellent value, and if you're missing eggs and bacon at breakfast, just ask!

rooms	8: 7 twins/doubles, 1 single.
price	€54–€64. Singles €40.
meals	Dinner €14, on request.
closed	Rarely.
directions	From Madrid, N-1 for Burgos. At km99, exit onto N-110 for Segovia. After 12km, right into Prádena. House off main square.

	Ramón Martín Rozas
tel/fax	+34 921 507260
email	acebo@tursegovia.com
web	www.el-acebo.com

Guest house

Map 11 Entry 142

La Tejera de Fausto

Ctra. La Salceda-Sepúlveda km7, 40173 Requijada, Segovia

The stone buildings of this rustic homestead stand in glorious isolation, a mile from the nearest village, close to the banks of the Cega river. Of course the roofs are terracotta: *tejas* were made here, hence the name. Decoration is warm, simple and appealing: bedrooms, in an outbuilding, have a mix of old and new furniture – and no phone or TV to distract you from the views. Hostess and restaurant make this place special. In a series of snug, interconnecting rooms where fires blaze in colder months, guests tuck heartily into the best of regional cooking; specialities are roast lamb, suckling pig and boar. The gardens are lovely, too, with many trees for shade. Next door is a romanesque chapel whose foundation stones were pillaged from a Roman villa. This is a remote corner of Castille: a fertile valley in the lee of the jagged Guadarrama mountains that cut like a scimitar between Madrid and the Meseta. Walk out along the old transhumance routes that criss-cross the region: Castillian to the core. Note that there are wedding parties on summer weekends, so treat yourselves to a midweek stay.

rooms	9: 7 twins/doubles, 2 suites.
price	€75. Suites €110-€150.
meals	Breakfast €6.
	Dinner from €27 à la carte.
closed	Rarely.
directions	From Segovia, N-110 for Soria to La Salceda. Then left for Pedraza. Hotel on left, after Val de San Pedro, by km7 marker.

	Jaime Armero
tel	+34 921 127087
mobile	+34 619 240355
fax	+34 915 641520
email	reservas@latejeradefausto.com
web	www.latejeradefausto.com

Guest house

Map 11 Entry 143

Saltus Alvus

c/Tejadillo 1, 40170 Sotosalbos, Segovia

Once a stopover for the Romans crossing the Sierra de Guadarrama, Sotosalbos was – still is – prime hunting territory. Begoña grew up here and, after years working in international business and the London theatre, has returned to settle. The house, newly built on land owned by the family, has a reassuringly solid, traditional feel, thanks to heavy beams and thick stone walls. Generous windows make the most of the mountain views and let in plenty of light to big, delightful, rustic rooms. Every last detail has been finely considered and all is brought together with style and panache – and yet the effect is homely and rural. The bedrooms have glowing terracotta tiles and rich pine ceilings, firm beds and comfortable armchairs or a sofa. The finest craftsmanship is evident throughout. Begoña and Víctor are a friendly and erudite couple with a young son. They have a great love for the area, and tremendous enthusiasm for this new venture. Saltus Alvus serves breakfast only, but there's a super restaurant nearby – ask Begoña to book you a table.

rooms	4: 1 double, 3 suites.
price	€80–€115. VAT included.
meals	Restaurant in village.
closed	Rarely.
directions	From Segovia N-110 for Soria. After 18km, Sotosalbos on left. At restaurant Las Casillas, sharp left up track. 2nd right ('residents only' sign); house opp. church on left.

	Begoña del Barrio & Víctor López
mobile	+34 639 891220
email	saltusalvus@terra.es
web	www.saltusalvus.com

Guest house

Map 11 Entry 144

Posada Fuenteplateada

Camino de las Rozas s/n, 40170 Collado Hermoso, Segovia

Here is a young hotel constructed from reclaimed materials, serving seasonal food and run by the nicest people. It's the sort of place that would appeal as much to couples looking for a quiet weekend in the country as business folk planning a brainstorming session. The delightful owner Maria is from the area so, if you're a walker or a history buff, make the most of her knowledge. After a day in Segovia (a 15-minute drive), how nice to return to a massage in the spa and a scrumptious dinner in the restaurant (or at their sister restaurant down the road). Followed, perhaps, by a nightcap in the living room, so cosy at night. There's a modern, rustic feel here, thanks to exposed stones and chunky terracotta, along with great attention to detail: mosaics set into the reception's stone floor, sweeping peachy fabrics, woven-rush dining chairs. Bedrooms come with king-size beds and pillows to suit every whim, plus spacious sitting areas in the bedrooms; the largest even gets a garden. Outside is a garden, a play area for children and a pretty terrace for breakfast. *Ask about painting & cookery courses.*

rooms	11: 3 twins/doubles, 8 suites.
price	€105. Suites €120–€230.
meals	Lunch & dinner €9–€18. Second restaurant in village run by owners.
closed	Rarely.
directions	From Madrid on A-6 to La Coruña. Just before Segovia, A-1 for Soria. At Collado Hermoso take track between church & bakery leading to the hills and hotel.

	María Jesús Martín
tel	+34 921 403077
mobile	+34 659 485862
email	info@fuenteplateada.net
web	www.fuenteplateada.net

Hotel

Map 11 Entry 145

La Abubilla

c/Escuelas 4 posterior, 40181 Carrascal de la Cuesta, Segovia

The delightful Oneto family have lavished love and decorative savoir-faire on this old farmhouse in a hamlet with a population of 12. La Abubilla (meaning 'hoopoe') is a typical Segovian farm, its house and outbuildings wrapped around a sheltered courtyard – good for summer breakfasts – where two ash trees provide shade during the Meseta's sweltering summer. Every detail of the bedrooms has been fussed over by Alfredo Oneto; even the light switches have been individually crafted. The best rooms are the pretty suites in the old hay barn: tiles are hand-painted, beds country four-poster, paints and fabrics sober, low-beamed bathrooms charming. The rustic, raftered, split-level sitting and dining room, where a log fire glows and classical music plays, is equally inviting. Indulge in a spot of hydrotherapy in the grounds before settling down to a delicious meal; the kitchen is the hub of this house. Segovia is near, and you could easily visit Madrid, Ávila *and* Salamanca, should you choose to stay several nights. Peaceful and friendly. *A Rusticae hotel.*

rooms	5: 1 double, 4 suites.
price	€94–€140.
meals	Dinner €24.
closed	24/25 December.
directions	From Segovia N-110 dir. Soria. In Sotosalbo, left for Turégano & Carrascal de la Cuesta. House on right as you enter village.

	Hermanos Oneto
tel	+34 921 120236
fax	+34 916 617278
email	oneto@oneto.com
web	www.laabubilla.com

B&B

Map 11 Entry 146

Casa de Hechizo

Co. de Torreiglesias s/n, Barrio de Abajo, 40181 Carrascal de la Cuesta, Segovia

Alfredo couldn't have chosen a better name for his hotel: it will indeed leave you 'spellbound'. A chunky adobe exterior, fronted by young, natural gardens, contains a refreshingly light interior. Enter a modernist mix of straight lines, smooth surfaces and polygon shapes, crisp white walls, immaculate wafer bricks and creamy open stones. Soothing taupes and splashes of red are the colours in characterful bedrooms, where Venetian blinds frame windows and beds are vast. The lighting is striking – alter the room's mood at the touch of a switch – while dark polished hardwoods reach from floors to bathrooms and radical flat-topped basins; some bathrooms are in alcoves, some blend into sleeping areas, others are divided by sliding doors. Our favourite rooms are those at the back: catch the sunsets from your bed. And then there's the spa – built directly under the roof and encased in glass, it is 'drenched' in Castillian light. Sink into the sauna, stoke the stove, slip into the jacuzzi, gaze at the stars (there's a telescope for that). The restaurant offers fresh, creative, imaginative food. Intimate, stylish, special.

rooms	8 twins/doubles.
price	€164-€201.
meals	Lunch & dinner €35.
closed	Rarely.
directions	N-110 Segovia-Soria; at km172, left for Sotosalvos. Continue 7km to Carrascal. House on right on exit of village; signs for Barrio de Abajo.

	Alfredo Oneto
tel	+34 915 753431
email	info@hotelesconhechizo.com
web	www.hotelesconhechizo.com

Hotel

Map 11 Entry 147

Posada El Zaguán

Plaza de España 16, 40370 Turégano, Segovia

People flock to cobbled, walled Pedraza, while little Turégano, with its porticoed main square and impressive castle, stays forgotten. On that very square is El Zaguán – every inch the grand Castillian house. Casement windows, dressed stone, stables, grain store and bodega… it is a warm, quiet and stylish posada. Downstairs is the restaurant, the hub of the place; expect pine timbers, wafer-brick pillars and terracotta floors, well-dressed tables and a wood-fired oven where roasts are prepared – beef and lamb as well as the inevitable suckling pig. The place oozes history; travellers have been fed and watered here since the 16th century. In the charming upstairs sitting room you could be stepping into the pages of an interiors magazine; softly lit bedrooms, no two the same, are undoubtedly handsome, while underfloor heating warms terracotta floors, a boon during Castillian winters. On the landing is a second sitting room with stylish sofas, huge woodburner and a prime view of the castle. Even more special: hardworking, cheerful and throroughly likeable Mario remains at the helm.

rooms	15 twins/doubles.
price	€66–€96. Singles €50.
meals	Breakfast €6. Lunch & dinner €18. A la carte €24–€30.
closed	22 December-8 January.
directions	From Segovia, N-601 Valladolid. After 7km, right for Turégano & Cantalejo. In main village square.

Mario & Jesús García Heredero

tel	+34 921 501165
mobile	+34 677 493946
fax	+34 921 500776
email	zaguan@el-zaguan.com
web	www.el-zaguan.com

Hotel

Map 11 Entry 148

Caserio de Lobones

Ctra. CL-605 km 5,5, 40140 Valverde del Majano, Segovia

The Marques de Castellanos – eminent 17th-century aristocrat – could scarcely have imagined that his countryside retreat would, at some stage, open its doors to all. Take an extraordinarily aristocratic Castillian farmhouse and add landscape gardeners, clock makers and curators from the Royal Palace of La Granja; spare no expense on furnishings; and add the spark and conviviality of an andalucían host. Back in 1847, an encyclopeadia gave a lengthy description of this exclusive rural retreat. Nearly two centuries on, Rocío and Jaime have created a series of sophisticated interiors without a hint of ostentation. Magnificent antique pieces rub shoulders with religious oil paintings and German architectural prints. Rooms flaunt fabrics in bold checks and elaborate florals. Massive mirrored wardrobes are unfazed by vast, high-ceilinged spaces; one wardrobe is genuine Louis XVI. Outside is as lovely, the interior walled garden a formal maze of lavender and box, while Sevilla roses grace romantic corners. The landscape encourages riding, walking and fishing, and monumental Segovia is five miles away.

rooms	10: 9 twins/doubles, 1 single.
price	€110-€130. Single €90.
meals	Breakfast €8.
	Dinner €25, on request.
closed	Rarely.
directions	From CL-605 exit km5.5 marker for Valverde del Majano & Hontanares de Heresma. Follow signs to hotel.

Jaime Pujadas & Rocío Morales

tel	+34 921 128408
fax	+34 921 128344
email	info@lobones.com
web	www.lobones.com

Hotel

Map 11 Entry 149

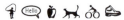

Natura

c/Colón 5-7, 40001 Segovia

This renovated 17th-century building in the heart of lovely Segovia makes a modest but comfortable place to stay. Its bedrooms are divided between three wings. Up from the slightly garish, Daliesque-themed entrance hall, the bedrooms, each different, are rag-rolled in warm colours and come with wood or terracotta floors – decent rooms for a *hotel hostería*, and spotless. Furniture is new but 'distressed' to look old, there are muslin curtains in many colours and plenty of space. You get all the mod cons and smart bathrooms too (hydromassage showers, a couple of baths), the odd balcony, even a few rooms set aside for smokers. If you're a light sleeper, ask for a room away from the road. You'll find more spirit at play in the modish cafeteria next door. And then there's historic Segovia: so much to see and enjoy… the Alcázar, the cathedral, the celebrated Roman aqueduct, the shops, the restaurants, the people. Don't miss out on the exquisite speciality of the region: *cochinillo asado*, or roast piglet.

rooms	17: 12 twin/doubles, 1 single, 2 family, 2 suites.
price	€40-€90. Single €40-€50. Family €40-€70. Suites €50-€90.
meals	Restaurants nearby.
closed	Rarely.
directions	In Segovia Old Town. Download map from hotel web site.

Miguel Espinosa de Frutos

tel	+34 921 466710
mobile	+34 685 429664
fax	+34 921 466711
email	info@naturadesegovia.com
web	www.naturadesegovia.com

Hotel

Map 11 Entry 150

Posada de Esquiladores

c/Esquiladores 1, 05412 San Esteban del Valle, Ávila

The granite exterior and rush blinds at the windows do not suggest the treats within. Enter a big inviting sitting room with a huge granite-fronted hearth and an exquisite restoration. In the lovely mountain village of San Esteban, the 18th-century posada was a village shop until 1989; some of the original goods are still on display. Today's interior is a harmonious and contemporary mix of stone, terracotta and serenely lovely fabrics; bedrooms are dreamy, bathrooms spotless. Ask María José, your charming hostess, to show you the old vaulted cellars below; they contain row upon row of ancient clay vats once used for storing the local red, Pitarra. If you book dinner you'll experience many of the dishes that have made Castillian cuisine famous. You can explore the wild villages of the region from here; there's a twice-yearly festival in honour of St Peter Baptist, the Franciscan missionary martyred at Nagasaki (whose skull rests in the church), and an annual horse race, El Vitor, in which riders race bareback from the square to the cemetery. A delicious retreat, run by lovely people. *A Rusticae hotel.*

rooms	12 twins/doubles.
price	€80–€120.
meals	Lunch & dinner €18. A la carte from €21. VAT included.
closed	Rarely.
directions	From Madrid, N-V/E-90 for Talavera de la Reina. At km123, right on N-502 for Avila to Ramacastaños. Here, N-502 for Mombeltrán. At entrance of village, right for San Esteban. In village, right at 'Ayuntamiento' to square & hotel.

	Maria José Quintanilla
tel	+34 920 383498
mobile	+34 652 915011
fax	+34 920 383456
email	posada@esquiladores.com
web	www.esquiladores.com

Hotel

Map 10 Entry 151

El Milano Real

c/Toleo s/n, 05634 Hoyos del Espino, Ávila

Surrounded by the Gredos mountains, this has the feel of a smart Swiss chalet, with shutters on all sides and the constant trickle of water in the oh-so-neat garden at the front. Inside, all is comfort and ease. Bedrooms are colour-coordinated and a good size, and include several rather plush suites. One is Japanese, stunning with futon and low furniture; another resembles a Manhattan penthouse; another is country English, with wall-to-wall carpeting and four-poster; and the Nordic room has its very own sauna. There are two lounges with matching sofas and armchairs, one up under the eaves, and a library and an observatory. The owner Francisco ('Paco'), is a keen astronomer, happy to share his passion with guests. But the dining room is the biggest draw, the food winning a mention in many guides; there's also a tempting wine list. Paco and his wife Teresa, outdoor enthusiasts both, have compiled their own walking guide: 20 GPS-referenced walks that take you into the heart of Gredos, one of Spain's best-kept secrets. *A Rusticae hotel.*

rooms	21: 13 twins/doubles, 8 suites.
price	€98–€140. Singles €86. Suites €180. Half-board €87.50–€120 p.p.
meals	Breakfast €12.50. Lunch & dinner €35–€45 à la carte.
closed	Rarely.
directions	Directions on booking.

	Yolanda Domínguez
tel	+34 920 349108
fax	+34 920 349156
email	info@elmilanoreal.com
web	www.elmilanoreal.com

Hotel

Map 10 Entry 152

El Canchal

c/de La Fuente 1, 05400 Arenas de San Pedro, Ávila

Not the Ritz, but perfect for walkers, who come for some of the most memorable routes in central Spain. Little Arenas de San Pedro, topped by a medieval castle and sculpted into the southern flank of the Sierra, is in the heart of the trails. This nobleman's residence – in the middle of town but not easy to find – dates from the Middle Ages and Isabel knows the history. She is the perfect innkeeper: unflappable, flexible, friendly. The feel is of a walkers' retreat, the furniture is darkly Castillian and the ceilings are low. Each bedroom is named after a variety of mushroom – the area is popular with gatherers – and is grandmother-cosy, thanks to antique beds and dressers, lace-edged curtains, antique washstands and dark beams. The lounge and dining room feel similarly homely, with their books, sofas, old tiles and ancient hearth. Try Isabel's homemade cake at breakfast and eat in at least once: meals are simple and excellent, and the house red is good. Don't miss the labyrinthine cellars deep below; one of Isabel's many projects is to fill them with her own judicious selection.

rooms	6 twins/doubles.
price	€50–€64.
meals	Breakfast €3. Lunch & dinner €18.
closed	Rarely.
directions	Madrid N-V for Badajoz. Exit 122 onto N-502 for Avila/Arenas de San Pedro. Here, over r'bout for 'Centro Urbano'. Before castle, left into c/Isabel La Católica. Round church; park in Plaza del Ayuntamiento. Walk up c/Cejudo, right; on left.

	Isabel Rodríguez
tel/fax	+34 920 370958
mobile	+34 607 958255
email	reservas@elcanchal.com
web	www.elcanchal.com

Hotel

Map 10 Entry 153

Posada Rincon de Alardos
Finca las Planas, El Raso, 05489 Candeleda, Ávila

A secluded microclimate where cool mountain air meets the warmth of the plains, and lemon and fig groves bow to forests of chestnuts and oaks. Jagged crests tower behind you…the Gredos is an ornithologist's dream. Susan, the vivacious British-Argentinian owner, said it was love at first sight. Not just for her, for this former tobacco-drying barn seduces anyone lucky enough to drift its way. Two huge tobacco leaves by the entrance pay homage to a once thriving industry. Rincon de Alardos has that rare quality, where you feel you're not staying in a house but in a home. Stone floors and ancient wooden beams lead to bright and spacious rooms, all of which ooze atmosphere, elegance and style: solid carved wardrobes, antique chests of drawers, polished bureaus. Our favourites are the two balconied rooms with breathtaking views over the mountains. As you sit on the vine-shaded terrace sipping spring-water lemonade, you may mull over whether to venture beyond the garden and explore the nearby Celtic village, or go walking in the Parque Natural de Monfragüe.

rooms	5 twins/doubles.
price	€66–€86.
meals	€12 tapas-style dinner.
closed	Rarely.
directions	A-5 from Madrid to Oropesa; continue to Madrigal, then C-501 for Candeleda. Outside Madrigal, left to El Raso immediately after river. Follow track for 2km; signed on left.

	Susan Reed
tel	+34 920 377075
fax	+34 920 377129
email	clientes@rincondealardos.es
web	www.rincondealardos.es

Guest house

Map 10 Entry 154

La Casa Inglesa
37700 Béjar, Salamanca

Many guests are Spanish: they come for fine food, good company and to escape the capital. La Casa Inglesa is both home and retreat, tucked away in a forest of chestnut trees from which the nearby village of El Castañar takes its name. Decoration has a traditional *Inglesa* feel: antique drop-leaf tables, crystal decanters, books, candelabras and oriental vases. Bedrooms have knick-knacks and chintz, bathrooms are dated but fine. Anna likes the good things of life so expect candles at dinner, classical music at most times and very good food: she had three restaurants in London during the Sixties and fed everyone from Nureyev to the Rolling Stones. Anna is no typical ex-pat: since setting up home in Spain she has never been one to search out fellow compatriots, and her cooking looks both west and east, with a fine choice for vegetarians. Dinners have a Lebanese slant and she will happily prepare you a cooked breakfast. A charming hostess and an easy-going home; stay a couple of nights and visit the exceptional village of Candelario, a ten-minute drive.

rooms	4: 3 twins/doubles, 1 triple.
price	€50–€60. VAT included.
meals	Lunch €25. Dinner €20.
closed	Rarely.
directions	From Salamanca for Cáceres & Béjar. In Béjar pass 2 petrol stations, left for El Castañar. Immed. opp. Hotel Los Duques, sharp left down cobbled track. At 3rd loop, sharp left to black gate. Ring bell.

Anna Antonios

tel	+34 923 404499
mobile	+34 636 363476
email	lacasainglesa@telefonica.net
web	www.casainglesabejar.com

B&B

Map 10 Entry 155

Hotel Residencia Rector

Paseo Rector Esperabé 10, 37008 Salamanca

In a city of ineffable loveliness, one of western Spain's most perfect small hotels. Señor Ferrán likes things to be 'just so' and examples of his meticulous care are found in every corner. There are two serene stained-glass windows in reception, and wood is used to fine effect: sparkling parquet floors in the public rooms, inlaid tables, writing desks and hand-crafted bedheads in the bedrooms. You may not need the phone in the bathroom, or the fax point in the bedroom, but you'll surely appreciate the double glazing, the air conditioning and the deeply comfortable beds. Bathrooms are quietly lavish: silver-grey marble, double basins, thick towels. Superb standards at breakfast too, where the staff are quiet, discreet and kind. Leave your car safe in the hotel car park – a big plus – and head out on foot to explore: the cathedral is two minutes away, the incomparable Plaza Mayor a step further, and next door is the Casa Lis, a fascinating museum dedicated to Spanish Art Nouveau and Art Deco. A charming and much-praised hotel. *Parking bookable in advance.*

rooms	13: 12 twins/doubles, 1 suite.
price	€116–€175. Suite €152–€190.
meals	Breakfast €11.
closed	Rarely.
directions	From Madrid on N-501, 1st right at 'Centro Ciudad'. At r'bout, left into P. Rector Esperabé. After 300m, hotel in front of two walls, by museum. Drop off bags & reception will direct you to car park.

	Julian Almaraz
tel	+34 923 218482
mobile	+34 958 452807
fax	+34 923 214008
email	info@hotelrector.com
web	www.hotelrector.com

Hotel

Map 10 Entry 156

Posada Real La Vadima

Ctra. Ledesma-Bermillo km7, 37100 Ledesma, Salamanca

If it is Old Spain you're seeking, come here. For generations this family have been living off the land, raising bulls, living in this 300-year-old, character-steeped house. The old granite and timbers embrace you and there's history at every turn. And kindness, from special, well-travelled hosts who cherish their B&B guests. Amalia's is a long established Castillian family, and her love for this place gives life to every ancient nook and cranny. The sitting room has checked sofas, hunting trophies and a roaring fire; idiosyncratic bathrooms, some more modern than others, have lashings of water; each bedroom, named after a family member, is different. Isobel's grandparents' room comes with matching Deco furniture and astonishingly effective plumbing, while the room with the best view has an Austro-Hungarian wardrobe and a library of rare books. Doors are carved and heavy, curtains handmade, ceilings solid chestnut. The wines and the cooking – whatever Amalia decides to produce that day – are as enjoyable as all the rest.

rooms	10: 7 twins/doubles, 1 single, 2 suites.
price	€80-€90. Singles €60-€65. Suites €100-€125.
meals	Breakfast €7. Lunch & dinner €25.
closed	10-31 January.
directions	From Salamanca cross Rio Tormes. Follow signs for Valladolid/N-620. Exit onto SA-300 for Ledesma. At bridge, right on SA-311 for La Vadima. Posada on right after 7km.

Jose Madrazo Ambrosio
tel   +34 923 570230
fax   +34 923 570329
email   info@lavadima.com
web   www.lavadima.com

Hotel

Map 10 Entry 157

Posada Real del Pinar

Pinar de San Rafael, 47450 Pozal de Gallinas, Valladolid

This small hotel, secreted away in 300 acres of pine forest at the end of a long track, exudes comfort. The low vaulted brickwork in the centre of the building is 17th century; the new brickwork is the colour of the earth in the fields. The sitting room, with its fire and plush seating, is an intimate and relaxed place to be; the dining room is elegantly vaulted and has a woodburning oven. Mouthwatering roasts are a speciality, there's a good little menu for children, and the local wines are delicious (and well priced). Behind the hotel is an old chapel, which has been converted into a library and whose airy grandeur is perfectly suited to business receptions and weddings; if you prefer not to clash with a party, check when you book. Bedrooms, named after *mudéjar* towns, are smartly furnished, the largest in the old part of the building. The older rooms are accessible by lift. The coloured mosaics in some of the bathrooms could be considered garish, but the overall impression remains classy. Historic Olmedo is worth a visit, there are plenty of natural marvels to see, and a thermal spa nearby. *A Rusticae hotel.*

rooms	19: 14 twins/doubles, 2 singles, 3 family.
price	€95. Singles €80. Family €150.
meals	Breakfast €6. Lunch & dinner €18.
closed	15-31 January.
directions	From Valladolid, A-6 for Tordesillas; A-6 for Madrid. Exit km157 for Olmedo. Follow CL-112 for 5km to Pozal de Gallinas. Posada signed on right as you pass through village; 3.2km down track.

	Ignacio Escribano
tel	+34 983 481004
mobile	+34 686 484201
fax	+34 983 449972
email	info@laposadadelpinar.com
web	www.laposadadelpinar.com

Hotel

Map 10 Entry 158

La Hoja de Roble

c/Costanilla 13, 49300 Puebla de Sanabria, Zamora

The ancient town's position on its isolated promontory is stunning. And just down from its 15th-century castle is this 17th-century Castillian inn. Young entrepreneur Gustavo devotes much time to his selection of wines in the cellar-bar, tempting visitors with the local red, Toro… or Albariño or Rioja – a delightful preamble to a meal in the beautifully dressed restaurant and a plate of habones (butter beans) and juicy beef from Sanabria. Or, perhaps, octopus, a local speciality – an exciting choice in a land-locked region. The nobleman who owned this house 300 years ago left behind furniture and complete sets of linen and china, stored on the ground floor where they have always been. Minimalist-rustic bedrooms are charming with local-linen curtains, intricately carved beds, chunky stone walls, reclaimed beams and subtle use of colour; some have balconies from which you may look down on the bustling street below. After a day wandering the serene shoreline of the Lago de Sanabria, what bliss to return to a deep bath in an exceptional bathroom. Worth a serious detour.

rooms	6 twins/doubles.
price	€60–€90. VAT included.
meals	Breakfast €6. Lunch & dinner €20–€25. VAT included.
closed	1-15 February; 4-20 November.
directions	From Orense/Madrid on A-52; exit 79 for Puebla de Sanabria. Cross river Tera and immediately turn left at T-junc. into town centre. After 300m, at fountain square, hotel on right beside kiosk.

	Gustavo Alonso
tel	+34 980 620190
email	info@lahojaderoble.com
web	www.lahojaderoble.com

B&B

Map 2 Entry 159

Casas Cueva Al-axara

Ribera de Cubas 102, Jorquera, Albacete

The Ribera de Cubas is an other-worldly gorge which runs into remoteness for miles and miles. Peeping enchantingly out of stunningly thick stone walls are these houses – sited in rocky caves that were the last refuges of the Moors. Al-Axara and El Jaraiz make rustic and special retreats; in both, an Arabic influence prevails. Dig deep into the nooks and crannies of blissfully cool interiors where wrought-iron Morrocan lamps create a warm glow against strong Mediterranean colours, and white-painted rockfaces create a background for bohemian paintings and pieces. Your bedrooms are simple, some with just futons on the floor – richly authentic! Be cheered by the colours – ochres and terracottas, scarlets and blues – and capacious showers built directly into the rock. El Jaraiz has one balcony-terrace, Al-Axara two, the biggest with a barbecue. Water is solar-heated, products are ecological; it is green, fun and original. You'll be all smiles when Ruth, the friendly manager who lives nearby, asks if she can improve your stay.

rooms	House for 2-4; house for 6-7.
price	House for 4, €90-€110.
	House for 6, €120-€150.
meals	Self-catering.
closed	Rarely.
directions	From Valencia on A-3 to Requena, then N-322 to Casas Ibáñez. Follow signs to Jorquera; from here, right into gorge following road by river (direction Valdeganga) to Cubas. Hotel 300m after church, on right.

	Cristina Villafañe
tel	+34 968 879219
mobile	+34 662 006742
email	al-axara@al-axara.com
web	www.al-axara.com

Self-catering

Map 17 Entry 160

Hotel Albamanjón

Laguna de San Pedro 16, 02611 Ossa de Montiel, Albacete

In the heart of Albacete – land of windmills and Don Quixote – is this sleepy corner. By a crystal lake, surrounded by small beaches and elephant grass, the Albamanjón, its terraces and its gardens dropping down from a rocky headland, is blessed with an extraordinary site. Built in the 70s with some curious features (including a windmill frontage), its cosy spaces are filled with much-loved collectables. The place may appear a little frayed at the edges but it reflects the geniality of its owners and feels cared for. Bedrooms, in which the rock sometimes appears unannounced, reveal a hotch-potch of furniture and hydromassage baths; go for a room at the top. Raul's succulent cuisine (suckling lamb, roast ham in honey) is the draw and the terrace sparkles with fairylights in summer; there's also a cosy café. But the biggest reason to be here is the stunning ribbon of translucent deep-water lakes in the Ruidera National Park. Swim from the hotel jetty, or hire rowing boats, kayaks and mountain bikes and explore, pioneer-style. The wildlife is rich, the peace profound.

rooms	12: 11 twins/doubles, 1 suite.
price	€89-€104. Singles €72. Suite €152. Half-board extra €20 p.p. VAT included.
meals	Lunch & dinner €18-€35. VAT included. Restaurant closed Tuesdays.
closed	Rarely.
directions	From N-IV, exit Manzanares & N-430 for Albacete. At Ruidera, signs to lakes. Hotel signed from lakes.

	Raúl Arés Espílez
tel	+34 926 699048
mobile	+34 607 723834
fax	+34 926 699120
email	hotel@albamanjon.net
web	www.albamanjon.net

Hotel

Map 16 Entry 161

Hotel Rural Antigua Casa de la Bodega
c/Clérigos Camarenas 58, 13200 Manzanares, Ciudad Real

From the dusty-hot streets of Manzanares, slip through handsome doors into a shuttered space of polished tiles, rich furniture and gleaming elegance. This 19th-century former bodega has all the slow, unhurried charm of a mature wine; one that demands you slip off your shoes, sink into a sofa and drink deeply. Isabel and Rafael spent three years lovingly restoring the house, giving it a swaggering exterior of white walls, wrought-iron balconies and gay awnings; the interior is classically traditional. Be soothed by plump upholstery, antiques, fine porcelain, bowls of fruit and acres of fabulously ornate floor tiles. The high-ceilinged bedrooms are all lace curtains, brass bedsteads, cool walls and dark wood. Elegant touches work their magic: monogrammed bed linen, a pretty glass chandelier, a petite writing desk, a cosy window seat. And always flowers. In one room, tiled steps lead up to a love nest. Bathrooms sparkle whitely. Beyond the shady, plant-filled breakfast terrace, a small pool is tucked into the high-walled garden. All this, and owners who are as charming, kind and refined as their house.

rooms	5 twins/doubles.
price	€70. VAT included.
meals	Restaurants nearby.
closed	February.
directions	From Madrid N-IV south; 1st exit for Manzanares. At r'bout follow signs for 'Centro Ciudad'; through tunnel; hotel on left.

	Isabel Blanco & Rafael Bermejo
tel	+34 926 611707
fax	+34 926 612105
email	info@antiguacasadelabodega.com
web	www.antiguacasadelabodega.com

Hotel

Map 16 Entry 162

La Casa del Rector

c/Pedro Oviedo 8, 13270 Almagro, Ciudad Real

An ornate jewel in the heart of Spain's hot, dry, central plain, Almagro was once tipped to become home to the next Spanish university. It never happened, and the Casa del Rector, a charming collection of 16th-century houses on the edge of town, passed into private hands. Some years ago, Juan Garcia, a restaurateur of some repute, bought the old place and, with the help of local craftsmen, gave its ashen features a rosy, healthy glow. Behind the sandstone façade are a number of originally furnished rooms and suites opening onto a galleried central atrium full of antiques and interesting paintings where water flows – a lovely place to unwind. Choose your bedroom before you arrive: Spanish traditional or rustic chic. Most have sofas, woodburning stoves, smallish windows and adventurous (even open-plan) bathrooms, perhaps a sauna/shower or a massive mosaic hot tub. The young, friendly staff serve excellent breakfast with Manchegan cheese and charcuterie; for a Castillian dinner, look no further than the owners' brilliant restaurant *A Rusticae hotel*.

rooms	16: 11 twins/doubles, 1 single, 4 suites.
price	€85–€132. Singles €75. Suites €180. Half-board €35 p.p.
meals	Breakfast €10. Lunch & dinner €25–€45.
closed	Last week in July.
directions	From Ciudad Real, CM-412 to Almagro. At 1st r'bout follow hotel signs; right, then 2nd on right.

Carmen Crespo Coello

tel	+34 926 261259
fax	+34 926 261260
email	recepcion@lacasadelrector.com
web	www.lacasadelrector.com

Hotel

Map 16 Entry 163

Casa Bermeja

Plaza del Piloncillo s/n, 45572 Valdeverdeja, Toledo

Angela has realised a long-nurtured dream: to escape the noise of Madrid and retreat to this peaceful village. Architect brother Luis took the renovation in hand; Angela, a designer, took care of the rest. Beyond the exuberant façade and the stately entrance is a seductive interior, its warm tones inspired by the red earth of Castille. Antique mingles with modern, there are huge rafters and polished tiles, immaculate checked sofas and contemporary wrought iron. The sitting room contains a multitude of smaller living spaces: choose from a plush sofa in front of the fireplace, an old rocking chair by the gallery, a baize-covered games table. Atlases, art books and magazines in many languages are casually scattered on tables. Bedrooms are elegant, comfortable and blissfully quiet. Clematis, roses, jasmine, lemon and orange trees populate the sunny garden; the impeccably kept pool is framed by original stone flags and is exceedingly alluring. This corner of the Meseta is an ornithological wonderland; children bored by birdwatching can look out for the resident one-eyed turtle. *A Rusticae hotel.*

rooms	9 + 4: 7 twins/doubles, 2 family. 2 studios; 2 apartments.
price	€72–€95. Singles €76. Suites €110–€170. Family €130–€170. Studio €110. Apartment €120.
meals	Lunch & dinner €25–€30.
closed	Rarely.
directions	Directions on booking.

Angela González

tel	+34 925 454586
mobile	+34 658 934865
fax	+34 925 454595
email	info@casa-bermeja.com
web	www.casa-bermeja.com

Hotel & Self-catering

Map 10 Entry 164

Hostal del Cardenal

Paseo de Recaredo 24, 45003 Toledo

Toledo is quintessentially, gloriously Spanish, having absorbed the richest elements of Moorish and Christian Spain. Tempting, then, to stay at the Cardenal, built 700 years ago as a mansion for the Cardenal Lorenzana, peacefully down on the city walls. All of Toledo's character and charm is reflected within its cool Castillian interior, and the gardens are lovely: fountains and ponds, geraniums and climbers. Go through the elegant main entrance to discover patios, screens, arches and columns... and rooms whose walls glow with fine old oils and *mudéjar* bricks. A peaceful mantle lies softly over it all, to the background tick-tock of the grandfather clock. Wide *estera*-matted corridors and a domed staircase lead to majestic, somewhat dated bedrooms, with gleaming parquet floors and dark furniture. Bathrooms are small, some are opulent. Choose between several small dining areas, one under the trees, and feast on roast lamb, suckling pig, stewed partridge. (Breakfasts are less impressive.) No views, church bells at 5am – but a truly great place. The El Greco museum is the shortest of strolls.

rooms	27: 23 twins/doubles, 2 singles, 2 suites.
price	€88–€112. Singles €54–€103. Suites €114–€145.
meals	Breakfast €7.80. Lunch & dinner €25.
closed	Rarely.
directions	From Madrid A-42 to Toledo. On arriving at old town walls & Puerta de la Bisagra, right; hotel 50m on left, beside ramparts.

	Luis González Gozalbo
tel	+34 925 224900
fax	+34 925 222991
email	cardenal@hostaldelcardenal.com
web	www.hostaldelcardenal.com

Hotel

Map 11 Entry 165

La Almazara

Ctra. Toledo-Argés y Polan km2, Apartado 6, 45004 Toledo

One of Toledo's sons, the infamous Cardinal Quiroga, built this delectable house
as a summer palace in the 16th century. El Greco used to visit for inspiration.
High on a hillside overlooking Toledo, wrapped in cypress trees and rosemary,
the building catches the breezes that sweep across the Meseta. Oil was milled
here and there are still vats of it deep below. You arrive via a grand old portal
and long drive to be greeted by the charming owner, Paulino, or one of his
welcoming staff. Downstairs is a large sitting room with vast fireplace for
winter; for summer, a white vaulted dining room overlooking the orchards to
Toledo. And take a closer look at those idiosyncratic oil paintings, the work of
Paulino's daughter. Bedrooms, feeding off long corridors, are straightforward
with a monastic feel; bathrooms have good repro taps and lush cotton towels.
Rooms 1-9 are our favourites, their French windows opening to large terraces
from where you gaze down on the ochre-roofed city. The private car park is a
plus and the town is a short drive downhill. Book ahead: this is well priced.

rooms	28: 26 twins/doubles, 2 singles.
price	€43-€58. Singles €30.
meals	Breakfast €4. Restaurants 2km.
closed	10 December-25 February.
directions	From Madrid, CM-401 to Navahermosa. Cross bridge; at r'about continue on CM-401. Hotel signed on right after 1.5km - turning easy to miss. Hotel at end of 400m track.

	Paulino Villamor
tel	+34 925 223866
fax	+34 925 250562
email	reservas@hotelalmazara.com
web	www.hotelalmazara.com

Hotel

Map 11 Entry 166

Casona de la Reyna

C/Carreras de San Sebastian 26, 45002 Toledo

The position is as close to perfection as it gets: within walking distance of the Casa del Greco and the Jewish quarter, yet in an off-the-beaten-track spot opposite the green banks of the Tajo, on the southern edge of the cobbled Old Town. This modern and stylish hotel, built on the site of a 16th-century house, is a welcoming, cool and relaxing haven to come back to after a long, and probably hot, day exploring one of Spain's most remarkable cities. Communal areas are cool and inviting: the elegant bar with its plush sofas; the miniature inner patio, with its fragant gardenias and trickling fountain. Graceful tapestries and reproduction oils decorate vividly painted bedrooms well-stocked with mod cons; large, comfortable beds with intricately carved headboards and fine cotton sheets ensure a good night's sleep. The bathrooms are among the best we've seen, with their gleaming fittings and mirrors, marble basin stands and Moorish tiles. And there's a bus stop right outside; hop on and discover Toledo.

rooms	25: 21 twins/doubles, 1 single, 3 suites.
price	€60–€117. Singles €60–€94. Suite €133–€176. VAT included.
meals	Breakfast €7.50. VAT included.
closed	Rarely.
directions	From Madrid exit 69 to Ciudad Real, then signs for 'Toledo Centro'. At r'about, follow signs for 'Centro Ciudad'. Hotel 1km, on left.

	Rosa Durán
tel	+34 925 282052
email	info@casonadelareyna.com
web	www.casonadelareyna.com

Hotel

Map 11 Entry 167

Casa Palacio Conde de Garcinarro
c/Juan Carlos I, 19, 16500, Huete, Cuenca

The owner spent his childhood further down the street – and gave the building back its dignity. He was helped in this formidable task by his wife Encarna, an artist and antique restorer; every corner shows an eye for detail and a feel for what's right. The village may be underwhelming but the mansion is finest Castillian: a fine portal of dressed sandstone with coat of arms above, grilled windows, and an enormous studded door leading to a central, colonnaded patio-garden with wooden balustrade above. Sweep up the wide walnut staircase to the first floor; to one side is a vast lounge (formerly the chapel) decked in rich burgundy colours, to the other, a second, less imposing living room. Uncluttered bedrooms are vast, high-ceilinged, terracotta-tiled and painted in wonderful pastel colours. There are old prints, window seats, cushions, easy chairs and hand-painted furniture – surprising extras given this hotel's prices. After breakfast served in the kitchen at brightly checked tables, head off to discover the delights of this wild, undiscovered corner of Castille. *A Rusticae hotel.*

rooms	14: 10 twins/doubles, 4 family.
price	€55-€66. Family €75-€86.
meals	Breakfast €6.
	Restaurants 5-minute walk.
closed	Rarely.
directions	Madrid-Cuenca on N-400/A-40; CM-310 to Huete. In village centre next to Santo Domingo church.

	Antonio Reneses Sanz
tel	+34 915 323307
mobile	+34 969 372150
fax	+34 915 327378
email	garcinar@teleline.es
web	www.casapalaciocondedegarcinarro.com

Hotel

Map 12 Entry 168

El Jardín de San Bartolomé

c/Juan Gavala 2, 16830 Carrascosa del Campo, Cuenca

Here are the vast, historic landscapes of the Spanish Reconquista, backdrop to battles between Christians and Berbers. In the library of this imposing 19th-century house, caressed by the warmth of a crackling fire, you'll recall the history. A monastic air pervades this place, in contrast to the witchcraft that prevailed here 500 years ago. There's even a prayer room – with confessional should you need one! The light-drenched inner courtyard, the heart of the house, conceals an ingenious smoke-heating system under the floor, devised to mitigate winter rigours; this is a land of climatic extremes. Vintage photographs and 19th-century manuscripts decorate the walls of the grand stone staircase, telling stories of prosperous times in Cuba. Beamed ceilings, 'hydraulic' floor tiles, flower-patterned bedspreads and curtains – a labour of love by Francisco's mother-in-law – add to the restrained comfort of the rooms. This is a cool and airy retreat to come back to after trips to Cuenca's 'hanging' houses and Segóbriga, one of the best-preserved Roman remains in Europe. Both are a day trip.

rooms	7: 5 twins/doubles, 2 quadruples.
price	€30-€60. Quadruple €40-€90. VAT included.
meals	Breakfast €5. Lunch & dinner €12, on request. VAT included.
closed	Rarely.
directions	From Valencia/Madrid on A-3; exit for Saelices-Segóbriga. Just before Sealices, take road for Carrascosa del Campo-Huete. Here, hotel on left opposite church. Park by road behind hotel.

	Francisco de Diego & Carmen Sarmiento
tel/fax	+34 969 124186
mobile	+34 639 665437
email	fdediego@sudistrito.com

Guest house

Map 12 Entry 169

Posada de San José

c/Julián Romero 4, 16001 Cuenca

Cuenca is a town that astonishes and engraves itself on the memory. Perched on the rim of its unforgettable gorge, this is an inn to match. A magnificently crumbling portal beckons you to enter; you would never guess what lies beyond. Inside, a multi-levelled and labyrinthine dwelling, where twisting staircases take you up, across and down…Your bedroom may be large or small, perhaps with a balcony or terrace or a canopied bed, probably its own bathroom. All have fresh white walls, uneven floors and are furnished with old country pieces and decorative flair; these owners value a vase of fresh flowers over trouser-presses and satellite TV. The best and quietest rooms are at the back and have views to make the spirit soar – but all of them are worth a night. Good smells waft from the welcoming little restaurant with its heart-stopping view; you'll be glad you cut across the Meseta to reach this out-of-time place. Cuenca is fascinating though parking is tricky; you may have to park at the bottom of the hill. Make time for the wonderful museum of contemporary art. *A Rusticae hotel.*

rooms	31: 20 twins/doubles, 2 singles; 9 doubles, singles & family rooms with shared baths. VAT included.
price	€35–€140. Singles €23–€55.
meals	Breakfast €8. Tapas in evenings.
closed	Rarely.
directions	From Tarancón, N-400 to Cuenca; signs to Casco Antiguo. Posada 50m from cathedral main entrance. Load at hotel; protected parking 150m down (avoid Plaza Mayor: cars often clamped).

	Jennifer Morter
tel	+34 969 211300
fax	+34 969 230365
email	info@posadasanjose.com
web	www.posadasanjose.com

Guest house

Map 12 Entry 170

La Posada de Tamajón

c/Enmedio 35, 19222 Tamajón, Guadalajara

A house with a colourful history: from wine store to 16th-century inn to Guardia Civil headquarters – and back to village inn. During the War of Independence the resident priest would hide religious artefacts from Napoleon's troops; the gracious Spanish family who live here now have unearthed many during their lengthy restoration. Now the house has reverted to its former status of posada. The owners, fond of local traditions, have also salvaged old farming implements and displayed them in the entrance hall. And they have a penchant for good antiques. (Some furniture is for sale – do ask.) The feel is of a rather grand manor house – at times ostentatious, at other times charming and homely. Shiny marble and brass, glittering silver, polished furniture and vibrant fabrics manage to co-exist. There are four bedrooms, one for each season, the most sumptuous being Invierno (Winter). It has marble and terracotta floors, lace bedcovers on a wrought-iron bed, a bathroom with luxurious brass basins, antique taps and jacuzzi, and a sunny private patio for breakfast. Quite a place.

rooms	4: 3 twins/doubles, 1 suite.
price	€80–€120. Suite €100–€150.
meals	Dinner on request.
closed	Rarely.
directions	From R-2, exit for Fontanar onto CM-101. Continue to Humanes; here, CM-1004 to Tamajón. Posada on main square, next to 'Ayuntamiento'.

	Javier Gamo Ruiz
tel	+34 949 211739
fax	+34 949 212934
email	info@laposadadetamajon.com
web	www.laposadadetamajon.com

B&B

Map 11 Entry 171

Hospedería Rural Salinas de Imón

c/Real 49, Imón, 19269 Sigüenza, Guadalajara

Prize-winning salt is still produced at Imón: you see the crystallising beds as you arrive. Just beyond is a tiny square and the Hospedería. This elegant house began life as a convent, then became a lowly salt warehouse. The heavy studded door now opens onto a second conversion: an unusual and exquisite mosaic of different styles. A sitting room hums with bright sofas, antiques and ornaments, old dolls and books, framed prints and huge repro paintings by Luis Gamo Alcalde, whose art enhances the whole house. Up the colourful stairway to bedrooms individually, historically themed. One has musical scores and signed photographs of musicians, another a Louis XVI-style cradle; Carlos III is graced by Empire beds and family photos; bathrooms are beamed and subtly lit. Right at the top, a cosy log-fired library leads to a patio and a stunning garden where the two towers of the original building rise… a secluded swimming pool blends in. There's a fine new spa close by – and furniture restoration and painting courses in three languages. Highly likeable, deeply cultural, and run with a personal touch.

rooms	12: 10 twins/doubles, 2 suites.
price	€57-€72. Suites €99.
meals	Breakfast €9. Dinner €25.
closed	Rarely.
directions	From Madrid A-2/E-90 for Zaragoza. Left to Sigüenza; here, C-110 for Atienza to Imón. Hotel on main square of village.

	Jaime Mesalles de Zunzunegui
tel/fax	+34 949 397311
email	sadeimon@teleline.es
web	www.salinasdeimon.com

Hotel

Map 11 Entry 172

Molino de Alcuneza

Ctra. de Alboreca km0.5, 19264 Alcuneza, Guadalajara

The quintessence of rural charm and fine taste: El Molino is proof of just
what can be achieved when love and energy are present in great measure.
Little remained of the 400-year-old mill when Juan and Toñi fell in love with it
and this swathe of delicious greenery. The rushing millrace still offers respite from
the baking summers of Spain's vast Meseta. Originally it was to be a weekend
bolthole for the family but the idea of a hotel was mooted and Juan was hooked.
Every last detail of the interior decoration has been carefully considered: pine
floors beneath dark beams; rich fabrics; a glass floor under which flows a rivulet
of crayfish and trout; an aunt's framed, pressed flowers; fine linen at beautifully lit
tables. Our favourite rooms are Nos. 3 and 4 but all are special. Guests are given
separate tables and dinner is a feast of local produce: partridge with chickpeas,
trout baked in Albariño wine, mushrooms from the forest. Breakfasts are hearty,
picnic hampers can be arranged and Siguenza and Atienza, two great medieval
villages nearby, are a cultural must. *A Rusticae hotel. Minimum stay two nights.*

rooms	10: 9 twins/doubles, 1 single.
price	€108–€190. Singles €70–€90.
meals	Breakfast €9. Dinner €33.
closed	Rarely.
directions	From Sigüenza towards Medinacelli. Molino well signed before you reach Alboreca, on right.

Blanca Moreno

tel	+34 949 391501
fax	+34 949 347004
email	informacion@molinodealcuneza.com
web	www.molinodealcuneza.com

Hotel

Map 12 Entry 173

Hotel Quinta de los Cedros

c/Allendesalazar 4, 28043 Madrid

Framed by 100-year-old cedars, this 'country house' retreat is remarkably close to the centre yet seems a million miles away. Ensconced on a quiet leafy avenue it has an elegant, old finca style, yet is brand new. Hold on to the happy illusion of residing on an estate, a feeling fuelled by the impressive main building and its apartments in the grounds. Extensive gardens and terraces for whiling away the hours complete the picture. Inside all is smart and traditional. Wander through the public sitting room and reading areas until you reach the conservatory – a choice spot, famed for its parties and just enough Spanish celeb spotting. Bedrooms reflect the overall mood, with their tasteful wallpapers and writing desks, and WiFi should you feel the need to contact the outside world. Quite a few have private terraces overlooking the gardens; all have nicely understated bathrooms with lush toiletries. And there's one more delight in store – the wizardry of renowned chef Perdo Larumbe. A swish escape from the hustle and bustle of Madrid life.

rooms	32: 20 twins/doubles, 2 suites, 10 apartments for 2.
price	€152–€210. Singles €121–€144. Suite €226–€268.
meals	Breakfast €10–€13.50. Lunch & dinner €45–€63.
closed	Rarely.
directions	From Madrid airport on A-1 then M-30. Exit 3 signed c/Arturo Soria. Pass 'Piscina Stella' on your right; under c/Costa Rica; 1st right into c/Allendesalazar. Hotel on left.

	Jorge Bardón Díez
tel	+34 915 152200
fax	+34 91 4152050
email	reservas@quintadeloscedros.com
web	www.quintadeloscedros.com

Hotel

Map 11 Entry 174

Abalú

c/Pez 19, 1st floor, 28004 Madrid

Bang in the city centre – an innovative and affordable alternative to luxury hotels. Bundles of designer bamboo on street-side balconies hint at what's in store. Young and enterprising, Antonio has not only transformed his career but also this, his parents' *hostal*. And he has done it in style. What a relief to find a reception area not brassy or formal, but staffed by cheerful people who welcome you in off the bustling streets behind Gran Vía. Each individual bedroom is Antonio's homage to modern urban design – very of-the-moment, all clean lines, rich colours and IKEA touches. Walls become artworks, with gentle florals and bold prints, and every space bathes in mellow lighting. As bathrooms gradually succumb to the Antonio treatment they too make their mark – stone walls and floors, walk-in showers, sleek basins, and a jacuzzi in the suite. The finish is less good in the public areas but the hotel is perfect for a long weekend in this buzzing city: walk your socks off, then retire to a cool, classy 'pad'. Antonio is working on the ground floor next.

rooms	10: 8 twins/doubles, 1 single, 1 suite.
price	€65–€87. Single 68–€77. Suite €120.
meals	Breakfast €6. Restaurants nearby.
closed	August.
directions	Metro: 'Noviciado' or 'Pza. de España'. From 'Noviciado' take exit for 'Ministerio de Justicia'. c/Pez is opposite as you come out of station. Hotel 300m up road, on right.

	Antonio Fernández
tel	+34 915 314744
fax	+34 915 214492
email	info@hotelabalu.com
web	www.hotelabalu.com

Hotel

Map 11 Entry 175

Levante

Molino del Río Argos

Camino Viejo de Archivel-Benablón, 30400 Caravaca de la Cruz, Murcia

Remote and beautiful, the fruit and walnut farm is secreted away beside a 135 million-year-old canyon cut by the Argos – paleontologist heaven. Its abundant waters explain why grain was milled here for centuries... now Carmen and Swedish Jan have restored the 16th-century mill and outbuildings and created an award-winning place to stay. The peachy colourwash makes the least possible impact on the setting, natural dyes have been used for doors and beams, floor tiles handmade according to an ancient technique, and organic orchards planted on the terraces. In earlier times peasants came to exchange goods for flour; now people come for a perfect night's sleep (lulled by the sound of fountains and streams) in a rustically simple apartment or room. Food is simple Mediterranean, occasionally Scandinavian, with wild meat a speciality. Patios, pergolas and outdoor pool, river walks and birdwatching, and a new 'centre for health and culture' with classes in yoga and relaxation. All this and more: Caravaca, the fifth holy city, and the Ethnologic Music Museum are just four kilometres away.

rooms	1 + 6: 1 double.
	6 apartments for 2-6.
price	€50. Apartment €55-€112.
meals	Breakfast €6. Lunch & dinner €22.
closed	Rarely.
directions	From Alicante A-7 for Murcia, then Andalucia/Granada. Exit at C-415 for Caravaca de la Cruz. Then signs to Andalucia. After 7km, hotel signed on right.

	Carmen Alvárez
tel	+34 968 433381
mobile	+34 606 301409
fax	+34 968 433444
email	molinodelrio@molinodelrio.com
web	www.molinodelrio.com

B&B & Self-catering

Map 17 Entry 176

Hospedería La Mariposa

Casa del Estanco 67, Gebas, 30840 Alhama de Murcia, Murcia

In the old days you climbed the winding road to stock up on vegetables, flour, eggs and baccy. Now the old farmstead has become a welcoming country hotel run by new owners, Mark and Sam, who upped sticks to move here in 2004 with their family. And what a site, on the edge of the Sierra Espuna Regional Park, in the heart of hiking country. Explore the park on foot or by car, see the old ice houses and the famous dinosaur footprints, and fit in some rock climbing and mountain biking; maps and info are provided at the hotel. But if nature won't tempt you away, stay put and lounge by the pool. There's even a playpool to keep little ones happy. Choose a book from the library, recline on the patio and soak up the views. Wrapped around a central courtyard, the bedrooms are beautifully uncluttered and a very good size. The dining room is open for breakfast and the *menú del día* is served daily, with an English roast on Sundays. Take a cool drink to the courtyard, sink into a sofa by the bar. Water is recycled, solar power used, and much of the fruit is organically home-grown.

rooms	8: 6 twins/doubles, 2 family.
price	€39–€65. Family €75–€90. VAT included.
meals	Lunch & dinner from €9.
closed	Never.
directions	From Alhama follow signs for Mula & Gebas. Hotel on right on entering Gebas.

	Mark Langton
tel	+34 968 631008
fax	+34 968 632549
email	info@hotellamariposa.com
web	www.hotellamariposa.com

Hotel

Map 17 Entry 177

Poco-a-Poco Orange Farm

50A Partida Carga, 03330, Crevillente, Alicante

Poco a poco ('little by little') was the neighbours' regular comment as they watched the Brettles building this house alongside the orange and pomegranate groves. 'Modern', 'roomy' and 'comfortable' best sum up the result. There are no stairs so it's ideal for little ones and the less nimble, and the bedrooms are large, one with a very fancy bathroom. Outside: an enormous gravelled garden with a large pristine pool, from whose plastic loungers you can admire great views. There are also a boules court, a sauna and a steam room. Pauline and Chris couldn't be more accommodating or more hands on. Rent the whole house and cook for yourselves, or book a room with breakfast; ask for an evening meal, eat out in Crevillente or, if you pick up the ingredients for a barbecue supper, the Brettles will cook it for you – over orange wood. Golfers will like it here, with seven courses within driving distance, and the motorway is close, so you can reach the airport in no time. There's the Vega Baja to explore, all those beaches and the dramatic Sierra Crevillente.

rooms	3 twins/doubles.
price	€55. €290-€385 p.w. Whole house available.
meals	Dinner from €10, on request. Self-catering option.
closed	Christmas.
directions	From Alicante A-7 for Murcia; exit 77 for 'Torrevieja'. Straight over at 1st r'bout; next r'bout right; under motorway; immed. right on tarmac road; left at fork & left again onto dirt track.

	Pauline Brettle
mobile	+34 676 169649
email	pauline@poco-a-poco-orangefarm.co.uk
web	www.poco-a-poco-orangefarm.co.uk

Casa 10-11

Pedanía de Úbeda, 03658 Pinoso, Alicante

Mavis and Karl, from Cumbria, have thrown themselves into their new Spanish retreat – rambling, colourful, chaotic – with gusto and joy. They are gregarious, fun-loving hosts. Enjoy their company along with sunshine and peace: this quirky hotel, once a bakery, winery and shoe factory, rests on the edge of a traditional village surrounded by vineyards and olive trees. Bedrooms are charactefully, eclectically themed in a mish-mash of Arabic, Spanish, French and English styles – and why not! Energy and love have been poured into the restoration, and guests' paintings and gifts only add to the feel. The bathrooms are particularly original, full of atmospheric bits and bobs and colourful tiles. The Bar Fuego – note the red flames on the wall – includes an area set aside for live music, while a rustic lounge with open fire blends into a dining room with a big sociable table. Outside is charming: Moroccan lamps, old sun loungers, a canopy of vines. Take breakfast out here, or watch the sunsets with your hosts over a barbecue and a glass of champagne. *Small beauty salon, sauna & gym.*

rooms	7: 4 twins/doubles, 2 family, 1 suite. Self-catering options: East Wing for 12; West Wing for 6.
price	€60-€90. East Wing €240 (€1,400 p.w.). West Wing €120 (€700 p.w.). VAT incl.
meals	Lunch €10. Dinner €15.
closed	Rarely.
directions	Directions on booking.

	Mavis Hanson
tel	+34 965 477335
mobile	+34 618 825304
email	info@casa1011.com
web	www.casa1011.com

Hotel & Self-catering

Map 18 Entry 179

Mas Fontanelles

Ctra. Biar-Bañeres km4, 03410 Biar, Alicante

Light-flooded rooms, burnished wood floors, high raftered ceilings – it is rustic, contemporary, beautiful. The huge, peaceful, 200-year-old farmhouse overlooks the pine, olive and almond trees of Benijama valley, and has been lovingly restored by Isabel and her Italian husband, Roberto. Colours are ochre and blue, fabrics are creamy, furniture is restored-antique or sleekly modern – chic but not pretentious. Bedrooms, named after trees, have a light designer touch making perfect use of natural colours and materials: creamy cotton bedspreads, rush-seated chairs, antique chests of drawers. Some rooms have balconies, one a terrace and two have loft-style additions, brilliant for children. There's a cosy sitting room with board games and a high-raftered, second-floor living room with comfortably elegant sofas and vast paintings. And, everywhere, stunning views. Isabel and Roberto will help you plan your days; walk, ride, quad-bike, paint, visit an Arab castle or two. Then back to a freshly prepared supper, and a terrace from which to gaze, wine in hand, on a perfect southern sunset.

rooms	8 twins/doubles.
price	€65-€70. Singles €56. VAT included.
meals	Dinner €20.
closed	Rarely.
directions	From Alicante N-330 to Villena. Here, signs for Biar. Hotel 4km outside Biar off road to Bañeres.

	Isabel Aracil & Roberto Medoro
mobile	+34 686 426126
fax	+34 965 979007
email	info@masfontanelles.com
web	www.masfontanelles.com

Hotel

Map 18 Entry 180

Almàssera Vella

Carrer de la Mare de Deu del Miracle 56, 03578 Relleu, Alicante

The village's old olive press still stands – in the dining room. Derelict when Christopher and Marisa arrived, the house is both a stylish and inviting home and a cultural centre. Spanish Marisa is an expert seamstress and interior designer, and cooks like a dream; Christopher is a prize-winning poet. Courses, run mostly during the spring and autumn, include writing, painting, photography, tapestry and mountain walking. The bright, airy living room is stuffed with books (3,000 at the last count), the dining room is homely. Also in the main house are four cosy, cottagey bedrooms with original artwork and photographs on the walls; two look over the terrace garden with pool and giant chess, and the valley with Moorish hilltop castle beyond. Opposite is a smaller house for self-catering – and an independent studio flat upstairs, an inspiring retreat for artists and writers. Not every room has its own but there are plenty of bathrooms in both houses. A place for grown-ups not children – there's far too much thinking and creating going on! *Min. two people in cottage & studio high season.*

rooms	4 + 2: 4 twins/doubles. 1 cottage for 6, 1 studio for 3.
price	€75. Cottage & studio €35–€40 p.p. (from €150 p.p. per week).
meals	Dinner €20. VAT included.
closed	Rarely.
directions	From exit 66 on A-7 (Villajoyosa); right (inland). After Orcheta, left to Relleu. Street opp. church; last property on right.

	Christopher & Marisa North
tel	+34 966 856003
fax	+34 966 856337
email	christopher@oldolivepress.com
web	www.oldolivepress.com

B&B & Self-catering

Map 18 Entry 181

El Almendral de Relleu

Partida Rural El Terme, Ctra. CV-775 km18, 03578 Relleu, Alicante

It's remote, the track is bumpy, there's little to do. It's just you, 2,800 almond trees and uninterrupted views of jagged peaks. This is switch-off and chill-out country. Bernard, a well-travelled French journalist, has renovated and extended his hilltop, 18th-century country house (20km, but a world away, from Benidorm) to provide quirky but sinfully commodious surroundings. Step inside and rooms spill off in all directions. Furnishings are stylish, spoiling and reflect Bernard's travels and his refreshingly irreverent attitude. The bedrooms, named after (most of) the deadly sins – Greed is yellow, Pride is purple – are furnished with elegance and comfort: huge American beds, gleaming French antiques, rich Catalan fabrics. The salon has Art Deco sofas and a cinema-size TV while the restaurant, with its cherry-red and white walls, oil paintings and thick napery, is classy and romantic. The Spanish/French menu is the big draw for returning guests. Cool off in the pool, doze on the shady terrace, wander among the palms, orange and lemon trees, gaze at the views… bliss.

rooms	6 twins/doubles.
price	€85-120.
meals	Lunch & dinner €18. A la carte from €25.
closed	Rarely.
directions	From Alicante on motorway; exit for Campello-San Juan. On CV-775 for Agues. At km18 marker, 1st left for El Almendral.

	Bernard Vassas
mobile	+34 659 165085
fax	+34 966 308875
email	info@almendral.com
web	www.almendral.com

B&B

Map 18 Entry 182

Casa Mosmai

Apartado 184, 03510 Callosa d'en Sarriá, Alicante

The setting is lovely: this new house, built with recycled wood and stone to a traditional design, is surrounded by hillsides dripping with oranges, lemons, avocados and figs. Organically grown, they find their their way in season to your table at breakfast; if you're self-catering, you may buy as much as you like – punnets of strawberries, baskets of nuts. The kind-hearted farmer and his family live upstairs, having set the lower storey aside for guests. B&B is an option here but we feel the layout of the rooms makes Casa Mosmai more suitable for one big group. You get a large airy, open-plan living room with repro furniture, board games and books, and a dining room and kitchen at one end, all very well equipped, from dishwasher to microwave to barbecue by the pool. Pastelly bedrooms are comfortable spaces to sleep in, nothing more, nothing less; bathrooms have brass shower fittings and taps. It's clean, simple, good value and ideal for two families: your hosts are relaxed, there's a pool with a view and the beaches are no distance at all.

rooms	5: 4 twins/doubles, 1 family. Lower floor available to rent.
price	€63-€75. Singles €50-€60. Family €85-€100. Whole lower floor €250-€360.
meals	Self-catering option. Restaurants 5km.
closed	Rarely.
directions	From Alicante on AP-7 for Valencia; exit 64. CV-755 for C. d'en Sarriá. 3km after Altea la Vella, 300m after bridge on Rio Algar; signed, on left.

	Joan Antoni Ferrando Pérez
tel	+34 965 972523
mobile	+34 666 411015
fax	+34 965 149242
email	casamosmai@telefonica.net

B&B & Self-catering

Map 13 Entry 183

Casa del Maco

Pou Roig 15, 03720 Benissa, Alicante

It's described as a rustic farmhouse but it's grander than that. An imposing paved terrace, statuesque trees and Lloyd Loom loungers around the pool give the Casa a gracious air. The 18th-century rooms, their beamed ceilings and deeply recessed windows betraying finca origins, are similarly special, the décor revealing flair and restraint. The restaurant, too, is sophisticated rather than rustic – food and wines are delicious, indisputably 'haute' (lobster is the house special) and served by impeccable staff. Bedrooms are romantic, bathrooms luxurious. The remote valley setting is stunning, and the gardens overlook vineyards, olive groves and almond orchards; behind, a bare shoulder of rock juts through the pine-covered hills. Excellent walks lead from the door; from Calpe, you can hike up to the flat top of the Peñón de Ifach (experienced crag rats like to tackle the rock climbs on its south face). Either way, you'll get great views of the saltpans, the mountains and the precipitous coastline to Cape La Nao. If you long for the sea and can face the crowds, the Costa is a short ride. A heavenly place.

rooms	6 twins/doubles.
price	€66–€99. VAT included.
meals	Breakfast €9. Lunch €19. Dinner from €35 à la carte. VAT included. Restaurant closed Tuesdays.
closed	January.
directions	From Alicante, A-7 for Valencia. Exit for Calpe & Altea; N-332 for Benissa. 900m after sign for Calpe, by BP petrol station, left for Casa del Maco, signed (easy to miss!).

Bert & Barbara de Vooght

tel	+34 965 732842
mobile	+34 699 069926
fax	+34 965 730103
email	macomarcus@hotmail.com
web	www.casadelmaco.com

Hotel

Map 13 Entry 184

Caserío del Mirador

Apdo. 180, 03727, Jalón, Alicante

Verdant mountains swoop around Johnny and Sarah's dream home with staggering views, some stretching to the sea. Splash amongst the hills in the fantastic pool, chat in comfort to your young, generous, humorous hosts under the bamboo canopy. Crisp, charming B&B bedrooms are bathed in whites and browns; solar-lit shower rooms display minimalist lines. Two spacious open-plan apartments (above which live the owners) are equally rustic-contemporary; the rest are self-contained. And you can tell that Sarah is a cook because your kitchen has absolutely everything you need (except, of course, for Sarah, to fill it with the delicious aromas of her tapas). Enjoy conversational dinners brimming with local produce and wine (made by the mayor himself); tempting to eat in every night. Families will love it here: the sandy coast is a breathtaking drive, there's a donkey sanctuary nearby, bustling Jalón (true Spain) is five minutes away, and there are fantastic walks in the hills. Best of all are the lazy days spent here, at this charming and happy home, in the company of Johnny, Sarah and their three young children.

rooms	2 + 5: 2 twins/doubles sharing shower. 5 apartments: 3 for 2; 2 for 4. Cots & extra beds.
price	€85–€145. Apartments €650–€1,000 per week.
meals	Breakfast €7.50. Lunch/picnic €15. Tapas €15–€20. Dinner with wine, €20–€30.
closed	Rarely.
directions	Directions on booking.

	Johnny & Sarah Robinson
tel	+34 965 973024
mobile	+34 607 811197
email	enquiries@villajalon.com
web	www.villajalon.com

B&B & Self-catering

Map 13 Entry 185

El Sequer

c/Traviesa 17, Partida Frontó, 03769 Benimelí, Alicante

Impossible to imagine it raining here, yet the lush fertility of the valley suggests that it must do sometimes. This beautifully restored *riu-rau*, where grapes were once dried, is full of light and colour. Orange trees, corn-yellow walls, blue shutters… there's a sunlit mood. You are nicely tucked away, too, at the top end of pretty Benimelí and with stunning views to the tiny villages ringed in a horseshoe around the valley. The garden is a delight, with its fig tree, vegetable patch, charming small pool and tile-clad tables and chairs for leisurely meals. Your living space is open-plan and airy, lovingly furnished – a few colourful paintings, a well-equipped kitchen, a woodburning fire. Smallish beds are dressed in soft pastels and ochres and the bathroom has a whirlpool bath. Bamboo-slotted ceilings, intersected with stout blue beams, are a hallmark of this type of cottage. You have all you need here, from CD player to mountain bikes. Jennifer, who lives in Denia, greets you warmly, and provides a little welcome pack. A sweet, simple place – and the peace is serene.

rooms	Cottage for 4.
price	€695–€950 per week.
meals	Self-catering.
closed	Rarely.
directions	A-7 from Alicante. Exit 62 Ondara (N-332); then CV-731 & CV-732 to Beniarbeig. At bridge, left to Benimelí. 1st road up on right, signed.

	Jennifer Pilliner
tel/fax	+34 966 424056
mobile	+34 626 200017
email	jpilliner@telefonica.net
web	www.mediterraneorural.com

Xaymaca

c/Pou 9, 03769 Benimeli, Alicante

Who would not love this 19th-century house in a sleepy village surrounded by almond and orange groves? The impressive wooden front door gives way to a spacious open-plan living area divided by a central kitchen, overlooking a plant-filled courtyard. Pass the Moroccan fountain and climb the lamp-lit stone staircase to a charming spot: a hidden garden with panoramic views, serene swimming pool and shaded barbecue area by an orchard. Bliss to spend time here on long warm days and sultry nights. Inside, all is vibrant and fun: happy Mediterranean yellows, reds and blues, natural fabrics and colourful little paintings of Jamaican scenes. The exposed stone walls and lofty wooden beams add to the homely mood, and there's comfy, cosy seating in two living rooms with log fires. High-ceilinged bedrooms have big comfortable beds and individual themes, two with a private terrace, one with a balcony. The owner is friendly, smiley, attentive and lives nearby – just in case you need anything more. Safe sandy beaches and nature parks wait to be discovered. *Minimum stay two to seven nights.*

rooms	House for 8.
price	€1,200–€1,800 per week.
meals	Self-catering.
	B&B option out of season.
closed	Rarely.
directions	A-7 exit 62; signs for Ondara, Valencia & Beniarbeig. In Beniarbeig, follow signs for Benimeli & Sagra.

	Jennifer Pilliner
tel/fax	+34 966 424056
mobile	+34 626 200017
email	jpilliner@telefonica.net
web	www.mediterraneorural.com

Self-catering

Map 13 Entry 187

La Casota

03791 La Vall de Laguart, Alicante

On a clear day you can see to Ibiza. The old farm is perched on the mountain side and has sensational views. Buildings ramble, flowers and herbs burst from pots, a big rectangular stone shades the fish pond, olive groves spread as far as the eye can see. Joaquina, friendly and kind-hearted, speaks excellent English, runs the farm on organic lines and has a team of girls to help look after the guests. It's a warm and inviting little place, simple, rustic, relaxing. Joaquina gives you four charming rooms in the *riu rau* where raisins were once stored, opening to a garden, and a delightful living area in another building, shared by all guests – comfy sofas, modern paintings and old farming implements on the walls, and glorious open fireplace in the corner. Self-caterers have an equally rustic studio-apartment and a two-storey house, the latter with a Moorish oven and all mod cons, both with a wood-burning stove for chilly nights. The food is a wonder – eggs from the hens, salads from the garden, fresh sorbets, homemade pastries, gilthead bream – and the pool overlooks the sea.

rooms	4 + 2: 4 twins/doubles. 1 house for 6, 1 studio for 4.
price	€60-€70. Single €45-€55. House €140-€160. Studio €85-€110.
meals	Breakfast €6. Picnic-style lunch €6. Dinner €17.
closed	Rarely.
directions	From Alicante on AP-7 for Valencia; exit 62 Ondara. CV-725 for Orba; here, signs to Vall de Laguar. Left on track just past signed entrance to Fleix. Hotel signed.

	Joaquina Garrido
tel	+34 965 583646
mobile	+34 629 501742
email	info@lacasota.com
web	www.lacasota.com

B&B & Self-catering

Map 13 Entry 188

Hotel Els Frares

Avda. del País Valencià 20, 03811 Quatretondeta, Alicante

Brian and Pat left the UK to head for the Spanish hills. Herculean efforts have borne fruit at their old village inn, once in a parlous state. Now its attractive frontage and constant flow of visitors are adding life and colour to the tiny hamlet, and your likeable hosts have made many Spanish friends. Behind, jagged peaks from which the hotel takes its name rise to almost 5,000 feet; the terrace, bliss for summery meals, looks out across the almond groves to its lofty crags. Good mattresses ensure deep sleep, fabrics are bright, there are framed photos of the Sierra Serrella, and ten bedrooms have terraces with views. More dramatic views from the new restaurant. There are four cosy sitting rooms, two with open log fires – the sort of rooms you'd want to return to after a hike in the hills, perhaps with Brian as your guide (though not in the height of summer). At supper choose from a menu that celebrates local dishes and tapas yet finds a place for imaginative vegetarian alternatives; the olive oil, fruit, vegetables and herbs are home-grown, the wines local and delicious. Walkers' heaven.

rooms	15 + 1: 15 twins/doubles. 1 cottage for 4.
price	€75-€95. Cottage €200 for 2, €300 for 4 (2 nights).
meals	Breakfast €10. Lunch €18. Dinner €20. A la carte from €24.
closed	Rarely.
directions	Directions on booking.

	Patricia & Brian Fagg
tel	+34 965 511234
mobile	+34 676 476148
fax	+34 965 511200
email	elsfrares@terra.es
web	www.inn-spain.com

Hotel & Self-catering

Map 13 Entry 189

Casa Rural Serrella

c/San Jose 1, 03812 Balones, Alicante

The steep, winding road passes almond and olive terraces while the air grows clear and pure. By the time you reach the mountain village of Balones (population 190) it's intoxicating – no wonder Mike and Demelza brought up their family here. Their large, peach-coloured village house is a true family home. Guests are greeted by an exuberant dog and everyone chats around the kitchen table. The guest rooms and the apartment (with terrace) have a comfy, lived-in feel, with much of the rustic-style furniture made by Mike. Colourful bedcovers, pastel coloured walls, terracotta floors and beamed ceilings create a simple but cared-for atmosphere. Summer meals are taken to the flower-filled terrace. Demelza, helped by daughter Melissa, cooks wholesome, unfussy, seasonally based dishes. After a day visiting historic Alcoy, or a long hike, return for a dip in the village pool – and time your visit, if you can, for one of the colourful village fiestas. The Whittocks are easy, relaxed people who are happiest treating guests as part of the family.

rooms	4 + 1: 4 twins/doubles. 1 apartment for 2.
price	€40. Singles €25. Apartment €25 p.p.
meals	Breakfast €5. Dinner €15. Packed lunch on request.
closed	Rarely.
directions	Directions on booking.

	Demelza & Mike Whittock
tel/fax	+34 965 511222
mobile	+34 697 441979
email	casaserrella@terra.es
web	www.quietspain.com

B&B & Self-catering

Map 13 Entry 190

La Casa Vieja

Carrer del Forn 4, 46842 Rugat, Valencia

This most peaceful of village houses combines 450 years of old stones with a contemporary feel for volumes and shapes. There are nobleman's arches and columns, ancient floor tiles, twisty beams, an indoor well and… a small, square, swimming pool in the verdant, Arabic courtyard. A double-height sitting area faces an immense inglenook where deep leather sofas envelop you as you sip a welcome sherry before dining. Many of the antiques have been in Maris's family for as long as she can remember – oil paintings and Persian rugs, a 16th-century grandfather clock, a carved mahogany table. Bedrooms, too, are stylish and homely, beds big and firm; there are terraces for some, books and baskets of fruit and no TV. Views stretch to the orange-clad hillsides, and summer meals are accompanied by jasmine and candles. People travel some way for the food which follows the seasons; fish, fruit and vegetables are fresh from the market and there are interesting vegetarian alternatives. We enjoyed the grilled goat's cheese with fig and orange confit, and the excellent Spanish wines.

rooms	6: 5 twins/doubles, 1 suite.
price	€70–€85. Singles €60. Suite €120.
meals	Dinner €24. Restaurants in village.
closed	15 December–15 January.
directions	Valencia A-7 for Alicante, exit 60; N-332 for Alicante. After tunnels, right onto CV-60 for Albaida. After 19km, right onto CV-619 for Rugat; through Montichelvo; Rugat 2nd village on left. Signed in village; behind church.

	Maris & Maisie Andrés Watson
tel	+34 962 814013
email	mail@lacasavieja.com
web	www.lacasavieja.com

B&B

Map 13 Entry 191

L'Agora Hotel

c/Sor Piedad de la Cruz 3, 46880 Bocairent, Valencia

Navigate the narrow, cobbled streets of this beautiful little town that stands in the shadow of the Sierra Mariola – a hill-walkers' paradise. Archaeologists will be fascinated by the comprehensive cave networks below – and will need no encouragement after a day of exploration to sit and savour the hearty regional food and rich wines served in the L'Agora Hotel. Indeed, behind its impressive and decorative modernist façade, L'Agora began life as a successful restaurant in a dear little square in the town's medieval centre. Picking up on the early 20th-century façade is an Art Deco interior, its replica antiques sitting soberly in 'themed' bedrooms: choose your country of choice and settle in for the night – Pakistan, China, Thailand. There's no hotel lounge, but the bedrooms are colourful, comfortable and the spacious bathrooms sparkle. After a fabulous dinner of paella and stuffed peppers, make a visit to the intricately decorated interior of the local church perched at the summit of the town. Not ideal for families but a comfortable stopover for couples. *Ask hotel about parking.*

rooms	8: 4 twins/doubles, 4 suites.
price	€83–€113. Singles €73–€80. Suite €132.
meals	Breakfast €9. Lunch & dinner €25–€30. Restaurant closed Sun-Thurs eves.
closed	Rarely.
directions	In Bocairent, follow signs for Casco Histórico. Park in Sor Piedad de la Cruz; hotel on right, not easy to find.

	Joaquín Piedra & María José Peidro
tel	+ 34 962 355039
fax	+ 34 962 355058
email	info@lagorahotel.com
web	www.lagorahotel.com

Hotel

Map 13 Entry 192

Hotel L'Estacio

Parc de l'Estacio s/n, 46880 Bocairent, Valencia

The station for the old narrow-track railway is today a light, bright hotel, run by friendly Dutch cousins Sebastian and Pascal. Reception is the station foyer, where an 'installation' of antique suitcases acts as a witty reminder of its history. Ultra-modern bedrooms, bathed in light from huge windows, have big comfy beds, elegant white blinds and a luxurious feel. The bathrooms match – generous and gorgeous. The large paintings you see everywhere are the work of Sebastian's talented mother. A vast building with vaulted ceilings – once the carriage shed – now houses a glass-roofed café/bar and a white-walled dining room, where you feast on regional dishes that make best use of local produce, flavoured with Mariola herbs grown in the garden. Wines are local and excellent. Stroll round the lovely medieval town of Bocairent, see the Sierra Mariola from a hot-air balloon, pop down to the coast – or simply unwind in the glass-canopied lounge or palm-lined, shady gardens, pretty with new pool. A stylish bolthole, a treat for all ages.

rooms	12: 11 twins/doubles, 1 single.
price	€66–€94.
meals	Breakfast €9. Lunch & dinner €10. (Only a la carte at weekends, around €25.)
closed	Rarely.
directions	From Alicante airport N-332. At Campello N-340 for Alcoi. There, take smaller road for Bocairent. Hotel to side of r'bout before town.

	Sebastian Lodder & Mats Lodder
tel/fax	+34 962 350000
email	reservas@hotelestacio.com
web	www.hotelestacio.com

Hotel

Map 13 Entry 193

Hostería Mont Sant

Ctra. del Castillo s/n, 46800 Xátiva (Játiva), Valencia

The Arab castle towers above; the views sweep dramatically over the red-roofed town and countryside way below. Terraced gardens glisten with orange trees and 1,000 young palms soften the habitat of fascinating archaeology… Iberian and Roman shards, Moorish fortifications, Cistercian walls. A Moorish irrigation system has guaranteed water in all seasons since the 12th century and the mountain streams are channelled, refreshing the air as they go, into a vast cistern under the garden. Javier Andrés Cifre is proud of his old family house, including the relics he has uncovered during excavations. The natural gardens are full of idyllic nooks and corners; terraces are charming with canvas parasols. Cool, beamed living areas have intimate alcoves; bedrooms above have antiques and great views; large, pine-clad cabañas (with air conditioning, TV, DVD) are dotted among the pines and the suite has its own pool. Bathrooms are luxurious. Tuck into elaborate Valencian dishes from state of-the-art kitchens, and, should you over-indulge, recover in the sauna, small pool or jacuzzi. *A Rusticae hotel.*

rooms	17: 16 twins/doubles, 1 suite.
price	€95-€140. Suite €260-€320. Half-board extra €45p.p. VAT included.
meals	Breakfast €12. Lunch & dinner available. VAT included.
closed	7-20 January.
directions	From Valencia A-7 for Albacete. Xátiva (Játiva) exit; follow signs for 'Castillo'. Signed. From Alicante to Madrid then A-7 to Valencia.

	Javier Andrés Cifre
tel	+34 962 275081
fax	+34 962 281905
email	mont-sant@mont-sant.com
web	www.mont-sant.com

Hotel

Map 13 Entry 194

Casa del Pinar

Ctra. Los Isidros-Venta del Moro, 46310 Venta del Moro, Valencia

Ping-pong among the fragrant pines – a joy on a summer's evening. And there is plenty more to delight the senses. Ana María and Phillipe took over the lovely old finca many years ago, its whitewashed buildings opening onto a central courtyard and enjoying a close relationship with the outdoors. He, a laid-back, modest host, loves his food and wine, while Ana knows a thing or two about tapas. This is a fully working vinegard and winery, producing over 16,000 bottles a year, and Phillipe, who sometimes runs cookery courses, uses the best of local produce (including the famous Requena sausage). There's a pretty restaurant and an elegant, galleried sitting room. Bedrooms are peaceful, traditional, simple and cosy, with attractive Spanish knick-knacks and good linen. Ask for one of the larger ones. More joy in the whitewashed self-catering houses, beautifully furnished and with many modern comforts. Flowers are everywhere, rambling across the courtyard or amassed in great urns in the garden; beyond, almond orchards, olive groves and vines. And a delicious pool of Olympian proportions.

rooms	6 + 2: 6 twins/doubles.
	2 houses for 7-8.
price	€82. Singles €65.
	Houses €800-€1,000 per week.
meals	Breakfast €8.
	Lunch & dinner €30-€35.
closed	December-January.
directions	N-322 for Albacete.
	After Los Isidros, right to Los Cojos.
	Pass turn for village; 1km, on left.

	Ana María Castillo Serna
tel	+34 962 139121
fax	+34 962 139120
email	diment@telefonica.es
web	www.casadelpinar.com

Hotel & Self-catering

Map 13 Entry 195

Hotel Mas de Canicatti

Ctra. Pedralba km2.9, 46191 Vilamarxant, Valencia

At the end of a twisting road, in the grounds of a working farm, is a spa hotel in two parts. The older building is in rustic style, the new is a Rubik's cube built into the hillside, its exterior a patchwork of coloured metal squares. Inside: a striking, stunning mix of Spanish antiques and modern design. The most charming rooms surround an inner courtyard with a fountain: boho tree trunks for bedside tables, warm bursts of modern art, private terraces with views. The new rooms are minimalist cool, equally lovely, and six of the suites have private pools. Then there are tennis courts, two bars, a superb spa (Turkish bath, massage, beauty treatments, sauna, jet pool), cooling, calm walls, polished parquet floors and piped chill-out music around the garden pool. You'll eat beautifully too: the kitchens are masterminded by seven chefs, each a specialist in his field. The extensive single-floor buildings – no stairs! – are surrounded by lawn, flowers, pines, palms, olive and carob trees; beyond: a hundred acres of orange groves. Blissful solitude very near to Valencia. *A Rusticae hotel.*

rooms	27: 14 doubles, 13 suites.
price	€191–€228. Singles €160–€191. Suite €260–€433. Half-board extra €46 p.p. Full-board extra €77 p.p.
meals	Breakfast €15. Lunch & dinner available.
closed	Rarely.
directions	From Valencia, A-3 for Madrid; exit Ribarroja del Turia. CV-320 for Pedralba. Hotel signed after 2.5km.

	María Angeles Fuertes Llopis
tel	+34 961 650534
fax	+34 961 650535
email	hotel@masdecanicatti.com
web	www.masdecanicatti.com

Hotel

Map 17 Entry 196

El Jardín Vertical

Carrer Nou 15, 12192 Vilafames, Castellón

Vilafames is a gorgeous hilltop village of red tiled roofs, turrets and towers, worn steps and an unmissable museum of contemporary art. And El Jardín Vertical is *the* place to stay, with its stylish décor and views that sweep across cherry and almond groves (a feast in early spring) to the mountains beyond. It's a 400-year-old house exquisitely styled, a sophisticated yet rustic hideaway. Floors are solid terracotta or 1920s cement-tiled, walls are open-stone or colourwashed plaster. Art work and pottery, wicker chairs and Moroccan mosaics add personality to the cool, serene reception and the sitting room with its open fire. Gloria's gift for design extends to the quirky patio and the big, harmonious bedrooms; the one in the attic (hot in summer) has sensational views. Pale tiled floors reflect the muted but warm colours, the bed linen is the best, the paintings are by Gloria's daughter. Double-glazing and shutters mute village traffic noise. Food is home-cooked and Mediterranean – so good that plans are afoot to open the restaurant to non-residents. *A Rusticae hotel. Minimum two nights at weekends.*

rooms	8: 6 twins/doubles, 1 family, 1 suite.
price	€135–€155. Family €175. Suite €185.
meals	Breakfast €15. Lunch & dinner €30.
closed	Rarely.
directions	From Barcelona A-7 exit 'Castellón Sur'. After toll to Benicassim, exit for Borriol onto CV-10; on for San Mateo. Exit 38 to Vilafames; at village entrance, right to hotel. Park by 'Ayuntamiento'; hotel at far right of square.

	Gloria Diaz-Varela Parada
tel/fax	+34 964 329938
email	casarural@eljardinvertical.com
web	www.eljardinvertical.com

Hotel

Map 13 Entry 197

Hotel Cardenal Ram

Cuesta Suñer 1, 12300 Morella, Castellón

Walled, hilltop Morella is a national heritage site: you'll realise why the moment you catch first sight of it. It's even better close to: traffic-free, cobbled and 14th-century. In one of its grandest mansions is a hotel as medieval as the town. Sited to one side of the colonnaded main street, its 15th-century arched windows give it a Venetian air – reflecting the one-time cultural exchange between Genoa and eastern Spain. Enter through the arched doorway beneath the Ram family coat of arms and you will be greeted by the genial Jaime Peñarroya or one of his friendly staff. A vaulted stairwell sweeps up to the bedrooms – big, cavernous even, with white walls and original chestnut beams up high. Rooms have recently been renovated and come with hydromassage baths. They are also wonderfully peaceful. You should eat well; truffles and sweet tarts are specialities. Book for several nights and discover the wild beauty of the Maestrazgo: there's a superb long-distance GR pathway that links these remote hilltop villages. But Morella will stay longest in the memory.

rooms	19: 16 twins/doubles, 1 single, 2 suites.
price	€70. Singles €45. Suites €80. Half-board extra €20 p.p. Full-board extra €35 p.p.
meals	Breakfast €6. Lunch & dinner.
closed	Rarely.
directions	Into old town thro' P. de San Miguel; follow road round town until hotel signs. 200m from cathedral. Unload & park by P. de los Estudios, outside city walls.

	Jaime Peñarroya Carbó
tel	+34 964 173085
fax	+34 964 173218
email	info@cardenalram.com
web	www.cardenalram.com

Hotel

Map 13 Entry 198

Extremadura

Monasterio Rocamador

Ctra Nacional Badajoz-Huelva km41, 06171 Almendral, Badajoz

The Franciscan monastery of Rocamador, long forgotten amid the wide spaces of Extremadura, has had new life breathed into old stones by celebrated model Lucía Bosé and actor Carlos Gómez. It is home and hostelry and so much more, for gastronomy is their life and their passion. So the Rocamador appeals hugely to well-heeled sophisticates who head here at weekends. Inner patios are filled with lush greenery and fountains, labyrinthine buildings fan out from cloister and chapel, and music and candlelight accompany dinners into the early hours. Bedrooms may not be the most brightly lit but are among the most extraordinary we've seen. Bathrooms are vast, some with shower heads ten inches wide, others with a chaise-longue next to the tub so you can recline like Madame Récamier. There are hand-painted tiles, enormous beds, three-piece suites, rich fabrics, wafer-bricking, vaulted ceilings, open hearths, incredible views. Never mind the hum from the main road as you linger by the pool... the Rocamador stands in a class of its own: sumptuous, daring, escapist, unique. *A Rusticae hotel.*

rooms	30: 26 twins/doubles, 4 suites.
price	€120-€190. Singles €130-€150. Suites €265.
meals	Breakfast €13-€19. Lunch & dinner €66. A la carte from €70. Restaurant closed Sun eve & Mon.
closed	24-25 December.
directions	From Madrid N-V; exit La Albuera (km382 marker). Into village, then towards Jerez de los Caballeros. At km41.1, right & over bridge; follow drive to Rocamador.

Carlos Gómez

tel	+34 924 489000
fax	+34 924 489001
email	mail@rocamador.com
web	www.rocamador.com

Hotel

Map 14 Entry 199

Hospedería Convento de La Parra

c/Santa María 16, 06176 La Parra, Badajoz

One of the most special small hotels in all Spain. This beautiful and tranquil place, formerly home to the nuns of the Order of St Clare, serenely evokes its monastic past. It is a place of understated elegance and charm: cool white walls, mellow floors, billowing muslin. Rooms open off a central cloister, with orange trees and fountain, on two levels; in winter, twin woodburning stoves add a glow to the raftered sitting room. Bedrooms have the simplicity of their former cell status but none of the austerity: the furniture is handmade, the tiling is impeccable. Some of the bathrooms have partly sunken baths and basins of beautiful earthenware or galvanised tin; others have double-arched ceilings; old and new have been brought together to provide comfort while preserving harmony. Set off on a donkey and take a picnic – it will be delicious; go paragliding, visit a castle. From the stork's nest on the bell tower to the exquisite turquoise pool to the sweet, kind staff, this is an exemplary place. No televisions or children to disturb the peace, and breakfasts served until twelve. *Spanish cookery courses.*

rooms	21: 15 twins/doubles, 4 singles, 2 suites.
price	€111-€133. Single €51. Suite €170.
meals	Lunch & dinner from €35 à la carte.
closed	24-25 December.
directions	From Sevilla, N-630 for Mérida. N-432 for Badajoz. Left for Feria & on to La Parra. Pass petrol station, left & up into village. Hospedería signed.

Javier Muñoz & María Ulecia

tel	+34 924 682692
fax	+34 924 682619
email	convento@laparra.net
web	www.laparra.net

Hotel

Map 14 Entry 200

Hotel Huerta Honda

Avda. López Asme 30, 06300 Zafra, Badajoz

Do visit Zafra. There is a castle, a beautiful arcaded main square, any number of churches to visit, and Huerta Honda is the best place to stay. It's larger than life and unmistakably southern: geraniums, bougainvillea, fountains in abundance and, in places, décor positively kitsch. In the guest sitting room are log fires in winter and a miscellany of decorative styles – fat modern sofas, rustic kilims, a deer's head on the wall. The dining rooms feel snug with their ochre walls, heavy beams and beautifully laid tables, but other parts of the hotel feel less intimate; wedding parties and business folk come here and the richly timbered bar is ever busy. The food is excellent, the cook is Basque and you may be tempted to splurge. Bedrooms have been recently redecorated, most with balconies overlooking the plant-filled patio; three much grander, theatrical suites have been added that take Moorish, Christian and Jewish Spain as their touchstone. On one of the large roof terraces is a tiny, decked pool – another reason to stay at this friendly hotel.

rooms	48: 45 twins/doubles, 3 suites.
price	€74-€96. Suites €150.
meals	Breakfast €8. Lunch & dinner €11. A la carte from €25. Closed Sunday evenings.
closed	Sunday.
directions	From Mérida south to Zafra. Hotel in city centre, near Palacio de los Duques de Feria.

Darío Martínez de Azcona

tel	+34 924 554100
fax	+34 924 552504
email	reservas@hotelhuertahonda.com
web	www.hotelhuertahonda.com

Hotel

Map 14 Entry 201

Casa Manadero

c/Manadero 2, 10867 Robledillo de Gata, Cáceres

What's so thrilling about Spain are these vast, untamed parts of its interior. All-but-unknown Robledillo lies at the heart of the Sierra de Gata, yet is still within easy reach of Salamanca and Portugal. This village – one of the region's prettiest – makes much use of the local slate: *arquitectura negra*. The tiny restaurant has heavy old beams, subtle lighting and excellent regional food – "one hundred per cent natural products," says young Caridad, who has pillaged the family recipe books for your benefit. There's plenty for vegetarians to get excited about, too, while Cervantes himself was fond of the local wines. The apartments, on three floors, vary in layout following the dictates of the original building; all are cosy yet airy and lofty, with kitchenettes and Caridad's cheerful décor. Outside is a basic, low-ceilinged cabin for two, with a geranium-strewn balcony for summer; views stretch over tiled roofs and endless vegetable gardens. You are surrounded by forests of oaks, olive groves and vineyards – marvellous for riding and biking. And there's a natural swimming pool close by.

rooms	1 studio for 3; 4 apartments for up to 6; 1 cabin for 3.
price	€42–€70 p.p. Half-board extra €14 p.p. Full-board extra €24 p.p.
meals	Breakfast €4–€6. Lunch & dinner €10–€15. Set menu weekdays only.
closed	Rarely.
directions	Through village of Descargamaría, right for Robledillo; 2km, left & down into village. Beware steep narrow roads. Contact owner re access.

	Caridad Hernández
tel	+34 927 671118
mobile	+34 610 332628
fax	+34 927 671173
email	info@casamanadero.com
web	www.casamanadero.com

Self-catering

Map 9 Entry 202

Finca El Cabezo

Ctra. Hoyos - Valverde del Fresno km22.8, 10892 San Martín de Trevejo, Cáceres

It is an awe-inspiring journey across the western reaches of Cáceres to the farm: rolling hills, cork oak forests, eagles above, the road to yourself. You are headed for a working farm (9,000 olive trees, 300 head of cattle) but don't expect a scruffy old ranch. Pass through the gates of this ivy-festooned building and you enter a magical inner courtyard of rambling virginia creeper and massed potted plants. The bedrooms are in the eastern wing and their size and elegance come as the greatest surprise: antiques on parquet or ancient terracotta, warm colours and modern art, chunky rafters and carved shutters. Bathrooms are fabulous. The sitting room, too, would have design mags purring: slate floors, open-granite walls, warm fabrics and good paintings. Feast on organic eggs fried in olive oil, goat's cheese and homemade cakes at breakfast; at dinner, choose between cheerful restaurants in San Martín or a Michelin-listed treasure down the road. This may be in one of Spain's furthest flung corners but it is worth a long detour and you couldn't hope to meet more special hosts. Sawday *Grand Cru!*

rooms	6: 5 twins/doubles, 1 suite.
price	€79. Suites €94.
meals	Restaurants nearby.
closed	Rarely.
directions	From Salamanca for Ciudad Rodrigo. Here, towards Cáceres; once over mountain pass 'Puerto de los Perales', right for V. del Fresno on EX-205. House on left at km22.8 marker. Signed.

Miguel Muriel

tel/fax	+34 927 193106
mobile	+34 689 405628
email	correo@elcabezo.com
web	www.elcabezo.com

B&B

Map 9 Entry 203

El Gallo Andante

Calle de la Pluma 7

Ana María, Juan and their extended family (it numbered seventy four at the last count) welcome guests to an unaffected, simple and unique living space. The philosophy here is very *lasissez-faire*: you simply pick a spot that looks comfortable and bed down. El Gallo's most memorable feature is its large, communal feather-and-straw mattress. It is not only a deeply comfortable cradle for the night but also provides for your supper in the form of the eggs laid by your fellow guests (yes, they are free range). At supper they come scrambled, poached, sunny-side up or fried: eggnogs are *the* alternative drink. One of the place's most original featuresis a nightly show after supper when various members of the Kiririki clan balance, asleep, on a number of high perches and old farm machinery. Late sleepers should note that the family are early risers and that alarm calls will never be the same once you have heard Juan crowing his guests awake. Prices, it must be said, are paltry, as it were.

rooms	1 space sharing bathroom & wc.
price	Mere chicken feed.
meals	Included and inevitable.
closed	It couldn't be more open.
directions	Follow your nose.

	Ana María & Juan Kikiriki
mobile	+34 111 111111
email	elgalloandante@itsa.con
web	www.itsa.con

Hovel

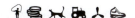

Map 10 Entry 204

Antigua Casa del Heno

Finca Valdepimienta, 10460 Losar de la Vera, Cáceres

The old farm stands superbly isolated on the southern side of the Gredos mountains, at the end of a long riverside track. You pass vineyards and olives, granite boulders and ferns to reach this enchanting spot. A crystalline stream meanders by, beyond are the mountains criss-crossed with footpaths. Inside: a sympathetic restoration, with granite, timber and cork the decorative leitmotif. A natural, earthy feel pervades this place and guest bedrooms get the balance just right: good beds, no modern intrusions and views across the farm. The valley is at its most magical in spring when thousands of cherry trees come into blossom; book ahead if you want to stay during this spectacle. Ornithologists come from all over Europe to focus their binoculars on kites, vultures, azure-winged magpie and great bustards. A reading room has recently been added, and your host brings the piano to life every now and again with pieces of Bach. There's a beautiful natural pool just a 20-minute walk, and the unmissable Monastery of Yuste, one of the residences of 16th-century King Carlos V, is a short drive.

rooms	7 twins/doubles.
price	€52–€68.
meals	Dinner €15.
closed	Rarely.
directions	From Madrid, N-V to Navalmoral de la Mata. Right onto EX-119 for Jarandilla, then to L. de la Vera. Pass 'Ayuntamiento'; left at sign 'Hotel Tipico Rural Casa del Heno'. Follow concrete road 3.3km to hotel.

	Miguel Millán Chaparro
tel	+34 927 198077
mobile	+34 609 603606
email	manoli.millan@terra.es
web	www.antiguacasadelheno.com

Hotel

Map 10 Entry 205

La Casa de Pasarón

La Magdalena 18, 10411 Pasarón de la Vera, Cáceres

Susana is young and friendly, proud of the 1890s village house in which her grandparents once lived. An elegant portal of carefully dressed sandstone in the unusual, burgundy façade leads into the entrance hall with its vaulted ceiling. The lounge mixes old and new furnishings piecemeal: cushioned sofas, a brass chandelier, photographic portraits and Impressionist prints. But the vaulted dining room has a really nice feel to it with just five attractively laid tables and the original marble-topped dressers; start your day here with a breakfast of oven-warm bread, local cheeses and fruit compotes made by the family. Dinner is excellent value, and homemade; perhaps soup followed by meatballs or kid stew. Bedrooms are reached via a heavy granite staircase: most are on the first floor and four are in the attic, with skylight windows. They are simple, spotless and quiet. At the back, a garden full of walnut and lemon trees (a pool and parking are planned). Do visit the nearby monastery of Yuste where Carlos spent his final months, in this very lovely corner of Spain. The village is a gem.

rooms	12 twins/doubles.
price	€70-€85. VAT included.
meals	Lunch €18. Dinner €10. VAT included.
closed	10 January-10 February; 2nd fortnight in June.
directions	From Plasencia towards Jaraiz to Tejeda del Tietar. Here, left to Pasarón. Enter village, 1st left. Signed.

	Susana Ayala
tel	+34 927 469407
email	pasaron@pasaron.com
web	www.pasaron.com

Hotel

Map 10 Entry 206

El Vaqueril

Ctra. Extremadura EX-207, 10930 Navas del Madroño, Cáceres

The big skies and cork-oaked hillsides make the area one of Spain's grandest visual feasts. Reached by an immensely long track, and in the middle of 320 hectares of cattle ranch, this old farmhouse stands amid carob, olive and palm. Its ochre and white frontage gives it a southern face and the house is classic cortijo: things gravitate towards a large central patio, the South's most effective technique for ensuring shade at any time of the day. No two bedrooms are the same: big, decorated with bright fabrics and family antiques, there are pretty tiles in the bathrooms, framed etchings and prints, open hearths. There is a vaulted lounge with a riotous ceramic hearth and a cavernous, candlelit dining room; expect simple, set menu dinners with some products straight from the farm. This is a hotel that specializes in catering for large numbers at local events – weddings, bullfighting spectacles etc – so it may get lively and staff may feel rushed. Laze by the big pool with views, rent a bike, stride off into the estate or jump into the car: Cáceres and Mérida are an easy drive. Unmistakably Spanish.

rooms	14: 13 twins/doubles, 1 suite.
price	€70. Singles €50. Suite €90.
meals	Breakast à la carte. Dinner €18. A la carte from €30. VAT included.
closed	Rarely.
directions	From Cáceres, N-521 for Valencia de Alcántara. Then EX-207 for Navas del Madroño. Just before village, left at sign for house; follow long track for 6km - always following signs.

	Javier Ruanu
tel	+34 927 375257
mobile	+34 659 101710
fax	+34 927 191001
email	elvaqueril@elvaqueril.com
web	www.elvaqueril.com

Hotel

Map 9 Entry 207

Dehesa Tres Riveros

10512 Herrera de Alcántara, Cáceres

The countryside is gorgeous rolling *dehesa*: open oak woodland dedicated to grazing Iberian pigs, cattle and sheep. This cluster of newly converted holiday cottages lies at the heart of a 400-hectare estate, within the boundaries of the national park that straddles the border between Spain and Portugal, the Rio Tajo. After an exhilarating drive, be greeted by the kindly farm manager, Eduardo. The cottages appear somewhat rectilinear from the outside but their unforgiving lines are softened by abundant greenery. Inside the feel is much more welcoming: warm colourwashes in sitting rooms and bedrooms, attractive stencilling and some unusual rustic Mexican furniture. Given the remoteness of the place – the nearest restaurant is eight kilometres away – you'll appreciate the well-equipped kitchens, while the makings of a simple breakfast are delivered to your door each evening by Eduardo. If you love a remote setting, and look forward to days spent hiking, riding, mountain biking and birdwatching, this is a superb place to stay.

rooms	3 houses for 4, 6 & 8.
price	House for 4, €91–€115. House for 6, €110–€135. House for 8, €146–€180.
meals	Self-catering with breakfast included. Restaurant 8km.
closed	Rarely.
directions	Cáceres N-521 Valencia de Alcántara; right for Cedillo. After 18.5km right for Herrera de Alcántara. After 4km, right for Santiago de Alcántara. Signed on left after 2km; 3km track to house.

	Gabriel Hernández García
tel	+34 923 238185
mobile	+34 606 434515
email	agroturismo@losbayones.com
web	www.losbayones.com

Self-catering & B&B

Map 9 Entry 208

Casa Salto de Caballo

La Fontañera s/n, 10516 Valencia de Alcántara, Cáceres

It has an intriguing position, this onetime shop and contraband centre, its front entrance in Spain and its back terrace in Portugal. Follow a narrow road across glorious, rolling hills to this, the furthest reach of the province of Cáceres – and, indeed, of Spain. This is where the smugglers plied their trade, saddlebags brimming with bread, coffee and garlic. These days you walk, or ride, straight out into Portugal's São Mamede Natural Park along those same secret pathways with not a thought for border patrols. Eva was so taken with it all she left Germany to restore this village house. The old floor tiles are still there, and the chestnut shutters and beams, along with a wholesome simplicity and a lack of modern luxury. Eva prepares innovative vegetarian meals if you would like them (she is a nutritionist and dietician) and three-course suppers. Generous hostess, generous prices and as far from the madding crowd as you could wish to get. A small pool is tucked into the pretty garden, and walking and fasting weeks can be arranged. Simple, no-frills, easy for families.

rooms	3 + 1: 3 twins/doubles. 1 apartment for 4.
price	€50. Apartment €90. VAT included.
meals	Lunch & dinner €15, on request.
closed	Occasionally in winter.
directions	From Cáceres N-521 for Portugal; through Valencia de Alcántara, then right for San Pedro. After 2km, right for La Fontañera; last house on left in village, signed.

	Eva Schuster
tel/fax	+34 927 580865
email	saltocaballo@gmx.net
web	www.saltodelcaballo.com

B&B & Self-catering

Map 14 Entry 209

Quinta de Luna

10500 Valencia de Alcántara, Cáceres

Just a hop away from Portugal, deep in a forest of chestnut and oak, is this new country retreat. Javier's three very private casitas were conceived with a maximum of comfort in mind, each a good distance from the next and with its own pretty terrace looking out across the valley. The feeling within is snug and welcoming: floors are make of slate and pine, contemporary prints rub shoulders with old agrarian implements and woodburning stoves provide the natural focus of the living and eating areas. Slump into a leather armchair and wind down a gear or two. All kitchen equipment – fridge, hob, juicer, oven, cutlery and crockery – is brand new, and the makings of a breakfast are provided on the day of your arrival. Bedrooms have the best of mattresses, attractive embroidered linen and sparkling shower rooms. Perhaps nicest of all is that you can walk from here along a leafy footpath to the little village of Aceña and its three friendly restaurants. Stay a few nights, slip across the border to the rolling Alentejo, and be sure to visit nearby Cáceres. *Minimum stay two to seven nights.*

rooms	3 casitas for 4-5.
price	€70-€120. VAT included.
meals	Self-catering. Restaurants 600m.
closed	Rarely.
directions	N-521 Cáceres-Lisboa; exit for Valencia de Alcántara. Turn off for Alcorneo & Aceña. On for 8km, just before Aceña de Borrega. House on left.

	Javier Hernández del Olmo
tel	+34 924 221157
mobile	+34 639 483667
email	info@quintadeluna.com
web	www.quintadeluna.com

Self-catering

Map 14 Entry 210

Finca El Jiniebro

Caserio Aceña de la Borrega, 10515 Valencia de Alcántara, Cáceres

Hidden away in a valley that borders on Portugal is this farm. For two centuries it housed farming folk; then the land was planted with pines and the stone buildings converted into self-catering cottages. All went swimmingly – until a fierce fire swept up the valley in 2003. Most people would have given up, but charming, vivacious Inocencia – and Luis, a carpenter by trade – are made of sterner stuff. El Jiniebro once again stands proud, the garden blooms and it is amazing how the valley has recovered: now it is awash with green. Luis's excellent handiwork can be seen in all the cottages, there are logs for winter, the pine furniture, some old, some new, is simple, and nothing is too much trouble for Inocencia, who has had years of experience in the hotel trade. In summer, the pool and the terraces, each with a barbecue, come into their own; even in July, the nights are cool. Walking is still a pleasure in this peaceful valley where there are megalithic stones and numerous birds, and you could be settling down to lunch in Portugal within minutes of shutting the door. *Please call to give arrival time.*

rooms	2 studios for 2; 2 houses for 3-4; 1 house for 9.
price	Studios €56. Houses €65-€185. VAT included.
meals	Self-catering. Restaurants 1km.
closed	Rarely.
directions	N-521 Cáceres-Lisboa; exit for Valencia de Alcántara. Turn off for Alcorneo & Aceña. On for 10km to Aceña de Borrega; right at signs for Jiniebro.

	Inocencia Rey
tel/fax	+34 927 584062
email	jiniebro@hotmail.com
web	www.turismoruraleljiniebro.com

Self-catering

Map 14 Entry 211

Finca Santa Marta

Pago de San Clemente, 10200 Trujillo, Cáceres

The farmer lived on the top floor and the olive oil was pressed below. Lost in a semi-wild Spanish landscape, surrounded by birdlife, the old farm has been transformed by designer Marta Rodríguez-Gimeno into a bucolic retreat. Bedrooms vary, and some are tiny, but each has a character of its own: antiques in some, hand-painted Portuguese furniture in others. Those in the next-door finca, the Santa Teresa, are more rustic in character, and the effect is equally pleasing. In the vaulted olive-pressing area is an enormous, cool and elegant sitting room with *estera* matting, neo-*mudéjar* ceiling, antique furniture and subtle lighting. And innumerable South American bits and pieces; husband Henri was Dutch ambassador to Peru and it was the Latin readiness to share that inspired him to open his home to guests. When the owners are away, charming housekeeper Inés and her staff step in. Lounge on the veranda in the evening and listen to the owls and the swallows. An enchanting spot, where peace wraps itself around you and sleep is deep. *A Rusticae hotel.*

rooms	14 twins/doubles.
price	€75–€120. VAT included.
meals	Dinner €28. VAT included.
closed	Rarely.
directions	From Trujillo, EX-208 for Guadalupe. After 14km, Finca on right where you see eucalyptus trees with storks' nests (km89 marker).

	Marta Rodríguez-Gimeno & Henri Elink
tel	+34 927 319203
mobile	+34 658 914355
fax	+34 927 334115
email	henri@facilnet.es
web	www.fincasantamarta.com

Hotel

Map 15 Entry 212

Casa Rural El Recuerdo

Pago de San Clemente, 10200 Trujillo, Cáceres

Extremadura is a land that is embracing and wild, one of vast, open landscapes, big skies and ancient stones. The Kelseys, recently returned from charitable work in India, were moved by the magic of the place – and its birdlife, which is exceptional. They happened upon a former 'lagar', a farm where wine was made, and, after some serious renovation, created a home of simple, solid comfort, the whole made spicier thanks to a quantity of furnishings and prints brought back from the East. The house's most memorable feature is its wafer-bricked, vaulted dining room where the wine was once made. You may be lucky and share dinner with Martin and Claudia, whose dishes are inspired by the recipe books of Spain, India and South America. There is high vegetable quotient and much of it fresh from the garden. Find time to take coffee in the square in nearby Trujillo, or laze beneath the willow beside the pool, perhaps perusing one of Martin's many books on birds (he's a professional ornithologist). Bedrooms are spotless, peaceful, traditional, just right for this type of rural retreat.

rooms	6 twins/doubles.
price	€70. VAT included.
meals	Dinner €20, on request.
closed	Rarely.
directions	From Trujillo EX-208 towards Guadalupe. After 11km, right for San Clemente. Signs to house.

	Martin & Claudia Kelsey
tel	+34 927 319349
mobile	+34 609 684719
email	info@casaruralelrecuerdo.com
web	www.casaruralelrecuerdo.com

B&B

Map 15 Entry 213

Andalucía

Finca Buen Vino

Ctra. CN-433 km95, 21208 Los Marines, Huelva

After years in the Scottish Highlands, Sam and Jeannie knew that to settle happily in Spain they would need to find another place of wild natural beauty; this divinely isolated spot hides among the thick oak and chestnut woods of the Aracena mountains. Buen Vino was built in the 1970s but many of the materials used were ancient, shipped in from far corners of Spain; the panelled dining room, the arched doors and the wooden staircase have a seductive, timeworn patina. The house's decoration is unaffected yet elegant, and the bedrooms Scottish-cosy, with our favourites in the attic. You get easy chairs and cushions, cheery oil paintings and family memorabilia, books and magazines, comfortable beds and good linen, perhaps a bath tub with a view (two rooms have their own). There are also three independent cottages to rent, hidden away on the edges of the estate, each with its own pool. The feel is house party, particularly over star-lit dinner (farm meat, eggs, veg cooked by Jeannie) or barbecue by the pool: friends, friends' children, guests, farm manager… all are free to join in the fun.

rooms	4 + 3: 4 twins/doubles. 3 cottages.
price	€100-€150. Cottage details on request.
meals	Lunch €15, on request (summer only). Dinner €35.
closed	Christmas & New Year.
directions	From Sevilla A-66; then CN-433 for Aracena/Los Marines. 1.5km after Los Marines; right at km95 marker.

Sam & Jeannie Chesterton

tel	+34 959 124034
mobile	+34 676 879989
fax	+34 959 501029
email	buenvino@facilnet.es
web	www.fincabuenvino.com

B&B & Self-catering

Map 14 Entry 214

Finca la Silladilla

21290 Los Romeros, Huelva

You couldn't wish for a more pastoral setting: the old textile mill stands in heavenly isolation surrounded by a forest of ancient oaks. Choose between B&B in the main house and self-catering in the farmhouses (well-equipped, one with three TVs!) that lie nearby, more isolated still. Bedrooms are pretty in their rustic garb: antique brass bedsteads, perhaps a Deco table, parquet floors. Bathrooms are snazzy, some with hydromassage tubs. And the views are gorgeous. Unusually there is no dining room in the main house, but breakfast is delivered to your room. There's a small farm shop, which doubles as a tapas bar, where you can buy the makings of a simple meal (accompanied by very good wines); they also make their own fragrant *jamón de Jabugo*: watch the semi-wild pigs rooting beneath the oaks. This is a fine place for birdwatchers, riders (they have seven horses) and peace-seekers. To the west of the market town of Aracena lies the Parque Natural of the same name, a huge 90% of it forested, and embracing some of Andalucía's prettiest villages. *Call for details of opening hours. A Rusticae hotel.*

rooms	2 + 4: 1 twin/double, 1 suite. 4 houses for 4, 6 or 10.
price	€76–€108. Houses €178–€445. VAT included.
meals	Lunch & dinner €25, on request. VAT included.
closed	Rarely.
directions	From Sevilla, N-630 for Mérida; N-433 through Aracena for Portugal. After El Repilado, left for Los R. Signed on left, 200m past cemetery.

Maia Araujo

tel	+34 959 501350
mobile	+34 647 913167
fax	+34 959 501351
email	silladi@teleline.es
web	www.jabugo.cc

B&B & Self-catering

Map 14 Entry 215

Finca Arroyo La Jara

Ctra. La Escalada km 4,5, 21350 Almonaster La Real, Huelva

Almonaster la Real is one of the prettiest of the white villages that pepper the wooded hillsides of the Aracena Natural Park. A few kilometers away is this cluster of casitas (little houses), placed in the perfect spot for exploring the park's ancient cobbled network of footpaths. And the walking is superb. With 32 hectares surrounding the original farm, Juan and Pilar, your amicable hosts, were able to give each of their newly-built casitas plenty of space, and athough the buildings look a mite rectilinear from outside, they are pretty inside. This was a labour of love for the owners, as revealed by bathrobes and hand-embroidered linen, curtains and bed covers stitched by Pilar, and sparkling kitchens with not a pan missing. Sitting rooms, like bedrooms, have masses of space and yet are toasty in winter thanks to excellent insulation and central heating. But what you'll remember most is the sheer peacefulness of the place, broken only by birdsong among the cistus and cork oaks, and the rasping of a thousand cicadas during the long, hot andalucían summers. *Minimum stay two nights.*

rooms	6 houses for 2, 4 & 10.
price	House for 2, €100; for 4, €145; for 10, €345. VAT included.
meals	Self-catering. Breakfast €9.
closed	Rarely.
directions	From Sevilla A-66/N-630 towards Mérida; then N-433 to Aracena. Pass Aracena; at km112 marker, left to Almonaster la Real. Here, towards La Escalada. Finca on right after 4.5km.

	Pilar del Cañizo
mobile	+34 661 341658/659
email	info@arroyolajara.com
web	www.arroyolajara.com

Self-catering

Map 14 Entry 216

Molino Rio Alájar

Finca Cabezo del Molino s/n, 21340 Alájar, Huelva

Rustling leaves and birdsong: it is as bucolic as can be. Come for the peace, or for the famously delicious ham or, in November, for the mushrooms. This gentle complex of self-catering stone cottages seems as much part of the natural scenery of this secret valley as the cork trees that surround it. Each has its own terrace, and each is finished to a high standard by the Dutch owners, Peter and Monica. Peter, who once walked from Amsterdam to Santiago de Campostela, has written a guide to local walks — you will not be left to wander aimlessly. The larger houses have underfloor heating, rafters and log fires, and steep stairs to the upper sleeping area; the smaller house is open-plan and has no kitchen (but you can cook in the reception building). Each dwelling is beautifully modern: tiles from Seville, woven rugs, painted ironwork beds, warm colours. Blissful for families: a pool, volley ball, trees to climb, and restaurants in cobbled Alájar, up the lane. Portugal is over the border — but you may not wish to venture far. *Four-week Spanish courses November & March.*

rooms	5 houses for up to 6.
price	€460–€770 per week.
meals	Self-catering.
closed	Rarely.
directions	From Sevilla, N-630 for Mérida; N-433 to Aracena. Left on A-470 to Alájar. After Alájar, at km13/14 marker, left; follow signs.

Peter Jan Mulder

tel	+34 959 501282
fax	+34 959 125766
email	rioalajar@wanadoo.es
web	www.molinorioalajar.com

Self-catering

Map 14 Entry 217

Hotel Rural Posada de Alájar

c/Médico Emilio González 2, 21340 Alájar, Huelva

Just as well that the Sierra de Aracena is famed for its walking: you'll need the exercise to justify your over-indulgence at this mouthwatering *posada*. Lucy and Angel's cooking, making full use of excellent local produce, is irresistible: *Ajo Blanco* (garlic soup), pork loin in sweet chestnut, layered apple pie… The vivacious young couple from Seville spent years searching for the right place but fell instantly for this 18th-century inn in Alájar village. It feels welcoming and warm the moment you step into the beamed, slate-floored and log-fired living room. As if by magic, you are drawn to the tiny bar beyond, then into the cosy, buttercup yellow dining room with its country tablecloths and Angel's collection of olive oils. The low-beamed bedrooms make the most of their limited spaces and are decorated in breezy colours with simple furnishings. Front rooms have French windows and balconies overlooking the street while those at the back are the quietest, but all assure a good night's sleep. Genuine warmth, a friendly welcome, five-star cooking and a great mountain position.

rooms	9: 8 twins/doubles, 1 family attic for 7.
price	€60. VAT included.
meals	Dinner €18. VAT included.
closed	Rarely.
directions	From Sevilla, A-66 towards Mérida; N-433 towards Portugal & Aracena. At Aracena on towards Alájar; 2nd entrance to village. Hotel just before main square, on left.

	Lucy Arkwright & Angel Millán Simó
tel	+34 959 125712
email	info@laposadadealajar.com
web	www.laposadadealajar.com

Hotel

Map 14 Entry 218

Palacio de San Benito

San Benito s/n, 41370 Cazalla de la Sierra, Sevilla

Four-star treatment and an informal feel... the sandy brick façade, nuzzling up to the 15th-century church with quirky triangular tower, gives no clue as to what lies within. The raised swimming pool with its spouting fountain, the sumptuous 19th-century library with its up-to-date CDs and DVDs, the curved, ornately-tiled stair: a splendid theatricality pervades this palacio. The owner, whose noble lineage is attested to in the stately interiors, was a set designer for the opera and inherited the palace from his grandmother. By a curious feat of stage management he had the building moved, brick by brick, then let his design flare run riot inside, using bold juxtapositions of colour and style. The Room of the Infanta is one of the least dramatic, with its rose-strewn sofas and fine potraits on aqua walls, while bedrooms on the ground floor have terraces and tinkling fountains. Bathrooms are sumptuous and the central sunny terrace with glazed cloisters is a gem. With a top-class chef and a memorable dining room, this place promises as much glamour as a night at the opera.

rooms	9 twins/doubles.
price	€140–€230. Singles €120.
meals	Lunch & dinner €30. A la carte from €35.
closed	Rarely.
directions	From Sevilla, N–630 for Mérida, right on A–431 Cantillana; A–432 to El Pedroso & onto Cazalla. Palacio on right, up hill, at village entrance.

	Manuel Sánchez
tel	+34 954 883336
mobile	+34 670 785624
fax	+34 954 883162
email	info@palaciodesanbenito.com
web	www.palaciodesanbenito.com

Hotel

Map 15 Entry 219

La Cartuja de Cazalla

Ctra. A455 Cazalla - Constantina km2.5, 41370 Cazalla de la Sierra, Sevilla

The 15th-century Carthusian monastery, one of the most remarkable buildings in Andalucía, lay empty for 150 years until Carmen Ladrón, visiting in the 1970s, nursed it back to life. Passionate about history and art, she has introduced a series of extraordinary paintings by Peruvian artist Espinoza to the five restored chapels and created a ceramics workshop in her 'centre for contemporary culture.' (Painters, sculptors and musicians have been known to exchange art for their stay.) The guest bedrooms, which finance the centre, are divided between a contemporary block and the original, well-restored, monks' cells, where light streams through a huge skylight. They have modern furniture and bathrooms, and, in keeping with the spirit of the place, no telephones or TV; heating is hit or miss in winter. Country cooking – fixed menu, no frills – is extremely good. Unwind in the healing centre, ride horses from the Cartuja stables, roam the surrounding 100 acres, slip into the spring-water pool. We have magical memories of wandering from chapel to chapel in the early morning light. *A Rusticae hotel.*

rooms	14 + 1: 8 twins/doubles, 2 singles, 4 suites. 1 apartment for 6.
price	€80–€90. Singles €50–€55. Suites €100–€120. Apt €120.
meals	Lunch €15. Dinner with wine, €25.
closed	24–25 December.
directions	From Sevilla C-431 to Cantillana; A-432 to El Pedroso & Cazalla. There, right onto A-455 for Constantina. La Cartuja at km2.5 marker.

	Carmen Ladrón de Guevara
tel	+34 954 884516
fax	+34 954 884707
email	info@cartujadecazalla.com
web	www.cartujadecazalla.com

Guest house

Map 15 Entry 220

Las Navezuelas

Ctra. A-432 km43.5, Apdo. 14, 41370 Cazalla de la Sierra, Sevilla

A place of birds and natural beauty, a 16th-century olive mill set in 136 hectares of green meadows, oak forest and olive groves – you are in some of Spain's loveliest countryside and the place is an ornithologist's dream. Water streams down from the Sierra, often along Moorish-built channels, swallows and storks nest, boar and deer roam, sheep bells jangle and pretty Cazalla is two miles away. The house and converted outbuildings are pure Andalucía with beams and tiles; the garden is a southern feast of palms and orange trees, wisteria, vines, jasmine and lazy pool. Bedrooms vary in shape and size, the most characterful in the rambling main house; all are whitewashed and well-lit, with old bits of furniture and a homespun feel. Apartments are attractive though minimally supplied. There are two sitting rooms and two dining rooms, the oldest aromatic with log fires in winter, and the menu includes truly delicious local dishes and produce from the farm. The town is a five-minute drive – good news for self-caterers.

rooms	6 + 6: 4 twins/doubles, 2 suites. 3 studios for 2; 3 apartments for 4-6.
price	€59-€63. Singles €45-€55. Studios €86-€90. Apt €110-€140.
meals	Lunch & dinner €20. VAT included. Lunch in summer only.
closed	7 January-25 February.
directions	From Sevilla 8006 to Cantillana. Here, A-432 for Cazalla. Pass km43 marker; after 500m, right at sign.

Luca Cicorella & Mariló Tena

tel	+34 954 884764
fax	+34 954 884594
email	navezuela@arrakis.es
web	www.lasnavezuelas.com

Guest house

Map 15 Entry 221

Hotel Rural El Olivo

Pza. Virgen de las Huertas 1, 41479 La Puebla de los Infantes, Sevilla

Chances are you won't have heard of Puebla de Los Infantes. It hides in the furthest corner of Seville province, on a quiet back road that cuts up from the Guadalquivir valley to the foothills of the Sierra Morena – the sort of place where a foreign number plate might turn heads. The sturdy white building, a labour of love for the Sáenz family, stands on a small square edged with citrus trees, and the owners are proud of what they have achieved. The décor is as andalucían as can be: marble and tiled floors, sugary prints of flowers on white walls, wrought-iron ballustrading and window grilles galore, potted palms and aspidistras and all is new and shiny. The sole communal space is a tiny sitting area by reception furnished with rattan chairs. However, the simple bedrooms, each named after a variety of olive, are so spruce and such brilliant value that you won't mind a bit. It might be nice to break the journey here, en route from Seville to Córdoba, and get to grips with that fabled 'real Spain'.

rooms	10: 7 twins/doubles, 2 singles, 1 suite.
price	€50–€60.
meals	Restaurants in village.
closed	Rarely.
directions	From Sevilla A-4 towards Madrid; exit for Carmona/Lora del Río. Continue to Lora del Río then on Via Ermita de Setefilla to La Puebla. Hotel on left of 1st square.

	Miguel Sáenz
tel	+34 954 808103
mobile	+34 619 239857
email	reservas@casaruralelolivo.com
web	www.hotelruralelolivo.com

Hotel

Map 15 Entry 222

Palacio de los Granados

c/Emilio Castelar 42, 41400 Écija, Sevilla

Push the boat out and come here – this 18th-century baroque palace makes every guest feel like a prince or princess, and charm oozes from every corner. Expect heavy tasselled fabrics, deep sofas, thick rugs; Moorish arches, lanterns and brassware, reflecting the city's Arabic past, add an exotic touch. The inner courtyards are magical: in one there are pillared archways, soothing fountains and glossy ferns; the other, with an elegant pool and 120-year-old palm, is scented with orange and pomegranate trees – sheer delight to breakfast in. The high-ceilinged bedrooms are grand in every detail: queen-size beds, jewel-bright fabrics, exotically coloured walls, mosaic-tiled bathrooms. Some have chandeliers, others Moorish alcoves, yet others get draped beds straight from *The Arabian Nights*. Dinner menus change daily – a mix of andalucían and South American. Explore Écija with its Roman remains and baroque churches, return to a nightcap by that lovely little pool. Pablo and his staff are as gracious as you would expect; you will be hopelessly spoiled.

rooms	14: 10 twins/doubles, 4 suites.
price	€145-€177. Suites €177-€220.
meals	Lunch & dinner €35-€40.
closed	Rarely.
directions	From Sevilla on A-4; exit for Écija & Osuna on A-351. At r'bout follow signs for 'Centro urbano, Ayuntamiento, Palacio de Granados'. At end of c/Emilio Castelar, on right.

	Pablo Ojeda O'Neill
tel	+34 955 905344
fax	+34 955 901412
email	info@palaciogranados.com
web	www.palaciogranados.com

Hotel

Map 15 Entry 223

Cortijo Aguila Real

Ctra. Guillena-Burguillos km4, 41210 Guillena, Sevilla

Aguila Real is every inch the classic, whitewashed cortijo. You are surrounded by fields of cotton, sunflowers and wheat, yet are no distance at all from the charms of Seville (catch a glimpse of the Giralda tower from the gardens). Passing under the main gate you enter a vast inner courtyard where bougainvillea romps; an old dovecote and water trough are reminders that this was a working farm. The public rooms, the best with beautiful barrel-vaulted ceilings, are decorated in ochres and terracottas with a smart mix of modern sofas and heavy antiques and the odd painting and hunting trophy on the wall. In the new, purpose-built dining room and on the elegant summer terrace dinner comes with silver cutlery and classical music; the food is regional and the wine list is long. Bedrooms, set around the inner courtyard, are swish affairs, with huge beds, patterned and coordinated fabrics and lots of space; bathrooms have double sinks, some bedrooms get a terrace and the tower room has views. The palm-filled garden where white doves coo is subtly illuminated at night – and there's a pretty pool.

rooms	13: 8 twins/doubles, 5 suites.
price	€82–€127. Suites €123–€202.
meals	Breakfast €12.
	Dinner from €26 à la carte.
closed	Rarely.
directions	Sevilla ring road SE-30 to Merida A-66. Exit 798 towards Guillena (SE-460). In Guillena, right at 2nd lights. Hotel on Guillena-Burguillos (A-461) road; signed.

	David Venegas
tel	+34 955 785006
fax	+34 955 784330
email	hotel@aguilareal.com
web	www.aguilareal.com

Hotel

Map 15 Entry 224

Hotel Simón

c/García de Vinuesa 19, 41001 Sevilla

Two steps from the third largest cathedral in the Christian world is the Simón – a friendly little place, well-worn but not shabby, and ideal if you don't feel like splashing out. The hotel is utterly Sevillian; pass through the main portal, then a second wrought-iron door, and into a cool, columned, inner patio. Here tables and chairs are dotted among an abundance of aspidistras and ferns: a retreat from the throbbing heat. The dining room has grand old mirrors and Moroccan-tiled walls, period tables and chandeliers, and bedrooms, a touch dated but reasonable for those on a budget, are set around the patio and reached via a marble staircase – another reminder that this was a nobleman's residence. Rooms are simply decorated and air conditioned, the best at the front; those at the back can be gloomy. Breakfast is table service although it appears to be buffet. There are innumerable restaurants and tapas bars outside the door; ask the helpful staff to advise. Light sleepers note that local bars stay open late.

rooms	29: 19 twins/doubles, 5 singles, 5 suites.
price	€75–€110. Singles €55–€60. Suites €125–€150.
meals	Breakfast €4.25.
closed	Rarely.
directions	Hotel just south of cathedral, in newly pedestrianised area. Park as near to bullring as possible; call hotel or take taxi.

	Enrique Aguayo
tel	+34 954 226660
fax	+34 954 562241
email	info@hotelsimonsevilla.com
web	www.hotelsimonsevilla.com

Hotel

Map 15 Entry 225

La Casa del Maestro
c/Almudena 5, 41003 Sevilla

You may be compelled to dance a flamenco inside this classic Sevillian townhouse. It was once the home of the maestro guitarist, Nino Ricardo, and photographs of his handsome face and passionate playing cover its walls, evoking the heady days of the 1900s. The house has kept that era's gracious style while carefully introducing 21st-century comforts. The focal point is the central covered courtyard with its mosaic floor, elegant chairs and tables and double tier of wrought-iron balustraded galleries. The upper galleries lead to the bedrooms. These are stylishly classic with creamy stucco walls, rugs on tiled floors, noble bedheads and embroidered bed linen. Antiques, fresh flowers and glossy magazines add a warm, homely feel; white and blue bathrooms reveal delicious toileteries. Breakfast is served by charming staff in the courtyard – or brought to your room. After a day's exploring the fascinating old Jewish quarter of Santa Cruz, return to sunset watching from the rooftop terrace. This place captures the intimacy and romance of Seville, and our readers love it.
A Rusticae hotel.

rooms	11 twins/doubles.
price	€105–€260.
meals	Restaurants nearby.
closed	Some days in August.
directions	In Sevilla S-30 for Córdoba, exit S. Justa. At S. Justa station, 1st right; 1st left; right for P. de Osario. Right on c/Escuelas Pías, pass church, 1st left. Straight to Plaza S. Leandro; turn into c/Francisco Carrión Mejías; 1st left.

	Patricia Zapardiel
tel	+34 954 500007
fax	+34 954 500006
email	reservas@lacasadelmaestro.com
web	www.lacasadelmaestro.com

Hotel

Map 15 Entry 226

Casa Numero 7

c/Virgenes 7, 41004 Sevilla

The owner, an aristocrat from Jerez, has a fondness for Britain and the British; the result: a touch of Chelsea in the heart of Seville. Perhaps it was memories of England's country houses that inspired his conversion of fine Moorish townhouse into exceptional small hotel. A mood of privileged intimacy prevails, with six bedrooms – very quiet for the centre of town – grouped around a central courtyard. And there's a roof terrace from which you can gaze on the Giralda. Bedrooms are regal affairs, every one different, from the smallest to the largest, the Yellow Room with its 'Juliet' balcony. All is immaculate, fabrics, furniture, lighting; beds are sumptuous and large. Yet there's a delightfully homely feel, thanks to books (*Who's Who!*), magazines and photos of the owner's famous forebears. The cool and elegant drawing room is a distinguished spot for a glass of sherry – from the family's Jerez bodega, of course – and breakfasts are perfectly English, served by two butlers in white gloves. Cristina is a sparkling manageress, and Seville lies outside the door.

rooms	6 twins/doubles.
price	€177–€275.
meals	Restaurants nearby.
closed	Rarely.
directions	Park in Aparcamento 'Cano y Cueto' at junc. of C/Cano y Cueto & Menendez Pelayo (next to Jardines de Murillo). Tell attendant staying at Casa No. 7. From here 5 minutes' walk to hotel.

	Gonzalo del Río y González-Gordon
tel	+34 954 221581
fax	+34 954 214527
email	info@casanumero7.com
web	www.casanumero7.com

Hotel

Map 15 Entry 227

Hotel Alminar

c/Alvarez Quintero 52, 41004 Sevilla

Hotel Alminar stands in the heart of graceful, characterful Seville. And because it gives onto a tiny pedetrianised street it is blissfully quiet – a treat in a city of 4am dust carts and midnight mopeds. Young staff take great pride in their work and could hardly be more helpful with tips and recommendations. This new renovation of a handsome townhouse opened in 2005 with a stylish sprinkling of rooms, the nicest being at the top; numbers 31 and 32 have their own small terraces and bird's-eye views of the Giralda. They are minimalist in style, with cream walls, clean lines, sober furniture in neutral shades, and fabulous bathrooms in immaculate mosaics. All feels spotless and well cared-for. There's no lounge, space at breakfast time is limited and breakfast is a modest buffet. But who cares where there are so many enticing bars so close to hand; it feels good to start the day with the locals over a *café con leche*. Soulful Seville lies at your feet. If you visit nothing else, visit the exquisite Moorish palace of Alcazar, and its oasis of a garden.

rooms	12: 10 twins/doubles, 2 singles.
price	€90–€155. Singles €60–€95. VAT included.
meals	Breakfast €6. VAT included. Restaurant close by.
closed	Rarely.
directions	Hotel 100m east of Cathedral. Best to park in c/Albareda car park next to Plaza Nueva, then walk.

	Francisco Naranjo
tel	+34 954 293913
mobile	+34 655 215261
fax	+34 954 121197
email	reservas@hotelalminar.com
web	www.hotelalminar.com

Hotel

Map 15 Entry 228

Casa el Marqués

c/En medio 40, 41950 Castilleja de la Cuesta, Sevilla

The dukes of Seville came to this area to escape the blistering heat. You might be tempted to do likewise; you'll still be a bus ride from Spain's sultriest city – birthplace of Carmen. There is a strong sense of being hidden away here, tucked behind the high wall of the Casa de Cultura, in the grounds of a former olive mill. This sweetly elegant holiday home belongs to Juan and Macarena, whose knowledge of Seville's palaces, museums and green spaces will set you on the right track. Via a small courtyard (your hosts live opposite) you enter a smartly furnished house, cool with white walls and tiled floors and stairs. Furniture is mostly antique (Macarena ran a shop in Seville). The two bedrooms, one with a balcony that overlooks the courtyard, are clean and uncluttered. Downstairs are the bathroom and living room, and chairs on the cobblestoned patio should so you can spill into the sun. There are flashes of colour from the pots outside. Those escaping the noise and dust of the city will be very happy here, and if you tire of self-catering, there are a number of restaurants a stroll away.

rooms	House for 2-4.
price	€70-€180. VAT included.
meals	Self-catering. Restaurants close by.
closed	Rarely.
directions	Sevilla-Huelva A-49. At km3, exit Castilleja. At 1st r'about, exit for Centro Comercial. Straight over 2nd r'about; at 3rd r'about, left. Just pass Telepizza right at sign 'Casa de Cultura'. Take 2nd right, house on left.

	Macarena Fernandez-Palacio & Juan Castro
mobile	+34 629 791188
fax	+34 954 165379
email	informacion@casaelmarques.com
web	www.casaelmarques.com

Self-catering

Map 14 Entry 229

Hacienda de San Rafael

Apdo. 28, Ctra. N-IV (km594), 41730 Las Cabezas de San Juan, Sevilla

The hacienda lies in glorious isolation amid the undulating farmlands of Seville's hinterland, half a mile of olive-lined drive leading to its sunny façade. Andalucía! The views are vast, golden with sunflowers in summer. You'll be greeted by one of San Rafael's staff with an iced drink — and will continue to be pampered at every turn. San Rafael has been in the brothers' family for nearly 150 years, and is lovelier than ever. Stunning bedrooms — split-level, stone-floored, with their own verandas and gorgeous bathrooms — give onto the exquisitely cobbled central patio, the inner sanctuary of any true cortijo. Geranium, jasmine and bougainvillea romp. In the gardens are three thatched casitas, beautifully furnished in a mix of country antique and modern, with a piece of terrace each and sharing an infinity pool. There are two elegant drawing rooms where oriental furnishings and prints collected on trips to the East blend with local pieces, and a thatched dining area in the garden for summer meals; the cooking is superb. There's even a little shop selling local blankets and Indian jewellery.

rooms	11 + 3: 11 twins/doubles, 3 casitas for 2.
price	€225. Casitas €480.
meals	Lunch from €25 à la carte. Dinner with wine, €55.
closed	15 November-15 March.
directions	From Sevilla south on N-IV, San Rafael is 1st turn on right-hand side after km594 marker, before Repsol petrol station.

	Anthony & Patrick Reid
tel	+34 955 872193
fax	+34 955 872201
email	info@haciendadesanrafael.com
web	www.haciendadesanrafael.com

Hotel

Map 20 Entry 230

Cortijo Alguaciles

Ctra. A-1828 km3.3, 41710 Utrera, Sevilla

Bed and breakfast in the rolling wheatlands of the Sevillian hinterland, where the only passing traffic is the tractor from the next village. Arrival is up a lovely palm-lined drive, then into a cobbled courtyard where beautiful whitewashed walls are offset by ferns, geraniums and jasmine. The housekeeper greets you and shows you the sprucely furnished bedrooms in the old grain stores, whose furniture and paintings form part of the collective memory of the Mencos family (who live in Madrid for most of the year). Our favourite is the massive Naranjo room whose swish bathroom is the size of a studio in London or Paris – but all are roomy, comfortable and full of original and interesting features. (And water is solar-heated.) No meals in the Cortijo, apart from a rudimentary breakfast, but for dinner there is a wonderfully authentic *venta* (roadside restaurant) a short drive away. The silence at night envelops you; after a day or two here you will feel closer to understanding the elusive andalucían character. This is great value, and an enchanting antithesis to chain hotels.

rooms	8 twins/doubles.
price	€53. Singles €40.
meals	Two restaurants nearby.
closed	1-15 August.
directions	N-IV Sevilla-Cádiz to Cabezas de San Juan. There, at crossroads left on A-371 for Villamartín; 6.5km; left again on A-8128 for Montellano. Farm on left after km3.3 marker.

	Maribel Gómez
mobile	+34 630 561529
fax	+34 915 641071
email	alguaciles@alguaciles.com
web	www.alguaciles.com

Hotel

Map 20 Entry 231

La Mejorana

c/Santa Clara 6, 11610 Grazalema, Cádiz

Push aside the carved wooden door and step into an apparently ancient, mountain village house – gleaming with polished tiles, dark rustic furniture and white walls. A shock, then, to discover La Mejorana, tucked into a quiet corner of Grazalema, is 20 years old. Its other trick is that its one-storey appearance opens up into three floors that tumble down the hillside to a jasmine-scented garden and swimming pool below. The guest rooms, and their neat, colourfully tiled bathrooms, are furnished, as is the rest of the house, in andalucían rustic style – with the cheerful addition of the modern art of Ana, one of the young and friendly owners. Beamed ceilings, tiled floors, shuttered windows, lacey bedcovers – there's a wholesome, uncluttered feel, while potted plants, decorative plates and checked cushions help create an individual atmosphere. Hope for a room with rooftop and mountain views! Breakfasts are taken in the glass-fronted gallery with more stunning vistas. An unpretentious but fetching place, close to Ronda and the wonderful walks of the Grazalema Natural Park.

rooms	5 twins/doubles.
price	€50. VAT included.
meals	Restaurants in village.
closed	Rarely.
directions	In main square right up c/de las Piedras; at fountain, right, then right again; park. Signed.

	Andrés Sánchez & Ana Vázquez
tel	+34 956 132327
mobile	+34 649 613272
email	info@lamejorana.net
web	www.lamejorana.net

B&B

Map 20 Entry 232

Hotel La Antigua Estacion
Antigua Estacion s/n, 11650 Villamartin, Cádiz

It never did become an *estación*. The project to link Arcos with Málaga by rail was put on hold during the second Republic, then abandoned after the Civil War. Thomas fell for the faded elegance of this Twenties' building when he came to visit the air strip next door; months later he opened it as a hotel. The delightfully jaunty La Antigua Estacion stands at the start of the scenic 'Green Line', bands of ochre highlighting its white and sculpted façade. These colours are repeated in a light and lofty sitting room, and again in first-floor bedrooms. They vary in layout and size, the nicest being those with balconies and views across the farmland. Air conditioning is a bonus during scorching summers, bathrooms are good and the restrained décor perfectly suits the rural setting. A simple, buffet-style breakfast is the only meal on offer, served outdoors when weather permits. But there is an exceptionally good value restaurant just one kilometre away: pass grazing horses and errant chickens and you arrive in the sleepy town of Villamartín and the Restaurant El Anafe.

rooms	15: 6 twins/doubles, 6 family, 2 singles, 1 suite.
price	€80. Family €100. Singles €60. Suite €100.
meals	Breakfast €6. Restaurant 1km.
closed	Rarely.
directions	From Jerez towards Arcos; bypass Arcos and continue towards Ronda. 2km before Villamartin left towards Las Cabezas de San Juan, then 1st right at sign 'Hotel/Aerodromo'; right at sign for hotel.

	Thomas Huster
mobile	+34 617 560351
fax	+34 956 730702
email	thuster@antiguaestacion.com
web	www.antiguaestacion.com

Hotel

Map 20 Entry 233

Cortijo Barranco

Ctra. Arcos-El Bosque (A-372) km5.7, 11630 Arcos de la Frontera, Cádiz

Grand Barranco stands alone, high on a hillside, across from the 'white' town of Arcos de la Frontera. Getting here is quite an adventure, at the end of a dusty one-mile track. This is every inch the classic olive-mill-cortijo, the private quarters and former stables wrapped around a central courtyard; they still make their own olive oil. The guest rooms and apartments are refreshingly sober with their terracotta floors, wrought-iron bedsteads, heavy linen curtains and hand-crocheted bedspreads; the most private of the apartments is charmingly authentic, with a big open-plan kitchen/living area. The sitting room is enormous with space for a billiard table, the dining room is lofty, with long tables and an open hearth at one end, and the huge, vine-clambered patio is a cool haven on hot days. A beautiful pool overlooking the Sierra de Grazalema completes the picture. Stroll out after dinner and abandon yourself to the beauty of the sun dipping behind the hills… later, let the owls hoot you to sleep. *The above address is for correspondence only.*

rooms	14 + 5: 14 twins/doubles. 5 apartments for 4.
price	€53-€83. Singles €43-€63. Apartments €80-€185.
meals	Lunch & dinner €21-€25, on request.
closed	Rarely.
directions	From Arcos de la Frontera, A-372 El Bosque. After 5.7km marker, at end of long straight section, left at sign onto paved track; 2km to farm.

Maria José & Genaro Gil Amián

tel	+34 956 231402
fax	+34 956 231209
email	reservas@cortijobarranco.com
web	www.cortijobarranco.com

Guest house

Map 20 Entry 234

Casa Margarita

Lista de Correos, 11630 Arcos de la Frontera, Cádiz

The house on the hill, one of a group of typically Spanish holiday homes, lies in the last reaches of the rolling Jérez country, its landscape gentler than the jagged limestone of the Grazalema Natural Park beyond. Laze by the pool surrounded by southern lushery, splashes of bourganvillea and dramatic views, the only sound that of the rooster crowing and the inevitable distant barking dog. The main terrace has Arcos views: spectacular at night when the churches are lit up. Guest bedrooms, set among the pine and citrus trees, have patios, simple shower rooms, breakfast in the fridge, orchard fruits on the table and a rustic, Spanish-Moroccan décor. The well-equipped apartment, in an independent part of the main house, has air-conditioning for summer and a woodburner for winter. Life at Casa Margarita is lived by Anne, her daughter Rebecca, horse Baltasar and two friendly dogs in a laid-back manner: expect to unwind. Anne also has lots of info on walks. The house takes its name from the healer who once lived here – these alternative doctors are still a part of life in the sierras of the south.

rooms	2 + 1: 1 twin, 1 double. 1 apartment for 2-4.
price	€45. Singles €30-€45.
meals	Restaurants 3km.
closed	21 December-6 January.
directions	From Arcos, A-372 towards El Bosque. Pass lake & petrol station; at km 5.5 marker, right for Girasol onto old road; 300m to 2nd Girasol sign; right; 5th on left. Name by gate.

	Anne Lacy
tel	+34 956 023070
mobile	+34 600 076273
email	annelacyarcos@hotmail.com

B&B & Self-catering

Map 20 Entry 235

Hacienda El Santiscal

Avda. El Santiscal 129, (Lago de Arcos), 11630 Arcos de la Frontera, Cádiz

This grand old cortijo overlooking the lake is a short drive from Arcos in a peaceful place where pigeons coo. Converted from a forgotten family home into an elegant but simple hotel, the building is Andalucian to the core: an austere whitewashed façade, a grand portal and the blissful peace and cool of that inner sanctum, the courtyard (pleasantly furnished with wicker chairs). The bedrooms lead off the patio, and almost all have magnificent long views across the estate. All are dark, classic Andaluz, with traditional beds and modern soft furnishings added. Bathrooms are good, with marble or tiles, and woodwork in Andaluz green. The suites are really special, and worth splashing out on. Children will enjoy the circular pool in the lawn. Mouthwatering aromas waft from the kitchen; dine in on classical Andalucian dishes (grilled meats, quail soufflé), or – when weddings are in the offing – head up to wonderful old Arcos where there are loads of tapas bars and a few good restaurants. Wonderful. *A Rusticae hotel.*

rooms	12: 7 twins/doubles, 5 suites.
price	€65-€99. Suites €84-€137.
meals	Breakfast €10. Lunch & dinner €25.
closed	Rarely.
directions	From Arcos A-372 for El Bosque; 1km after crossing bridge, left into Urbanización Dominio El Santiscal; follow signs (carefully) to El Santiscal.

Francisca 'Paqui' Gallardo

tel	+34 956 708313
mobile	+34 616 309310
fax	+34 956 708268
email	reservas@santiscal.com
web	www.santiscal.com

Hotel

Map 20 Entry 236

La Casa Grande

c/Maldonado 10, 11630 Arcos de la Frontera, Cádiz

La Casa Grande nudges right up to the very edge of whitewashed Arcos – a spectacular site. At night, from its terrace-of-terraces, you gaze onto two floodlit churches and mile after mile of surrounding plain. The house is almost 300 years old and many of the original features have survived to tell the tale. In true Andaluz style, a central, colonnaded, plant-filled patio is the axis around which the house turns; vaulted rooms lead off to all sides, nooks and crannies appear at every turn. A cosy lounge doubles up as a library with thousands of books – some of them written by delightful, multi-talented Elena. The decoration of the house reflects her eclectic, bohemian taste: tiles from Morocco, blankets from Grazalema, a Deco writing table topped by a designer lamp, a wickerwork chair. Stylish yet homely – and everywhere, the smell of woodsmoke and coffee. Guest bedrooms (two below street level but with balconies and views) are full of antiquey bits and pieces, with double glazing to protect you from night-time hum. Then wake to breakfast on that unforgettable terrace. *A Rusticae hotel.*

rooms	8: 6 twins/doubles, 2 suites for 4.
price	€65–€85. Singles €55 (low season only). Suites €77–€148.
meals	Breakfast €80.
closed	7 January–7 February.
directions	In Arcos follow signs to Parador. Park in square in front of Parador & walk to end of c/Escribano (just to left of Parador). Right, past Hotel El Convento, then left. House on right.

	Elena Posa Farrás
tel	+34 956 703930
fax	+34 956 717095
email	info@lacasagrande.net
web	www.lacasagrande.net

Hotel

Map 20 Entry 237

Casa Viña de Alcántara

Autovía A-382, salida 3, 11400 Jerez de la Frontera, Cádiz

Senor Gonzalo del Rio y Gonzalez-Gordón is linked to the Gordon-Byass sherry dynasty – which means you'll be served a very decent glass of fino before dinner. A fervent anglophile, Gonzalo (who divides his time between the family estate and his hotel in Seville) is a charming man with a gift for gracious living. The 1890 hunting lodge, built by great-grandfather, has an instant allure, and is equally inviting within. First it was gutted, then subtly and exquisitely restored: polished limestone downstairs, oak parquet up. Bedrooms have refined elegance *and* warmth, thanks to fine family furniture and Gonzalo's mother's paintings. All is perfection, from taps to towels, and the bathrooms are some of the best in this book. Breakfast – English, with southern touches – is served by a white-gloved butler, as is dinner, simple and delicious. The Casa is fringed by a small forest of palms and pines, and surrounded by the vine-braided hills that nurture the palomino grape. Jerez, an architectural gem, is two minutes by car, thanks to the motorway (just a gentle hum). The beaches are not much further.

rooms	9 twins/doubles.
price	€150-€300.
meals	Dinner on request.
closed	Rarely.
directions	From Sevilla A-4 to Jerez. 1st exit for Jerez, follow signs Arcos & Circuito de Velocidad. Pass 'Meson La Cueva'. On right after 500m surrounded by trees.

	Gonzalo del Río y Gonzalez Gordon
tel	+34 956 393010
fax	+34 956 393011
email	info@vinadealcantara.com
web	www.vinadealcantara.com

Hotel

Map 19 Entry 238

Casa de Medina

c/Tintoreros 5, 11170 Medina Sidonia, Cádiz

House-hunting in the town's oldest quarter, the Bistons stumbled upon an ancient dwelling, fell in love with it and, 24 hours later, bought the place. A year of renovation followed and now they have the guest house of their dreams. The old building wraps itself around an inner patio where wafer-bricked columns support drop arches, and potted palms and jasmine add splashes of green to floors of sandy marble. You could breakfast here, or in the dining room to one side, but the temptation would be to grab a tray, clamber up to the roof terrace and drink in the view – of Cádiz, the Atlantic and, on a clear day, the mountains of the Moroccan Rif. The decked plunge pool above the terrace gives blessed relief in summer. Bedrooms are fresh, inviting and hugely comfortable: white walls, marble floors, excellent linen, feather pillows, Casablanca fans to keep the heat at bay. There are several lively tapas bars around the main square, a short stroll away: easy to make new friends. Then back up the hill to Gary and Kirsty, your good-humoured hosts who look after you brilliantly.

rooms	4 twins/doubles.
price	€60-€100. VAT inc.
meals	Occasional dinner with wine, €25. Restaurants nearby.
closed	Rarely.
directions	From Jerez A-381 for Los Barrios; exit 24 Medina Sidonia. Signs into town & 'Oficina de Turismo'. Park on square; walk down hill thro' alleyway to left of tourist office; 1st left then 1st right onto c/Tintoreros. Or call hotel for pick-up.

	Gary & Kirsty Biston
tel/fax	+34 956 410069
mobile	+34 646 489069
email	gary@casademedina.com
web	www.casademedina.com

B&B

Map 20 Entry 239

Hotel Sindhura

Patria s/n/, La Muela, 11150 Vejer de la Frontera, Cádiz

The position couldn't be finer. In the hills, ten minutes from the charming coastal town of Vejer de la Frontera, the hotel has amazing views across the Costa de la Luz and Cape Trafalgar. In defiance of the isolated and treeless surroundings (we are in classic bull-rearing territory here), the owners are enthusiastically landscaping the site with Mediterranean plants and shrubs. A buddha welcomes you to their serene hotel-retreat, and their styling is oriental and soothing. White walls run into burgundy washes and there are a series of comfortable wicker sofas in jasmine-scented internal patios; so, plenty of space to sit quietly and unwind. The restaurant, in a separate building, does buffet breakfasts and a choice of delicious Spanish dishes at lunch and dinner. The prices are reasonable for the area and your hosts, a Spaniard brought up in England and her psychologist husband, are wonderfully welcoming. Bedrooms, some spacious, some less so, are simply and pleasingly furnished. Go for one with a balcony and a spectacular view.

rooms	15: 13 twins/doubles, 2 suites.
price	€60–€95. Suites €75–€180.
meals	Lunch & dinner €20.
closed	15 December–1 February.
directions	From Málaga on N-340; at x-roads continue for La Muela, then for Patría; follow signs to hotel.

	Ana María García Varra
tel	+34 956 448568
mobile	+34 956 448550
email	reservas@hotelsindhura.com
web	www.hotelsindhura.com

Hotel

Map 19 Entry 240

Hotel La Breña

Avda. de Trafalgar 4, 11159 Caños de Meca, Cádiz

What immediately strikes you about this place is the friendly, light-hearted mood. The staff are happy and helpful and genuinely enjoy what they do. It's a modern, beach-side hotel which only opened recently, although it has been a successful restaurant for five years. And the food is fresh and very good – try the seafood carpaccio and the luscious homemade puddings. Local wines as well. If you eat out on the wide, bamboo-covered terrace, you'll have the additional pleasure of an uninterrupted view across the sea to Morocco – the hotel is on the very edge of the Atlantic. Inside is an enormous dining/reception area with acres of honey-coloured marble and lots of interesting modern art. The bedrooms are all big, too, and pleasingly decorated in earthy colours. Some have their own private terraces and all have excellent bathrooms. The beaches are good – if you're into skinny dipping, you'll appreciate the nudist beach to the left of the hotel – and a Parque Natural runs all the way from here to Barbate, so there's no difficulty in finding somewhere attractive to walk. A great place to unwind.

rooms	7 twins/doubles.
price	€60–€110. VAT included.
meals	Breakfast €5. Lunch & dinner €19. VAT included.
closed	November–February.
directions	From Cádiz N-340 for Tarifa. At km35, right for Vejer; at r'bout, right for Caños. Here, through village parallel to sea; signed at far end of Caños.

	José Manuel Morillo
tel/fax	+34 956 437368
mobile	+34 627 424343
email	info@hotelbrena.com
web	www.hotelbrena.com

Hotel

Map 20 Entry 241

Casas Karen

La Fuente del Madroño 6, Los Caños de Meca, 11159 Vejer de la Frontera, Cádiz

Recline among the broom and mimosa in your Mexican hammock on one of the last wild coastlines of southern Spain. Casas Karen feels like a mini village hidden in a wild expanse of garden between the pinewoods and the beach, the sort of place to meet friends for life. All thanks to musical, artistic Karen, the life and soul of the place. While the overall feel is distinctly rustic, all the houses have their own privacy and are surprisingly comfortable, with bright flowing fabrics and stylish local touches – and local here means andalucían and Moroccan. Many have open fires for winter and the straw houses are particularly light and airy. The place attracts an interesting clientele (artists, lawyers, surfers) and the atmosphere is totally laid back – like Caños itself, a celebrated hang-out for hippies until its 'discovery' two decades ago. There's massage, reiki, tai chi, yoga, and a life coaching session on the house; few places to stay are greener than Casas Karen. It's perfect for individuals, families and groups, and if self-catering seems daunting, a friend of Karen's can come and cook for you.

rooms	1 + 8: 1 double. 4 houses & studios for 2-4; 2 houses for 4-6; 2 thatched houses for 2-4.
price	€40-€80. Houses €60-€150. Studio €45-€118.
meals	Self-catering.
closed	Never.
directions	Directions on booking.

	Karen Abrahams
tel	+34 956 437067
fax	+34 956 437233
email	info@casaskaren.com
web	www.casaskaren.com

Guest house

Map 20 Entry 242

CasaCinco

c/Sancho IV el Bravo 5, 11150 Vejer de la Frontera, Cádiz

Fascinating Vejer de la Frontera is perched on a hilltop, its winding, cobbled streets brimful of shops, restaurants and cafés. CasaCinco stands in its middle, a townhouse wrapped around a small patio, with a beautiful arch of wafer brick. The tiled floors and beamed ceilings add to the traditional feel, but what makes this place special is your hosts' exquisite feel for contemporary design. Peaceful bedrooms fuse andalucían pieces with English antiques, the functional with the frivolous, and every room is unique… grey-blue ceiling beams here, a metal Deco bed there, an orange glass bowl in a rose-red alcove. Delightful bath and shower rooms, tiled, light and clean, are en suite and open plan (no doors). Colette and Glen are a friendly pair who serve great breakfasts – accompanied by flamenco music, if you so desire – and like to get everything right. The living room is small, but its books, magazines, woodburner and leather sofas make it intimate. A tiny door leads to a roof terrace with views that sail over the rooftops to the beach at Zahara and the mountains of Morocco. Superb.

rooms	5 doubles.
price	€75-€120.
meals	Restaurant 1-minute walk.
closed	Rarely.
directions	From Algecíras N-340; exit at km36 for Vejer. On uphill; follow signs for 'Ayuntamiento' to Plaza de España. Park; through arch, right; CasaCinco on left.

	Colette & Glen Murphy
mobile	+34 626 481301
fax	+34 956 451125
email	info@hotelcasacinco.com
web	www.hotelcasacinco.com

B&B

Map 20 Entry 243

Tripería no.1

Plaza de España 16, 11150 Vejer de la Frontera, Cádiz

The diminuitive Plaza de España is the neural centre of old Vejer. Its swaying palms, beautiful ceramic-tiled fountain and lively bars and restaurants can't fail to put you in that 'I'm on holiday' mood. Tripería, just a few steps down from the square, is, in essence, an annexe to the neighbouring Casa de Califa (see entry 245, right). An unassuming door on the street takes you through to the inner patio and the large swimming pool, a bonus in the sweltering centre of town. Bedrooms are big on space and have been decorated in the same Andaluz/Moroccan style as that of the sister hotel, with the same excellent mix of eastern artefacts and contemporary art. It all feels light, airy, clean and welcoming. From the private terrace of your room you can feast on a vista that sweeps across the rooftops to the distant pines of the Natural Park of Las Marismas, cutting a delicious green swathe between Vejer and the ocean. There is a basement kitchen where you can prepare your own breakfast – but it's much nicer to eat next door in Casa de Califa's leafy, lovely courtyard restaurant.

rooms	6: 1 double, 2 twins, 2 suites, 1 family suite for 4.
price	€69–€103. Suites €84–€121. Family suite €126–€158.
meals	Breakfast €6. Meals served next door, at Casa del Califa.
closed	For 3 weeks after Epiphany.
directions	From Algeciras E-15/N-340 towards Cádiz. Take 2nd turnng left for Vejer at km36. Up hill then follow signs for 'Ayuntamiento' to Plaza de España. Casa del Califa on left.

	James Stuart
tel	+34 956 447730
mobile	+34 956 451625
fax	+34 956 451625
email	reservas@lacasadelcalifa.com
web	www.grupocalifa.com/triperia

Hotel

Map 20 Entry 244

Hotel La Casa del Califa

Plaza de España 16, 11150 Vejer de la Frontera, Cádiz

No fewer than five village houses are woven into the fabric of La Casa del Califa, and their gradual union has created a seductively labyrinthine structure: the antithesis of the made-to-measure hotel. Parts of the building are ancient and have seen occupation since the time of the Moors, so corridors and rooms follow the twists and turns of the building, and bedrooms have oodles of character. There are vaulted ceilings and beamed ones, some private terraces, and some original, geometric-tile floors. Expect brightly coloured cushions and bedspreads, interesting lamps, contemporary paintings and a stylish debt to all things Moroccan. Best of all is the courtyard bar and restaurant with its *A Thousand and One Nights* buzz, thrilling on spring nights when the lamps are lit and the citrus trees are in blossom. The menu offers a delightful change from the look-alike menus of so many of andalucía's restaurants: interesting salads, Islamic flavours and an interesting selection of wines. Califa is one of the most seductive of Spain's small hotels; it shouts 'romantic break for two'!

rooms	18: 15 twins/doubles, 1 single, 2 suites.
price	€69-€103. Single €53. Suites €120.
meals	Lunch & dinner €25-€30.
closed	For 3 weeks after Epiphany.
directions	From Algeciras E-15/N-340 towards Cádiz. Take 2nd turning left for Vejer at km36. Up hill, then signs for 'Ayuntamiento' to Plaza de España. Casa del Califa on left.

	James Stuart
tel	+34 956 447730
fax	+34 956 451625
email	reservas@lacasadelcalifa.com
web	www.lacasadelcalifa.com

Hotel

Map 20 Entry 245

Hotel Restaurante Antonio

Bahía de la Plata, Atlanterra km1, 11393 Zahara de los Atunes, Cádiz

A short walk to the laid-back fishing village of Zahara, with gardens that lead straight onto one of the least spoilt beaches on the southern coast, these sister hotels share a stunning spot. We prefer Antonio Mota's first, smaller, family-run affair, popular with the Spanish. The newer venture is modern and four-star. Both are southern in spirit, with some uninspiring prints on the walls (romantic swans, bullfights), but you're here for the site, which is superb. Choose dinner in the 'old' restaurant: lobster fresh from the tank and excellent local wine; breakfasts display eggs, fruit, cheeses and hams. Bedrooms in the new hotel are a good size and come with balconies, somewhat basic furnishings and air con; ask for a view of the sea. Older rooms have more character; go for a terrace room overlooking the palms and the breakers crashing 100 metres away. There's a lovely pool, a beach bar too, and horses for hire – ride along the beach to Bolonia, and find Roman ruins and restaurants. Note that this stretch of coastline is unlikely to remain unspoilt for ever!

rooms	Old hotel: 22 doubles, 3 singles, 5 suites. New hotel: 17 doubles, 16 family, 2 suites, 1 wheelchair room.
price	€61–€125. Singles €36–€64. Suite €74–€125.
meals	Lunch & dinner €19. A la carte from €30.
closed	November–January.
directions	Algecíras E-5/N-340 to Cádiz. 25km after Tarifa left to Barbate; Zahara on left after 10km. Signed.

	Antonio Mota Pacheco
tel	+34 956 439141
mobile	+34 649 843018
fax	+34 956 439135
email	info@antoniohoteles.com
web	www.antoniohoteles.com

Hotel

Map 20 Entry 246

Dar Cilla Guesthouse

c/Cilla, 11380 Tarifa, Cádiz

As you laze on the roof terrace you gaze on Morocco: Zoe's spiritual home. With energy and flair, English Zoe has created a corner of Morocco in Tarifa. Handsome, 100-year-old Dar Cilla (once a ruin!) was built against the 12th-century town wall and wraps itself round not one but two patios. These studios and apartments are truly lovely: wafer bricks, sienna-washed plaster, polished stucco, illuminated nooks and crannies and kilims on terracotta; the finishes are superb. You get bedrooms and dining/sitting areas, shower rooms and kitchenettes in the fashionable – but in this case, low-key – Arab-Andaluz style, dotted with decorative features and fabrics that Zoe has picked up on her trips to Tangier. No lounge, but that amazing roof terrace, cosy and convivial with loungers, fridge for drinks and shower. Da Cilla's Café Gusto, a breakfast café managed by Zoe's daughter-in-law, is open June to August. Surf the golden beaches of the wind- and kite-surfing capital of Europe, gallop in pine forests, dip into the many bars of the old, labyrinthine town – or do that ferry hop to Morocco. *Minimum stay three nights.*

rooms	7 studios/apartments for 1-5.
price	Single studio €30-€40. Apt for 2, €65-€130. Apt for 4-5, €170-€195. VAT incl. Reduced rates Oct-March.
meals	Breakfast €3-€5. Restaurants 5-10min walk.
closed	Rarely.
directions	N-340 Algecíras-Cádiz; 1st exit for Tarifa. Dar Cilla 1km, on left.

	Zoe Ouwehand-Reid & Martina de Rijke
mobile	+34 653 467025
fax	+34 956 627011
email	info@darcilla.com
web	www.darcilla.com

Guest house

Map 20 Entry 247

Huerta Las Terrazas

c/Sierra de Lucena, Pelayo, 11390 Algecíras, Cádiz

Climb up through honeysuckle, mimosa, oleander, cypresses and shady corners, and reach the cool, blue pool. Turn and gaze southwards to the exotic outlines of the Moroccan mountains. The three-acre terraced gardens, dizzy with scent and colour, are the draw of this white casa, teetering below the foothills of the Sierra de Ojen, on the edge of the Alcornocales Natural Park. In the bedrooms – choose La Casita for a self-contained hideaway – the eager young English owners have blended cool modern design with traditional furnishings. Seagrass matting, white walls and soft bed linen mixes with dark wooden furniture, rich cushions and hints of Morocco. The sitting and dining rooms are emboldened with warmer colours, lamps and candles. Breakfasts are from their organic fruit and veg garden while their own spring feeds the pool as well as the taps. But don't forget this is the countryside: neighbouring farm dogs are not always quiet. Swim, surf or ride on the beaches, explore cosmopolitan Tarifa, enjoy one of Amy's expert massages or birdwatch; the house is under the African migration route. *Minimum stay two nights.*

rooms	3 + 1: 3 doubles twins/doubles. 1 cottage for 2.
price	€85–€110. Cottage €600–€750 per week.
meals	Light lunch €12. Dinner €30.
closed	Rarely.
directions	From Algecíras, N-340 for Cádiz. Pass km97, under foot bridge; next right, past restaurant Las Piedras. On uphill; 2nd left at fork. Follow road up to green gate.

	Alistair & Amy Farrington
tel	+34 956 679041
email	alandamy@huertalasterrazas.com
web	www.huertalasterrazas.com

B&B & Self-catering

Map 20 Entry 248

Cortijo La Hoya

Ctra. N-340 Tarifa-Algecíras, km96, 11280 Tarifa, Cádiz

Two miles of cork tree-fringed track lead to the farm and Fabiola's casitas, tucked among the eucalyptus and cork oaks in an exquisite corner of the Alcornocales Park. Their chicken-shed origins are hard to credit. Charming, intelligent Fabiola has great decorative nous, her colour schemes inspired by the earthy washes of the Mahgreb, her patterned fabrics gorgeous. Kitchenettes are well-equipped and there's central heating for winter. The wonderful garden, full of intimate corners, all created by Fabiola, leads to a sensationally situated 'infinity' pool where the water of the pool merges with that of the Straits of Gibraltar – above which rises the Moroccan Rif, its colours changing as subtly as the iridescent coastal light. Fabiola is mindful of guests' privacy, but, should you ask, will tell you all you need to know. Do note her recommendations about where to eat in Tarifa. This ancient town pulsates on a Friday and Saturday night, and its white sand beaches are superb. And then there are the dogs… four of them, of all shapes and sizes, ever ready with a wag. *Minimum stay two to seven nights.*

rooms	3 casitas for 2-3.
price	€90-€115. VAT included.
meals	Self-catering. €30 hamper on request. Restaurants in Pelayo, 3km.
closed	Rarely.
directions	From Algecíras, N-340 for Cádiz. Through Pelayo; at youth hostel, U-turn & head back. 100m past km96 marker, sharp right. Follow signs for 3km.

	Fabiola Dominguez Larios
tel	+34 956 236070
mobile	+34 609 520227
email	cortijohoya@hotmail.com
web	www.cortijolahoya.com

Monte de la Torre

Apdo. de Correos 66, 11370 Los Barrios, Cádiz

Puzzling to come across this Edwardian building in the very south of Spain
– it was built by the British when they were pushing the railway through the
mountains to Ronda. This commingling of northern architecture and southern
vegetation and climate is as seductive as it is unexpected. The house stands alone
on a hill, surrounded by resplendent gardens; bask in the shade of the trees,
gaze onto the Bay of Gibraltar, dip into the pool. Quentin Agnew's family has
farmed this estate for generations. The drawing room is panelled, the dining
room elegant, there are masses of books, family portraits, a grandfather clock,
dogs... this is a home, not a hotel. The bedrooms (reached by a grand staircase)
are high-ceilinged, decorated with family heirlooms and have period bathrooms –
a festival of tubs and taps. Each is different, all lovely in an old-fashioned way.
The self-catering apartments are in the former servants' quarters, and the garden
is a birdwatcher's paradise. Sue and Quentin are charming hosts, and there are
many good restaurants within easy reach. *Children welcome in apartments.*

rooms	3 + 2: 3 twins/doubles. 2 apartments for 5.
price	€110-€130. Apts €550-€850. VAT incl.
meals	Restaurants & tapas bars nearby.
closed	15 December-15 January; July/Aug.
directions	Málaga A-7/E-15 Algeciras. Exit 110B onto A-381 towards Jerez; exit 85 into Los Barrios. 2nd left at 3 r'abouts onto C-231 Algeciras. At km2.8 marker, right to house.

	Sue & Quentin Agnew Larios
tel	+34 956 660000
mobile	+34 677 591311
fax	+34 956 634863
email	montedelatorre@gmail.com
web	www.andalucia.com/montedelatorre

B&B & Self-catering

Map 20 Entry 250

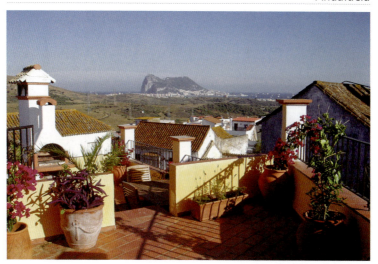

Casa Julio Verne

Plaza de las Viudas 9, 11360 San Roque, Cádiz

Cross the sleepy square to Rose and Sagi's guest house, unmissable with its smartly painted exterior and tumbling geraniums. Inside is stylishness at every turn. The living area has luscious linen sofas, Moroccan lamps, books and games, while against a neutral palette are vivid flashes of colour – a bowl of scarlet gerberas on the breakfast table, a magenta bougainvillea bloom gracing white bathroom towels. All the bedrooms are lovely here, particularly the capacious, light-filled Nautilus suite with its double jacuzzi, soaring beams and woodburner. Down in the courtyard are a small pool and a hammam; up on the roof terrace, views that stretch all the way to Africa on a clear day, the great rock of Gibraltar in between... a stunning spot to sit and relax over a drink from the honesty bar. Your young hosts are great fun, and they'll tell you all about the area over a breakfast spread (Sagi's lavender-infused orange juice is inspired). But why is it called Casa Julio Verne and why are there copies of the great man's books in 'Nautilus', 'Nemo' and 'Lidenbrock'? Book in and find out! *Min. two nights July-Sept.*

rooms	3: 1 twin/double, 2 suites. Whole house available to rent.
price	€85-€90. Suites €90-€115.
meals	Self-catering option. Restaurants nearby.
closed	Rarely.
directions	Málaga A-7/E-15; exit 119 San Roque/Gibraltar. Right at bottom of slip road; right again after bus stop. Over r'bout; 1st first left to top of hill & Plaza Espartero. On left in c/Sagasta.

	Rose Favell & Sagi Ifrach
tel	+34 956 782623
mobile	+34 655 699841
email	enquiries@casajulioverne.com
web	www.casajulioverne.com

B&B & Self-catering

Map 20 Entry 251

Hostal El Anón

c/Consuelo 34-40, 11330 Jimena de la Frontera, Cádiz

Five wonderful old townhouses have been amassed into a catacomb of beamed and low-ceilinged rooms on a myriad of levels and intimate terraces: such a delicious little piece of authentic Spain. Suzanna has lived here for years, knows the people and country like her own, and always has time for tea and a chat. She will delight in disentangling the rich web of local history for you, and can organise riding, painting, birdwatching, walking and flora-spotting expeditions. The countryside has treasures galore: see it from the little rooftop swimming pool – salty water rather than chlorine – with views over the tile-topped village all the way to Gibraltar. Enjoy the cool peace of the arched main courtyard and the exotic banana and custard-fruit trees, rejoice in the furnishings collected over the years (wall-hangings, paintings, sculptural bits and pieces), then dine on delicious spare ribs or tapas on the verdant terrace or in the bustling restaurant/bar. Rooms – and plumbing! – are basic; come for quantities of Spanishness in an unusually laid-back place.

rooms	14: 11 twins/doubles, 1 single, 2 suites.
price	€60. Single €37. Suite €70. VAT included.
meals	Lunch & dinner from €25 à la carte. VAT included.
closed	2 weeks June; 2 weeks November.
directions	From Málaga, N-340 Algecíras; at r'bout in Pueblo Nuevo de Guadiaro, right for Jimena. In village centre, left by taxi rank; 2nd right. Parking tricky.

Gabriel Delgado & Suzanna Odell

tel	+34 956 640113
mobile	+34 649 954775
fax	+34 956 641110
email	reservas@elanon.net
web	www.andalucia.com/jimena/hostalanon

Guest house

Map 20 Entry 252

Cortijo El Papudo

11340 San Martín del Tesorillo, Málaga

An authentic old farmstead in the fertile valley of the Guadiaro river; there's a special feel here. And fruit trees flourish, thanks to the exceptional climate: everything from citrus to custard fruit, pomegranates to avocados. More recently a number of plant nurseries have sprung up and the Harveys have set up one of their own – an obligatory shop-over for the coastal ex-pat community. They are, of course, highly knowledgeable about all things botanical. Their own garden is an exotic, multi-coloured ode to southern flora, and laps up to the high, solid old cortijo whose rooms are simple and pleasing. The original wooden ceilings give character to the bedrooms, which have Casablanca-style ceiling fans for the summer, and central heating for the colder months. All have views of the garden and across the farm to the surrounding orange groves; one has a balcony overlooking the flower-fringed pool. The rustic breakfast room has a handsome flagged floor and a woodburner, and there's an honesty bar here. The beach is a 15-minute drive.

rooms	11 twins/doubles.
price	€70. Singles €46. VAT included.
meals	Restaurants 2km.
closed	Rarely.
directions	A-7 Málaga-Cádiz; exit 133 Sotogrande/Torreguadiaro on A-2102 towards San Martín del Tesorillo. Drive through Secadero, turn right just before bridge. 1.5km; then up hill for 50m; sharp left for hotel.

	Michael & Vivien Harvey
tel/fax	+34 952 854018
email	papudo@mercuryin.es
web	www.andalucia.com/gardens/papudo

Andalucia Yurts

Rio Genal 24, La Huerta, Gaucín, Málaga

Few places sit in such natural seclusion – astonishing that you are only ten miles from the Costa del Sol. Sited by a river so clean you can drink from it (with otters and wild boar as fellow guests), the place is engulfed by cork and pine plantations to a backdrop of sheer soaring peaks. With only one building in sight – the castle in Gaucín – it is the sort of wild escape nature lovers crave. The B&B centres on a pretty cottage, sensitively restored using old wooden beams and sustainable materials. Its nerve centre is the veranda, which is covered in long concrete benches, comfortably decked in exotic Indian fabrics. Your bedrooms are under canvas, but don't worry – these yurts are spacious, airy and utterly private, tucked away in different corners of the smallholding. The Hoggs – tree surgeons by trade – are engaging people, and passionate about the environment. Fellow guests may include yogis, birdwatchers and writers. As well as being an organic farm, water is pumped from the river and solar panels are de rigeur. The African Bush comes to Spain – hurrah!

rooms	1 + 2: 1 double. 2 yurts for 2.
price	€60. VAT included.
meals	Dinner €15.
closed	Rarely.
directions	From E-15 exit 142 onto A-377 for Gaucín/Casares. At km21 turn right after bridge. Follow track for 3.8km; get to gate and the second right.

	Penny Hogg
mobile	+34 686 888409
email	hoggs@vsatmail.com
web	www.andaluciayurts.com

B&B & Self-catering

Map 20 Entry 254

Hotel Casablanca

c/Teodoro de Molina 12, 29480 Gaucín, Málaga

Gaucín is one of Andalucía's most spectacular mountain villages. Its labyrinthine, car-challenged streets huddle against a hillside beneath a Moorish castle; eagles wheel overhead, the views stretch for ever. The Casablanca's restoration is majestic; pass through enormous wooden doors, beneath lofty inlaid ceilings, to emerge in the bar. Beyond is a glory of a garden, giving you both sanctuary and breathtaking views. Palms, magnolia and jacaranda lend colour and shade, a fountain murmurs beside the pool, sun-dappled terraces on varying levels look out across rooftops to the castle and the mountains of Morocco, and the sunsets are sensational. The Van Gogh and Goya bedrooms in the old house are perhaps the finest, but every room is special: polished parquet or terracotta floors, warm colours, huge beds, heavenly bathrooms (three with shower only). All bar two have private terraces – and those are studios a step from the pool. Dine in at least once; the new chef is working wonders in the kitchen, and his food follows the seasons. The owners live in Britain but regularly drop by to check all is perfect.

rooms	9 twins/doubles.
price	€140–€200. VAT included.
meals	Lunch & dinner from €25 à la carte. VAT included.
closed	November–February.
directions	From Málaga N-340 for Algecíras. After Estepona, right on MA-539 via Manilva to Gaucín (not Casares). In centre, find street of San Sebastián church; follow one-way system right for Ronda; on left, signed.

	Ian & Lisa Clark
tel	+34 952 151019
fax	+34 952 151495
email	enquiries@casablanca-gaucin.com
web	www.casablanca-gaucin.com

Hotel

Map 20 Entry 255

El Nobo

Aptdo. 46, Camino de Gibraltar, 29480 Gaucín, Málaga

The gardens are tremendous, showing clearly what a dozen years in Spain can produce. And the organically shaped pool – its views stretching to Gibraltar and the mountains of Africa – is magical. Gaucín has long been popular among the more adventurous of the ex-pat community and the Von Meisters live in one of the area's most charming homes. At the end of a dusty old track, anchored to a rocky hillside… a Moorish courtyard, a Spanish villa, two stone cottages, one fountain and several sun terraces; impossible to believe that a shepherd's hut once stood here. The drawing room pays full homage to that view-of-views thanks to enormous French windows and is an enchanting spot for breakfast and dinner. Gregarious Sally runs the place with aplomb, has created a colourful mix and match décor, cooks confidently (two nights a week) and adores her dogs. Tuffy knows his wines. The bedrooms at El Nobo are relaxed spaces, comfortably flamboyant; bathrooms have mosaics and Moroccan mirrors. As for precariously perched Gaucin, it has the best views in all Spain.

rooms	3: 2 twins/doubles, 1 suite.
price	€125. Suite €145.
meals	Dinner €35 twice a week.
closed	July/August; Christmas; New Year.
directions	AP-7 to exit 142; on to Gaucín. Right into village at T-junc; tricky turns, then sharp right onto road marked 'Camino de Gibraltar'; 1km down hill on left.

	Sally & Christopher Von Meister
tel/fax	+34 952 151303
mobile	+34 680 453899
email	elnobo@avired.es
web	www.elnobo.co.uk

B&B

Map 20 Entry 256

La Herradura

Camino Romano, 29480 Gaucín, Málaga

Unforgivable not to make the most of a panorama like this. And the designers of the little pink-washed house have done just that: house, terrace and pool are perfectly positioned for maximum effect. Behind and to either side is wild, green mountainside; ahead, breathtaking views to Africa. La Herradura, owned by Christopher and Sally next door, has been newly built in an unobtrusive, rustic style, while flair and imagination have created an effect of rural simplicity tempered with sophistication inside. Pastel colours – pinks, blues and golds – glow gently against pale cream walls. In the airy, open-plan living room, a big woven rug contrasts with the austere white fireplace; a squashy sofa and armchairs are grouped companionably around. The ceiling is chestnut-beamed and slopes down towards two sets of double doors that open onto the terrace. There's a fireplace in the attractive kitchen/dining area, too – but you'll want to eat outside whenever you can. Below: a gorgeous pool, poised on the very edge of hillside; beyond: those unbelievable views.

rooms	Villa for 4.
price	€1,150–€1,700 per week. VAT included.
meals	Self-catering.
closed	Never.
directions	AP-7 to exit 142; on to Gaucin. Right into village at T-junc; sharp right onto road marked 'Camino de Gibraltar'; 1km downhill on left.

	Sally & Christopher von Meister
tel/fax	+34 952 151303
mobile	+34 680 453899
email	elnobo@avired.com
web	www.elnobo.co.uk

Self-catering

Map 20 Entry 257

Banú Rabbah

Sierra Bermeja s/n, 29490 Benarrabá, Málaga

A good little place in a very grand setting. You're pretty much left to your own devices but all you need is here – restaurant, terraces, pool, nightlife. (Local legend has it that the Moors built a secret tunnel between here and Gaucín.) The hotel, named after the first Berber tribesman who settled here, was built as a local council initiative, and is now run by a friendly group of six from the village. The lofty setting is what makes Banú Rabbah special: 2,000m up a mountain, with a magnificent sweep of rocky range, white village and densely wooded hillsides. The hotel has a rather cumbersome design but bedrooms are cosy, light and clean and come with generous terraces. The restaurant – open to the public, along with the pool, in summer – features local produce: try the *saltavallao* (a hot gazpacho) and the almond cakes. After dinner take a stroll through this very Spanish village: you are unlikely to meet many foreigners here (unlike in neighbouring Gaucín). There's a trek down to the sparkling waters of the Genal for the energetic – route maps provided – and mule rides and 4x4 trips for the idle.

rooms	12 twins/doubles.
price	€48–€60. Singles €39–€49. Extra bed €10. Half-board extra €13.50 p.p. Full-board extra €21 p.p.
meals	Breakfast €3. Lunch & dinner available.
closed	February.
directions	From Málaga N-340 for Cádiz; A-377 via Manilva to Gaucín. Here, towards Ronda on A-369; after 4.5km, right to Benarrabá. Signed.

Jesús García

tel	+34 952 150288
fax	+34 952 150005
email	hotel@hbenarraba.es
web	www.hbenarraba.es

Hotel

Map 20 Entry 258

La Casa del Arriero

c/Cantón 8, 29380 Cortes de la Frontera, Málaga

No fewer than three of Andalucía's most beautiful natural parks are on your doorstep. The Guadiaro valley is criss-crossed with ancient drovers' paths and these young owners know its loveliest corners. They organise walking and riding holidays and have route maps of all their rambles. They've given new life and a twist of style to this traditional village house – all yours – with a roof terrace that looks to the church tower and across the rolling pastures of the valley. Things within work beautifully: an open-plan kitchen and diner, a small plant-filled patio for summery meals, a cosy lounge with a woodburning stove. There are two bedrooms, one vast with its own sun terrace, the second much smaller but fine for kids. The house takes its name from the muleteer who once lived here and the equine tradition continues: Mel, a rider all her life, organises full or half day rides from Cortes. Even if you're idle, this is just the place to recharge your batteries. Buy veggies fresh from the market, rub shoulders with the locals in any number of bars, get a taste of that fabled 'real' Spain.

rooms	House for 2 + 2 children.
price	€400–€490 per week. VAT included.
meals	Self-catering.
closed	Rarely.
directions	From Málaga E-15 for Algeciras; exit for Gaucín. Here right to Ronda, left to Cortes de la F. Here, right opp. bullring then left up c/Alta. Park at top. Down pedestrian street; 1st left; last house.

	Melanie & Tiger Templer
tel/fax	+34 952 153330
mobile	+34 690 822860
email	enquiries@casaarriero.com
web	www.casaarriero.com

Self-catering

Map 20 Entry 259

The Hoopoe Yurt Hotel

29380 Cortes de la Frontera, Málaga

Under the shade of cork and olive trees, up a rocky, muddy track – best avoided at night – these authentic Mongolian and Afghani yurts sit in splendid andalucían isolation. On raised wooden platforms, the felt-lined white circular tents are reinforced with arching roof poles that support a domed crown; wicker baskets, ethnic furniture, sheepskin rugs and bold colours create a rustic and romantic mood. The charming and well-travelled young owners Ed and Henrietta have made the yurts stylish while maintaining a 'back to nature' feel (there's a compost loo and solar-heated water in the lovely bamboo-walled shower rooms). Wonderful views of the soaring mountains are best enjoyed from a hammock slung between two cork trees or on a bamboo sun bed beside the freshwater pool. Wake to birdsong, cowbells and the distant rumble of trains; at night, tiptoe your way to bed past twinkling lights in the trees. Henrietta, a talented cook, uses the best local and organic ingredients; the village, one of the most organic in Spain, is a 20-minute walk. Bliss. *Minimum stay two nights.*

rooms	4: 3 yurts for 2, 1 yurt for 2 (under 12s only), each with separate shower.
price	£80 (sterling). VAT included.
meals	Lunch €20. Dinner €30.
closed	Mid-October to end March.
directions	After Benaojan, cont. for C. de la Frontera; there, 1st left after fountain. Before petrol station, left on track, then left at fork; after 1km, right onto track before white house.

	Ed & Henrietta Hunt
tel	+34 952 117055
mobile	+34 696 668388
email	info@yurthotel.com
web	www.yurthotel.com

SPECIAL GREEN ENTRY
see page 13

Hotel

Map 20 Entry 260

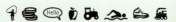

Molino del Santo

Barriada Estación s/n, 29370 Benaoján, Málaga

Pauline and Andy moved south in search of the good life, and restored a century-old mill surrounded by national park. The setting is exquisite: water tumbles past flowered terraces, under fig trees and willows and into the solar-heated pool. (When it comes to things environmental, these owners are exceptionally green.) Pretty rooms and restaurant wear warm local garb – terracotta tiles, beams, carved beds, rush-seated chairs. Fresh flowers are everywhere and the Molino's reputation for good Spanish food is established – as organic and free-range as possible. Most hotel guests are British but the locals flock in at weekends to enjoy local hams and sausages, rabbit, fish and imaginative vegetarian. Staff and owners are generous with advice on walks from the hotel. From the sleepy little station you can take a train to Ronda or, in the other direction, pass some of the loveliest 'white' villages of Andalucía. The Molino, one of the Sierra's most enjoyable small hotels, has achieved the perfect balance between warmth and professionalism. Pay extra for a superior room with a terrace – and book in advance!

rooms	18: 15 twins/doubles, 3 suites.
price	€80-€140. Suites €100-€180. VAT included. Half-board extra €25 p.p.
meals	Lunch & dinner €25. VAT included.
closed	Mid-November-mid-February.
directions	From Ronda, A376 Sevilla; after km118 marker, left for Benaoján on MA-505. After 10km, having crossed railway & river bridges, left to station & follow signs.

	Pauline Elkin & Andy Chapell
tel	+34 952 167151
fax	+34 952 167327
email	info@molinodelsanto.com
web	www.molinodelsanto.com

Hotel

Map 20 Entry 261

El Tejar

c/Nacimiento 38, 29430 Montecorto, Málaga

You gaze out from a high-up terrace near Ronda to a panorama of oak forest, almond and olive groves and distant peaks. Guy stumbled across El Tejar, once a tile factory, when out walking over 20 years ago. Now it is a deliciously labyrinthine series of spaces built on a dozen different levels. Decoration was inspired by andalucía's Moorish past and travels in the East; there are rugs from Kashmir, Rajastani throws, carved Moroccan mirrors and beautiful pots from Fez. Home this most definitely is, thanks to books and magazines, paintings and Guy's photographs of distant lands. But best of all are those views from the terraced areas and pool, stretching southwards to the peaks of the Grazalema Park. The four airy bedrooms look south too, and have excellent beds, big wardrobes, CD players and cooling fans. A friendly housekeeper, Francisca, cleans and tidies each morning (if that's what you'd like) and can prepare meals. If you're looking for a smaller place there is Dar Hajra ('House of the Rocks') higher up; sculpted around a limestone outcrop, it has an infinity plunge pool and more sublime views.

rooms	House for 6-8. Rock house for 2-4.
price	€1,350-€1,785. Rock house €1,150-1,350. Prices per week.
meals	Self-catering. Dinners on request.
closed	Rarely.
directions	From Ronda A-374 towards Sevilla for 20km. Right into Montecorto; cobbled track opp. church; at end, right. Pass left of no. 54; at last house, right up track to El Tejar & Dar Hajra.

	Guy Hunter-Watts
mobile	+34 616 057184
email	info@rondatejar.com
web	www.rondatejar.com

Cortijo Las Piletas

Apdo. 559, 29400 Ronda, Málaga

Play the country squire: there are 100 hectares of wheat and sunflower fields, oak woodland and cattle grazing at your disposal. This sprawling cortijo, with its brilliant white walls and tomato-red shutters, is a fine example of an andalucían country estate, owned by Pablo's family for 200 years. Staying here is like staying as a guest of the family. Light-filled bedrooms are elegant with polished furniture, pretty coloured or carved bedheads and soft white curtains. Flowers or plants add a fresh, country touch. The old farmhouse hall has been turned into a comfortable drawing room enriched with antiques, tapestries and oil paintings; a fire in winter and an honesty bar add to the relaxed feel. The beamed dining room – with terrace for summer eating – is small and cosy, its tables set with pretty china. This is terrific walking country with three natural parks, including Grazalema, on the doorstep. Return to a dip in the pool, a snooze on your private terrace, and binoculars and books to borrow. From the gardens, watch the sun set over Grazalema, glass of wine in hand. Pablo keeps an excellent cellar.

rooms	8: 7 twins/doubles, 1 family.
price	€79-€84. Singles €64-€68.
meals	Dinner €24. Picnic-style lunch €9.
closed	November & January.
directions	From Ronda A-376 for Sevilla. Ignore first turn to Benaoján/Montejaque. Continue towards Sevilla; after 20km, left for Montejaque on MA-505. Las Piletas is 1st farm on the left, with red windows.

	Elisenda Vidal & Pablo Serratosa
mobile	+34 605 080295
fax	+34 951 230603
email	info@cortijolaspiletas.com
web	www.cortijolaspiletas.com

B&B

Map 20 Entry 263

La Fuente de la Higuera

Partido de los Frontones, 29400 Ronda, Málaga

Tina and Pom have travel in the blood; he chartered yachts, she worked for one of the big airlines. Then the Ronda mountains wrapped them in its spell and they realised their dream: a luxurious retreat to ease away urban cares. Tina is the 'spark', a charming and vivacious woman who has decorated the hotel with an understated panache. Pom is born to the role of host: a raconteur by nature and a connoisseur of wine. The conversion of their old mill has been accomplished with local expertise, smooth plastering and planked floors adding to the immaculate furnishings and the stylish feel; a refreshing change from the more rustic beam and terracotta. Each lovely suite has an open fire for cosy winter stays; Indonesian beds, muslin drapes, lamps, chairs and tables add an exotic feel. Bathrooms are generous. An honesty bar in the library, a laid-back feel… La Fuente is more home than hotel. The focus is poolwards; beyond, groves of olives and the changing colours of the mountains – a blissful backdrop to your sundowner. At dinner, feast on local food impeccably presented, and excellent wines.

rooms	11: 3 twins/doubles, 8 suites.
price	€135-€280. Suites €179-€280.
meals	Dinner €35.
closed	Rarely.
directions	Bypass Ronda on A-374 towards Sevilla. Pass turning to Benaoján; right at sign for hotel. Under bridge, left at 1st fork; over bridge; left after 200m.

	Pom & Christina Piek
tel	+34 952 114355
fax	+34 952 165609
email	info@hotellafuente.com
web	www.hotellafuente.com

Hotel

Map 20 Entry 264

Finca La Morera
Ronda, Málaga

The narrowest of country lanes passes sleepy bars, errant chickens and groves of medlar, quince and olive before eventually looping round, then ending, at La Morera. *The* classical vision of Arcadia: two solid whitewashed farmhouses, swaying palm fronds, jasmine-clad terraces, orchards stretching to a river. Inside, a meticulous division of space and design from a team of friends from England. Their aim? To create one of the plushest, most exciting rent-a-homes in Andalucía. Enter a lofty hall-dining room with a huge fireplace and a table for 14, then a twin sweep of stairs that arcs one way to the master suite (with a claw-footed tub in the bedroom itself), the other to a gorgeous chestnut-floored drawing room with enticing valley views. Bedrooms, all en suite, are fabulous; each has a balcony or private terrace, mattresses from England, cotton sheets from Egypt, perhaps a four-poster from Indonesia. Add to this a games room and cinema, two state-of-the-art kitchens, underfloor heating in the main house, a choice of two pools and a chef available at 24-hours notice. Exceptional. *Short lets out of season.*

rooms	House for 12.
price	€3,000–€6,000 per week.
meals	Self-catering. Restaurant/bar 1.5km.
closed	Rarely.
directions	5km off Ronda-Seville A-376 road. Directions on booking.

Richard Johnston
& Nicholas Smallwood

tel	+44 (0)1749 814811
email	info@fincalamorera.com
web	www.fincalamorera.com

Self-catering

Map 20 Entry 265

La Alcantarilla

Apdo. 504, 29400 Ronda, Málaga

It was the Moors who turned this corner of Ronda's Llano de la Cruz valley into a verdant paradise. Named after the water course ('alcantarilla') that they installed during their 8th-century stay, their legacy is obvious in this smallholding, its five acres of orchards and Roman-brick aqueduct functioning to this day. The house itself owes its charms to the local vernacular, with a little help from its current English owners, an artist and a writer. They have preserved most of its features – from the pantile roofs to the window grills and doors. Inside is a quarry of calm, with cool stony hues and stylish décor. Outside, a choice of private patios; one is a formal rose garden, its pergola decked in wisteria and vines, its views to distant, shimmering mountains. Across a bridge, hidden almost completely by walnut trees, is the simple, 13-metre pool. Expect a fridge full of local products (perhaps some plums, figs or pears from the garden) and an excellent fully, functioning-kitchen. There is a log-burning stove and central heating in winter. *Owner's house also available for rent July/August.*

rooms	House for 6.
price	€500–€1,100 per week. VAT included.
meals	Self-catering.
closed	Rarely.
directions	Directions on booking.

	Gabriella Chidgey
mobile	+34 696 843704
email	enquiries@alcantarilla.co.uk
web	www.alcantarilla.co.uk

Self-catering

Map 20 Entry 266

Finca La Guzmana

Apdo. de Correos 408, 29400 Ronda, Málaga

You'll want to stay here for at least a week – such a happy, relaxed place to be. The house, a 150-year-old, single-storey andalucían cortijo, is surrounded by five acres of olive trees and vines and, apart from the occasional train, or the put-put of the tractor as Peter works his fields, it's truly peaceful. At the heart of the place is a tiled courtyard, wrapped around by the three whitewashed wings of the house. A dappled terracotta roof juts forward to provide cloister-like shade; vivid geraniums spill from supporting pillars; dogs scamper and cats doze. Breakfast out here by the lion fountain is a delicious way to start the day. The bedrooms – and the open-plan kitchen that guests are free to use – open off the courtyard: pleasant rooms, with square, deep-set windows and lots of light and space. Outside is a superb, 20m salinated pool where you can swim and gaze up at the mountains. There's masses to do in the area, and Peter is happy to provide a packed lunch. For dinner, good food can be found at the *venta* at the end of the track.

rooms	7 twins/doubles.
price	€70-€90. VAT included. Weekly rates available.
meals	Packed lunch €6. Restaurant 300m.
closed	Rarely.
directions	Ronda-El Burgo road to km4 marker. Take track ('Camino Privado') opp. La Venta; 300m.

Peter McLeod

tel	+34 951 160269
mobile	+34 600 006305
email	info@laguzmana.com
web	www.laguzmana.com

Guest house

Map 20 Entry 267

Alavera de los Baños

c/San Miguel s/n, 29400 Ronda, Málaga

A very fetching small hotel on the edge of the old Tanners Quarter — sheep-grazed pastures to one side, cobbled (steep!) ascents to Ronda on the other. *A la vera de* means 'by the side of' — your hotel is next to the first hammam of the Moorish citadel. Christian and Inma brim with enthusiasm for both hotel and restaurant, and staff are friendly. The new building is in keeping with the Hispano-Moorish elements of its surroundings: thus terracotta tiles, wafer bricks, keyhole arches without and, in the cosy little bedrooms, a softly oriental feel: kilims, mosquito nets, colour washes of ochres, blue and yellow. Shower rooms are compact but charming. Book one of the terrace rooms if you can; they lead to a lush little garden and delicious pool (crowded in high summer) with views. The dining room is lily-filled and candlelit, cut across by an arched central walkway leading to the rooms at either end. Breakfasts are freshly different each day; dinners have a Moorish slant: lamb is the speciality and there is tasty veggie food too, much organically grown. Come out of season for the Alavera as its best.

rooms	10: 9 twins/doubles, 1 single.
price	€85–€105. Single €65–€75. VAT included.
meals	Dinner €22–€25.
closed	December–January.
directions	In Ronda, directly opp. Parador hotel, down c/Rosario. Right at end & down hill to Fuente de los Ocho Caños. Here left; 1st right to Arab Baths; hotel next door. Park here.

Christian Reichardt

tel/fax	+34 952 879143
email	alavera@telefonica.net
web	www.alaveradelosbanos.com

Hotel

Map 20 Entry 268

La Cazalla

Tajo del Abanico, Apdo de Correos 160, 29400 Ronda, Málaga

If you want 'off the beaten track', make for Ronda's valley. Spectacularly positioned at its head and built into the craggy rockface is La Cazalla. A Roman road once ran beside it – you can almost imagine the legionnaires trudging by. It is a place of astonishing nature and peace, and the house, part Roman, part Arab, is exquisitely restored. On the big terrace, with views to the breathtaking escarpment of Tajo del Abanico, shade is provided by willows and vines. Keep cool in the big, beautiful pool – or the small spring water one. Everywhere there are fruit trees and the soothing sound of water; indoors is piped flamenco and jazz. Natural rock walls and white paint contrast with rich kelims and piles of books in the sitting room – delightfully different. Bedrooms upstairs are airy and elegant, and sport binoculars for watching the wildlife. No baths, but fabulous power showers in domed Moorish recesses. María rules this sanctuary and her son Rodrigo is the chef; his three-course dinners are "always a surprise".
A Rusticae hotel. Minimum stay two to five nights.

rooms	5 doubles.
price	€102–€130.
meals	Dinner €40.
closed	Rarely.
directions	From Ronda, C-369 for Algeciras. Pass 1st r'bout; at next r'bout, turn right taking left fork, avoid track for 'ermita'. Follow blue-painted marks on stones for 2.8km.

	Maria Ruiz González
tel	+34 952 114175
fax	+34 952 114092
email	reservas@lacazalladeronda.com
web	www.lacazalladeronda.com

Hotel

Map 20 Entry 269

Los Castaños

c/Iglesia 40, 29452 Cartajima, Málaga

You will be charmed the moment you step through the huge studded door. The Moorish influence seduces so easily: water trickles in a little tiled fountain, arches beckon, geraniums splash the dazzling walls with colour. There's a fireplace, too, for the nippier months. Climb to the next floor and you'll find cool, airy bedrooms – four with balconies – and windows framing the loveliest of mountain views. Handmade beds, old Spanish rocking chairs, low tables, Moroccan lights and super bathrooms add to the sense of well-being. Go up again and you emerge onto an entrancing roof terrace, benignly presided over by the white tower of next door's church. Set among pillars and pierced terracotta screens is a small, round, brilliant blue plunge pool: irresistible. A pampering, grown-up place, where Di and her daughter Lu, smiling and generous, know how to soothe and spoil. The food is delicious, the village is charming and there are good walks to the other villages glimpsed through the trees. As if that wasn't enough, there are fascinating Roman and Phoenician ruins to explore.

rooms	5 twins/doubles.
price	€110.
meals	Dinner €35. Not Sunday.
closed	Rarely.
directions	From San Pedro to Ronda on A-376/A-397. 10km before Ronda, left after petrol station to Cartajima. There, bear right, pass recycling bins, then 1st hard right; park by phone box. On right.

	Di & Lu Beach
tel	+34 952 180778
mobile	+34 696 081354
fax	+34 952 180901
email	reservations@loscastanos.com
web	www.loscastanos.com

B&B

Map 20 Entry 270

Albero Lodge

Urbanización Finca la Cancelada, c/Támesis 16, 29689 Estepona, Málaga

A private villa reborn as a romantic beach hotel. Young trees stand sentinel in front of the modern, ochred exterior (*albero* describes the sandy colour of the bull ring) lending it a ceremonious air. The interconnecting dining room, sitting room and bar are similarly formal. The bedrooms, by contrast, are triumphantly, stylishly individual, each inspired by a different city: Florence, Deauville, Berlin, Dover, Ronda, Madras, Djerba, Fez and New York. Those with an eastern theme are especially luscious. Walls are colourwashed, every room gets its own patio, Djerba is peaceful and Fez's bathroom oozes rustic chic. The gardens are similarly groomed, resplendent with palm trees, jasmine, hibiscus, plumbago. Living areas have stylish wicker sofas and chairs, the terrace a delicious pool, and charming staff serve breakfast until 12. Albero Lodge is part of a smart development of villas fairly close to the N-340; from outside there's a distant hum, but indoors the insulation is good. 'Secret' footpaths lead you to the beach, Gibraltar is a short drive to the west, and Morocco is a day trip away.

rooms	9: 4 twins/doubles, 5 suites.
price	€75–€110. Suites €95–€155.
meals	Breakfast €7. Restaurants nearby.
closed	10 January–10 February
directions	From Málaga, N-340 for Estepona. Exit after km164.5, signed Cambio de Sentido. Under bridge, left twice, right twice, past Park Beach. Hotel on right.

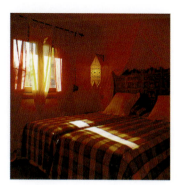

	Myriam Pérez Torres
tel	+34 952 880700
fax	+34 952 885238
email	info@alberolodge.com
web	www.alberolodge.com

Hotel

Map 20 Entry 271

Amanhavis

c/El Pilar 3, Benahavis, 29679 Marbella, Málaga

There's a real warmth to this place, thanks to Burkhard, Leslie and staff, and you sense it the moment you enter. The oasis-like Benahavis has long been known to Costa residents for its string of restaurants, and the most renowned is this one. Make the most of Burkhard's "creative Mediterranean cuisine" in this intimate restaurant-hotel: fresh tiger prawns, fillets of monkfish, raspberry cream cake, mountain cheeses… no wonder they're popular with the Marbella set. Bedrooms, radiating off the gorgeous inner courtyard with plunge pool, are lavish and regal – nine flights of fantasy with themes harking back to Spain's Golden Age: the Astonomer's Observatory, the Spice Trader's Caravan, the Philospher's Study. Satellite TV, air conditioning and the internet speak of a more modern era. Bathrooms have a Moroccan feel and there's comfort and attention to detail throughout, from the snugs in the suites to the aromatic oils. In summer you dine by the pool, indoors is a convivial bar. This excellent place is five kilometres from the sea and all those golden beaches – and golf clubs abound.

rooms	9 twins/doubles.
price	€119-€159.
meals	Breakfast €11. Dinner €37.50. Restaurant closed Monday in low season & Sunday all year.
closed	1-15 December.
directions	From Málaga for Cádiz. Just past San Pedro, right for Benahavis. Hotel on far side of village, signed.

Leslie & Burkhard Weber

tel	+34 952 856026
fax	+34 952 856151
email	info@amanhavis.com
web	www.amanhavis.com

Hotel

Map 20 Entry 272

The Town House

c/Alderete 7, Plaza Tetuán, 29600 Marbella, Málaga

Maria is eager for people to discover the simple elegance that is the real Marbella and there couldn't be a better launch pad than this. Plaza Tetuán is a lovely square in the very heart of the old town. It's not on any through route, so is surprisingly quiet (except during the Feria in the second week of June). The house is a rare and striking place to stay, with a peachy marble entrance placed at the corner of the building and bisected by a single white pillar. Originally an old family house – seven brothers lived here – it has been closed for the last eight years and gradually restored. Inside, Moorish and Modern have been married to arresting effect; the whole place has an air of supremely tasteful decadence! The luxurious bedrooms are decorated in neutral colours or lustrous pastel shades and furnished with restraint: sumptuous beds, fine mirrors, the occasional superb antique… Each room is different; all are marble floored and subtly lit, with exuberant plants and suitably sybaritic bathrooms. You'll have to eat out but that should be a pleasure, with the fine array of good restaurants close by.

rooms	9 twins/doubles.
price	€95–€130. VAT included.
meals	Restaurants nearby.
closed	Rarely.
directions	From Málaga airport for Cádiz; exit for Marbella 'Centro Urbano'. On for 2km; right at junc.; follow signs for Hotel Lima. Last exit at r'bout into Avda Nabeul. On c/Najera to Plaza Tetuán. On corner.

	Maria Lundgren
tel/fax	+34 952 901791
email	info@townhouse.nu
web	www.townhouse.nu

Hotel

Map 20 Entry 273

La Villa Marbella Charming Hotel

c/Principe 10, 29600 Marbella, Málaga

Spiritual home to Europe's *nouveaux riches*, and the most upmarket resort in Spain? Dig deeper and you uncover a gentler and more enticing spot to stay. In the old Arabic heart of town, lost down a maze of charming cobbled streets, lies this 150-year-old townhouse decked in bougainvillea, with an earthy and subtle décor. Brazilian Marcus is a congenial host, who oversees his domain with broad smiles, helpful information and the odd joke. The heart and soul of his small hotel is the roof terrace where breakfast is happily served until 1pm… flowing seamlessly into shady afternoon siestas and chilled aperitifs as the sun drops over the Ronda mountains. But don't nod off and forget the children – there's a bit of a drop. Pot plants, squidgy sofas and wooden cabinets give an Asian edge – such is the style that infuses the place. Batik wall hangings and bamboo lights accent the cosy bedrooms, colours are easy on the eye, bathrooms stylish. Nearby, one of the newer suites has its own roof terrace. Forget designer labels, here is Marbella in a new light.

rooms	15: 12 twins/doubles, 2 family, 1 suite.
price	€85–€135. Family €105–€165. Suite €125–€185.
meals	Restaurant 5-minute walk.
closed	21–26 December.
directions	From Málaga/Algeciras on N-340; follow signs to Marbella, Centro Ciudad & Casco Antiguo. Detailed map on web site.

	Marcos Torres
tel	+34 952 766220
fax	+34 952 765748
email	info@lavillamarbella.e.telefonica.net
web	www.lavillamarbella.com

Hotel

Map 20 Entry 274

El Oceano Hotel & Beach Club

Ctra. N-340 km 199, Urbanización Torrenueva, 29649 Mijas, Málaga

One of the best on the Costa del Sol. El Oceano may not be particularly Spanish, but it is as spoiling as can be, and the people who run it are delightful. Mooch around all day in a white bathrobe in the spa, get your nails polished, your hair done, then slip into something fabulous for dinner. Double bedrooms look onto the mountains, suites face the ocean; several have terraces, a few have outdoor jacuzzis, and the newest are truly stylish. There's a hint of Florida in the lounge/bar and a touch of the Far East in the outdoor pool, lush with palm trees and thatched bar – glide up for a generous measure of pink gin. The restaurant is one of the best around and the cuisine, accompanied by fine wines and live, mostly classical, music, is international and delicious. In warm weather you dine on the wooden broadwalk overlooking the sea. Beyond the pool: a long sweep of ocean; the blue water shimmers, waves lap onto the rocks and the beach feels as though it's yours. Yes, you are off the N-340 and close to Marbella's sprawl, but El Oceano sits on its own rocky outcrop with clean, empty beaches nearby.

rooms	38: 14 twins/doubles, 24 suites.
price	€140. Suites €195–€260.
meals	Lunch €24.50.
	Dinner €30–€50 à la carte.
closed	Winter months.
directions	From Málaga, N-340 for Marbella. Exit Riviera del Sol. At r'bout, left under m'way, back onto N-340 for Fuengirola. After footbridge, 1st exit. Hotel on right.

	John Palmer
tel	+34 952 587550
fax	+34 952 587637
email	info@oceanohotel.com
web	www.oceanohotel.com

Hotel

Map 20 Entry 275

The Beach House

Urbanización El Chaparral, CN-340 km.203, 29648 Mijas Costa, Málaga

Marlon Brando was once photographed by the pool… alongside which the Mediterranean splashes and sparkles. An arresting spot: you may be sandwiched between the devil (the N-340) and the deep blue sea, but once you've negotiated the slip road, it's easy to forget the devil. In a previous life, this was the ritzy villa of a wealthy Arab. Now Swedish Kjell is the owner, and, although he cannot often be here, his spirit lingers. This boutique hotel has a zen-like calm and is a haven of special touches – from the orchid floating in a bowl by your bed to the music on the hotel's compilation CD. Staff are professional and charming, serving you breakfast, a fine-looking buffet, on the decked terrace in summer. The whole beautiful place exudes a Nordic chic – buckskin rugs in reception, baskets brimful of magazines – yet is irresistibly inviting. It is like staying in a friend's exquisite villa. The pool is heated all year, the (beautiful) beach waits below, and Marbella, spiritual home to Europe's *nouveaux riches*, is a shake away. Ask for one of the quieter rooms in the main villa.

rooms	10 twins/doubles.
price	€125–€175. VAT included.
meals	Snack bar nearby.
closed	Mid-December–mid-February.
directions	From Málaga N-340 Cádiz. Keep on N-340; past km202, exit Cala de Mijas. Follow signs Fuengirola & Málaga; back onto N-340. Keep hard right; past 1st footbridge, slip road to right. On right after 250m.

Irene Westerberg & Jes Jensen

tel/fax	+34 952 494540
email	info@beachhouse.nu
web	www.beachhouse.nu

Hotel

Map 20 Entry 276

Posada del Torcal

Partido de Jeva, 29230 Villanueva de la Concepción, Málaga

The fruit of the owners' conversion from bustling Costa to harshly beautiful Sierra is this award-winning small hotel. Inside and out feels thoroughly Andaluz, and the setting – not far from the Dalí-esque limestone formations of the Torcal Park – is sublime. Bedrooms are dedicated to Spanish artists and are lavish. The oils are local copies of originals, while many of the trimmings come from further afield; the beds, some brass, some gothic, some four-poster, were shipped out from England. The balcony rooms have the most outstanding views. Underfloor heating warms in winter, air conditioning cools… the only sound is that of the gardener clipping the meadow in summer. Food is elaborate: prawns in filo pastry with coconut milk, lamb wrapped in a spinach mousse, the range of vegetarian dishes wide and the wine list long. Terraced gardens run down to the pool, heated all year round, and there's tennis, sauna, mountain bikes and gym. Professional staff will point you in the right direction if walking or riding is your thing. Even helicopter trips can be arranged – not bad for a 10-bed hotel!

rooms	10 twins, doubles & suites.
price	€95-€175. Suite €190-€225.
meals	Lunch & dinner from €35 à la carte. VAT included.
closed	11-19 December.
directions	Málaga N-331 for Antequera, exit 148 for Casabermeja. There, right for Almogía; next left to V. de la Concepción. At top of village, left at junc.; 1.5km, right for La Higuera. Hotel 3km on left.

Karen & Geoffrey Banham

tel	+34 952 031177
mobile	+34 629 534055
fax	+34 952 031006
email	hotel@laposadadeltorcal.com
web	www.laposadadeltorcal.com

Hotel

Map 20 Entry 277

Hotel La Fuente del Sol

Paraje Rosas Bajas, La Joya, 29260 Antequera, Málaga

High up in the Torcal mountains, the little village of La Joya must have been so named on account of the feeling that stirs within as you gaze towards Africa. Set against a teetering backdrop of national park and sheer rock, la Fuente del Sol is actually the spring that waters the grounds and burgeoning gardens. The epitome of rustic-deluxe, the hotel is surprisingly new, although there's little to distinguish it from the other century old white-walled cortijos in the area. Modern spaces come with authentic touches to the reconditioned beams, wooden doors and windows, even an 1879 Dodge City station clock that still seems to work. Siesta-inducing chaise-longues line the hallways in between the plants; and if you make it that far, a heated pool or massage is only a flop away. Ratchet up the tempo in the gymnasium. A young cook caters for the hungry in modern Andaluz style with excellent salads and dishes such as smoked salmon on a bed of spinach and pine nuts. Bedroom eyries with raffia rugs, neutral tones and quirky lamps let you spread your wings.

rooms	14: 11 twins/doubles, 3 suites.
price	€150–€250. Singles €120. Suites €200–€250.
meals	Lunch & dinner €30–€40.
closed	Rarely.
directions	From Málaga exit 148 for Villanueva de la Concepción on to A-45. In Villanueva, signs for La Joya & hotel.

Luis Lozano

tel	+34 951 239823
mobile	+34 670 467210
fax	+34 951 232090
email	info@hotelfuentedelsol.com
web	www.hotelfuentedelsol.com

Hotel

Map 20 Entry 278

Santa Fe Hotel-Restaurante

Ctra. de Monda km3, Apartado 147, 29100 Coín, Málaga

The Santa Fe, taken on by two energetic and multi-lingual Dutch brothers over a decade ago, goes from strength to strength. The old farmhouse sits among the citrus groves of the Guadalhorce valley, to one side of the road from Marbella up to Coín (traffic is audible, but never intrusive). The transformation from farm to guesthouse has been faithful to local tradition; simple bedrooms have been rustic furniture, terracotta floors (tiles fired with the dog-paw print bring good luck!) and stencilled walls. Those with small windows are darkish in winter. No sitting room, but a great garden and pool, and a terrific little restaurant, popular with the locals – Spanish or Costa-cosmopolitan. Two brilliant new young chefs rustle up the likes of marbré from breast of duck and salmon and turbot carpaccio. There's a good selection of vegetarian dishes too, and wines. The dining room has a log fire in winter and the conservatory and bar are cosy – but most of the year you dine beneath the huge and ancient olive tree or the pool-side pergola. A friendly, relaxed atmosphere – and late breakfasts – reign.

rooms	5 twins/doubles.
price	€66. Singles €58. VAT included.
meals	Lunch & dinner €25-€35 à la carte. VAT included. Not Tuesday.
closed	2 weeks in November; 2 weeks in February.
directions	From Málaga on N-340 for Cádiz. 1km after airport A-366/C-344 for Coín. Nera Coín on A-355 for Monda/Marbella; take exit Coín signed A-7102. Hotel 500m, on left.

	Warden & Arjan van de Vrande
tel	+34 952 452916
fax	+34 952 453843
email	info@santafe-hotel.com
web	www.santafe-hotel.com

Hotel

Map 20 Entry 279

Hotel Cerro de Híjar

Cerro de Híjar s/n, 29109 Tolox, Málaga

On a clear day you can see — well, if not forever, at least to the sea. It has a remote and unrivalled position, this hotel, on a bluff 700 metres high. From the sleepy Arab village of Tolox (known for its old-fashioned spa), you follow the winding road up and up… to a new hotel built with rare vision. Inside: a terrific sense of light and space, creamy stucco walls, bright rugs and pleasing furniture, a winter fire and andalucían paintings on every wall. Bedrooms range from big to massive, each with its own stylish lighting, a designer bathroom, colourwashed walls, tapestries from Morocco. You'll eat and drink wonderfully well: Martín's cooking is traditional andalucían with an inspired touch, while the excellent buffet breakfast is laid out with care and served on bone china. Martín, Guillermo and Eugenio run the place in an eco-friendly manner (every guest is given a sapling to plant before they leave) and manager María is a gem. The málaga valley reaches out before you; closer are the peaks of the Sierra Nevada, snow-capped until March. The walking is magnificent, the place is a treat.

rooms	18: 14 twins/doubles, 4 suites.
price	€68-€82. Singles €61-€73. Suites €95-€108.
meals	Breakfast €8. Lunch & dinner €27.
closed	Rarely.
directions	From Málaga, to Cártama. Filter right to Coín, then onto A-366 for Ronda. Left to Tolox, through village to Balneario (spa); right up hill for 2.5km to hotel.

Guillermo Gonzalez;
Eugenio Llanos & Martín Jerez

tel	+34 952 112111
mobile	+34 605 885480
email	cerro@cerrodehijar.com
web	www.cerrodehijar.com

Hotel

Map 20 Entry 280

Molino de las Pilas

Ctra. Vieja de Ronda km1, 29327 Teba, Málaga

The lofty, atmospheric dining hall of the Molino, liberally adorned with restored farm machinery from the 1880s – the decade in which it was built – is one of the best places to eat in the interior of andalucía. The hotel next door is equally charming. The old mill was in ruins when gentle Pablo found it, and the restoration took three years. Simply but comfortably furnished in an elegantly rustic style, bedrooms have excellent beds, fine bathrooms and log-burning stoves, and there's a big sitting room that's cosily beamed. In summer you'll want to be outside, in the courtyard – a riot of bougainvillea and honeysuckle – or on the terrace at the back, where views soar across rolling fields of olives and wheat to the Serranía de Ronda. In the restaurant the old workings are in place: great grindstones for mashing the olives, a massive beamed press, and huge *tinajas* set in the floor to store the oil. Equally remarkable is Esmeraldas's cooking: superb fish, fabulous marinaded partridge, salads a delight – all at amazingly reasonable prices. The Molino gets better and better.

rooms	6 twins/doubles.
price	€70. VAT included.
meals	Lunch & dinner from €25 à la carte.
closed	3 weeks in January.
directions	From Málaga, A-357 for Campillos. After Ardales, cross bridge at lake, left at km11 to Teba, on A-341. After 6km, right at petrol station, up hill. 1km, signed on left.

	Pablo Moreno Aragón
tel	+34 952 748622
fax	+34 952 748647
email	info@molinodelaspilas.com
web	www.molinodelaspilas.com

Hotel

Map 20 Entry 281

La Casa de la Fuente

c/Málaga 18, 29310 Villanueva de Algaidas, Málaga

Comfortable, spick and span B&B in an untouristy Spanish village, run with charm. Linda and John chanced upon the big old Aldalucian house after five years of searching. He worked on the restoration, she the décor. Lovely old floor tiles have been restored, the furniture is in traditional country style, and each bedroom is named after a favourite artist – Van Gogh, Picasso, Monet, Constable, Cézanne – with prints of their works on the walls. Bathrooms are hugely luxurious, big enough to tango in and graced with John's tiling. Painted frescos decorate the oriental-tiled staircase that leads to the nicest rooms on the second floor. The building centres on a courtyard with a heated plunge pool and ceramic-topped tables, a fountain, potted plants and welcome shade. Book dinner here – they do a simple *menú del día* – or drop in on the wonderful Bar la Tasca nearby. Great value – and excellently sited for day trips to Granada, Córdoba, Ronda and the old town of Málaga. Lovely old Antequera is even closer.

rooms	5: 4 twins/doubles, 1 family.
price	€70–€85.
meals	Dinner €20.
closed	Rarely.
directions	From Antequera N-331 N for Córdoba; right for Villanueva de A. on MA-206. In village, left at junc. Down hill, left for Cuevas Bajas; after 75m, left into c/Málaga. House on left.

	John & Linda Collie
tel/fax	+34 952 745030
mobile	+34 690 205351
email	lacasadelafuente@yahoo.com
web	www.lacasadelafuente.com

B&B

Map 20 Entry 282

Cortijo Valverde

Ctra. Alora-Antequera km 35.5, 29500 Álora, Málaga

The 40 acres around Valverde are still farmed (sunflowers, olives, citrus) and the farmhouse adheres well to its rustic past. In a landscape of hills and rocky outcrops, it looks in one direction up to the Torcal, in the other, to the Moorish castle and city walls of Álora. Dinner here after a day exploring the treasures of Granada or Seville is something to come home for: seven days a week you are treated to Caroline's cooking, created from the freshest produce brought in daily from the market (and it's full Spanish on Fridays). After aperitifs on the terrace, try delicious tapas and paella in the house-party atmosphere on the terrace. New owners Caroline and Ali are enthusiastic hosts. Bedrooms are in their own very private casitas, with walk-in showers and pretty terraces; the spaces are light, airy and comfortable, and you get log-burning stoves, heating and air con. Scented maturing gardens, southern views, a blissful pool – and views with snowy peaks till April if you're lucky. Pretty villages are a half-hour drive. *Airport pick-up extra charge. Car hire can be arranged.*

rooms	7 casitas for 2.
price	€96-€118.
meals	Lunch €3-€12. Dinner €25-€30.
closed	Rarely.
directions	From Málaga, A-357 for Campillos; A-343 to Álora. Don't go into village but cross river; at T-junc., by Bar Los Caballos, left for V. de Abdaljis. Pass km35.5; sign to right; 300m; sharp left up to hotel.

	Caroline & Ali Zartash-Lloyd
tel/fax	+34 952 112979
email	info@cortijovalverde.com
web	www.cortijovalverde.com

Guest house

Map 20 Entry 283

Cortijo Jacaranda

Apdo. de Correos 279, 29500 Álora, Málaga

The problem with holidaying with young children is that so few places answer
your needs and theirs. This is different; Lorna and Lee are as family-friendly as
can be; they'll even run you to and from the airport. Their 16-acre farm in the
hills, once the property of an enthusiastic planter of rare trees, has two purpose-
built and simply styled casitas and an apartment – plus three small terraces
with barbecue and a shared pool (replete with circular shallow area at one end
and inflatable toys)… a boon during the blistering summer. You also get a big sun-
trap terrace, purpose-built play area, giant patio chess, videos and cd's to rent,
mountain bikes to borrow and loads more – a rare set-up for a remote mountain
setting. Your hosts are also happy to provide a babysitting service on Tuesdays,
ferrying you to and from your chosen restaurant. They put on a BBQ once a week
and also a Paella evening once a week. Golf and riding can be arranged, as well as
other activities such as archery, and skiing is possible (a two-hour drive) between
January and April. Quite a place ! *Laundry €10 per load.*

rooms	2 houses for 4–6. 1 apartment for 2–4.
price	House €110–€120. Apartment €75–€85. VAT included.
meals	Self-catering.
closed	Rarely.
directions	From Málaga A-357 for Campillos. After 25km, exit for Álora; 6km right at T-junc. Left onto track after 0.7km, opp. bus shelter; 1.5km, right fork; 2.8km on, at x-roads.

	Lee & Lorna Rickwood
tel	+34 952 112703 +44 208 1339005 (SKYPE)
mobile	+34 679 091689
email	bookings@cortijojacaranda.com
web	www.cortijojacaranda.com

Self-catering

Map 20 Entry 284

Finca Las Nuevas

Apdo. Correos 171, 29500 Álora, Málaga

Since living the dream in the West Country, sisters Sarah and Jane have been deeply involved in the sustainable idyll. They've recreated it perfectly here in Spain, among the remote, rolling peaks of the untouched Alora region. With their partners, this delightful pair have turned a 200-year-old ruined farmhouse into a magical hideaway — simple rooms, staggering setting. As the crow flies it's just five miles from málaga, but in reality an hour's drive, worth every twist and turn. Self-catering it may be, but a cook is on hand to tempt you with lunch and dinner, or picnic baskets for days out in the mountains. The casitas are uncomplicated and rustic, just white walls, wooden beams and pine furniture; each has a living and kitchen area and a wood-burning stove. Bathrooms are white-tiled and plain. Laze on the terraces under shady vines; dip in the pool with the housemartins. Solar panels, recycling, home-grown veg — the green credentials shine through. You're welcomed with a basket of food essentials and they'll do a weekly shop — there for when you arrive. Ask nicely and they may be able to babysit too.

rooms	3 houses: 1 for 6-8; 1 for 4; 1 for 2.
price	€75-€150 (€400-€900 per week).
meals	Self-catering. Lunch, dinner & hampers on request.
closed	Rarely.
directions	Detailed directions on booking.

Sarah & Mike Russell;
Jane & Mark Howlett

mobile	+34 629 833420/618 882703
email	enquiries@lasnuevasalora.com
web	www.lasnuevasalora.com

SPECIAL GREEN ENTRY
see page 13

Self-catering

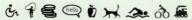

Map 20 Entry 285

Casa Domingo
Arroyo Cansino 4, 29500 Álora, Málaga

Dynamic young Belgians Robin and Sylvie have thrown themselves into their new venture. And they've really shaken up the kitchen, hosting big riotous meals on the veranda in summer. Meet them and you'll realise why they were bound to succeed: their enthusiasm is infectious. Guests can choose between B&B rooms or self-catering studios with terraces (note that the kitchenettes have hobs not ovens). It's a super place, rich in creature comforts, with good new beds and bright rugs on terracotta floors. Modernist paintings add an artistic touch, mature gardens offset the stylish house and, being positioned so high above Álora, there are stunning views of the eastern ranges of the Ronda Sierra. Life in the warmer months centres on the poolside terrace with open kitchen and barbecue; guests mingle easily, perhaps over a game of boules or tennis. It's bliss for families, with swings, sand pit and wendy house for little ones. Hop in the car for Granada, Cordoba, Seville, visit the Picasso Museum in málaga, or cycle, hike or ride – Robin and Sylvie have five beautiful horses. *Minimum stay one week July/August.*

rooms	2 + 3: 2 twins/doubles. 1 apartment for 5; 2 studios for 2.
price	€70-€85. Apt €695-€815 per week. Studio €495-€570 per week. VAT included.
meals	Dinner €20. Half-price children. Restaurant 1km.
closed	Rarely.
directions	Málaga A-357 for Campillos; A-343 Alora. Ignore 1st left to village; cross river, continue to T-junc, then straight over; signed.

Robin & Sylvie Condic Begov
tel/fax	+34 952 119744
mobile	+34 692 249970
email	casadomingo@vodafone.es
web	www.casadomingo.be

B&B & Self-catering

Map 20 Entry 286

Los Limoneros

Apdo de Correos 314, 29560 Pizarra, Málaga

Drift off to sleep in Morocco, China or Japan.. The bedrooms in this andalucían farmhouse – half an hour inland, but a world from the Costa del Sol – are globally themed. 'Japan' is neat with white walls, simple black furniture and pretty fans; 'Africa' has rich red walls, exotic prints and mosquito netting. Enfolded by citrus groves and with views to the Arab town of Álora and the mountains and valleys of Guadalhorce, this hotel is guaranteed to help you unwind. Furnishings in the beamed and tiled public rooms are rustic and simple, enhanced with second-hand finds. While Anne-Marie looks after the cooking – menus are varied and flavoursome – Yvette, a complementary therapist, offers reflexology, massage and crystal healing. She and Anne-Marie are easy, laid-back people who have created a happy, wholesome place to stay. Lazing by the pool, in the shade of the bamboo-clad terrace, may be all you wish to do – the garden, with its lemon, fig and orange trees, is a soporific spot – but Granada, Seville and Ronda are too close to ignore, and the walking and riding are magnificent. *Yoga pad in garden.*

rooms	7 twins/doubles.
price	€90. Singles €60. VAT included.
meals	Light lunch €7. Dinner €20.
closed	Rarely.
directions	From airport towards Málaga, then Motril. Exit on A-357 for Cártama. From A-357 exit on A-343 to Pizarra. Here, left; at km49 marker, right at sign 'Ermita de N.S. de la Fuensanta'. House 2nd on left.

Anne-Marie Walker & Yvette Winfield

tel/fax	+34 952 484072
mobile	+34 639 551743
email	loslimoneros@hotmail.com
web	www.loslimoneroshotel.com

Hotel

Map 20 Entry 287

Hacienda San José

Camino 1, Entrerrios, 29650 Mijas, Málaga

This hilltop hacienda is a cool, calm sanctuary from the concrete and heat of the Valle del Golf, and looks down on seven golf courses with views to Mijas and the sea. Delightful Nikki opened one of the first small country hotels in Spain years ago; now she and Pepe have created another classy and comfortable Andaluz retreat. The building is not ancient but the smell of woodsmoke and beeswax, the terracotta floors, the high wooden ceilings and the many antiques give the place a traditional feel. Huge bedrooms have underfloor heated tiles, colourwashed walls, new beds and generous drapes; bathrooms come with double sinks and fancy handmade tiles. The high-raftered, ochre-walled sitting room has warmth and charm, and you breakfast on a cobbled patio – homemade patisserie and fruits from the orchard. Your hosts are mindful of your privacy yet there when you need them. Riding and golf in summer, sightseeing (Granada, Ronda) in winter – and one of the mildest climates in Europe. A genuine cortijo feel, a great garden (palms, tennis, pool) and bags of class.

rooms	7: 2 twins/doubles, 5 suites.
price	€105–€110. Suites €140–€150.
meals	Dinner €25.
closed	Rarely.
directions	From Fuengirola for Marbella on N-340 (A7). In Cala de Mijas turn for La Cala Golf. At 1st r'bout, right; at next fork, right for Entrerrios; 1.8km; hotel signed.

Nikki & José García

tel	+34 952 119494
mobile	+34 639 790517
fax	+34 951 313141
email	haciendasanjose@yahoo.co.uk
web	www.hotelruralhaciendasanjose.com

Hotel

Map 20 Entry 288

Rancho Sentosa

Ctra. Mijas km4, La Alcaparra 7, 29650 Mijas, Málaga

A few miles inland from the Costa del Sol, hilltop Mijas keeps its Spanish charm. Its web of cobbled streets, the prettier the higher you go, are stuffed with tiny shops and traditional bars, while donkey-taxis line the main square. Rancho Sentosa hides in a leafy glade just below, the last villa in the road. Ex-London restaurateurs Vanessa and Slawek, in search of seclusion, fell in love with the place. Now, after a year of hands-on restoration, they have created both a home for themselves and two fabulous guest apartments. Living/dining rooms are airy and generous, bedrooms are immaculate with king-size beds, chic kitchens and mosaic'd shower rooms sparkle, and a brimming welcome hamper gets you off to a flying start. Modern art sits serenely with traditional beams and tiles. Masses of space outside too, with terraces for each bedroom and another for the shared pool – a lush and lovely spot with a sundeck, covered barbecue and wicker-chaired dining area. Vanessa and Slawek may join you but are mindful of your privacy; lovely hosts, they want you to go home with happy memories.

rooms	2 apartments for 2.
price	€65–€129. VAT included.
meals	Self-catering. Restaurants 1km.
closed	Rarely.
directions	From Málaga N-340 take A-7/E-15; 2nd exit for Mijas/Fuengirola at km213. Up hill towards Mijas on A-387; just before Bellini restaurant, right; signs down hill to Rancho Sentosa.

Vanessa Schon & Slawek Bolesta

tel	+34 952 590755
email	info@ranchosentosa.com
web	www.ranchosentosa.com

Self-catering

Map 20 Entry 289

Rancho del Inglés

Camino del Convento, 29130 Alhaurín de la Torre, Málaga

Now the children have flown, David and Miyuki have transformed their old rambling ranch into a quirky, fascinating place to stay. While the farmhouse itself is from the 1860s, complete with cobbled floor and fireplace, the rest is a fabulous cornucopia of building materials 'salvaged' from Europe to Asia and furnished with some apocryphal pieces. A shelving unit from a Surrey post office, an ancient Salamanca door, the headrest of a raised-iron Punjabi bed, a shower room open to the elements. No two rooms are alike and yet there are constants: in the beautiful old *barro* tiles and the arched shuttered windows that give onto delicate balconies. Various living areas have large log-burning stoves and huge dining tables; loggias have space and views; the citrus trees glow. Few British couples in Spain come more interesting than David and Miyuki. He a former advertising mogul, she a designer, they now market their own avocados and grow mountains of bougainvillea to defend their three-hectare oasis of charm from the inexorable sprawl of Alhaurin. *Min. stay two nights. 15 minutes from airport. Cook available.*

rooms	4 + 3: 4 twins. 1 house for 2; 1 house for 4-6; 1 house for 8.
price	€50-€80. Houses €105-€550.
meals	Breakfast €10. Restaurants in Alhaurín, 3-minute drive.
closed	Rarely.
directions	A-366/A-404; exit Parador del Golf/Churriana onto A-366. Thro' Alhaurín to BP-petrol. At r'about, exit Málaga/Coín; at 3rd r'bout, onto A-404; 1st right after 100m; on left before road bears right.

	Miyuki Taylor
tel	+34 952 410692
mobile	+34 677 167551
email	miyuki1@uk2.net
web	www.ranchodelingles.com

B&B & Self-catering

Map 20 Entry 290

Cortijo Padre Avilés

Ctra. de Olias km 7.5, 29197 Padre Avilés, Málaga

If it's solitude you're after, Padre Avilés is one of the quietest, remotest and most relaxing spots in andalucía, up in the hills 20 minutes from málaga – and only half an hour from the airport. It's a converted 17th-century convent steeped in history. And behind its walls lie two excellently equipped and spacious apartments, each with its own front door and private terrace. From one you slip straight out through French windows to the pool. Rooms have a nautical bent; the owners are super-keen sailors. And ideal hosts, very much around should you need them. Everything is shipshape: bedrooms light and airy, bedding crisp and white, mattresses orthopaedic; bathrooms have decent sinks and pretty mosaics; the cabin-style kitchen-diners have immaculate white sofas. Familes will not want to leave: there are two separate play areas, tennis courts, hammocks and a big pool. Take a well-worn path round the 180-acre estate scattered with olive and almond trees, or make for the national park just up the road. Views out to sea are awesome; on a clear day you can see Africa.

rooms	2 apartments for 5.
price	€850–€1,150 per week.
meals	Self-catering.
closed	Rarely.
directions	From Málaga airport towards town; exit for Motril/Almería onto A-7. After 20km & 3 tunnels, exit 246B dir. La Cala del Moral/Olías on M-24. Exit 5 for Olías; right at T-junc; house gate 6.5km, after telephone posts.

	Claire & David Parish
tel/fax	+34 952 294242
mobile	+34 666 148149
email	dave_claireparish@yahoo.co.uk
web	www.padre-aviles.com

Self-catering

Map 20 Entry 291

Hotel Humaina

Parque Natural Montes de Málaga, Ctra. de Colmenar s/n, 29013 Málaga

Hotel Humaina is hidden deep in a forest of oak and pine, at the end of a mile and a half of steep, unbeaten track. It was a hunting lodge before being reborn as a small hotel; the area was popular with the shooting brigade, but its new status as a Parque Natural means that the rabbits, foxes and hares are more likely to be of this world than the next. What strikes you when you arrive is the tranquillity of the place and it seems fitting that you should be greeted in such a gentle manner. The dining room and bedrooms are plainly furnished and nothing special; bedrooms at the front have the best wooded views. The cosiest space is the small lounge with chimney piece, furnished with books on walking and nature; set time aside to hike along the waymarked trail. This is an eco-aware hotel: water is recycled, heated by solar panels, then re-channelled into the garden; food comes from the vegetable patch. Try the *plato de los montes* if you like fry-ups, followed by a glass of *vino de pasas*, the local raisin wine. Birds sing, wild boar nose by at dusk: a delightfully simple forest getaway.

rooms	14: 10 twins/doubles, 2 family, 2 suites.
price	€71–€92. Singles €52–€56. Suites €106–€118. Half-board extra €22–€29 p.p.
meals	Breakfast €7. Lunch & dinner €25.
closed	Rarely.
directions	Málaga-Motril, exit 244 for Limonar. On for Camino Colmenar. After 15km onto C-345, at Fuente de la Reina, road on left for 3.8km.

	Juan María Luna
tel	+34 952 641025
fax	+34 952 640115
email	info@hotelhumaina.es
web	www.hotelhumaina.es

Hotel

Map 21 Entry 292

Fountainhead

Partido del Río el Terral, Fuente la Camacha, 29180 Riogordo, Málaga

One of the hippest hotels to open in recent years, Fountainhead surveys andalucía at its wildest – a mere 15 miles from Málaga. Sierra de Caramolos unfolds behind an unadulterated scene of olive groves and almond trees; the peace is incredible. A carob tree marks your entry onto the walled patio where a circular hole in the wall portals the cane covered walkway to your own casita, bordered by wild flowers and trim cacti. Just four – Indian, Sultan, Oriental, Arizona – they have been conceived with clean zen-like lines that belie Helen's fiesta of designer-savvy touches and glorious patterns. The fridge is packed full of goodies from manchego cheese to strawberries, while hot croissants and fresh bread are delivered to your door each morning. Architects by trade, Helen and Peter are your thoughtful hosts, zealous about organics and up for a laugh. They now produce their own olive oil, vegetables and delicious almonds. Unsurprisingly, the menu is local sophistication par excellence with staples of lemon grass and cumin soup and a salad of langoustine, orange and chicory. Even the wheelbarrows are stylish.

rooms	4 suites.
price	€225.
meals	Dinner €30.
closed	Mid-November-mid-December. Ask about weekend breaks.
directions	Directions on booking.

	Helen Bartlett & Peter Jewkes
mobile	+34 696 183309
email	info@fountainheadinspain.com
web	www.fountainheadinspain.com

Hotel

Map 21 Entry 293

Molino de Santillán

Ctra. de Macharaviaya km3, Apdo. de Correos 101, 29730 Rincón de la Victoria, Málaga

Carlo Marchini, tired of the cut and thrust of business in Madrid, moved to the softer climes of Andalucía, bought an old farmhouse and, after years of restoration, is harvesting the fruits of his efforts. The building is inspired by the hacienda-style architecture of the New World, its arched patio opening at the southern end to catch the light and a distant view of the sea. One wing is given over to the restaurant, an ochre rag-walled room where you may be treated to home-grown aubergines stuffed with hake, or loin of pork in a honey and apple sauce; the paella is excellent, too. Bedrooms feel properly Andalucían; stencilling and warm colours add zest, Casablanca fans keep the temperatures down, wrought-iron beds are prettified with mosquito netting. A new extension has been created for further rooms; they may lack the personality of the old ones but have French windows to private terraces and a well-finished feel. Outside: a pool and a verdant courtyard garden. Carlo, his daughter Adriana and their staff have created a comfortably laid-back restaurant-hotel. *A Rusticae hotel.*

rooms	22: 20 twins/doubles, 2 suites.
price	€90-€138. Singles €68-€89. Suites €142-€258.
meals	Breakfast €9. Lunch/dinner €20.
closed	Rarely.
directions	From Málaga for Motril on N-340. Exit for Macharaviaya; right at signs before reaching village. 1km of track to hotel.

Carlo Marchini

tel	+34 902 120240
fax	+34 952 400950
email	reservas@molinodesantillan.es
web	www.molinodesantillan.es

B&B

Map 21 Entry 294

Hotel Paraíso del Mar

c/Prolongación de Carabeo 22, 29780 Nerja, Málaga

Nerja is one of the busiest resorts of the Costa del Sol – hardly an auspicious beginning. But the Paraíso is a friendly little place, and pleasantly quiet, away from the main drag of restaurants and bars, and on the edge of a cliff looking out to sea. The main house was built in the Sixties by an English doctor (no lift, several stairs); the annexe is newer, and all has all been thoroughly revamped thanks to charming young Enrique and his wife Alicia. Most remarkable perhaps are the hotel's terraced gardens that drop down towards the beach: a tumble of jasmine, palms, bougainvillea, bananas, morning glory and a washingtonia… an exotic, southern air prevails. Bedrooms are pleasant – ask for one of the less dated – and most are roomy; the suites have jacuzzis; all have fluffy bathrobes and good towels. From some, a spiral stair leads you up to your own patch of roof terrace – perfect for sunset-watching, or topping up the tan as you gaze over the sparkling bay. Beneath the hotel are a sauna and a hot tub dug out of solid rock – and you breakfast on the terrace overlooking the Med.

rooms	17: 9 twins/doubles, 8 suites.
price	€77–€125. Singles €67–€115. Suites €108–€150.
meals	Restaurants nearby.
closed	Mid-November–mid-December.
directions	From Málaga N-340 for Motril. Arriving in Nerja, signs to Parador; Paraíso del Mar is next door.

	Enrique Caro Bernal
tel	+34 952 521621
fax	+34 952 522309
email	info@hispanica-colint.es
web	www.hotelparaisodelmar.com

Hotel

Map 21 Entry 295

Hotel Rural Almazara

Los Tablazos 197, Ctra. Nerja-Frigiliana, 29788 Nerja, Málaga

There's an unexpectedly rural feel to this new hotel, built above the coastal road in the vibrant resort of Nerja. After braving the beach or the shops, return to attractive grounds lined with palm trees and seating spots, decorative jasmine and acacia. The entrance is guarded by the olive press from which the hotel gets its name; the communal areas are comfortable in classic Spanish rustic style. And there's plenty of opportunity to splash: a pool on the terrace, perfect for families, and a plunge pool in the natural cave in the basement (extra charge, for couples only). There are also a jacuzzi and sauna. The restaurant, which has an adventurous menu and a good wine list, is a hive of activity in summer, and is considered one of the area's best. Dine outside with views of the sea. Spotless bedrooms have terraces and wicker chairs, and some traffic hum. Staff are friendly and helpful; take a copy of this guide and they will give you a discount. It's worth staying at least a night: in spite of encroaching urban sprawl, the beaches are some of the best in the region.

rooms	22: 21 twins/doubles, 1 single.
price	€79-€112. Singles €60-€80.
meals	Breakfast €9.50. Lunch & dinner €21.
closed	Rarely.
directions	From Málaga, N-340 for Motril. At Nerja (exit 292), MA-105 to Frigiliana. On right after 100m.

José Antonio Gómez Armijo

tel	+34 952 534200
mobile	+34 637 515532
fax	+34 952 534212
email	info@hotelruralalmazara.com
web	www.hotelruralalmazara.com

Hotel

Map 21 Entry 296

La Posada Morisca

Loma de la Cruz s/n, Ctra. Montaña Frigiliana-Torrox, 29788 Frigiliana, Málaga

Stylish comfort, stunning views. Lounge under a thatched parasol by the pool and gaze up at the mountains or down to the village and the distant sea… spectacular. The building, gleaming white and terracotta on the hillside, employs the best of andalucían design – Cordoban cobble-pattern floors, old wafer-brick thresholds – and is surrounded by verdant planting. Sara, from Frigiliana, has stamped her personality on this place, and her warmth and charm add greatly to the atmosphere. There is a sense of gaiety and simplicity about the whole establishment… brightly coloured tiles, latticed wardrobes, wood-burning stoves (each bedroom has one). Simple casita rooms, with private terraces and generous baths, are individually and appealingly decorated. Enjoy colourful food at well-dressed tables in the cosy, cream-walled dining room or on the terrace, where there's a choice of traditional and 'creative' menus. The wine list is small but select. And when your batteries are thoroughly recharged, head for Nerja, where there's lots going or – or inland. *A Rusticae hotel. Reserved parking, no charge.*

rooms	12 twins/doubles.
price	€72–€90. Singles €50–€60. VAT included.
meals	Dinner €20–€40 à la carte. VAT included.
closed	January.
directions	From Málaga m'way to Almería. Exit 292 for Nerja. There, MA-105 to Frigiliana. Round to the left; left at Taller los Cobos for Torrox. Signed on left after 1.5km; tricky to find.

	Sara Navas Sánchez
tel	+34 952 534151
fax	+34 952 534339
email	info@laposadamorisca.com
web	www.laposadamorisca.com

Hotel

Map 21 Entry 297

Finca El Cerrillo

29755 Canillas de Albaida, Málaga

From the delightfully sleepy square of whitewashed La Axarquía, a narrow road zigzags steeply down into the valley, crosses the river, then loops up to the old finca where olives and raisins were once farmed. When you reach the shady front terrace – with its heart-stopping view south to the Med – you can't fail but slip into that 'I'm on holiday' mood. Everyone loves El Cerrillo, where bedrooms and living spaces are traditionally andalucían and contemporary comforts have been integrated with style. Gordon was a set designer and has an eye for what works, in terms of colour and use of space. Bathrooms are tiled and gleaming, mattresses and linen are first class, and most rooms have the ocean view. Add to this an enchanting garden, a spectacular pool, fabulous breakfasts and dinners, hiking in the sub-tropical valley below, and relaxed and charming hosts. Indeed, it's all so lovely that we recommend you book for several nights. You could also reserve a place on one of their 'Arts at the Finca' events: birdwatching, painting, scriptwriting – just ask.

rooms	12 twins/doubles.
price	€100–€110. Singles €65–€80.
meals	Dinner €25 (4 days a week). Buffet lunch €10. Packed lunch €8. Restaurants 1.5km.
closed	Mid-November–mid-December.
directions	Exit Algarrobo/Caleta, then signs towards Competa. Pass Sayalonga; left to Archez, dir. Sedella/Salares. Cross bridge, up hill; right at sign 'Fogarate'. On right before Canillas.

	Sue & Gordon Kind
tel/fax	+34 952 030444
mobile	+34 636 921252
email	info@hotelfinca.com
web	www.hotelfinca.com

Hotel

Map 21 Entry 298

El Amparo

Cortijo Lorenzo, Santa Cruz del Comercio, 18129 Alhama de Granada, Granada

If you're anything like the Arabic king Abu al-hacen, you'll leave the historic spa town of Alhama de Granada with the same agonised parting – "Ay de mi Alhama!" No doubt Jeff and Sally shared a similar sentiment when they realised that they couldn't save the original 200-year-old farmhouse from collapse. Left with four exposed acres to rebuild upon, they have worked industriously to incorporate as many of the historic touches as possible. The gloss has yet to mellow with its surrounds, but a fountain courtyard, old beams and original roof pantiles all remember a past grandeur. Jeff, a one-time baker, now your chef, knows his crust from crumb and has an eye for the innovative – such as the old tile lights cut into the walls and a curved bar made from an ancient sledge – as well as essentials like a roaring fire in winter. All the furniture in modern and TV-free bedrooms is shiny and new, neat shutters close out the day and fans keep you cool in front of full-length mirrors. Pretty *azulejo* tiles in the bathroom complete an indulgence of Italian marble. Mountain bikes are on the house!

rooms	6: 5 twins/doubles, 1 family.
price	€85–€125. Singles €60.
meals	Lunch & dinner €20, by arrangement.
closed	Rarely.
directions	A-92 to Granada, exit 211 for Moraleda de Zafayona & Alhama de Granada. At Santa Cruz, left opposite bar Ferubi; cross square; pass church & take left fork. Up track for 1.5km.

	Jeff & Sally Webb
mobile	+34 628 867755
email	info@elamparo-granada.com
web	www.elamparo-granada.com

Hotel

Map 21 Entry 299

Hotel La Tartana

Urbanización San Nicolás, 18697 La Herradura, Granada

This has always been a focal point for the people of La Herradura and never more so than now; Penny, Barry, and Jo spent years on cruise ships catering for the rich and famous before coming here to roost. La Tartana, surrounded by trees, its arched entrance swathed in bougainvillea, is right by the coastal road — noisy, yes, at certain times of the day, but there is an almost uninterrupted view of the sea, and a big terrace from which to enjoy it. The hotel is built andalucían style, around a patio, with a fountain at the centre and rooms leading off, and the interiors, mixing old with new, are a delight. Doors and beams come from a 16th-century convent, boutique bedrooms are white-walled with splashes of colour. Downstairs is a vaulted bar — a great place to get to know your relaxed hosts over a drink and a salsa dip before settling down to enjoy Jo's inspired cooking. Both food and dining room are colourful. Dishes are American with an international 'fusion' (ribs, Irish beef, Thai curries, salads) and there is a good and unusual selection of Navarra wines. Save room for some fine desserts.

rooms	7: 4 twins, 3 doubles.
price	€55-€79.
meals	Dinner €15.
closed	Rarely.
directions	From Málaga, N-340 for Motril. Urbanización San Nicolás on left hand side of road, just before entrance to La Herradura. Hotel 1st house on left on entering Urbanización.

	Penny Jarret & Barry Branham
tel/fax	+34 958 640535
email	reservations@hotellatartana.com
web	www.hotellatartana.com

Hotel

Map 21 Entry 300

La Casa de los Bates

Ctra. Nacional 340 km329.5, Apartado de Correos 55, 18600 Motril, Granada

It was built in 1898: a bad year for Spain with the loss of its last American colony. But not a hint of depression in this flamboyant Italianate villa. It stands just far enough back from the coastal highway for noise not to be intrusive, and is shielded by one of the most exquisite gardens in the south: huge and exuberant palms, catalpas, magnolias and Atlas cedars to make a plant-lover's heart quiver. Many of the trees and fishponds pre-date even the villa. When the Martín-Feriche family acquired the house it had long lain empty but thanks to careful restoration and the skill of an accomplished interior designer it is once again an elegant, beautifully furnished home. Marble-floored lounges flourish Deco lamps, Japanese lacquered tables, screens and oils, a Bechstein piano, family photos, gilt mirrors, mounted pistols, a harp; bedrooms have a classic 1950s period feel, bathrooms are attractive modern. The mahogany table in the dining room sits up to 20 (great for small weddings); give your blue-blooded hosts enough warning and a formal, candlelit dinner can be prepared. *A Rusticae hotel.*

rooms	4: 3 twins/doubles, 1 suite.
price	€132–€180. Suite €240.
meals	Dinner €25–€45 à la carte. VAT included. On request.
closed	Rarely.
directions	From Málaga N-340 east. Pass Salobreña; after 2km, large warehouses on right of 'Frutas de Cara'. Exit, then N-340 back for Salobreña; 200m; right for house.

	Borja Rodríguez Martín-Feriche
tel	+34 958 349495
fax	+34 958 349122
email	info@casadelosbates.com
web	www.casadelosbates.com

Hotel

Map 21 Entry 301

Palacete de Cazulas

Caserío de Cazulas s/n, 18698 Otívar, Granada

It's thanks to the irrigation skills of the Moors that this palace and its delightfully informal gardens are as verdant as anywhere in Europe. Structurally, everything is as it was centuries ago when a local aristocrat added to the former Arabic palace turning it into an Italianate masterpiece. While neither modern nor stylish inside, it keeps its old charms. Rooms are elegant, fabrics luscious, furniture antique; there are sparkling bathrooms, a couple of four-posters, delightful curios and sweeping views, and the vaulted-ceiling salon has an honesty bar and books. Five miles from the nearest village (three restaurants, two bars), at the end of a subtropical valley, you are blissfully secluded, the goatherd's flock the only traffic. Come with a family party and take over the whole place: basic maid service is included, and there are cooks should you need them. Outside are walled grounds and hidden corners, a private chapel, a long pool flanked by high clipped cypress, tennis… and a heavenly walk along the valley floor to a towering gorge and crystalline rock pools. One of the best.

rooms	11 + 1: 11 twins/doubles. Cottage for 2-4.
price	From €120. Whole house (16): €9,900 per week. Extra guests: €550 p.p. p.w. Cottage €700 p.p. per week.
meals	Restaurants in village.
closed	May-August self-catering only.
directions	From Almuñecar, A-4050 to Granada past Otívar. On for 5km to km43.3 marker; left at 'central Cazulas'. On for 1.5km.

Brenda & Richard Russell-Cowan

tel	+34 958 644036
mobile	+34 619 040309
fax	+34 958 644048
email	info@cazulas.com
web	www.cazulas.com

Hotel & Self-catering

Map 21 Entry 302

Cortijo del Pino

c/Fernán Núñez 2, La Loma, 18659 Albuñuelas, Granada

Little-known Albuñuelas is only a short drive from the Costa and 30 minutes from Granada. It's a fetching little place surrounded by citrus groves, with wonderful walks along the rocky canyon that cuts south from the village. El Cortijo del Pino sits high on a bluff above, taking its name from the gargantuan Aleppo pine that stands sentinel over house and valley. The sober lines of the building have an Italian feel and the sandy tones that soften the façade change with each passing hour. Perhaps it was the endlessly shifting light that attracted artist James Connel. His painterly eye and his wife Antonia's flair for decoration have created a warm, enveloping place to stay, an open house for guests and friends. Bedrooms are big, beamed and beautiful, with comfortable beds and very good bathrooms. Outside, birdsong and church bells, roses, wisteria and a terrace with sweeping views, a dreamy pool... if you are inspired, grab a canvas and an easel and retire to James's studio. Art lovers be warned: his paintings are on every wall and you may be tempted to part with your money! *House available for rent in summer.*

rooms	5: 4 twins/doubles, 1 suite.
price	€85–€110. Singles €65. Whole house €2,000 p.w. VAT included.
meals	Restaurants nearby.
closed	Rarely.
directions	From Málaga dir. Granada; m'way to Motril, exit 153 for Albuñuelas. Opp. bus stop, right & follow steep road to house.

James Connel & Antonia Ruano

tel	+34 958 776257
mobile	+34 607 523767
fax	+34 958 776350
email	cortijodelpino@eresmas.com
web	www.elcortijodelpinolecrin.com

B&B & Self-catering

Map 21 Entry 303

Molino del Puente

Puente de Durcal s/n, 18650 Durcal, Granada

The water that gushes from the high Sierras is the raison d'être for this old mill —
and explains the prolific greenery and birdlife. Dori and Francisco started off
making organic biscuits and jams; now they have a successful restaurant-hotel.
The dining room has already made quite a name for itself with the locals, and
rightly so: the food is Andaluz, the meats char-grilled, the desserts wood-fired,
the fruits, vegetables and liqueurs home-grown. Note that they get very busy
with wedding and christening parties at weekends. Bedrooms are modest affairs
but full of creature comforts, there are cosy rafters and Impressionists on rag-
rolled walls, and shower rooms full of towels. The sound of rushing water is never
far away (competing with the cars crossing the bridges to either side) so a first-
floor room might be a wise choice during winter. The newest bedrooms are in a
separate wing, but our favourite is room 102 — a waterfall plunges down outside
its window! Come for the food, the people and the lush setting; children will
enjoy the new outdoor pool.

rooms	15 twins/doubles.
price	€75–€90. Singles €50. VAT included.
meals	Lunch & dinner €20–€30 à la carte.
closed	2 weeks in November.
directions	From Motril, m'way north for Granada. Exit Durcal; just after crossing bridge, sharp right down hill.

Francisco Maroto Caba

tel	+34 958 780731
mobile	+34 629 415144
fax	+34 958 781798
email	biodurc@teleline.es
web	www.elmolinodelpuente.com

Hotel

Map 21 Entry 304

Alojamiento Rural Cortijo del Pino
18194 Churriana de la Vega, Granada

Farmhouse B&B 15 minutes from the city, and a delightful family. Kind, artistic Concha and her mother make this place, and their grand old farmhouse, topped with tower and pigeon loft, is hard to resist. The approach is marvellous, the beautiful surrounding trees creating a warm, out-of-time atmosphere. The apartments in their converted cattle stalls are supremely comfortable – one a nest for two, another sleeping six, two sleeping four. Come for underfloor heating, woodburning stoves and characterful and well-equipped kitchens. Furnishings are antique, the beds a delight; ceilings are high, walls thick, tiles handmade. A gorgeous wisteria covers some of the outside patio, and each of the houses has its own terraced area. The swimming pool and laundry are shared. For the green-fingered and green-minded, there are workshops on recycling and nature, while summer guests are offered products from the holding's own *huerta ecológica*. And when you've had enough of home cuisine, there's an excellent *venta* nearby. Who would not love this place? *Minimum stay two to seven nights.*

rooms	4 apartments for 2-6.
price	€68-€123 (€408-€861 per week). VAT included.
meals	Self-catering.
closed	Rarely.
directions	From Ronda de Granada, exit 128. At r'bout to 'Depuradora Aguas Residuales' and 'Campo de Golf'. Cross river to Churriana de la Vega. At r'bout to C. de la Vega. 1.4km; right for 'Camino Viejo de Cullar'. Follow signs.

	Concha Lopez
tel	+34 958 250741
email	info@cortijodelpino.com
web	www.cortijodelpino.com

Self-catering

Map 22 Entry 305

Hotel Reina Cristina

c/Tablas 4, 18002 Granada

A big 19th-century townhouse, two steps from the cathedral and the Bib Rambla square. The hotel comfortably strides past and present, able to please the most demanding of modern travellers. Carpeted corridors lead to marble-floored bedrooms with a pot-pourri of printed bedspreads and drapes and comfortable beds. Ask for one of the larger rooms set around the furnished, fountained courtyard (neo-*mudéjar* ceiling, pretty andalucían tiles, marble columns: blissfully cool): they should be quieter than most. In one corner is a reproduction of the painting depicting the rendition of Granada; the dining room has the original Art Deco fittings and a collection of photos from the time of one of Spain's most revered poets, García Lorca, whose friend, Luis Rosales, lived here. Make sure you eat in at least once: the Rincón de Lorca restaurant has won awards, the chef conjuring up a mix of traditional regional dishes and in-house specialities. The wine list is judicious and long. Excellent tapas in the café, too, and homemade cakes. Maria and her staff are relaxed and friendly – and the position is perfect.

rooms	60 twins/doubles.
price	€80–€119.
meals	Breakfast €7.50. Lunch & dinner €23. A la carte from €35.
closed	Rarely.
directions	From A-92 exit 128 onto Mendez Nuñez which becomes Avda. Fuentenueva. Before Hotel Granada Center, right into Melchor Almagro which becomes Carril del Picón. Left at end into c/Tablas. Intercom to open gate. Hotel on left.

	María Gómez & Federico Jiménez
tel	+34 958 253211
fax	+34 958 255728
email	clientes@hotelreinacristina.com
web	www.hotelreinacristina.com

Hotel

Map 21 Entry 306

Casa Morisca ✓

Cuesta de la Victoria 9, Bajo Albaycín, 18010 Granada

Imagine yourself outside a tall, balconied, 15th-century house on the south-facing slopes of the Albaycín. The street drops steeply away and opposite towers the Alhambra. You are in the old Moorish quarter of Granada and Casa Morisca is an exquisite example of the old style. Rescued and restored by Carlos, its architect owner, it won the Europa Nostra prize; easy to see why. A heavy door leads from the street to a galleried inner courtyard, where slender pilasters, wafer-brick columns, delicate mouldings and pool create serenity and space. The same subtle mastery of effect runs throughout. In one of the blissful bedrooms you lie on your bed and espy the Alhambra from a specially angled bathroom mirror. One top-floor room with astonishing views has been turned into the most romantic of eyries; another has a magnificent *mudéjar* ceiling, stripped of its plaster shroud. Bathrooms are ultra-chic. On a more prosaic note, the eateries of Acera del Darro are a step away – or you may climb the labyrinthine streets to the restaurants of Plaza San Miguel Bajo and rub shoulders with the Granadinos.

rooms	15: 12 twins/doubles, 2 suites, 1 family.
price	€114-€144. Suites €196. Family €154-€194.
meals	Breakfast €10.
closed	2 weeks in January.
directions	Detailed directions on booking.

María Jesús Candenas & Carlos Sánchez

tel	+34 958 221100
mobile	+34 609 817859
fax	+34 958 215796
email	info@hotelcasamorisca.com
web	www.hotelcasamorisca.com

Hotel

Map 21 Entry 307

Casa del Capitel Nazarí

Cuesta Aceituneros 6, 18010 Granada

At the heart of this 16th-century *palacete* is a superb Granadino courtyard. Half a dozen slender marble columns, two of which are Roman, surround the pebble-mosaic. There's also a Nasrid carved capital from which the hotel takes its name, and several carved ceilings are still in place, too; look skywards and you'll see the elegant, encircling galleries of the floors above. Generally speaking, this is an attractive if slightly disorganised place, with pretty communal spaces but less impressive bedrooms, some of which are on the poky side and whose shower rooms are tiny! Best to ask for one of the quieter rooms, away from the courtyard. Modest buffet breakfast is at glass-topped tables in the little dining room; in summer you spill into the courtyard, delightful with plants and wicker chairs. No dinners here, but restaurants, cafés, tapas bars and Moroccan tea houses just outside the door. Although parking is a taxi ride away, the position, in Granada's oldest quarter, is superb – 200 metres from the Plaza Nueva and a 20-minute walk up the wooded Alhambra hill to the palace.

rooms	17 twins/doubles.
price	€72-€99. Singles €65-€79.
meals	Breakfast €8. Restaurants 50m.
closed	Rarely.
directions	A-44, exit 131 for Armilla – Palacio de Congresos. Follow signs to Parking Plaza Puerta Real (€13 per day). Take taxi to hotel; hotel will reimburse with taxi receipt.

Angela Caracuel Vera

tel	+34 958 215260
fax	+34 958 215806
email	info@hotelcasacapitel.com
web	www.hotelcasacapitel.com

Hotel

Map 21 Entry 308

El Ladrón de Agua

Carrera del Darro 13, 18010 Granada

Captivated by a visit to Granada in 1924, the poet (later Nobel prize-winner) Juan Ramón Jiménez wrote *Olvidos*, a spiritual journey inspired by the water found throughout the city. Raúl, the sympathetic young manager of El Ladrón, hopes his beautiful, unusual hotel will be a source of inspiration too. The place fuses poetry, water, architecture, luxury and friendliness in an irresistible blend. A vast new painting in the hall pays tribute to the poet but the most memorable part of the 16th-century building is its central patio. Slender columns of Tuscan marble support a graceful gallery and the fountain has been sculpted from a block of sombre marble. In the high-ceilinged bedrooms nothing has been stinted or forgotten: sumptuous beds, oriental rugs on terracotta floors, lovely writing desks… Each room has been named after a character or poem connected to Jiménez. Eight look across to the Alhambra hill; those at the front of the hotel are above the busy thoroughfare of the Carrera del Darro. You're right in the middle of old Granada, a short walk from Sacro Monte and the Alhambra itself.

rooms	15 twins/doubles.
price	€105–€218. Singles €79–€172. Half-board €30 extra p.p.
meals	Breakfast €9.50.
closed	Rarely.
directions	In Granada head for city centre & Plaza Nueva. Here, drive up Carrera del Darro (parallel to river Darro). Hotel 50m from Plaza Nueva. Park in any central car park & take a taxi.

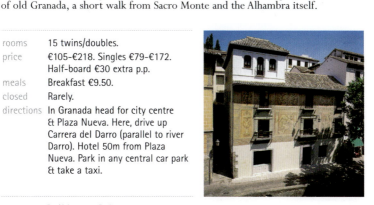

	Raúl Lozano Ruiz
tel	+34 958 215040
fax	+34 958 224345
email	info@ladrondeagua.com
web	www.ladrondeagua.com

Hotel

Map 21 Entry 309

Migueletes ✓

c/Benalúa 11 (Plaza Nueva), 18010 Granada

Slip through doors into a quiet courtyard cooled by a fountain and scented with citrus; gaze up to a handsome tier of wooden galleries; catch a glimpse of tiled staircases and inviting archways. Hard to believe you are in the heart of dusty Granada. The 17th-century nobleman's house is as richly atmospheric as the Moorish Albaycín quarter that surrounds it, and has been sympathetically restored. It keeps its grandeur yet is quietly, luxuriously, 21st century. Rooms have beamed ceilings, tiled floors and carved, hand-crafted beds. Polished antiques, plump sofas and rich hangings add to the high-comfort factor while bathrooms spoil with gorgeous soaps, masses of towels and classy tiles. Some rooms overlook the Alhambra, one has a domed bathroom, another is in a tower. Pull out all the stops and choose the four-poster suite in the old chapel. Traditional andalucían breakfasts are taken in the glowing, brick-arched cellar. Manageress Ingunn makes you feel like family and has an enviable knowledge of Granada's best tapas bars and restaurants: ask for the owners' guide.

rooms	25: 24 twins/doubles, 1 suite.
price	€129-199. Suite €349.
meals	Breakfast €9.50. Restaurant 20m.
closed	8-31 January.
directions	Granda 'circunvalacion', exit 129 for Centro-Recogidas; right for Palacio de Congresos. In square, park in underground Plaza Puerta Real (special rates for hotel guests); taxi to hotel (receipt required). Check web site for detailed directions.

	Karl Otto Skogland & Ana Raczkowski
tel	+34 958 210700
fax	+34 958 210702
email	info@casamigueletes.com
web	www.room-matehotels.com

Hotel

Map 21 Entry 310

Hotel Rural Alicia Carolina

c/Granada 1 (Cruce Colinas), Monachil, 18193 Granada

The modern façade of this roadside hotel belies a homely interior of gleaming terracotta, dark polished wood and shining brass candlesticks. Bedrooms – simple and beautiful with their gleaming floors, richly coloured bedspreads and creamy voile – look as though someone pops in to plump up the pillows when the guests are out. Each room has its individual touch, an embroidered cushion, a hand-painted headboard, a pair of antique chairs, a pile of books. And, always, fresh flowers. Choose a second-floor attic room for sloping ceilings. Then there are the views... the hotel's plumb-perfect position, outside the village of Monachil, eight minutes from Granada, means one side looks towards the city's skyline while the other gazes on the snow-capped peaks of the Sierra Nevada. There's skiing a half-hour drive, a bus stop outside for jaunts to the sea, and fine walking. In the evening, relax with a drink in the cosy sitting room while Alicia, the young, energetic owner, cooks an authentic Portuguese supper using her grandmother's recipes. Simple, gracious, good value – and what a spot! *Frequent buses to Granada.*

rooms	10: 8 twins/doubles, 1 single, 1 family.
price	€52–€66. Single €39. Family €52; €15 extra bed. VAT included.
meals	Dinner €25 on request.
closed	First 3 weeks in July.
directions	Granada ring road, exit for Alhambra & Sierra Nevada; then exit 2 for Monachil. At lights, ahead for 700m to crossroads. On right.

	Alicia Higueras Rodríguez
tel/fax	+34 958 500393
mobile	+34 639 203196
email	info@hotelaliciacarolina.com
web	www.hotelaliciacarolina.com

Hotel

Map 21 Entry 311

La Molín Private Guest House

Cortijo Pitel Bajo, 18247 Moclín, Granada

Locals tell of a mill standing on this site for 400 years, and history buffs will love it here – as will anyone who craves peace in a spectacular, undiscovered area. The doors and windows of the old flour mill have been lovingly restored by Brian, a carpenter, and new tiles and metal gates added. Bedrooms and bathrooms are light and clean; nooks and crannies create cosy spaces to hole up with a book (yours to borrow). The welcoming British owners are good people who like to eat with their guests, and take enormous pride in the old place; they also know lots about the local history. Romans, Moors and Christians swept through the area, the final frontier before Granada, and tales of ancient fortifications and bloody battles abound. As you saunter among the custard-apple and plum trees, the silence is broken only by the liquid tones of rare golden oriels and spring water tumbling into a stone trough. If the history inspires you, help 'dig' the remains of the Roman settlement next door. *Minimum stay two nights.*

rooms	3: 2 twins/doubles, 1 family.
price	€48. Family €58. VAT included.
meals	Picnic €10. Dinner €20. VAT included.
closed	Rarely.
directions	N-432 from Granada towards Alcala La Real & Moclín. Just before Moclín, take road to the left for Tozar. Hotel on left, at bottom of hill.

Janet & Brian Shields

tel	+34 958 403035
mobile	+34 686 393792
email	janshields@gmail.com
web	www.lamolin.com

B&B

Map 16 Entry 312

La Almunia del Valle

Camino de la Umbría s/n, 18193 Monachil, Granada

Secluded terraces, soothing fountains, little channels ferrying water to every part of the grounds… In the Moorish period, an *almunia* was a summer residence and there's a distinctly Moorish feel to this hillside garden. The farmhouse, once lived in by a German artist, stands in its own orchards, its crisp white lines softened by an abundance of chestnuts, olives and figs. The interiors have been touched by a masterly hand in a mix of period and modern – traditional slate floors and contemporary art, leather chairs and woven hangings – plus some arresting colours and masses of books. Bedrooms smell deliciously of cherrywood and are lavishly equipped… bright kilims, Casablanca fans and unexpected detail add interest to the understated elegance. From the vast sitting room, painted a warm rose, you step out onto the wide terrace and take in the dramatic sweep of mountains and the Monachil valley below. You're 20 minutes from Granada but it all feels rural, remote and tranquil. Terrific food, too, and a small but good selection of house wines. Perfect for sybarites. *A Rusticae hotel.*

rooms	9 twins/doubles.
price	€103–€120. Singles €85-103.
meals	Dinner €30-€36.
closed	13-30 November; 22 December-2 January.
directions	Follow signs for Alhambra & Sierra Nevada on Ronda Sur ring road; exit 2 Monachil. Follow signs for Monachil & Casco Antiguo; through hamlet; follow signs along narrow road to La Almunia.

	José Manuel Plana & Patricia Merino
tel	+34 958 308010
mobile	+34 619 130508
fax	+34 958 304476
email	laalmunia@infonegocio.com
web	www.laalmuniadelvalle.com

Hotel

Map 21 Entry 313

Alojamiento Rural El Molino

Avda. González Robles 16, 18400 Órgiva, Granada

Wander round the weekly market to see just how New Age this multi-ethnic community has become. This is bustling, hippy-shabby Órgiva, and you are in the heart of it. But behind the heavy grille lies an enclosed walled patio and another world. Esteban is a young and delightful host, who ran this old olive mill as a bar before turning it into a wonderful *turismo rural*. Terracotta floors, massive beams, a potted palm – there's an andalucían feel. In the vast and lofty bedrooms – those at the back the quietest – is a mix of simple wooden furniture and the odd antique; one wardrobe was once a confessional. Breakfast is an excellent spread, served, for much of the year, on the patio by the fig tree. Bliss in the heat of the day to float in the small, jacuzzi-style pool under an azure andalucían sky. This lush, exuberant area, put on the map by Chris Stewart's *Driving Over Lemons*, has some great walks: take advantage of the GR7 long-distance footpath that traverses the southern flank of the Sierra Nevada, or explore the remoter villages of the Alpujarra.

rooms	5 twins/doubles.
price	€58. VAT included.
meals	Dinner on request.
closed	Rarely.
directions	From Málaga, N-340 for Motril; N-323 for Granada. Exit Lanjarón; N-322 to Órgiva. El Molino on right just before 1st set of lights. Free parking at municipal car park behind Guardia Civil station.

	Esteban Palenciano
mobile	+34 646 616628
email	elmolino@casaruralelmolino.com
web	www.casaruralelmolino.com

B&B

Map 21 Entry 314

Hotel de Mecina Fondales

c/La Fuente 2, 18416 Mecina Fondales, Granada

The walking here is wonderful and this small modern hotel a comfortable place to return to after a day of trail-bashing. It looks out across the lush Guadalfeo valley; read more about the area – and its people – in Chris Stewart's *Driving Over Lemons*. In spite of its large reception area, the hotel has a cosy feel. The dining room is especially inviting, with its dark chestnut beams, patterned curtains and ladderback chairs. Pizza is on the menu – but if you fancy something authentic, try the *plato alujarreño*; this Spanish fry-up has several local variants but will certainly include 'poor-man's potatoes' and sweet green peppers. Victor the owner is keen to promote traditional dishes and local wines. Bedrooms are medium to large, squeaky clean and as smart as can be, with fridge, kettle and central heating; a winter stay would be a cosy one. For views, ask for a room looking south to the valley. The hamlet sits high on the Sierra Nevada, a cluster of whitewashed houses with the flat slate roofs and rounded chimney stacks typical of the area.

rooms	21 twins/doubles.
price	€75–€100. Singles €50.
meals	Breakfast €6. Lunch & dinner €12–€18. A la carte €20–€25.
closed	Rarely.
directions	N-323 for Motril; C-333 through Lanjarón. Before Órgiva, Pampaneira road to Pitres. 1km before village, right for Mecina. At entrance to village, right.

Victor Fernández

tel	+34 958 766254
fax	+34 958 766255
email	victor@hoteldemecina.com
web	www.hoteldemecina.com.es

Hotel

Map 21 Entry 315

Los Piedaos

Las Barreras, 18400 Órgiva, Granada

At the end of the long winding track, on a tree-covered ridge beneath the soaring Sierra Nevada, the multi-levelled farmstead has been renovated by its architect owner with shade, privacy and huge views in mind. Each white casita reveals old tiles and timbers, recycled shutters and doors and a colourful hotch-potch of terraces and furnishings: convivial dining tables, throws over sofas, simple bedrooms/bathrooms and plenty of novels. The owners – keen hispanophiles, welcoming but discreet – are passionate about the organic growth of the Orgiva area and are aiming for carbon neutrality. Roofs are painted white to reflect sunlight, grey water is channelled into pretty gardens, hot water comes from solar panels, the pools are cleansed by copper/silver purification, air conditioning is low energy, olives and oranges are organically grown. Trails lead to quiet spots, swallows swoop above ancient olives and a 40-minute walk brings you to popular Orgiva, one of Spain's hippy towns (yoga, tai chi, meditation). Exceptional peace, subtle architecture, soaring views. *Minimum stay five nights.*

rooms	4 cottages: 3 for 4, 1 for 2-3.
price	€325-€750 per week.
meals	Self-catering. Restaurants in Orgiva, 3km.
closed	Rarely.
directions	Detailed directions & map on web site.

	Shujata & David Dry
tel	+34 958 784470
email	david@lospiedaos.com
web	www.holidays-in-southern-spain.com

Los Tinaos de la Alpujarra

c/Parras s/n, 18412 Bubión, Granada

These simple, 12-year-old apartments have been built on terraces in local style: slate walls, flat-topped roofs, rounded chimney stacks, rough plaster – and pink potted geraniums in brilliant contrast to white walls. What lifts them into the 'special' bracket is the beauty of their position, close to the village church and looking out over terraced groves of cherry, pear and apple all the way to the Contraviesa Sierra… on a clear day you can make out passing ships on the Mediterranean. Each house has an open-plan sitting, dining and kitchen area giving onto a small terrace – perfect for meals and sundowners. There are open hearths and central heating, workaday pine furniture, smallish bedrooms and bathrooms, and locally woven fabrics to add a dash of colour. At the lower end of this village you shouldn't hear a thing, apart from the murmur of the river and the tolling of the church bells. Wood is supplied in winter for a small charge and Isabel and José, who own the café-bar opposite (breakfasts and snacks), happily advise on where to eat and what to do.

rooms	12 apartments for 6.
price	Apartment for 2, €59; for 4, €78; for 6, €102. VAT included.
meals	Self-catering includes breakfast. Snacks in café.
closed	Rarely.
directions	From Granada N-323 for Motril. Exit V Benaudalla. Here to Órgiva; there; right to Bubión. Enter; left into c/Lavadero. 25m 1st (sharp) left; at small fountain right.

	Isabel Puga Salguero
tel	+34 958 763217
mobile	+34 660 515333
fax	+34 958 763192
email	info@lostinaos.com
web	www.lostinaos.com

Self-catering

Map 21 Entry 317

Las Alpujarras Retreat

Cortijo Los Hurtados, 18430 Torvizcon, Granada

As renovations go, this is one of the best. A flat-roofed Alpujarran cortijo has been painstakingly converted using old-fashioned methods, and almost everything is sustainable, from the pretty hydraulic tiles to the local-slate floors. Like the houses in the Rif mountains of Morocco, the roofs are a mix of cane, cardboard and clay. Patio doors lead onto countless shady terraces and contemplative corners. Be charmed by fresh flowers, cushions and a stylish mix of old and new. Previously owned by Robert Graves' granddaughter, this retreat was admired by Chris *Driving Over Lemons* Stewart — until he found his own place around the corner. Your widely travelled hosts are witty and warm, dedicated to running this breathtakingly lovely place as sustainably as possible. You are close to a hamlet that hasn't changed for centuries, with views onto soaring snow-capped mountains in winter… and not a new building in sight. The ancient watering system brings mountain water to the land and fills a spring-water pool, food comes from local produce and all products are green. Inspirational.

rooms	House for 6.
price	€900–€975 for 4. €185 extra p.p. Prices per week. VAT included.
meals	Self-catering. Picnic-style lunch €15. Dinner €30.
closed	Rarely.
directions	From Granada for Motril & Lanjarón. Continue through Orgiva; after bridge left for Torvizcón. Call owner to meet in village.

	Dominic Momcilovic & Martina Hunt
tel	+34 958 343299
email	retreat_espana@hotmail.com
web	www.lasalpujarrasretreat.com

Self-catering

Map 21 Entry 318

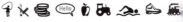

Alquería de Morayma

Ctra. A-348 Cádiar-Torvizcón, 18440 Cádiar, Granada

Mariano and his family built this fascinating hamlet-hotel in the local architecture, successfully recreating the rambling feel of an Alpujarran village. The main farmstead and the individual houses (one in the old chapel) are set amid olive groves, vineyards and kitchen garden — all organic. Your immensely likeable host has a commitment to the organic life — and hopes that guests will leave La Morayma with a deeper understanding of the traditions of mountain village life. Inside: antique brass bedsteads, Alpujarra bed covers, marble-topped dressers, good paintings, and photographs of the old farming days. Each room differs from the next, each feels warm and cared-for. Food is important here, a celebration of all things local, from delicious olive oil to charcuterie to the semolina cakes typical of this area. There are two restaurants, and wine from Morayma's new bodega in the cellars. See olives being milled during the the winter, or join in with the grape harvest or the sausage-making! The walking is wonderful — Mariano knows these hills well. *Reiki & relaxation courses available.*

rooms	13 + 5: 13 twins/doubles. 5 apartments for 4.
price	€54-€59. Singles €43-€47. Apartments €63.
meals	Breakfast €2.40. Lunch & dinner €12-€15.
closed	Rarely.
directions	From Granada N-323 south for Motril, then A-348 via Lanjarón, Órgiva & Torvizcón. 2km before Cádiar, signed on left.

Mariano Cruz Fajardo

tel/fax	+34 958 343221
email	alqueria@alqueriamorayma.com
web	www.alqueriamorayma.com

Hotel & Self-catering

Map 21 Entry 319

Sierra y Mar

c/Albaycín 3, 18414, Ferreirola, Granada

Take the blue door to paradise: enter a sunny, shady, flowery, leafy-walled garden
– a world apart. Mention breakfast: a minor feast shared with others under the
spreading mulberry tree. This is a gorgeous place run by two delightful people
(Italian and Danish) who know and love Andalucía; they are relaxed, intelligent
and 'green'. The ancient labyrinthine house has been extended with total respect
for its origins, and is furnished with old rural pieces and natural materials for
curtains and bedcovers, all in simple, wholesome taste. Each room has its own
shower or bath, and there's central heating for winter. Giuseppe and Inger
organise walking tours: do make time for the half-day circular hike that begins and
ends at the house. There's a well-equipped kitchen for guests, and a great family-
run restaurant you can walk to; also, a couple of vegetarian restaurants nearby.
The atmosphere is easy, the village is beautiful (you're in the heart of it) and your
hosts know the Alpujarras like few others. Wholly special B&B — book well in
advance. *Minimum stay two nights.*

rooms	9 twins/doubles.
price	€56. Singles €36. VAT included.
meals	Kitchen for guests. Restaurant 2km.
closed	Rarely.
directions	From Málaga dir. Motril, then dir. Granada. Cross small bridge after Vélez Benaudalla for Orgiva, then dir. Trevélez. 2 km before Pitres, down hill; in Mecina, left for Ferreirola. Park in square.

	Inger Norgaard & Giuseppe Heiss
tel/fax	+34 958 766171
email	reservas@sierraymar.com
web	www.sierraymar.com

Guest house

Map 21 Entry 320

Las Terrazas de la Alpujarra

Plaza del Sol 7, 18412 Bubión, Granada

You are high up in the Alpujarra – so high that on a clear day you can see down to the coast, across the Mediterranean and all the way to Africa. Las Terrazas, as the name implies, stands on a terraced hillside on the southern edge of Bubión. Enter the quietest inn in Spain: this is the only place – monasteries and churches aside – where we have ever seen 'Silencio Por Favor' signs on the walls! You breakfast in the modest lounge, on cheese and charcuterie. No other meals are served but there are plenty of good little restaurants and bars in the village. Bedrooms have terracotta floors, locally-woven blankets, framed photographs on the walls – small, nothing fancy and remarkably good value. Ask for one at the top with a view, or for one with a terrace. You can self-cater here, too – Paco's House nearby or the House of the Mill would be perfect for a vast party of hikers. Your hosts, the kindest of folk, have several mountain bikes and will happily help you plan your expeditions, speaking Spanish, on wheel or on foot.

rooms	20 + 5: 20 doubles. 3 apartments for 6; 2 houses for 20.
price	€29. Apt €37-€72. Houses €120-€180.
meals	Restaurants in village.
closed	7 January-7 February.
directions	Granada N-323 for Motril; C-333 through Lanjarón; just before Orgiva road to Pampaneira, left to Bubión. In village on left.

	Francisco Puga Salguero
tel	+34 958 763034
fax	+34 958 763252
email	info@terrazasalpujarra.com
web	www.terrazasalpujarra.com

Guest house

Map 21 Entry 321

Hotel La Fragua

c/San Antonio 4, 18417 Trévelez, Granada

Just to the south of the highest peak in the Sierra Nevada, this is one of the prettiest villages of the Alpujarra. Climb (steeply) up to its middle and find La Fragua, made up of two old village houses by the town hall. In one building is the friendly little bar; above, an eagle's nest of a pine-clad restaurant with a terrific view across the roofs — sit and gaze between courses. The food reflects the hostelry: simple and authentic. The locally-cured ham is utterly delicious and the puddings a treat. A few yards along the narrow street is the second house; this one holds your rooms. New terracotta floors, old beamed ceilings, comfy beds, no frills, perfect for walkers. Up above is a roof terrace with tables and another heavenly view. And there's a new annexe, right on the edge of the village, where the rooms are somewhat plusher — worth the extra euros. Your host, Antonio, knows walkers and their ways and will gladly help you plan your hikes. From May on, Trévelez attracts the trippers; come hiking — or riding — out of season, and return to wood-burning stoves.

rooms	24 twins/doubles.
price	€38. Singles €28.
meals	Breakfast €3.50. Lunch & dinner €12. A la carte €12–€15.
closed	10 January–10 February.
directions	Granada N-323 for Motril; C-333 through Lanjarón; just before Orgiva, take road to Trévelez. There, ask for 'Barrio Medio'; park in Plaza Las Pulgas. Next to town hall.

Antonio y Miguel Espinosa González

tel	+34 958 858626
fax	+34 958 858614
email	reservas@hotellafragua.com
web	www.hotellafragua.com

Hotel

Map 21 Entry 322

Casa Rural El Paraje

Ctra. Granada-Bérchules s/n, 18451 Bérchules, Granada

A short track cuts through groves of almonds, past chestnuts, olives and oak trees and brings you to this old farmhouse just above Bérchules. From the terrace in front – originally the threshing circle – are the most glorious views. And all around, superb walking country; one of the reasons Anita and Walter chose to settle here was so they could indulge their passion for walking. They're Dutch but completely at home in their adopted country – Anita and Walker spent many years exploring Spain and know it intimately. This is a relatively new venture for them: the farm covers about 20 hectares and the house was semi-derelict when they bought it; they've done a lot of the restoration themselves. The simply furnished bedrooms are attractively austere but provide everything you need – and the underfloor heating is a plus in the long Alpujarran winter. Downstairs is a small bar and restaurant, and the food is a treat. Walter, a terrific cook, uses good, fresh produce and serves local wines. He and Anita are the kindest, friendliest hosts and the area is refreshingly tourist-free.

rooms	4 + 1: 4 twins/doubles. 1 apartment.
price	€40-€45. Apartment €50. VAT incl.
meals	Dinner €15. VAT included.
closed	Rarely.
directions	From Málaga, east on N-340. Pass Motril, then left on N-345 to Albuñol. Just after Albuñol, right on N-340 to Cádiar, then A-4127 for Mecina; left to Bérchules. Here, left for Trévelez on A-4130; 2km, right at sign.

Anita Beijer & Walter Michels

tel	+34 958 064029
mobile	+34 626 186035
email	info@elparaje.com
web	www.elparaje.com

Guest house

Map 21 Entry 323

Hotel Los Bérchules
Ctra. de Granada 20, 18451, Bérchules, Granada

All that a walker could hope for: cosy, inexpensive, with good food and wine and a wonderful welcome from Wendy and son Alejandro. The hotel sits just beneath the village of Bérchules, 1,322m above sea level – about as high as Ben Nevis… Things are on a human scale here: a small, new-pine-clad lounge bar with a brick hearth and a collection of walking guides; a beamed dining room full of good things. Choose between à la carte and the great value *menú del día*; if you like rabbit, try Alejandro's paella. Guest bedrooms are sober and clean, pleasingly furnished with bright Alpujarra-weave curtains and blankets, with their own balcony-terraces and central heating for the cooler months. The best views are from those at the front. The long-distance footpath that runs the length of the southern flank of the Sierra Nevada passes right by; Wendy knows every route, and will run you to and from your hikes. A heated outdoor pool has been added, open from April to October. Don't be put off by the façade: this is a special place.

rooms	13 + 1: 10 twins, 3 singles. 1 apartment for 4.
price	€41-€49. Singles €30-€36. Apartment €70. VAT included.
meals	Breakfast €4. Lunch & dinner €10-€20.
closed	Rarely.
directions	Málaga, East on N-340. Pass Motril, left to Albuñol. Just after Albuñol, right on GR-433 to Cádiar, then Mecina; left to Bérchules. Enter village, on left.

Alejandro Tamborero Gibson
tel +34 958 852530
fax +34 958 769000
email hot.berchules@interbook.net
web www.hotelberchules.com

Hotel & Self-catering

Map 21 Entry 324

El Rincón de Yegen

Camino de Gerald Brennan, 18460 Yegen, Granada

Yegen is the village where Gerald Brennan came to live in the 1920s: his *South from Granada* is essential reading. Getting here is easier than in Brennan's day – and, although the 21st century has caught up with the villages of the Alpujarra, there is still beauty here in great measure. This small village inn, set just back from the road (some noise) fits well with its older neighbours – local slate, beam and bamboo are everywhere. Masses of shade-giving greenery means it's darkish inside, but the beamy dining room is inviting. Agustín, a trained cook, reworks local dishes in a light way, and the food is great value. The onion and goat's cheese tart makes a heavenly starter... and there's partridge, braised lamb with grapes, raspberry fool. Bedrooms are at the back of the restaurant, built high to catch the views from the hotel's 3,500-foot perch – they are large, with loads of space, new pine, stripey bedspreads, white walls, shining floors (warm underfoot in winter). It's as clean and as cared for as can be. If you prefer the independence of self-catering, the cottages have all you need.

rooms	4 + 3: 4 twins/doubles. 3 cottages for 4.
price	€42. Singles €30. Cottage €450 p.w. VAT incl.
meals	Breakfast €4.50. Lunch & dinner €14. A la carte €20-€30. Not Tuesday.
closed	First two weeks in February.
directions	Málaga N-340 Almería. Exit Albuñol; via Cádiar & Mecina Bombarón to Yegen. Signed left in village.

	Agustín Martín Rodríguez
tel/fax	+34 958 851270
email	elrincondeyegen@telefonica.net

B&B & Self-catering

Map 21 Entry 325

Casa Rural Las Chimeneas

c/Amargura 6, 18493 Mairena, Granada

Modest Mairena has barely changed since the advent of tourism – a gem of a village at the eastern end of Sierra Nevada. David and Emma are keen walkers and the majority of their guests come to explore the little-trodden paths that radiate from the village. The old house has been restored with particular sensitivity and you feel it the moment you enter. The guests' sitting/dining room is a light, lofty, serene space; four rocking chairs gather around a wood-burning stove, rush matting warms new stone floors, there are plants, books and views across the terraced hillsides. A plant-filled terrace with a tiny plunge pool shares the same view – with tantalizing glimpses of North Africa on a clear day. Guest bedrooms are as special, artistically furnished with antique dressers and beds (and modern mattresses!). Bathrooms, too, are a delight – uncluttered, stylish, homespun – as are the self-catering studios nearby. Dinner and breakfast are enjoyed at one table: the spirit of Las Chimeneas is relaxed and friendly. A perfect place for a long, restful stay.

rooms	3 + 3: 3 twins/doubles. 3 studios for up to 4.
price	€105. Singles €45. Studios €50-€90 (€300-€500 per week). VAT incl.
meals	Packed lunch €5. Dinner €20. VAT incl.
closed	Rarely.
directions	From Laroles, 2nd right into Mairena, by willows. Park in square; down narrow street at south-east corner; 10m to house.

David & Emma Illsley

tel	+34 958 760352
fax	+34 958 760004
email	info@alpujarra-tours.com
web	www.alpujarra-tours.com

B&B & Self-catering

Map 21 Entry 326

Cuevas Al Jatib

Arroyo Cúrcal s/n, 18800 Baza, Granada

A cave hotel may sound uncomfortable but Al Jatib takes you by surprise. This is the hot, cave-dwelling region of inland andalucía, and thousands of grotto-dwellers still live in Baza and Guadix – with good reason. Al Jatib is a super-stylish collection of cave houses and (excellent) restaurant that plunge up to 100 metres into the rock. Some caves are interlinked, all are huge fun, especially for families, with touches like a miniature 'clown cave' for children. The whole amazing, warren-like place was created by a Parisian interior designer: expect polished cement floors, ornate doorways, super kitchens, wide mantelpieces carved out of the rock, traditional wooden pergolas, earthy hues and cobalt blues – there's a lovely, laid-back, fishing shack mood. Cool ambient music is played throughout the day, both in the trendy bar and the Moroccan *tetería* (tea room); along one tunnel is a scented Turkish bath. Clever water-resistant planting adds to the drama – along with great sunsets and the swooping of the swallows. Peace reigns supreme.

rooms	4 + 4: 4 twins/doubles.
	4 cave houses for up to 11.
price	€79-€102. Cave houses €80-€185.
meals	Breakfast €4.50.
	Lunch & dinner €15-€25.
closed	Restaurant closed in June.
directions	Detailed directions on booking.

	Luc Compoint
tel	+34 958 342248
mobile	+34 667 524219
email	info@aljatib.com
web	www.aljatib.com

Hotel & Self-catering

Map 17 Entry 327

Hotel Zuhayra

c/Mirador 10, 14870, Zuheros, Córdoba

The Zuhayra's monolithic exterior may have you wondering. But do visit this small village at the wild heart of the Subbetica Park: quintessentially andalucían, its houses hug the hillside beneath the castle. Up above, the mighty mountains; below, mile upon mile of olives – and you are given a bottle of olive oil when you leave. Two delightful, gentle-mannered brothers and their wives manage the hotel. The downstairs café-bar is vast and utilitarian but on the first floor is a smaller room where you can tuck into local delicacies such as partridge, *clavillina* (thick stew served with a fried egg) and *remojón* (potato, onion and pepper salad with oranges). Delicious bread is locally made. Bedrooms are functional: modern pine, coordinated fabrics, hot-air heating, comfy beds. Bathrooms are spotless, all with baths; second-floor rooms get the best views. Walkers love it here and footpaths radiate from the village. Nearby there are cave paintings at The Cave of the Bats, you can hire a bike and head off along the *vía verde*, and Córdoba is an hour's drive.

rooms	18 twins/doubles.
price	€48-€60.
meals	Lunch & dinner €12. A la carte €16-€20.
closed	Rarely.
directions	Málaga for Córdoba; passing Lucena, A-339 on right to Cabra; cont. 4km; A-316 to Dona Mencia; pass town on left; right for Zuheros. In same street as Castillo 200m down hill (use castle car park).

	Juan Carlos & Antonio Ábalos
tel	+34 957 694693
fax	+34 957 694702
email	hotelzuhayra@zercahoteles.com
web	www.zercahoteles.com

Hotel

Map 16 Entry 328

Cortijo La Haza

Adelantado 119, 14978 Iznajar, Córdoba

An old farmhouse lost in the olive belt that stretches from here north and eastwards across almost half of Andalucía. If you like olive groves (it helps) and little-known corners of Spain, stay here – and use it as a base for your visit to the glories of Granada and Córdoba, the famous beaches of the Costa del Sol, and málaga, whose charming Old Town is often passed by. New owners Patriek and Bernadette have backgrounds in travel and tourism and are enthusiastically putting their stamp on this delightful small hotel. Opened five years ago, the renovation feels new yet the 'rustic' air of a 250-year-old andalucían cortijo has been beautifully preserved: walls have a rough render, old country pieces have been restored. Beamed bedrooms have Egyptian cotton sheets on wrought-iron bedsteads; bath and shower rooms are en suite. The sitting room and dining rooms are deliciously cosy with log-burning stoves, and in summer you spill into the white-walled courtyard. It is quiet, remote, friendly... and the pool and the garden share a spectacular view.

rooms	5 twins/doubles.
price	€75. Singles €65.
meals	Dinner €20.
closed	Rarely.
directions	From Málaga airport, A-7 for Málaga; A-45 & A-359 for Granada. After 24km, exit 1 onto A-333 for Iznajar. After km55 marker, left on CV-174 for 100m; left by small school for 2.6km. Signed on right.

	Patriek Defauw & Bernadette van der Heijden
tel	+34 957 334051
email	info@cortijolahaza.com
web	www.cortijolahaza.com

Hotel

Map 21 Entry 329

Hotel Huerta de las Palomas

Ctra. Priego–Zagrilla km3.5, 14800 Priego de Córdoba, Córdoba

Cascades of wrought-iron chandeliers, columned archways and a lofty central hall evoke the gracious style of a traditional cortijo. Yet this rural hotel, wrapped among olive groves, is brand new. Authentic grandeur cleverly combines with 21st-century comforts (large bathrooms, outdoor jacuzzi, gym) and not a trick has been missed – the garden's water feature even plays music. Bedrooms are hotel-stylish with warm pastel shades, wrought-iron bedheads, sleek repro furniture and shuttered windows. Bathrooms are rich in marble and ceramic tiling with plenty of multi-starred extras. You'll want to dress up for dinner, the dining room is so prettily elegant; the menu is andalucían with a modern twist. You could spend the whole day relaxing around the pool and gardens but it would be a shame not to make the most of where you are. Córdoba and Granada are an hour away, and the baroque architecture of Priego de Córdoba is just down the road. And there's the Subbetica National Park. A tranquil, friendly, well-planned hotel, surprisingly intimate for its size.

rooms	34: 30 twins/doubles, 4 suites.
price	€78–€100. Suites €110–€155.
meals	Lunch & dinner €20. A la carte €30–€35.
closed	Rarely.
directions	From Málaga A-45 for Antequera, then Lucena. Right onto A-339 to Priego de Córdoba. On entering Priego, left on CP-99 for Zagrilla. Hotel on left after 3.5km.

Salvador Ábalos

tel	+34 957 720305
fax	+34 957 720007
email	huertadelaspalomas@zercahoteles.com
web	www.zercahoteles.com

Hotel

Map 16 Entry 330

Palacio de la Rambla

Plaza del Marques 1, 23400, Úbeda, Jaén

The old towns of Úbeda and Baeza are often missed as travellers dash between Madrid and the coast, yet they are two of the brightest jewels in the crown of Spanish architecture. At the heart of old Úbeda, the exquisite Palacio de la Rambla dates from the Renaissance and has never left the Orozco family. You enter through an ornate Corinthian-columned portal into the cloistered patio; opulently colonnaded on two levels, smothered in ivy and wonderfully cool on a sweltering day. Lounge, dining room and bedrooms are large to massive and a perfect match for their setting: antique beds, chests, trunks, lamps, pretty washstands, claw-foot tubs, religious mementos, family portraits, and native terracotta softened by *estera* matting. Young, bubbly, glamorous staff will serve you one of the best breakfasts in this book: eggs, toast with olive oil, baskets of fruit, cheese, charcuterie, homemade cakes and jams. Palacio de la Rambla has a long tradition of regal welcoming; King Alfonso XIII stayed here when he was in town. A delectable, peaceful retreat. *A Rusticae hotel.*

rooms	8: 7 twins/doubles, 1 suite.
price	€115-€125.
meals	Restaurants nearby.
closed	16 July-10 August.
directions	From Madrid south on N-IV. At km292 marker, N-322 to Úbeda. There, follow 'Centro Ciudad' until Palacio is in front of you, between c/Ancha & c/Rastro, opposite cafetería La Paloma.

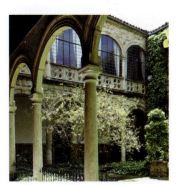

	Elena & Cristina Meneses de Orozco
tel	+34 953 750196
fax	+34 953 750267
email	hotel@palaciodelarambla.com
web	www.palaciodelarambla.com

Hotel

Map 16 Entry 331

Alojamientos La Torrecilla

Herredamiento s/n, 23480, Quesada, Jaén

The whitewashed farmhouse surrounded by ancient olive groves has held onto its rustic charm, while the spectacular views of precariously positioned Quesada are only matched by the distant glimpses of Ubeda and Baeza across a patchwork spread of fields. On the edge of the Cazorla National Park, this is one of Spain's best places for spotting deer, mountain goats; even the rare bearded vulture. The celebrated GR-7 international footpath goes right past the gate and gets you to Cazorla in three hours; continue and you'll eventually reach the terminus in Athens. Return to a spot beneath the garden's leafy walnut tree, or a dip in the small plunge pool. Your host is a personable and down-to-earth chap who spends his time renovating old buildings. He also knows the area well, having moved here from Granada ten years ago. Expect a cobbled terrace, a big old fireplace, pitted terracotta floors, a simple kitchen, few frills, and lashings of character. La Torrecilla is popular with the style-conscious French in summer, so book early. *Minimum stay one week July-Sept.*

rooms	House for 4-6.
price	€100-€120 (€500-€650 per week). VAT included.
meals	Self-catering. Restaurants 5-minute drive.
closed	Rarely.
directions	Directions on booking.

Enrique González

mobile	+34 689 776861
fax	+34 953 733323
email	latorrecill@hotmail.com
web	www.turismorurallatorrecilla.com

Self-catering

Map 16 Entry 332

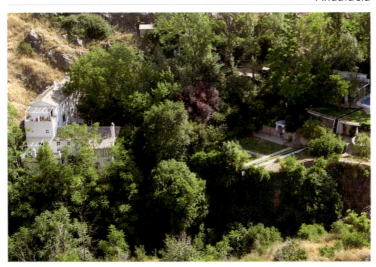

Molino La Farraga

c/Camino de la Hoz s/n, Apartado de Correos 1, 23470 Cazorla, Jaén

As gorgeous a setting as you could hope to find: a verdant river valley just beneath
the breathtaking Cazorla mountains. This mill's gardens are an ode to water: it's
everywhere, in ponds, channels, races and falls. These enchanting acres were
planted by an English botanist, then nurtured for years by an amiable American.
Once you've negotiated the very steep path up, you will revel in buckets of caring
in this cool valley retreat. Expect an interlocking puzzle of stairways, corners,
niches and turns, and an interior that is a confused mix of furniture styles;
original features appear to be an afterthought. However, super-enthusiastic new
owners from Madrid are about to give the old place the overhaul it deserves.
For now, bedrooms are a lucky dip, the best by far being the two with patios and
views; bathrooms are adequate (more showers than baths). Communal spaces have
a timeless feel and the great hall, where you breakfast at a Castillian oak table, is
as good as it gets. Most guests are walkers – find maps in the hall – and the town
has a magical atmosphere in the evening. Look out for the rare bearded vulture!

rooms	8: 7 doubles, 1 suite.
price	€70. Singles €50. Suite €100.
meals	Restaurant 250m.
closed	10 December–10 February.
directions	In Cazorla, signs for Ruinas de Santa María. Pass between ruined church & restaurant towards 'Castillo'. Park just below castle; walk 250m up stone path, over bridge, to Mill.

	Nieves Muñoz & Félix Gómez
tel/fax	+34 953 721249
email	farraga@terra.es
web	www.molinolafarraga.com

Hotel

Map 16 Entry 333

Finca Mercedes

Ctra. de la Sierra km1, 23476, La Iruela, Jaén

La Iruela's crowning glory is the castle fortress built by the Templars; make it to the top for an amazing view. La Finca Mercedes is just outside the village, a simple modern roadside restaurant with rooms. It takes its name from its bright and charming owner, ably helped by her two young daughters. You are just next to the road so do ask (in Spanish!) for a bedroom at the back – not just for peace but for glorious views, across the olive groves and far beyond. In bitter winter the dining room is as cosy as can be, when a fire burns in the corner hearth throughout the day. Decorative flourishes include old copper saucepans, dried flowers, hunting trophies and piano; the food is simple, regional, flavoursome and good value. So too are the bedrooms, a standard size with stained pine furniture and good bathrooms (full-size baths!). There's a garden with a pool, and six new bedrooms at the family's stone farmhouse, Cortijo Berfalá, a five-minute walk down a steep road. Brilliant for walkers, and people on a budget. *Advance bookings preferred.*

rooms	11: 8 twins/doubles, 2 singles, 1 suite. Cortijo: 6 twins/doubles.
price	€36–€39. Single €24–€27. Suite €39–€42.
meals	Breakfast €3.30. Lunch & dinner €12.60. A la carte from €18.
closed	Rarely.
directions	From Cazorla into village centre; at large square, left for La Iruela. Follow road for 1km round bottom of La Iruela; Finca just to left. Do not confuse with hotel next door!

	Mercedes Castillo Matilla
tel	+34 953 721087
email	info@lafincamercedes.com
web	www.lafincamercedes.com

Hotel

Map 16 Entry 334

La Joya de Cabo de Gata

Paraje La Joya, 04149 Aguamarga, Almería

She calls it her "miracle in the desert". Charo García discovered the landscape of Almería, the dry river beds and dunes, the dazzling white dwellings, the tough vegetation… and was captivated. So she built two farmhouses and imported a bedouin tent, added a terrace shaded by parasols of scrub and heather, a small pool for midnight swims, an open-air shower in a grotto… now her dream appears in glossy magazines. The farmhouses, run on solar energy and recycled water, are ancient yet modern: whitewashed walls, muslin drapes, rustic floors, stainless steel hobs, TVs and DVDs, and terraces that face east and north. The *jaima*, set among olive trees and palms, has an ecological stove for winter (just a few chilly days), ventilation for summer, a vast bed, a perfectly equipped kitchen and colourful Arabic décor. Breakfasts, based on "respect for the environment", are served on the communal terrace. Coves, inlets and empty beaches await, there's Garrucha for sea food, Mojacar for its hippy beach, Nijar for pottery. Rides on horses, ponies and camels can be arranged. *Uninspected at time of going to press.*

rooms	2 houses for 2-4; 1 bedouin tent for 2.
price	€120-€190 for 2; €210-€320 for 4. Tent €80-€140. VAT included.
meals	Self-catering includes breakfast.
closed	7-30 January.
directions	A-7/E-15, exit 494 for Carboneras. After 3.5km, right for Aguamarga. Paraje La Joya is just before Aguamarga.

	Charo García
mobile	+34 639 773759/619 159587
email	reservas@lajoyadecabodegata.com
web	www.lajoyadecabodegata.com

Self-catering

Map 22 Entry 335

Hotel Family

c/La Lomilla s/n, 04149, Aguamarga Almería

Gentle-mannered Michele and René came to Aguamarga on French leave; seduced by what was then a remote fishing village, they dreamed of moving here. They have given this little place their all, and run it with much energy, helped by their son and his wife – hence the name. A bumpy track takes you to the whitewashed hotel, restaurant and palm-backed pool – there's an exotic, southern feel. You are in a quiet part of the village, yards from one of the area's most gorgeous beaches. Rooms are simply furnished, the nicest and newest on the first floor, air-conditioned, well-equipped and with their own balconies. Those at the front have sea views. Come for Michele's food: huge portions and amazing value. Breakfasts are a feast of yogurts, fruits, tortillas and good toast for homemade jam. Stay at least two nights and discover the Cabo de Gata National Park: the walking is wonderful and the park holds some of Spain's most beautiful beaches. Aguamarga is more developed than it was, but remains an enchanting spot – particularly out of season. Readers are full of praise.

rooms	9: 7 twins/doubles, 2 family.
price	€45–€120. Singles €40–€115.
meals	Lunch & dinner with wine, €18. Lunch weekends only.
closed	1 November–15 December.
directions	From N-344 exit 494 Venta & Carboneras. On for Carboneras; right for Aguamarga. Signed to right in village as you arrive.

Marc Bellavoir

tel	+34 950 138014
fax	+34 950 138070
email	riovall@teleline.es

Hotel

Map 22 Entry 336

Mikasa

Calle Carboneras s/n, 04149 Aguamarga, Almería

The ingenious desert-style planting in the front garden and the metal replica door from the castle nearby say it all: this is one of the hippest hotels in andalucía. Two pools lie by side, one covered with a sundeck and solarium in summer, there's a fabulous spa and a fully equipped gym, and the floors are a mix of Portuguese marble and natural seaweed matting. A place for fashionistas to pick up ideas and the rest of us sit back and dream. The owners, a lawyer and an interior designer, multi-lingual, well-travelled, know their market and serve it perfectly. Bedrooms vary in style and size but all are immaculate, the attic suite particularly fine because of its views. Mosaic'd bathrooms are irresistible; one room has a huge round tub opposite the bed, others have balconies or terraces. Feeling active with six hours to spare? Walk the arid windswept coast to San Jose, where lunch and taxi can be waiting for you; return for superb dinner. Or stroll to one of the eating places in peaceful Aguamarga and a midnight swim; its sweeping sands are a delight, even in season.

rooms	20: 15 twin/doubles, 5 suites.
price	€90–€185. Suites €145–€235.
meals	Dinner €35.
closed	10 January–10 March.
directions	N-344 exit 494 for Venta del Pobre/Carboneras. Continue towards Carboneras, then right for Aguamarga; signed in village.

	Manuel Lezcano & Lydia Griffith
tel	+34 950 138073
fax	+34 950 138129
email	mikasa@mikasasuites.com
web	www.mikasasuites.com

Hotel

Map 17 Entry 337

Cortijo Los Malenos

04149 Aguamarga, Almería

At any minute, Clint Eastwood could come riding over the hill. Perched above a canyon, encircled by barren hills and semi-desert, this is a gem. The low, white cortijo lies in one of Spain's most alluring, harsh and unexpected landscapes, with all the classic hallmarks of the Wild West. Guarded by stocky date palms, this 'ranch' flaunts its finer features – a rose patio, a double-fireplaced living room – while a warren of courtyards and rooms makes up the space. Drawing deeply on Spanish and Indian influences, bedrooms are beautifully designed, comfortable and serene. Neutral and natural is the look, and stunning images of the landscape pepper the walls. Borrow whichever sunhat takes your fancy and brave the sun. Cacti, palms and carobs find their natural home here, creating a perfectly adapted garden. Round each quiet corner you may absorb staggering desert vistas, then cool off in the saltwater pool. Hot flamenco concerts in summer, laid-back winter nights by the fire, delightful staff all year round. Reminiscent of the silver screen, this is even more extraordinary in real life.

rooms	8 + 1: 8 twins/doubles. House for 4.
price	€80-€130. House €120-€190.
meals	Picnic €10. Dinner €20.
closed	Rarely.
directions	From Almería on E-15; exit 494 for Carboneras. 8km after exit, right to Aguamarga. Cortijo 2km beyond, on left, opposite turn-off for Fernán Pérez.

Aurora Cacho Quesada

mobile	+34 618 286260
email	contactar@cortijolosmalenos.com
web	www.cortijolosmalenos.com

Hostal Mirador del Castillo

Mojácar Pueblo, 04638 Mojácar, Almería

Its slogan is *el punto mas alto* ('the highest point') and that it most certainly is. Built as a private home, the Mirador now houses the cultural events of the Foundation FAMA. This Sixties' interpretation of a Moorish fortification, its concrete fabric a little frayed, may not be to everyone's taste, but don't be put off: the setting is sensational. And the views are enhanced by the recent addition of an Egyptian-Arabic style restaurant from which Arabic music soars out into an andalucían walled garden – verdant with palms, willows and bright bougainvillea. Regular concerts and plenty of jazz add to the cultural feel. For late breakfasts (11am on), light meals and matchless views there's the terrace. Bedrooms are very charming but due for some upgrading. Come for multi-levelled B&B, or make up a party of friends and rent the whole place. This would be fun for a party of ten; you get a small pool, a vast salon, a grand piano and, in winter, a Moroccan-style open fire. Note that Mojacar is at its best out of season. *Reservations for whole house required three months in advance.*

rooms	5: 3 twins/doubles; 2 twins sharing bath.
price	€48-€76. VAT included.
meals	Breakfast €6. Lunch & dinner €15-€20. VAT included. Café closed Wed afternoon & Thurs out of season.
closed	November.
directions	Directions on booking.

	Juan Cecilio Cano Tello
tel	+34 950 473022
mobile	+34 655 512346
email	information@elcastillomojacar.com
web	www.elcastillomojacar.com

Guest house

Map 22 Entry 339

Hotel Tikar

Ctra. Garrucha - Vera s/n, 04630 Garrucha, Almería

A restaurant with rooms and a great stopover if you want to be near the beach in Almería. Don't worry that the Tikar is in a built-up area next to a main road – wait and see what's inside. It's a gem, a hotel, restaurant and art gallery too, run with warmth and charm by Beatriz and Sean. The sitting room is cosy with modern sofas, small bar and woodburning stove, and the bedrooms are large, cool and comfortable, their lively, even eccentric colours offset by dark parquet and teak. And paintings – dozens of them – on every wall. Children are welcomed and well catered for, too; Beatriz and Sean have two young sons of their own. Relax on the rooftop terrace with walled garden and fountains, watch the sea, take a dip in the small pool. But the main event is the food. Sean's El Azul restaurant gets a Michelin mention and has a devoted local following, the menu being an inventive mix of Californian (light sauces and seafood) and Spanish. Plenty of vegetarian dishes too, and a list of over 75 wines. Don't miss the lively afternoon fish market of Garrucha.

rooms	6 suites.
price	€59-€115.
meals	Lunch €15. Dinner €24.50.
closed	December.
directions	From N-340/E-15, exit 534 for Garrucha. Pass Vera & pass through outskirts of Vera. Straight on at r'bout. Hotel on right at entrance of Garrucha.

	Beatriz Gallego & Sean McMahon
tel	+34 950 617131
fax	+34 950 617132
email	hoteltikar@hoteltikar.com
web	www.hoteltikar.com

Hotel

Map 22 Entry 340

Cortijo el Ciruelo

04825 Chirivel, Almería

You are just five minutes from the motorway yet all around are the hills and pine forests of the breathtaking Sierra Maria-Los Velez National Park. Even nearer is a nest of Booted Eagles, who soar away on the thermals at dawn and return at dusk. You might also see red squirrels, wild boar and genets dropping by for a feed. Walks start from the door – with the promise of a rescue in a 4x4 should it be needed. A former hunting lodge, the 300-year-old cortijo still has its original tiles and some of its beams; the rest is pretty new. The interiors are spic and span with comfortable matching furniture. Bedrooms are impeccably clean and share a well-stocked minibar (on the house). There are several set menus, which can be chosen in advance; meals are served at a lovely large table, they grow their own veg and Gillian bakes a fabulous almond cake. Packed lunches are also available for your jaunts around the region; don't miss the interesting town of Velez Rubio, and Velez Blanco with its famous castle, just ten minutes away.

rooms	4 twins/doubles.
price	€45. VAT included.
meals	Tapas lunch €1.50 per tapa. Dinner €15.
closed	Rarely.
directions	From Granada on A-92-N. 9km after junc. 385, exit for 'Area Descanso Ciruelo Picolo'; left over motorway, left again following signs for hotel.

Gary & Gillian Williamso

mobile	+34 667 477673
email	enquiries@elciruelo.net
web	www.elciruelo.net

B&B

Map 17 Entry 341

Balearics
Canary Islands

Les Terrasses

Ctra. de Santa Eularia km1, 07840 Santa Eularia del Río, Ibiza

Françoise Pialoux has crafted, planted and furnished a remarkable vision in this hidden corner of Ibiza. She is an immensely likeable, vivacious woman and her character infuses every corner of her exquisite terraced hotel. The old farmstead (a bus ride from Ibiza) stands alone on a knoll surrounded by Ibizan lushery and bamboo-fringed terraces; every room gets one. Steps lead to secret corners, shaded hammocks and expansive views, there's a state-of-the-art tennis court and two delicious pools. In the sitting room are deep sofas, books, a piano. The bedrooms are on different levels, some in the main house, others outside, perfectly private and secluded. Expect pure colours, white embroidered bedspreads, open hearths, Moroccan tiles, candelabras, heavenly bathrooms; no two are the same. Choose where and when you'd like to breakfast – by one of the pools, in the house or in your room. And stay for dinner; Tuesdays is couscous night and people come from everywhere. A chic, bohemian retreat; there's no more tranquil place to unwind. Be sure to book in advance.

rooms	10: 9 twins/doubles, 1 suite.
price	€165-290. Singles €115-€175. Suite €220-€310.
meals	Lunch €20-€25. Dinner €35.
closed	15 November-end February.
directions	From Ibiza for Santa Eularia; 9km, on right, at blue-painted rock; right & up track; farm on left.

	Françoise Pialoux
tel	+34 971 332643
fax	+34 971 338978
email	info@lesterrasses.net
web	www.lesterrasses.net

Hotel

Map 23 Entry 342

Sant Jaume
c/Sant Jaume 6, 07400, Alcudía, Mallorca

Coming down the pretty wrought-iron staircase to strains of jazz in the morning puts you in a relaxed frame of mind. Taking breakfast in the shrub-filled patio – a haven for birds with its giant palm, bougainvillea and jasmine – only adds to the mood. Built by a ship's captain 150-years ago, everything about San Jaume is spacious and serene… the very opposite of a cramped cabin on a ship. Slowly renovated by its current owners and keeping most of its original features – high wood-beam ceilings, hydraulic baldosa floor tiles – it reveals tasteful, retro furniture and calm colour schemes. Best of all, it is on a quietish side street just a few yards from the market square in Alcudia, a charming town with Roman remains and much of its medieval masonry still intact. Due to Alcudia's closeness to the brash development of Alcudia Puerto, the old town is perhaps best off season and not on Sundays, when the hordes decend for market day. Sant Jaume's lovely bedrooms have wood-panelled floors, antique beds and fashionable touches; large, stylish bathrooms are some of the best around. A joy.

rooms	6 twins/doubles.
price	€89-€146. VAT included.
meals	Restaurants nearby.
closed	December & January.
directions	Detailed directions on web site.

Rosi Speer & Sebastian Tuvyols

tel	+34 971 549419
mobile	+34 667 664755
email	hotelsantjaume@terra.es
web	www.hotelsantjaume.com

Hotel

Map 23 Entry 343

Posada de Lluc

Roser Vell 11, 07460 Pollensa, Mallorca

Pollensa, as old as the Middle Ages, is a charming town, long a favourite of painters; 21st-century galleries are mushrooming in the old town, and art furnishes many of this hotel's walls. The Posada has an interesting history. Built for a medieval nobleman it became a sanctuary for monks in 1459 – a handy place to decamp to after visiting the monastery at Lluc; today it is a more prosperous retreat. The two-year-old hotel stands in a quiet, narrow street, so don't expect lavish views or acres of land. But do expect space: behind that inconspicuous façade lie an unexpectedly large, airy, cobbled entrance hall, eight immaculate bedrooms and a super new pool. Furniture is antique Mallorcan, sofas are modern, chandeliers come from the glass factory in Campanet, and all is modesty and elegance, down the chess set (do play). Joana ensures you get the best local produce at breakfast and is always happy to advise. The bedrooms are large, peaceful (particularly the poolside ones), uncluttered and cool, with beams, stone floors and white or open-stone walls. A perfect, small-town hotel.

rooms	8 twins/doubles.
price	€70–€155. VAT included.
meals	Restaurants nearby.
closed	December & January.
directions	From airport for Palma; m'way for Inca & Alcudía. 20km after Inca, left exit to Pollensa. After 11km, left into Pollensa. Follow road left up Carrer Roser Vell.

	Joana Vives Cánaves
tel	+34 971 535220
fax	+34 971 535222
email	info@posadalluc.com
web	www.posadalluc.com

Hotel

Map 23 Entry 344

Son Siurana

Ctra. Palma-Alcudia km45, 07400 Alcudía, Mallorca

You may be close to Puerto Pollensa and Alcudia but this stunning stone finca is enveloped by almond groves and sheep-grazed pastures. And few places are reached via such a long, sweeping driveway. In the family since 1748, the house is a long, low and graceful stone building, its doors and windows highlighted by light and elegant *marés*. Life in summer centres around a large terrace with woodburning stove that looks onto a large and lovely swimming pool with a glorious view. Beyond, 100 hectares of ancient pines, lakes and a charming walled kitchen garden that supplies visiting chefs: guests can pick their favourite vegetables for the twice-weekly dinners. You stay in one of eight stylish self-catering cottages which have been slotted into the farm's outbuildings. The beautiful rooms are furnished with a rustic charm and have hand-painted tiles, terracotta or wooden floors, smart sofas and natural fibres, sisal car and country antiques. Breakfast is served in the main house, on the terrace or in your cottage. A very special place. *A Rusticae hotel.*

rooms	1 + 8: 1 suite. 5 cottages for 2; 1 cottage for 4; 2 apartments for 4. Extra beds available.
price	Suite €105–€152. Cottages/apartments €114–€244.
meals	Breakfast €12. Lunch €12. Dinner €36 (Tuesday & Thursday only).
closed	Rarely.
directions	From Palma towards Alcudía. Left for Son Siurana, opposite km45 marker.

	Sofia & Montse Roselló
tel	+34 971 549662
mobile	+34 610 608313
fax	+34 971 549788
email	info@sonsiurana.com
web	www.sonsiurana.com

Hotel & Self-catering

Map 23 Entry 345

Agroturismo Finca Son Pons

Ctra Búger-Sa Pobla, 07311 Búger, Mallorca

This pink and cream farmhouse is several centuries old, set deep in a vast country estate and surrounded by woodland – an impressive, lone palm tree, dwarfing the rough stone walls, stands guard. Sit on the wide terrace edged with stone water troughs, or in a wicker chair by the 16th-century well, and savour the silence. Behind the house is a big garden, with well-kept lawns and plenty of shady patios – perfect for watching the wildlife. Rabbits hop across the grass and exotic birds from the nearby nature reserve drop by. There's a large modern pool, too, beside a bougainvillea-swathed patio. The house is equally appealing inside, with stone walls, beams and lots of old Mallorcan furniture. The big bedrooms are all different, full of intriguing features and original artwork. Your hosts are an immensely friendly, multilingual family. Toni and his son do the cooking which is excellent – a super breakfast, and dinner on request a couple of times a week. They'll even do you a packed lunch if you want to spend the day exploring the countryside on foot or on horseback. And the beaches are 12 minutes away.

rooms	6 suites.
price	Suites €70-€85.
meals	Dinner €25, available twice a week.
closed	Rarely.
directions	From Palma dir. Alcudía; here, signs for Búger. From centre of Búger, take road to Sa Pobla (also signed Son Pons). Hotel 1.3km on left.

Inés Siquier & Christophe Bedos

tel	+34 971 877142
mobile	+34 649 453776
fax	+34 971 509165
email	finca@sonpons.com
web	www.sonpons.com

B&B

Map 23 Entry 346

Can Furiós

Camí Vell de Binibona 11, 07314, Binibona-Caimari, Mallorca

A year ago Can Furiós was one of the most upmarket of Mallorca's country house hotels. Then Adrian and Susy swept in with an impeccable broom and turned it into an even better place to stay. It is in the hamlet of Binibona – no shops, six small hotels – on the stunning, sheltered, eastern flank of the Tramuntana mountains. Impossible to believe that a decade ago the building was in ruins… now terraced gardens with palm, olive and citrus trees wrap themselves luxuriously round both pool and smartly renovated 16th-century house. There's a lovely sociable terrace for pre-dinner drinks – and dinners, served at formally dressed tables in the old farm's almond press, are delectable, fresh seafood being the house speciality. The bedrooms are in the main house and the suites in the farmworkers' cottages: all are cosy, traditional and very comfortable, with oriental rugs on tiled floors, best English mattresses and patterned drapes. Extra touches include white bathrobes and Crabtree & Evelyn soaps – and torches for jasmine-scented strolls after dark. Adrian and Susy have thought of everything.

rooms	7: 3 twins/doubles, 4 suites.
price	€150-€200. Suites €180-€280.
meals	Lunch €10-€14. Dinner €37.
closed	Rarely.
directions	From Palma, PM-27 N to Inca. There, signs to Selva & Binibona. Final journey on small country roads. Can Furiós on village square.

	Adrian & Susy Bertorelli
tel	+34 971 515751
fax	+34 971 875366
email	info@can-furios.com
web	www.can-furios.com

Hotel

Map 23 Entry 347

Finca Es Castell
c/Binibona s/n, 07314 Caimari, Mallorca

One of the oldest fincas on the island has become one of the loveliest hotels. These 750 acres once yielded olive oil; today a hammock sways between the olives and a lazy pool beckons. The rambling farmhouse has been in the family for ever – along with a small mountain behind (let Paola's puppy be your guide). Now it is rented to this young English couple and has been infused with new life. A huge old olive press, a 12th-century fireplace, ancient beams: old and modern meet in a glowing restoration. New are the chunky terracotta floors, the chestnut tables twinkling with night lights, the curly wrought-iron terrace chairs, the pretty beds, the fresh bathrooms, the paintings on whitewashed walls. The inner courtyard is rustically dotted with pots and overflows with green. You can't help but warm to this lovely place, and the setting is sensational: watch the sun dipping down over the Tramuntana mountain ranges as you dine (well) on one of three terraces. The old finca is surrounded by palms, pines, olives – and a grassed area where classes are sometimes held (best to check). Mallorcan heaven.

rooms	12 twins/doubles.
price	€110–€165.
meals	Dinner €35. Not Sunday.
closed	January.
directions	From airport for Palma; exit 3 for Viá Cintura; exit for Inca. There, towards Lluc & Selva. After Selva, road on right for Es Castell; on for 3km. At entrance of Finca-Hotel Binibona, right; 0.5km.

	Paola Cassini & James Hiscock
tel	+34 971 875154
fax	+34 971 875154
email	info@fincaescastell.com
web	www.fincaescastell.com

Hotel

Map 23 Entry 348

Ca'n Reus

Carrer de l'Auba 26, 07109, Fornalutx, Mallorca

Few villages in southern Europe have quite such a heart-stopping natural setting. Fornalutx is in the middle of Mallorca's rumpled spine, sandwiched between the craggy loveliness of the Puig Major and the Puig de l'Ofre. Artists, sculptors and writers discovered the village long ago yet the place has kept its charm. Light, elegant C'an Reus was built in faux-Parisian style by a returning emigrant – with none of the ostentatiousness that some of the *casas de indianos* are wont to display. The entrance hall is stunning and the bedrooms are to die for, with their original floors, 19th-century Mallorcan beds, crisp white bedcovers and simply mesmerising views. Owner Sue Guthrie has breathed new life into the whole gorgeous place, and introduced a delightful mix of Englishness and exoticism: deckchairs in the garden, candles up the stairs, perfect towels from John Lewis. At breakfast, local cheeses and sausages, homemade marmalades and tarts as you gaze on more loveliness from the steeply terraced garden – and sociable dinners cooked once a week by Sue. It's friendly, peaceful, special.

rooms	8 twins/doubles.
price	€110–€150. VAT included.
meals	Dinner €30; Mondays or Thursdays to coincide with local restaurant's closure.
closed	Rarely.
directions	Round Palma on ring-road; exit for Soller. Through (toll) tunnel, round Soller for Puerto de Soller. At 2nd r'bout, right at signs for Fornalutx. Park in village & walk; C'an Reus in lowest street.

	Susan Guthrie
tel	+34 971 638041
mobile	+34 699 098031
fax	+34 971 631174
email	info@canreushotel.com
web	www.canreushotel.com

Hotel

Map 23 Entry 349

Fornalutx Petit Hotel
c/Alba 22, 07109 Fornalutx, Mallorca

Whether the nuns who lived here until the 1920s chose this spot for its setting we'll never know – but this is its trump card. Fornalutx is said to be the loveliest village in Spain and this peaceful hotel has inspirational views. (Pay more for a room with a view – it's worth it.) In the tranquil garden, stretch out with a book in the shade of the citrus trees – source of the wondrous orange juice squeezed and served at breakfast by Isabel and her helpers. A delicious small pool and jacuzzi provide cool in high summer, and there's a sauna. Indoors, a series of bright, appealing rooms with a rustic-minimalist feel. Large, high-ceilinged bedrooms are simply furnished, colourful abstracts by local artists brightening the cool colours of the walls, while a breakfast room in the cavernous cellar makes a charming wet-weather alternative to the alfresco version on the terrace. The cobbled cul-de-sac street outside (traffic is virtually non-existent) is your departure point for the beautiful town of Soller just down the valley, and the pretty resort of Puerto de Soller lies a few miles beyond.

rooms	8: 6 twins/doubles, 2 suites.
price	€141–€152. Singles €77–€106. Suites €198–€247.
meals	Restaurants nearby.
closed	Rarely.
directions	From airport ring road west; exit for Puerto de Soller. After Bunyola through tunnel. At Soller towards Fornalutx. There, park in public car park after shops; head down towards river; c/Alba on right.

	Patricio Roig Monjo
tel	+34 971 631997
fax	+34 971 635026
email	info@fornalutxpetithotel.com
web	www.fornalutxpetithotel.com

Hotel

Map 23 Entry 350

Scott's Hotel

Plaza de la Iglesia 12, 07350, Binissalem, Mallorca

Your English and cosmopolitan hosts have created a glamorous, intimate, very English hotel out of a grand seignorial townhouse in the centre of old Binissalem; you'll be blissfully comfortable. Enormous beds were handmade in England, goosedown pillows were brought over from Germany, and bedspreads and Percale sheets from New York. "Pretty came second," says George, but pretty Scott's most certainly is and a night here is an experience to remember. Suites have any number of exquisite decorative touches and the feel is fresh, light and elegant; here an 18th-century Japanese print, there a grandfather clock, perhaps a Bokhara rug or a chaise-longue. All are large and luxurious, at the front overlooking the church square, at the back the lovely patio-courtyard. Breakfast out here till late, and dine in the hotel's bistro, a seven-minute walk: candles, damask, fresh flowers, Gershwin tinkling in the background and simple but sumptuous food. You get your own front door key, an honesty bar and a small indoor pool: more lavish private house than hotel.

rooms	17: 11 twin/doubles, 6 suites.
price	€175–€205. Singles €131–€154. Suites €235–€330.
meals	Dinner €23. A la carte from €32.
closed	Rarely.
directions	From airport for Palma, PM-27 (Via de Cintura) for Inca. Exit km17 for Binissalem. Next to church; discreet brass plaque by entrance.

	George Scott
tel	+34 971 870100
fax	+34 971 870267
email	stay@scottshotel.com
web	www.scottshotel.com

Hotel

Map 23 Entry 351

Son Porró

Diseminados Poligono 3, Parcela 223, 07144 Costitx, Mallorca

You are at the heart of the Plá – all ancient farmhouses and equally ancient fig and almond groves. Son Porró's stone walls look old, too; the house, however, is new. It owes its existence to Pilar Sánchez, who greets you (in Spanish!) as she would an old friend: nothing is too much trouble and when guests arrive unavoidably late she'll rustle up a meal at midnight. Her bedrooms are comfortable and roomy, one with huge views, the nicest off the pretty cobbled courtyard at the back; all have modern bathrooms, satellite TV, minibar and bowls of apricots or cherries. Two apartments with kitchenettes are in the stone-built outhouses that lie just beyond the lovely pool. In Son Porró's vast lounge the bright Mallorcan *lenguas*-weave of the curtains adds zest; reddish-brown leather sofas are more sombre. What makes this place special are Pilar's lunches, dinners and barbecues – on that patio in summer, at the polished dining table in winter. She tailors her cooking to suit her guests and uses ingredients from the local markets. And friends of hers can take you out on a guided walk or ride.

rooms	6 + 3: 1 twin/double, 5 suites. 2 apartments for 4; 1 house for 7.
price	€96–€120. Suites €126–€150. Apartments €120. House from €210. VAT included.
meals	Lunch & dinner €15.
closed	Rarely.
directions	From Palma towards Alcudía on m'way. Exit for Inca & at 2nd r'bout follow signs for Sineu; 9km; Son Porró signed; down narrow bumpy road for about 1km.

Pilar Sánchez Escribano

tel	+34 971 182013
fax	+34 971 182012
email	sonporro@gmail.com
web	www.fincasonporro.com

B&B & Self-catering

Map 23 Entry 352

Leon de Sineu

Carrer dels Bous 129, 07510, Sineu, Mallorca

Hilltop Sineu is one of the most charming small towns of Mallorca – and one of the oldest: people have been coming to its market since 1214. (Don't miss it: it's on Wednesdays.) The bars and restaurants are another draw. The Leon is equally delightful, a bit scuffed around the edges perhaps, but welcoming, sensitively decorated and with a lovely symmetrical façade. The reception leads into a walled garden full of ponds and quiet corners, with a pool: a peaceful escape at the end of the day. From the Winter Room, a covered terrace, one can sit and enjoy it out of season. The bedrooms, opening off a balustraded staircase of wrought-iron splendour, have a mix of dark antiques and fresh white walls; the best have terraces and the suite has stupendous views. Hospitable Señora Gálmez Arbona manages to recreate the atmosphere of a Mallorcan home, and the terrace restaurant (serving good food from a German chef) is charming. Breakfasts are traditional Mallorcan – cheese, salami, pâté, eggs, fruit, cake. Just the thing before you squeeze into your bikini and head for the cool pool – or the beach.

rooms	8: 6 twins/doubles, 1 single, 1 suite.
price	€100–€140. Single €80–€92. Suite €140–€162. VAT included.
meals	Lunch from €30 à la carte. Dinner €20. A la carte from €30. VAT included.
closed	Rarely.
directions	Head for town centre. Hotel signed.

	Francisca Gálmez Arbona
tel	+34 971 520211
mobile	+34 696 943370
fax	+34 971 855058
email	reservas@hotel-leondesineu.com
web	www.hotel-leondesineu.com

Hotel

Map 23 Entry 353

Torrent Fals

Ctra. Sta. María-Sencelles km4.5, Aptdo Correos 39, 07320 Santa Maria, Mallorca

What a position! Flanked by the Tramuntana mountain range, this low, golden, 15th-century farmhouse is surrounded by vineyards and plains. The views are phenomenal – especially if you get the suite with the roof terrace – and inside is just as alluring. In three years Pedro and his English wife Victoria have transformed this once-desolate ruin. Throughout, the effect is one of airy spaces and understated elegance. In the striking, uniquely-shaped sitting room (once the wine cellar), the walls are creamy stone and the high ceiling is striped with beams. Shapely arches lead from uncluttered bedrooms to delectable marble bathrooms. Cool chic and latest mod cons notwithstanding, the place has a real feeling of warmth and comfort, much enhanced by Pedro's friendliness and energy. He's receptionist, gardener and cook: duck and fish are a house special and the fruit and veg are grown on his brother's allotment. He can even be found hard at work cleaning the swimming pool – vast and magnificent, and designed to allow water to escape in a tantalising trickle at either end. *A Rusticae hotel.*

rooms	8: 2 twins/doubles, 6 suites.
price	€145. Suite €165. VAT included.
meals	Dinner €30, on request. VAT included.
closed	Rarely.
directions	From Palma PM-27 for Inca/Alcudía. Right on PM-303 before Santa María for Sencelles. Torrent Fals on left short way up track, before Biniali. Look out for sign.

	Pedro Cañellas Llabrés
tel	+34 971 144584
mobile	+34 696 508003
fax	+34 971 144191
email	pjcanellas@terra.es
web	www.torrentfals.com

Hotel

Map 23 Entry 354

Fínca Son Gener

Ctra. Son Servera-Artá km3, Apartado de Correos 136, 07550, Son Servera, Mallorca

Not a family hotel, nor a place for the gregarious, but an architect-owned paradise on the brow of an olive-groved hill. The once-dilapidated farm buildings have become an understatedly elegant small hotel, miles from the bronzing crowds. Impeccable lawns frame the house with its gently luminous *maré* façade; there are palms, roses, bougainvillea, exotic trees. The interior is a celebration of light and form: old rafters, limestone floors, neutral natural colours and carefully selected sofas, plants and flowers. Art ranges from striking abstact-modern to rich mock-renaissance. It is calming and uplifting, each lofty bedroom being a cool haven in summer, and as snug as toast in winter. Ground-floor rooms overlook the courtyard, upstairs ones get the views; all have fine Mallorcan linen and private terraces. Some rooms have a more rustic mood, and their own fireplaces. The gym, spa and saltwater swimming pools, one out, one in, share the same purity of style, and you breakfast and dine on one of many patios, each lovelier than the last. Exclusive and exquisite.

rooms	10 suites.
price	€260. VAT included.
meals	Lunchtime snacks. Dinner €42. VAT included. Restaurant closed Tuesday.
closed	1 December–15 January.
directions	From Palma to Manacor. There, towards Artá; through Sant Llorenc; 2km before Artá, right on 403-1. Signed on left after 3km.

Aina Pastor

tel	+34 971 183612
fax	+34 971 183591
email	hotel@songener.com
web	www.songener.com

Hotel

Map 23 Entry 355

Es Passarell

2a Vuelta No. 117, 07200 Felanitx, Mallorca

As rambling farmhouses go, this takes some beating. Hidden up a mile-long track, its sprawling stone walls bedecked in bougainvillea and vines, it is a companionable place where you might expect to make new friends. The sunny, verdant garden has plenty of seats and shade, and a big sociable terrace. Es Passarell feels like it's been lived in for centuries, as indeed it has, and, while some of the spaces can feel dark and monastic, most are clean, light and airy. New licensees Joy and Spencer add a friendly English touch. The rambling house is great for families, with a 'nursery' in the video room should you be planning the occasional escape. Bedrooms are big, cool and mostly on the ground floor, with attractive old beams and floors; expect bright rugs and cushions, lace drapes, dried flowers, intimate terraces. Apartments are simple, with an extra sofabed and a private terrace. Breakfast is buffet and big – freshly made cakes, lemon curd, plenty of fruit – and the cellar is stocked with Mallorcan wines. *A Rusticae hotel.*

rooms	5 + 5: 5 twins/doubles. 5 apartments for 1-4.
price	€65-€135. Apartments €110-€142.
meals	Lunch €6-€15 on request. Dinner €22-€25.
closed	December & January.
directions	From Palma to LLucmajor, then on to Porreres; here, towards Felanitx. Between km2 & km3 markers, at sharp bend, right; after 2.5km, house on right, signed.

	Joy & Spencer Rennie
tel	+34 971 183091
fax	+34 971 183336
email	info@espassarell.com
web	www.espassarell.com

B&B & Self-catering

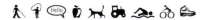

Map 23 Entry 356

Son Mercadal

Camino de Son Pau s/n, Apartado de Correos 52, 07260 Porreres, Mallorca

If you are looking for a blissfully comfortable bed, kind hosts, delicious food and a secluded setting, head here. The family derive great pleasure from welcoming guests to their rambling, beautifully restored farmhouse, whose every last corner is a delight. The house is a 'painting', as the Spanish would say, a measured still life of things old and rustic. José's son Toni is responsible for the decoration and his artistic eye has created a warm and harmonious mood. Most of the country antique pieces were already in the family: the grandfather clock, piano, old washstands, a complete Art Deco bedroom set, the engravings of Mallorca. And the food is of the best the island has to offer: Toni is keen for you to try the local specialities. Breakfast on the vine-shaded terrace on local sausage, cheeses, eggs from the farm, wonderful bread and Mama's watermelon jam; at dinner, on *tumbet* (the local meat-and-veg delicacy) and some of the island's very best wines. Much of what graces your table is straight from the farm, there are prize-winning horses in the stable and a large and lovely pool.

rooms	8 twins/doubles.
price	€105. Singles €85. VAT included.
meals	Lunch & dinner €28, on request. VAT included.
closed	Rarely.
directions	From Palma towards Santanyi. At Campos, left to Porreres. 1km before Porreres, left at sign 'Son Mercadal - Camí de Son Pau'. 2km track to house; tucked away on right.

	José Roig Ripoll
tel	+34 971 181307
fax	+34 971 181300
email	son.mercadal@todoesp.es
web	www.son-mercadal.com

Hotel

Map 23 Entry 357

C'an Bassa Coll

Ctra. Alquería Blanca-Porto Petro 55., 07691 Alquería Blanca, Mallorca

The low-tiled roof, characterful windows, the pergola on its front terrace, the majestic mountain views – these were the reasons that Harvey, the urbane owner, fell in love with this place 20 years ago. Never mind the road that runs nearby, the 'home at the foot of the hill' is a delightful and rustic oasis. The old building and the ultra-modern annexe are joined by a palm and fountain walkway, making them ideal for two parties. Children will roam the grounds, surprising parents around hidden corners, before everyone settles down to lunch under the deep shade of the loggia tree. Take time to digest among a natural bounty of creeper, hibiscus, plumbago and cypresses, as you watch an abundance of lemon, níspero and grapefruit that seem to grow more ponderous with every thought. Uncluttered bedrooms clean the senses for sleep and three lead out to a peaceful terrace. Marble floors and inlaid mirrors reflect decently sized bathrooms. Whether you're relaxing in the garden, gazing out to sea or exploring the rugged coastline around Portopedro – this is Mallorca at its prettiest. *Minimum stay one week in summer.*

rooms	House for 11.
price	€1,250-€3,150 per week. VAT included.
meals	Self-catering. Breakfast €10. Lunch €15. Dinner €30. Restaurant 100m.
closed	Rarely.
directions	Detailed directions on web site.

	Harvey Herrmann
tel	+44 (0)20 8747 1851
mobile	+44 (0)771 423 0838
fax	+44 (0)20 8995 0903
email	harvey@mallorcancountrysideholidays.com
web	www.mallorcancountrysideholidays.com

Self-catering & B&B

Map 23 Entry 358

Es Pins

c/Convento 35, Alquería Blanca, 07691 Santanyi, Mallorca

Unravel slowly in the peculiar charm of Es Pins within sight of pretty Porto Petro. Beautifully renovated, each room in the 18th-century manor has a history to tell, such as the separate suite with arched ceilings that sheltered a Republican soldier during the civil war. A system to feed him was adapted by means of holes, a dining etiquette that has since changed; feasting on fresh tumbet, a local speciality and favourite of the Filipino housekeeper/cook, is no hardship. The gardens are another delight. Stone paths lead from the huge raised pool, one through a sea of oleander, another into an olive grove and a short cross-country walk to the village. Enormous rocks surround a Japanese zen garden and vegetables grown on site are yours for the picking. Original terracotta and hydraulic tiles have been preserved with the old fireplace, while antiques from Lots Road in Chelsea – Harvey's favourite haunt – fill bedrooms without disguising their peachy afternoon glow. The farmhouse has a superb kitchen and all the electro-domestics you could need. Great for families. *Minimum stay one week in summer.*

rooms	House for 12.
price	€1,500-€3,950 per week. VAT included.
meals	Self-catering. Breakfast €10. Lunch €15. Dinner €30. Restaurants 10-minute walk.
closed	Rarely.
directions	Detailed directions on web site.

	Harvey Herrmann
tel	+44 (0)20 8747 1851
mobile	+44 (0)771 423 0838
fax	+44 (0)20 8995 0903
email	harvey@mallorcancountrysideholidays.com
web	www.mallorcancountrysideholidays.com

Self-catering & B&B

Map 23 Entry 359

Biniarroca Country House Hotel
Camí Vell 57, 07710 Sant Lluís, Menorca

Once a working farm, now a place of luxurious beauty. Sheelagh, a designer, once ran a guest house on the island, Lindsay is a painter whose light-filled creations grace antique-filled rooms. Together they have created something very special on this flat tract of land that leads down to Menorca's southern coast. A solitary palm stands sentinel over the cobbled courtyard; to one side is an elegant pool. Plumbago and bougainvillea festoon the façade of the old farmhouse; the oleander- and tamarisk-strewn gardens and shaded terraces are enchanting. More beauty in the bedrooms, stylish with generous beds, antiques, oil paintings and optional extras including the internet. Those in the old stables have their own private terraces and a second pool. The restaurant is another draw, the food sophisticated Mediterranean: fish ocean-fresh, vegetables organic and home-grown. Breakfasts are as delicious as you would expect: a cornucopia of cheeses, breads, fruits, pastries. Peace reigns – apart from the cockerel's crow. Impossible to imagine a prettier or more peaceful little hotel – perfect for couples.

rooms	18 twins/doubles.
price	€120–€130. Singles €75. Half-board extra €25 p.p.
meals	Light lunch €10. Dinner from €40 à la carte.
closed	December.
directions	From airport towards Maó, then to Sant Lluís. Here, follow signs on left for Es Castell. Biniarroca signed on left after 1.5km.

	Lindsay Mullen & Sheelagh Ratliff
tel	+34 971 150059
mobile	+34 619 460942
fax	+34 971 151250
email	hotel@biniarroca.com
web	www.biniarroca.com

Hotel

Map 23 Entry 360

Hotel Rural Las Calas

c/El Arenal 36, La Lechuza-Vega de San Mateo, 35320 Las Palmas, Gran Canaria

Hide in the hills, below the peaks of Gran Canaria. This is a relaxed and relaxing little hotel for summer (friendly dogs, an easy feel), converted from a century-old building. Abundant wood, stone walls, warm colours and traditional Canarian furnishings are tempered by splashes of restrained modernism; the predominating peace may be broken by the laughter of friends popping in for one of owner Magüi's parties. The generously sized rooms, each with its own personality, open onto a courtyard garden – a peaceful spot for browsing your pick of the hotel's library. If you get restless, scrump some fruit from the orchard – with Magüi's permission, of course; she turns most of it into jam. When evening comes, you could dine in on some typical Canarian cuisine – around the canopied table much of the year. Beyond the hotel lie the protected natural havens of the Cumbre and Pino Santo. Explore on horseback; there's an equestrian centre nearby. Vega de San Mateo is the nearest small town with a colourful cattle fair and farmers' market at the weekends, an ethnographic museum and a pretty church.

rooms	9: 7 twins/doubles, 2 suites.
price	€86–€98. Singles €76–€86. Suite €116–€126. Half-board extra €20 p.p.
meals	Dinner available.
closed	Rarely.
directions	Airport Tafira; after Santa Brigida, Vega de San Mateo; follow sign at end of village for Tejeda; cont. to lane on left, signed La Lechuza; pass football field on left & down lane (opp. main road); signed.

Magüi Carratala

tel	+34 928 661436
fax	+34 928 660753
email	reserva@hotelrurallascalas.com
web	www.hotelrurallascalas.com

Hotel

Map 19 Entry 361

Hotel Rural El Patio

Finca Malpaís 11, El Guincho, 38450 Garachico, Tenerife

Much comfort, a fabulous setting and not a whisper — other than the dawn chorus and the swish of waves breaking on the distant shore. El Patio sits in one of the oldest and lushest banana plantations in Tenerife. Rustically elegant bedrooms, each opening out onto a balcony, are housed in three separate buildings, each with a fascinating history. The listed 16th-century mansion and its 25-acre estate have been in the Ponte family for 500 years, and signs of the past are delightfully present: a 1565 chapel at the entrance to the estate, a 400-year-old dragon tree on the exuberant patio. But time has not stood still, and now you have a heated swimming pool, a solarium, a fitness room, a tennis court and even a golf-practice area for your pleasure. Canarian aristocrat Baltasar Ponte Machado is a plain-speaking man who has strict rules — rules designed to make you feel at home. He gives you keys to the bar — just help yourself and settle up when you leave — and to the front door, so you may come and go as you please. It's good value, too.

rooms	26 twins/doubles.
price	€69 –€110.
meals	Dinner from €17.
closed	1 May–14 July.
directions	From airport for Puerto de la Cruz & Icod de los Viños. Hotel 4km after Icod, on Garachico road.

	Baltasar Ponte Machado
tel	+34 922 133280
fax	+34 922 830089
email	reservas@hotelpatio.com
web	www.hotelpatio.com

Hotel

Map 19 Entry 362

Hotel Rural La Quinta Roja

Glorieta de San Fransisco s/n, 38450, Garachico, Tenerife

If you have never ventured beyond the coastal resorts of Tenerife, Garachico is a treat. Its baroque architecture includes palaces, convents, churches – and this mansion, built for the Marquis of La Quinta Roja, Lord Bailiff of Tenerife. If you're interested in the history of the building and the region, Paloma knows it all. The 17th-century exterior may seem forbidding, and, disconcertingly, you enter via a shop selling local products. But, once inside, visions of a grand lifestyle are instantly realised. Hand-carved wood on a monumental scale, a vast wraparound gallery, oak planked floors, ancient stone and, in the middle of it all, a richly planted courtyard patio with original marble fountain. The building has been effectively and sympathetically converted, wood being the dominant feature. Bedrooms vary in size but all are comfortable and well furnished in modern style. Some were once used as grain stores for the Marquis's cattle – hard to imagine now. If you feel like being pampered, visit the spa: treatments are free. And so are the mountain bikes – explore!

rooms	20: 16 twins/doubles, 4 suites.
price	€96–€160. Suites €130–€180.
meals	Restaurants 20m.
closed	Rarely.
directions	From Tenerife airport towards Puerto de la Cruz, Icod de los Viños & Garachico. Detailed directions on booking.

	Paloma Moriana
tel	+34 922 133377
fax	+34 922 133360
email	hotelquintaroja@quintaroja.com
web	www.quintaroja.com

Hotel

Map 19 Entry 363

Hotel San Roque

Esteban de Ponte 32, 38450, Garachico, Tenerife

The brochure will lure you straight to the Isla Baja: 'secret Tenerife'. The 17th-century mansion has been transformed into a peaceful, exclusive, family-run hotel – the first to open in Garachico. Wood and steel, geometric shapes and earthy colours have been introduced with a flourish. It is bold yet subtle, and lavish. An immaculately dressed bed floating on a sea of dark-polished parquet, a new Deco rug, heavy linen curtains, contemporary art. Each room is different, each good-looking, with big old rafters and a passing nod to 1930s design. At every turn the eye is drawn to something striking, such as the soaring steel sculpture in the courtyard – a chic outdoor space with original wraparound wooden balcony transformed by terracotta walls, white armchairs and potted aspidistras. Puritans will be unsettled for there are far too many opportunities for decadence: sauna, pool, music, tennis, Canarian cuisine, breakfast as late as you want. Garachico is ancient and intimate, enveloped by mountains and sea. There is everything, and nothing, to do. *A Rusticae hotel. Golfing discounts available.*

rooms	20: 16 doubles, 4 suites.
price	€175–€250. Suite €280–€350.
meals	Light lunch €10. Dinner €25.
closed	Rarely.
directions	From southern airport m'way past Santa Cruz, La Laguna & Puerto de la Cruz. On past San Juan de la Rambla & Icod de los Viños to Garachico. Here, 4th left into cobbled street; 1st left. On right.

	Dominique Carayón Sabater
tel	+34 922 133435
fax	+34 922 133406
email	info@hotelsanroque.com
web	www.hotelsanroque.com

Hotel

Map 19 Entry 364

Useful vocabulary

Before arriving

Do you have a room free tonight?
¿Tiene una habitación libre para hoy?

How much does it cost?
¿Cuánto cuesta?

Do you have any wedding or
conference parties booked?
*¿Tienen alguna boda, comuniones o
conferencia esos dias?*

We'll be arriving at about 7pm.
Vamos a llegar sobre las siete.

We're lost.
Estamos perdidos.

We'll be arriving late.
Vamos a llegar tarde.

Do you have animals?
¿Tienen animales?

I'm allergic to cats/dogs.
Soy alérgico/a a los gatos/los perros.

We'd like to have dinner.
Nos gustaría cenar.

On arrival

Hello! I'm Mr/Mrs Sawday.
¡Hola! Soy el señor/la señora Sawday.

We found your name in this book.
Le hemos encontrado en este libro.

Where can we leave the car?
¿Dónde podemos dejar el coche?

Could you help us with our bags?
¿Podría ayudarnos con las maletas?

Could I put this food/drink in your
fridge?
*¿Podría dejar esta comida/bebida en
su nevera?*

Could I heat up a baby's bottle?
¿Podría calentar este biberón?

Can you put an extra bed in our
room?
¿Podría poner una cama supletoria?

Things you need/that go wrong

Do you have an extra pillow/blanket?
*¿Podría dejarnos otra almohada/
manta?*

A light bulb needs replacing.
Hay que cambiar una bombilla.

The heating isn't on.
No está encendida la calefacción.

Photo Guy Hunter-Watts

Can you show us how the AC works?
¿Como funciona el aire acondicionado, por favor?

We have a problem with the plumbing.
Tenemos un problema de fontanería.

Do you have a quieter room?
¿Tiene una habitación más tranquila?

Where can I hang these wet clothes?
¿Dónde puedo colgar esta ropa mojada?

Where can I dry these wet boots?
¿Dónde puedo secar estas botas?

Could we have some soap, please?
¿Podría darnos jabón, por favor?

Could we have some hot water please?
¿Podría darnos agua caliente, por favor?

Do you have an aspirin?
¿Tendría una aspirina?

Could you turn the volume down?
¿Podría bajar un poco el volumen?

How the house/hotel works
When does breakfast begin?
¿A partir de qué hora dan el desayuno?

We'd like to order some drinks.
Querríamos tomar algo.

Photo Julia Richardson

Can the children play in the garden?
¿Pueden jugar fuera los niños?

Can we leave the children with you?
¿Podemos dejar los niños con vosotros?

Can we eat breakfast in our room?
¿Podríamos desayunar en nuestra habitación?

Local information
Where can we get some petrol?
¿Dónde hay una gasolinera?

Where can we find a garage to fix our car?
¿Dónde hay un taller de coches?

How far is the nearest shop?
¿Dónde está la tienda más cercana?

Useful vocabulary

We need a doctor.
Necesitamos un médico.

Where is the nearest chemist's?
¿Dónde está la farmacia más cercana?

Can you recommend a good restaurant? (to me/to us)
¿Podría recomendarme/nos un buen restaurante?

Where is the nearest cash dispenser?
¿Dónde hay un cajero automático?

On leaving

What time must we vacate our room?
¿A qué hora tenemos que dejar libre nuestra habitación?

We'd like to pay the bill.
Querríamos pagar la cuenta por favor.

This is a wonderful place.
Este lugar es maravilloso.

Eating in/or out

What is today's set menu?
¿Qué tienen hoy de menú?

What do you recommmend?
¿Qué recomienda?

What vegetarian dishes do you have?
¿Qué platos vegetarianos tienen?

We'd like to see the wine list.
Nos gustaría ver la carta de vinos, por favor.

Do you have some salt/pepper?
¿Me podría traer sal/pimienta, por favor?

Where is there a good tapas bar?
¿Dónde hay un bar que sirva buenas tapas?

Please keep the change.
Quédese con la vuelta.

Where are the toilets?
¿Dónde están los servicios?

It was a delicious meal.
Estaba muy rica la comida.

I'd like a white/black coffee.
Un café con leche/un café solo.

We'd like some tea, please.
Quisiéramos tomar un té, por favor.

Photo Toby Sawday

Recommended reading

• *The Face of Spain and South from Granada* Gerald Brennan
Fascinating perspectives on 1930s' Spain.

• *Death in the Afternoon*
Ernest Hemingway
Touches on the Spanish passion for bullfighting.

• *The Seville Communion*
Arturo Pérez-Reverte
Ignore the swear words – the prose is superb.

• *Driving over Lemons* Chris Stewart
An Englishman in Andalucía: on its way to becoming a classic.

• *El Manuscrito Carmesí*
Antonio Gala
Set in the Andalucía of La Alhambra times - a novel of character.

• *Roads to Santiago* Cees Noteboom
A modern day pilgrimage through Spain.

• *Don Quixote Delusions; Travels in Castilian Spain* Miranda France
"A fascinating romp through the Spanish psyche."

• *As I Walked Out One Midsummer Morning*
Laurie Lee
Irresistible account of his walk across Spain at the time of the Spanish Civil War.

• *Viaje a la Alcarria* Camilo José Cela
Travel literature – quirky and funny.

• *A Stranger in Spain* H V Morton
Classic travel guide through untouched Spain.

• *Duende* Jason Webster
An entertaining account of an Englishman's attempt to infiltrate the flamenco scene.

• *Spain* Jan Morris
Out of print, but available from abebooks.co.uk.

• *El Jardín de las Dudas*
Fernando Savater
A much-acclaimed novel by this professor of ethics.

• *Culture Shock: Spain*
Marie Louise Graff
A must if you intend living here, even for a short time.

• *Xenophobes Guide to the Spanish*
Drew Launay
Mostly accurate and very funny.

• *Blindness* José Saramago Winner of the 1998 Nobel Prize for Literature.

• *The Last Jew* Noah Gordon
An action-packed novel set in the time of the Spanish Inquisition.

A short selection compiled by Jose Navarro

Vías Verdes

Discover the hidden corners of Spain. *Vías Verdes* or Greenways - are breathing new life and new jobs into many of the rural communities – and, slowly but increasingly, drawing crowds away from the hectic coastal resorts into the countryside. Now visitors and locals alike can cycle, ride or stroll along more than 1,550 kilometres (and growing) of disused, narrow-gauge railway lines – 81 at the last count.

It's not just the tracks that have been given a new lease of life but the stations too. Some have metamorphosed into bike-hire shops, others into cafés or restaurants, yet others into hotels, the La Parada del Compte (entry 87) in Aragon being

one (surprisingly luxurious) example. At the old stations of Puerto Serrano and Olvera on the Vía Verde de la Sierra, a couple of simple hotels have been created, so you can leave your car at one end and cycle both ways over one or two days.

The *Vías Verdes* project was launched in 1993, its aim to rejuvenate a total of 7,600 kilometres of abandoned line (some private industrial but most authority-owned). More than €50m has been invested to date. Where trains once passed, pushchairs, wheelchairs, horses and bikes now proceed - every means of non-motorised transport is welcome. It's a novel resource for active tourism in Spain, and has an attractively ecological slant.

In spite of Spain's rugged landscape, the vías run mostly on the flat: unscary terrain for children and the elderly. The fascinating *Carrilet Vía Verde* (102km), which crosses a volcanic region in the foothills of the Pyrenees, includes the ancient city of Gerona, touches the Costa Brava, and draws 120,000 visitors a year, many from the city of Barcelona. But you'll often find the tracks are virtually people-free. Dig out the binoculars as you pass through stunning nature reserves; dwell on the history as you cross viaducts 100 years old (one designed by Gustave Eiffel).

Photo Jose Navarro

No need to be spooked by the cool, dark tunnels – they're reassuringly illuminated by solar power as you enter. Stay at the charming Etxatoa (entry 68) in the Navarra and cycle the length of the Vía Verde Plazaola: it has no fewer than 14 tunnels along its 12km track.

Vías Verdes Day

Walking and cycling en masse on the second Sunday in May.

Guia de Vías Verdes is a two-volume Spanish guide (€17), including maps, pictures, railway connections, bike hire etc. Worth it if you're planning a cycling or walking holiday based around the Vías Verdes.

www.viasverdes-ffe.com
viasverdes@ffe.es

IGN maps

www.ign.es
1:2,5000, 1:50,000, 1:100,000 are the equivalent of OS maps, although nowhere near as accurate and user-friendly as their British counterparts. Best to order them from Stanfords before you go.

Editorial Pirineo

www.editorialpirineo.com
Possibly the best topographic maps of the Spanish Pyrenees you will find.

Editorial Alpina

www.editorialalpina.com
Classic walking maps of mountainous areas of Spain. Not the most accurate maps in the world but very user-friendly and they keep the spirit of adventure alive.

Photo Fundacíon de los Ferrocarriles Españoles

Our offices

Beautiful as they were, our old offices leaked heat, used electricity to heat water and space, flooded whole rooms with light to illuminate one person, and were not ours to alter. We failed our eco-audit in spite of using recycled cooking oil in one car and gas in another, recycling everything we could and gently promoting 'greenery' in our travel books. (Our Fragile Earth series takes a harder line.)

After two eco-audits we leaped at the chance to buy some old barns closer to Bristol, to create our own eco-offices and start again. Our accountants thought we were mad and there was no time for proper budgeting. The back of every envelope bore the signs of frenzied calculations, and then I shook hands and went off on holiday.
Two years later we moved in.

As I write, swallows are nesting in our wood-pellet store, the fountain plays in the pond, the grasses bend

Photos above Quentin Craven

before a gentle breeze and the solar panels heat water too hot to touch. We have, to our delight, created an inspiring and serene place.

The roof was lifted to allow us to fix thick insulation panels beneath the tiles. More panels were fitted between the rafters and as a separate wall inside the old ones, and laid under the underfloor heating pipes. We are insulated for the Arctic, and almost totally air-tight. Ventilation is natural, and we open windows. An Austrian boiler sucks wood-pellets in from an outside store and slowly consumes them, cleanly and – of course – without using any fossil fuels. Rain-water is channelled to a 6,000-litre underground tank, filtered, and then flushes loos and fills basins. Sun-pipes funnel the daylight into dark corners and double-glazed Velux windows, most facing north, pour it into every office.

We built a small green oak barn between two old barns, and this has become the heart of the offices, warm, light and beautiful. Wood plays a major role: our simple oak desks were made by a local carpenter, my office floor is of oak, and there is oak panelling. Even the carpet tiles tell a story; they are made from the wool of Herdwick sheep from the Lake District.

Our electricity consumption is extraordinarily low. We set out not to flood the buildings with light, but to provide attractive, low background lighting and individual 'task' lights to be used only as needed. Materials, too, have been a focus: we used non-toxic paints and finishes.

Events blew our budgets apart, but we have a building of which we are proud and which has helped us win two national awards this year. Architects and designers are fascinated and we are all working with a renewed commitment. Best of all, we are now in a better position to encourage our owners and readers to take 'sustainability' more seriously.

I end by answering an important question: our office carbon emissions will be reduced by about 75%. We await our bills, but they will be low and, as time goes by, relatively lower – and lower. It has been worth every penny and every ounce of effort.

Alastair Sawday

Photo above Paul Groom
Photo below Tom Germain

www.special-escapes.co.uk
Self-catering from Alastair Sawday's

Cosy cottages • Sumptuous castles • City apartments • Hilltop bothies • Tipis and more

A whole week self-catering in Britain with your friends or family is precious, and you dare not get it wrong. To whom do you turn for advice and who on earth do you trust when the web is awash with advice from strangers? We launched Special Escapes to satisfy an obvious need for impartial and trustworthy help – and that is what it provides. The criteria for inclusion are the same as for our books: we have to like the place and the owners. It has, quite simply, to be 'special'. The site, our first online-only publication, is featured on www.thegoodwebguide.com and is growing fast.

www.special-escapes.co.uk

Where on the web?

The World Wide Web is big – very big. So big, in fact, that it can be a fruitless search if you don't know where to find reliable, trustworthy, up-to-date information about fantastic places to stay in Europe, India, Morocco and beyond....

Fortunately, there's www.specialplacestostay.com, where you can dip into all of our guides, find special offers from owners, catch up on news about the series and tell us about the special places you've been to.

www.specialplacestostay.com

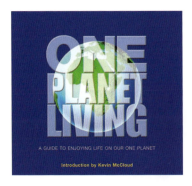

One Planet Living
Edition 1, £4.99
By Pooran Desai and Paul King

A practical guide providing us with easy, affordable and attractive alternatives for achieving a higher quality of life while using our fair share of the planet's capacity.

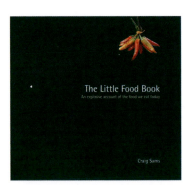

The Little Food Book
Edition 1, £6.99
By Craig Sams,
Chairman of the Soil Association

An explosive account of the food we eat today. Never have we been at such risk – from our food. This book will help clarify what's at stake.

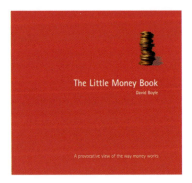

The Little Money Book
Edition 1, £6.99
By David Boyle, an associate of the New Economics Foundation

This pithy, wry little guide will tell you where money comes from, what it means, what it's doing to the planet and what we might be able to do about it.

www.fragile-earth.com

Order form

All these books are available in major bookshops or you may order them direct.
Post and packaging are FREE within the UK.

British Hotels, Inns & Other Places	£14.99
British Bed & Breakfast	£14.99
British Bed & Breakfast for Garden Lovers	£14.99
Croatia	£11.99
French Bed & Breakfast	£15.99
French Holiday Homes	£12.99
French Hotels, Châteaux & Other Places	£14.99
Greece	£11.99
Green Places to Stay	£13.99
India	£11.99
Ireland	£12.99
Italy	£14.99
London	£9.99
Morocco	£11.99
Mountains of Europe	£9.99
Paris Hotels	£10.99
Portugal	£11.99
Pubs & Inns of England & Wales	£14.99
Spain	£14.99
Turkey	£11.99
One Planet Living	£4.99
The Little Food Book	£6.99
The Little Money Book	£6.99
Six Days	£12.99

Please make cheques payable to Alastair Sawday Publishing   **Total £**
Please send cheques to: Alastair Sawday Publishing, The Old Farmyard, Yanley
Lane, Long Ashton, Bristol BS41 9LR. For credit card orders call 01275 395431
or order directly from our web site **www.specialplacestostay.com**

Title   First name   Surname

Address

Postcode   Tel

SP7

If you do not wish to receive mail from other like-minded companies, please tick here ☐
If you would prefer not to receive information about special offers on our books, please tick here ☐

Report form

If you have any comments on entries in this guide, please let us have them.
If you have a favourite house, hotel, inn or other new discovery, please let us
know about it. You can return this form, email info@sawdays.co.uk, or visit
www.specialplacestostay.com and click on 'contact'.

Existing entry
Property name:_____

Entry number:_____ Date of visit: ___ / ___ / ___

New recommendation
Property name:_____

Address: _____

_____

Tel: _____

Your comments
What did you like (or dislike) about this place? Were the people friendly?
What was the location like? What sort of food did they serve?

_____

_____

_____

_____

_____

_____

_____

_____

Your details
Name: _____

Address: _____

Postcode: _____ Tel: _____

Please send completed form to ASP, The Old Farmyard, Yanley Lane,
Long Ashton, Bristol BS41 9LR

Wheelchair accessible

At least one bedroom and bathroom accessible for wheelchair users. Phone for details.

Limited mobility

These places have at least one bedroom and bathroom accessible without steps.

Budget

These places have double rooms for under €100 (£70).

Quick reference indices

Quick reference indices

No car

Places within 10 miles of a coach or train station and the owners can pick you up.

Quick reference indices

Secure parking

Seure parking is available at these places. Please check when booking.

Tennis

These places have a tennis court on the premises. Use by arrangement.

Index by property name

Index by property name

Photo Jose Navarro

Index by place name

Index by place name

Photo Jose Navarro

How to use this book

1 Basque Country

Urresti
Barrio Zendokiz 12, 48314, Gautegiz de Arteaga, Vizcaya

2 A dream come true for Urresti's two friendly young owners – they have transformed the ruins of the farmhouse they found in green Vizcaya. From the outside it looks 17th century; inside is more contemporary in feel. Breakfast is excellent value, served in the large sitting/dining room: local cheeses, homemade jam, fruits from the farm, plenty of coffee. For other meals guests share an open-plan, fully-equipped kitchen/living area. Smart, impeccably clean little bedrooms have laminate floors and new, country-style furniture; the one under the eaves (hot in summer!) has a balcony; another is big enough for an extra sofabed. En suite bath and shower rooms are excellent. Outside: a small organic plot – you can buy the vegetables. The house stands in beautiful rolling countryside with stunning beaches not far away – bring buckets and spades. Gernika, too, is close. A brilliant place for families, with emus, sheep, goats, horses and hens to fuss over, and ancient forests of oak and chestnut to explore (borrow the bikes). The whole area is a Parque Natural and many come just for the birdlife.

3 rooms	6 + 2: 6 twins/doubles.	
	2 apartments: 1 for 2, 1 for 4.	
4 price	€47–€55. Apartments €71–€77.	
5 meals	Breakfast €6.50.	
6 closed	Rarely.	
7 directions	From Gernika for Lekeitio. At fork, lower road for Lekeitio. After 6km, left for Elanchobe. On right, below road level, after 1.2km at sign 'Nekazal Turismoa Agroturismo'.	

María Goitia & Jose María Rios

tel	+34 946 251843
fax	+34 946 251843
email	urresti@wanadoo.es
web	www.toprural.com/urresti

9 Guest house

10

8 Map 5 Entry 63